THE POLITICAL ECONOMY OF GLOBAL POPULATION CHANGE, 1950–2050

THE POLITICAL ECONOMY OF GLOBAL POPULATION CHANGE, 1950–2050

Paul Demeny
Geoffrey McNicoll
Editors

POPULATION AND DEVELOPMENT REVIEW

A Supplement to Volume 32, 2006

POPULATION COUNCIL
New York

Library of Congress Cataloging-in-Publication Data

The political economy of global population change, 1950–2050 / Paul Demeny and Geoffrey McNicoll, editors.

    p. cm.

    "Population and development review, a supplement to volume 32, 2006."
    ISBN 0-87834-114-5 (pbk. alk. paper)

    1. Population—Economic aspects. 2. Population—Political aspects. 3. Population—Environmental aspects. 4. Population—History. I. Demeny, Paul George. 1932– II. McNicoll, Geoffrey. III. Population and development review ; vol. 32, 2006 (Supplement)

    HB849.41.P635 2006

    304.6'2—dc22   2006046445

ISSN 0098-7921
ISBN 0-87834-114-5

Printed in the United States of America.

CONTENTS

Over the two centuries 1750–1950, the global frontrunners in political and economic development—states initially containing some 20 percent of the world's people—transformed institutional and technological invention into systems of democratic governance, industrial production, and dynamic consumer economies. The following century, 1950–2050, is the turn of the rest of the world.

The demographic accompaniment of such transformations is a surge in population growth, set off by falling mortality and (for a time) rising fertility. Historically, a doubling or trebling of population was the common experience. Soon, however, sharp fertility declines took hold and again slowed the growth rate—and created the top-heavy age structures of "modern" demographic regimes. The demographic transitions now underway will result in much greater proportional increases in population, and from much larger base populations. In the half-century since 1950 the world grew from 2.5 billion to 6 billion people; by 2050 another 3 billion are likely to be added. But by then the expansion may be nearly over, with at most another billion or two to come in the later decades of the century. Low fertility will likely have spread worldwide—with negative population growth rates possibly entrenched in some regions. The regional divergence in demographic regime begun in the eighteenth century will have mostly disappeared, though leaving a vastly more populous world and a very different global pattern of relative population sizes.

The extent to which the development effort is made more difficult by rapid population growth has been and remains a contentious matter. Whatever the interpretation of the economic data of past decades, however, few would dispute that both the size and the rate of growth of populations have profound effects on human societies and their governance, on their built environments and rural hinterlands, and on most of the rest of nature.

Moreover, the demographic convergence that is now anticipated does not necessarily signal convergence in other domains. Speculations about economic, political, and environmental trends range widely. Worldwide economic prosperity and benign "end of history" political scenarios are familiar forecasts but are balanced by others that foresee continued large regional inequalities in economic performance and expect no lessening of international tension and political turmoil. And large-scale environmental change may be shifting the ground under these human systems at a discernible rate, creating problems for the international order of unknown dimensions. These uncertainties themselves derive in part from the pace and scale of underlying population change.

These broad issues and relationships warrant far more attention than they receive—and not just by population experts, whose disciplinary focal length, many would argue, is poorly suited to the task. The present volume aims to be a step in this direction. It brings together historians and social scientists interested in contemporary global change, its origins, and implications to reflect on the demographic dimensions of that change. The chapters deal with the processes of convergence and differentiation in the global economy over the period since 1950, with key past and emerging issues examined from selected regional perspectives, and with population-linked challenges for public policy that will likely have to be met in the first half of this century.

Early versions of most of the chapters were presented at a conference on the political economy of global population change held at the Rockefeller Foundation's Bellagio Conference Center in 2002. That meeting and the subsequent work that has brought the material to publication have been supported by a generous grant from the Rockefeller Foundation. We also thank the Population Council for its support.

Paul Demeny
Geoffrey McNicoll

World Population 1950–2000: Perception and Response

PAUL DEMENY
GEOFFREY MCNICOLL

The second half of the twentieth century witnessed the vast political transformation that followed the ending of the Western colonial era, the breakup
of the Soviet Union, and the emergence of new aspirants to global influence. It was a period, too, of unparalleled economic growth: a sevenfold
increase in the size of the world economy, and major increases in income
per head, most remarkably in Asia. Despite intermittent regional turmoil
and setbacks, in comparison to the previous 50 years punctuated by two
World Wars and a global economic depression, it was also an era of peace
and of spreading social and political freedoms. It was marked by increasing
interconnectedness of economies and civilizations within a world that technological advances seemed to shrink, yet one that globalization also widened. In the background of these changes, but linked to them in many different and significant ways, was a huge expansion of the size of the world's
population—unprecedented in pace and magnitude—generated by improving health and longevity, especially in the world's poorer regions.

Competition for influence in these regions, denoted the developing
countries or (with a misleading sense of coherence) the third world, was a
major component of the Cold War struggle between the United States and
the Soviet Union in the first four decades of the period. American—and
more broadly, Western—perceptions of the potential implications of rapid
population growth for economic development, international security, and
geopolitical balance were powerfully shaped by that competition. Population policy issues, once strictly in the domain of domestic concerns, emerged
as a legitimate if perennially controversial topic for international discussion and advice-giving, with results sometimes beneficial for both giver and
taker but often less than felicitous. Foreign aid programs, a postwar invention as an enduring facet of international relations, eventually came also

to embrace programs intended to lower third-world birth rates and hence to moderate the tempo of population growth. International organizations also played a role in promoting such endeavors, and intergovernmental conferences set out principles and designed plans of action. More important, national elites in some of the more populous countries of the developing world, motivated by ambitions for social and economic modernization, were prompted to seek their own distinctive solutions for speeding up the process of demographic transition toward balancing low death rates with low birth rates.

By the end of the twentieth century, although expansion of population numbers in the developing world still had far to run, the pace had greatly slowed: widespread declines in birth rates had taken place and looked set to continue. To what degree population policies played a significant role in this epochal transformation of demographic regimes remains a matter of conjecture and controversy. It seems likely that future observers will be impressed by the essential similarities in the path to demographic modernity that successive countries have taken in the last few centuries, rather than discerning a demographic exceptionalism in the most recent period—with achievement of the latter credited to deliberate policy design. But that eventual judgment, whatever it may be, needs to be based on an understanding of how demographic change over the last half-century has been perceived and the responses it has elicited—an exercise in political demography. Such an exercise, inevitably tentative given the recency of the events, is essayed in this chapter.

The question of world population

The concept of world population is simple enough. Demographers count or estimate the population of each of the distinct national or political units to which the terrestrial three-tenths of the globe is divided and add up the numbers. For 1950, this arithmetic yields the figure of 2.5 billion. For 2000, the corresponding figure is 6.1 billion. For an estimate of the world population in 2005, add to that number roughly 380 million.[1]

Are such global totals merely figments of demographers' imagination—proofs of their skill in compiling data? Or do they also represent a reality that has a bearing on things that do matter—international relations, economic welfare, adequacy of natural resources, population policy? Is there a "world population problem"—as distinct from diverse problems affected by population size, structure, and dynamics, more or less tightly compartmentalized within individual countries, regions, or social strata?

This issue was addressed in a notable article published in 1949, entitled "The 'false problem' of world population." The author was Alfred Sauvy, a prominent public intellectual in France and for many years probably the most influential student of population in Europe. To talk about a world population problem, Sauvy argued, is largely meaningless—it is a problem incorrectly posed and, as a result, its explication leads to erroneous and useless conclusions.

> To demonstrate this, let us carry the reasoning to its absurd limit. Let us imagine that we could enumerate human beings, like ourselves, who live on other planets. Considerations relating to the total population of the solar system would then be no less meaningful than those about the population of the globe. Without claiming that the lines of separation within the latter are equally wide, the terrestrial compartmentalizations are sufficiently well established to render any global calculus that ignores them quite pointless.

He continued with a more down-to earth argument:

> For the time being, there exists no world government, nor are there institutions that would come close to such a construct. Even if some political conflicts are adjudicated at international tribunals, and even if some studies are carried out internationally and some principles are established on that level, such coordination of efforts falls far short of the degree of solidarity that would be needed to make the expression "world population" acquire real meaning.

There is such a thing as a French population or a Japanese population, Sauvy allowed, but that is because there exist corresponding linguistic, ethnic, or political units. Within the frontiers that delineate such populations, persons and goods can move freely, and transport and communication are relatively easy. "Thus, when strong imbalances emerge, a tendency toward evening out of differences also manifests itself, which to a large extent also shapes the demographic problem inside those frontiers into a single problem."

Measures that would give substance to international solidarity have had little effect. In international migration, creation of global institutions— the League of Nations, in particular—might even have had the opposite effect, by providing forums for the voicing of parochial concerns. In other domains, too, notably with respect to international trade, national interests similarly intrude, preventing serious action to lessen economic differences and relieve demographic pressures. In all, such institutions "constitute...a denial through deeds of the notion of world population." (Sauvy 1949.)

This view of the question of population was broadly representative of European attitudes at the middle of the last century. Emerging from a devastating war and acceding (in retrospect at least, with some relief) to the pressures for independence from their former colonies, the countries of Western Europe were preoccupied with rebuilding their economies and dealing with their own social problems. Domestic population policies were a natural part of that endeavor, continuing a long process of expanding governmental functions within the modern state system. The central element of government involvement had to do with population "quality"—the increasingly socialized provision of health and educational services. (Formerly, such matters were largely left to lower-level social units, and often ultimately to the family and to individuals.) But population size, structure, and change also often emerged as important concerns of governments. France can serve as perhaps the clearest illustration of this. Indeed, in the article cited above, Sauvy was anxious to enunciate a principle: "Even if judgments on the existence of global overpopulation were fully confirmed, they should not persuade the insufficiently populated countries to adopt a policy of renouncing population growth or a policy of neglect. In particular, such judgments can in no way change the nature of the French population problem, nor mitigate the necessity for a strong rejuvenation through the upturn of fertility." Promotion of such demographic rejuvenation through higher fertility was an explicit policy goal in France: a response to the challenge of below-replacement-level fertility and impending population decline.

Population policy and development as international public goods

The underlying cause of governmental concerns with population and the justification for policies that might be adopted as a result are fairly well understood. With respect to fertility, for example, an individual or a couple may be satisfied with their own preferred choices but still take an interest in and be critical of their fellow citizens' fertility behavior. If well informed, they might perceive, for instance, that it would be in their interest for their own children to grow up in a country that is less crowded, more affluent, better educated, and healthier than it would likely be if average fertility remained high. In other circumstances, they might discern economic or even aesthetic disadvantages for themselves and their children arising from population aging and wish for higher fertility by the rest of the citizenry in order to rejuvenate the population. But even if their judgment on this score were indeed well informed—a tall order for most individuals—acting alone they would be powerless to further their interests in this domain. They cannot bargain with a multitude of other individuals and couples, trying to persuade them, or, if need be, in effect to bribe them, to change their behavior appropriately. A potential welfare gain thus remains unattainable. In such a situation the objective assumes the property of a public good—a desired service or modification of institutional arrangements that only government can provide or put into effect.

Extensions of this simple model of public action are readily envisaged. Instead of isolated individuals, the would-be bargaining parties may be larger groups—distinguishable by demographic, economic, or social criteria. In a democracy, the central task of the political process is to reconcile and harmonize such interests, whether they are in conflict or broadly congruent, and to make arrangements through which the cost of the resulting policy changes is acceptably distributed. Needless to say, that political task is fraught with problems even in fields that would seem relatively noncontroversial, such as collective provision of elementary education or basic health services. In population policy, the difficulties are well illustrated by the sharply conflicting interests that must be reconciled in formulating a consensus on immigration. Reaching an analogous consensus on policies aimed directly at modifying fertility is likely to be even more demanding, especially if the aim is to decrease rather than increase fertility. The comparative rarity of such measures in a democratic polity is therefore hardly surprising. When the political costs are high, laissez faire will be the better part of wisdom.

Is there an international equivalent of the domestic case for population policy? The answer at first sight would seem to be negative. Certainly, as Sauvy noted, there is no supranational authority that could play the role of the national government in attempts to adjust demographic behavior in a desired direction. Yet nations have good reason to be aware of population change in their neighborhood, and what they find may sometimes be a cause for anxiety or alarm. France, for example, in the decades that followed its military defeat by Prussia in 1870, worried that its own population growth was significantly slower than that of unified Germany. With distances shrunken by modern transportation, communication, and military technology, such concerns could become legitimate and rational even on a global scale.

The example of French–German demographic rivalry is now mainly of antiquarian interest. France could do nothing to bring the German birth rate down; the relative population sizes and, with them, the relative economic weights of the two countries shifted to the disadvantage of France. Over time, German fertility rates fell to the French level and eventually below it. And technological changes made population size and territory less relevant components of military might.[2] After World War II, however, another aspect of differential rates of population growth emerged as a source of concern in the international arena. This was the potential adverse impact of rapid population growth on economic development and international economic inequality, with likely unwelcome implications for international peace and security. Development, peace, and security were key international public goods, and newly designed institutions, notably the United Nations, were intended to secure them. Achieving these goals required establishing their social, political, and economic underpinnings. The Preamble of the United Nations Charter, adopted in 1945, spelled this out concisely, signaling members' determination "to promote social progress and better standards of life in larger freedom," and, for this end, "to employ international machinery for the promotion of the economic and social advancement of all peoples."

The "international machinery" the UN Charter referred to had obvious shortcomings. Some of these had to do with population size. The United Nations was to be an organization of sovereign states, with equal rights. But at the time of its founding, large parts of the globe were still in colonial or otherwise dependent status. The losers of World War II were also not part of the organization. And the 45 founding members represented vastly different demographic and economic weights. China, with a population of over one-half billion, and Luxembourg, with a little more than one-quarter million, each had the same vote in the General Assembly. As membership expanded over time—it was 192 in 2006, with the prospect of more to come—these contrasts only became more pronounced. Important matters therefore were to be handled by the Security Council. There, five great powers—the World War II victors—had veto power over decisions, an arrangement that for over 60 years has successfully resisted all attempts at reform. At the time of the founding, the combined population size of two of these five, Britain and France, represented less than 4 percent of the global population (it is now less than 2 percent). China, with more than one-fifth of the world's population, was in a demographic class of its own. But between 1949 and 1971 the Chinese seat was occupied by the Republic of China—Taiwan—whose de facto population amounted to less than one percent of the global total. Finally, and most importantly, the remaining two members of the Security Council, the Soviet Union and the United States, soon after the UN's founding turned from wartime allies to Cold War adversaries for a period that lasted more than four decades.[3]

Thus, soon after World War II, it became obvious that constructive action requiring international cooperation would have to take place mainly in the traditional frames of intercourse between countries: through regional alliances and institutions with less than global reach and through bilateral negotiations. There were soon "three worlds," first, second, and third.[4] The "third world" broadly defined the same mosaic of countries that UN terminology variously called "underdeveloped," "less developed," and finally, and more optimistically, "developing." The first world was the "West": North America and the western part of Europe, and also Japan and Australia and New Zealand. In the immediate postwar years, Western Europe benefited from major economic transfers, notably through the Marshall Plan, from the United States—an innovation with no precedent in international relations. (For some beneficiaries it may have served to keep them within the Western fold.) Japan, whose recovery from wartime devastation was even more spectacular than that of West Germany and of Western Europe at large, also received substantial economic assistance, as well as assistance in institutional redesign, from the United States. This assembly of economically advanced capitalist countries, within which a preponderant role was necessarily played by the United States, competed with the second world—the Soviet Empire and its newly conquered satellites—for access to and influence in the third world.

The first world was rich, and, especially during the first three decades after World War II, became ever more affluent. Those decades also saw an unexpected development: a temporary baby boom (relative to low-fertility expectations), hence reinvigorated population growth.[5] The recipes for economic advance—markets lightly regulated and competitive, international trade unimpeded between willing partners, entrepreneurship and technological innovation given free reign, political stability and the rule of law maintained—which had seemingly been forgotten during the interwar years, were found again.

The second world, led by the Soviet Union, which was still relatively poor but militarily powerful, contrasted sharply with the West. It was guided by a universalist ideology that had a strong if intermittent appeal in many of the newly independent countries and in Latin America. This was, perhaps, mostly because it also offered a prescription—central planning and social engineering—that seemed to promise a key to rapid progress from poverty to wealth. It was seen as a shortcut to the goal shared by all less developed countries, especially those with a sizable and expanding population and a strong identity rooted in a distinctive national history: to catch up with and eventually to surpass the West.

Third-world attempts to find a stable and productive "third way" between the two power blocs—a noncapitalist and noncommunist route to economic development—remained largely fruitless. Instead of nonalignment, various mixtures of cooperation with and influence exercised by the West and the Soviet Union ensued, with varied outcomes.[6] In terms of its economic, social, and political makeup, and with respect to the historical background that lay behind these features, the third world was of course already highly differentiated at the time of its christening. Over the following decades that differentiation sharpened, and the collective label stuck on this diverse group of countries lost much of its meaning.

From the vantage point of the immediate post–World War II years the future appeared fraught with danger. Demography played a major role in that perception. Around 1950, minor exceptions apart, the third world had one conspicuous common trait: high fertility and high demographic growth potential. Seen by many in the West, and with less consistency by many third-world leaders themselves, this put an ominous shadow on the economic prospects of the less developed countries, and, by the same token, lowered the chances for an outcome advantageous for the West in the Cold War competition with the Soviet bloc.

Demographic prospects at midcentury

The demographic characteristics of the third world attracted little attention until the 1950s.[7] Prior to World War II, fertility remained high, more or less at its premodern level. Population growth was slowly increasing, however, as a result of improvements in mortality. Following the end of the war, mortality decline accelerated greatly and as a result so did population growth. In 1950, some 1.7 billion of the then world population of 2.5 billion were in countries classified as less developed, with an average annual birth rate of 44 per thousand population—twice the rate in the developed world. Unless there was a substantial decline in the birth rate, starting soon, a large increase in human numbers was inevitable. This was well understood: it was a clear implication of demographic transition theory, a generalization of the historical pattern of change from a traditional demographic regime characterized by high fertility and high mortality to a modern demographic regime characterized by low fertility and low mortality. Mortality decline in the early phase of the transition is followed only later by the decline of fertility. For a time, the birth rate exceeds the death rate, resulting in population growth. If the drop in the death rate is precipitous, as was clearly observed to be the case in the early postwar years, and if the decline in the birth rate is tardy, as was expected to be the case in the less developed countries, the population will grow fast and will do so for an extended period.

Realization of how extraordinarily large that population expansion would be was slow to come. In 1945, Frank Notestein, America's most influential demographer, published a population projection elaborated in regional detail and arrived at a 2000 world population of 3,345 million (Notestein 1945). The actual figure turned out to be some 82 percent higher.[8] Similar forecasts a decade later came closer to the actual trend, but still fell well below it. For example, in a widely read study, the geophysicist Harrison Brown anticipated a global population of 4.8 billion in 2000—more than 1.2 billion short of the actual population at that year (Brown 1954). In a paper presented at the 1954 World Population Conference in Rome the economist E. F. Schumacher (later of *Small is Beautiful* fame) used the figure of 3 billion for the expected global population in 1980 (Schumacher 1955). The actual figure was nearly 50 percent larger: 4.4 billion. But by that time United Nations estimates had started to draw a more accurate picture of the world's medium-term demographic future, although subject to substantial uncertainty. At the same conference, the UN projected a 1980 global population between 3,295 million and 3,990 million (United Nations 1955). Subsequent estimates kept shifting upward. Just a few years later the range was revised by the UN to "low" and "high" estimates of 3,850 and 4,280 million—closer to but still failing to straddle the actual 1980 population (United Nations 1958).[9]

Assessments of future population growth for individual countries were also often badly off the mark. Thus, for example, in an analysis of China's demographic prospects, published in 1950, Notestein and Irene Taeuber foresaw the annual population growth rate in the one-half to one percent range and, taking the then current population as 400 million, put the expected absolute increase by 1980 in the range of 65 to 140 million (Balfour et al. 1950). The actual increase of China's population between 1950 and 1980—notwithstanding a precipitous fertility decline during the latter part of that period—was 444 million. As for Asia's other demographic giant, the encyclopedic study of the demography of the Indian subcontinent by Kingsley Davis offered no formal projections. But Davis fitted a logistic curve to adjusted Indian census data up to 1941. He commented that in the exercise he found it satisfactory to posit 700 million as the upper asymptote, a figure he took to be roughly attained by the middle of the twenty-first century (Davis 1951). In the course of events, by 1980 the population of the subcontinent had already exceeded that envisaged upper limit by 150 million. The UN medium projection for the combined three successor states of prepartition India foresees a 2050 population of 2.14 billion, more than triple Davis's figure, and still adding 10 million per year.

Economic forebodings at midcentury

What did this acceleration of population growth—soon labeled with the attention-catching, if plainly ill-fitting term "population explosion"—imply for economic development? The trigger of that acceleration was a welcome achievement: falling death rates represented a clear welfare gain for the populations experiencing them. It was also an achievement for which the developed world could take substantial credit. The major cause of falling death rates was transmission of technological advances from the first world to the third in controlling infectious and parasitic diseases. Yet at the same time many observers saw the suddenly rapid expansion of human numbers as a major obstacle to economic development. To some, it raised the specter of coming Malthusian conditions, with food supplies unable to keep up with population growth.[10] Others, more numerous among academics, saw it as a factor retarding economic progress or even wiping out all the gains. As the often-quoted Red Queen said to Alice, "Now, here, you see, it takes all the running you can do, to keep in the same place. If you want to go somewhere else, you must run at least twice as fast as that."

But how fast was twice as fast? Quoting Lewis Carroll could not substitute for realistic, fact-based estimates of the economic growth potential of third-world countries. Economic theory was not much help either. Beginning in the 1940s, a distinct branch of economics applicable to the study of the less developed world was emerging, although the need for such specialization was highly questionable. The new development theory focused on the shortages of savings and investment as the main barriers to growth, and it emphasized the role of the state in overcoming those shortages. This effectively downplayed the relevance of the past experience of the pioneer countries of industrialization. An appraisal of that experience would have pointed to the dominant role of systemic factors in economic development—in particular, institutions that encourage entrepreneurship and innovation. It would have stressed that the state's best contribution to development lay in the provision of physical security and a stable legal system, in the protection of property rights, and in the development of human capital through provision of public health and educational services. Instead, the crucial variable in the midcentury growth models was the capital–output ratio, recording the effectiveness of invested savings in generating economic growth. Estimates of likely capital–output ratios were typically high and measured savings rates low, imparting pessimism about the feasible tempo of economic advance.

The peak country-level population growth rates came in the early postwar decades and only rarely exceeded 3 percent per year: fast population growth typically meant an annual rate between 2.5 and 3 percent. If economic growth could be appreciably faster than that, demographic expansion might still be seen as a drag on development, but much of the crisis atmosphere generated by stagnant per capita income would have been dispelled. At that time, however, few people thought that economic growth at such rates would be possible in countries that were poor and predominantly agricultural. Underlying and justifying this somber outlook was the dismal economic record of the decades that preceded World War II. In most countries, including countries of the developed world, economic progress in that period was slow or nonexistent, even with the relatively low rates of population growth then prevailing.[11] Protectionism practiced by the developed countries allowed international trade to grow only slowly or not at all—to the disadvantage of all, but especially the less developed countries. Anticipating a radically different postwar economic environment seemed unwarranted.

A penetrating analysis of the economic problems and prospects of the less developed countries, combined with recommendations on how to improve those prospects, was offered in a report completed in 1951 by a group of eminent economists appointed by the UN Secretary-General Trygve Lee (United Nations 1951).[12] Although its authors paid due attention to savings and capital accumulation and endorsed the need for economic planning, their prescriptions were predominantly in the spirit of classical economics, emphasizing the importance of the human and institutional preconditions for growth and of technological development. The 108-page report devoted a short chapter (pp. 45–48) to population growth. At the outset, it signaled dissent from the then prevailing gloomy outlook:

The belief that economic development must inevitably be dissipated in population growth causes pessimism in some quarters. We do not share this view. If vigorous effort is put into developing the under-developed countries, we see no reason why their national incomes should not rise at rates higher than the rates at which their populations are currently increasing, or may be expected to increase. The problem is difficult, but it is not insoluble.

Neither do we share the view that population growth can be substantially diminished by refraining from economic development. The rate of growth of population is now first and foremost a function of the extent to which medical knowledge is made available to the people. It is true that the spread of medical services is itself to some extent a function of the rate of economic development. But we believe that, over the next ten years or so, these factors will remain largely independent. Medical knowledge will spread, and the population will increase, whether economic development takes place or not.

The report went on to discuss the effect of population growth on the standard of living. It distinguished cases where the effect is positive or neutral—these are situations where a larger population presents opportunities for specialization or for the use of indivisible resources, not available to a smaller population, or where natural resources are abundantly available for the extra population. It invoked the experience of the Western countries: fears in the early stages of industrialization that population growth would outrun production proved groundless. But the report also noted the costs of population growth even when the standard of living was unchanged. If the population of an underdeveloped country is increasing "at the not uncommon rate of 1½ per cent per annum," it needs nearly as much as it is normally likely to save merely to cope with population growth. Yet, the report noted, historical experience suggests that "the combination of a rising standard of living, and the new ways of life associated with economic development" are the factors needed for the birth rate to fall. It also suggested that the gap between mortality and fertility declines might take a long time to close.

Thus, with reference to situations that the report clearly implied were typical in countries making up the large majority of the less developed world, the closing paragraph of the population chapter squarely signaled the need for policies addressing fertility:

There are many countries where a further increase of population must, all things considered, be found to be an adverse factor. Such countries cannot afford to wait on the slow cultural effects of modernization to bring their fertility and mortality rates into balance, since in the meantime their populations will increase with disastrous consequences. It is, therefore, important that thought be given to discovering ways and means, which are consistent with the values and culture of each of the peoples concerned, of speeding up the reduction of fertility rates.

Thought indeed *was* given to discovering those ways and means that could avert the disastrous consequences. The central issue in the political economy of global population change in the second half of the twentieth century was human fertility: how to initiate its decline where it was high—"premodern"—and how to speed the process toward low levels once it was underway.

Why does fertility change from "high" to "low"?

To this question the experience of the West should provide a ready answer. After all, nearly all Western countries had low fertility, indeed often below-replacement fertility, by the 1930s. The causes of that decline from formerly high birth rates were generally agreed upon; for many observers they represented merely common sense.[13] By the late 1920s a coherent theory of the demographic transition had been worked out—independently by Adolphe Landry in France and Warren Thompson in the United States—and by the end of World War II had been more fully developed by other American demographers, notably Notestein, Davis, and Kirk.[14] The transition was seen as a byproduct of economic and social change, manifest in processes such as industrialization, urbanization, and the secularization of social values. The micro-level units of society—individuals and families—responded to the changing structural conditions of the economy and the society in demographic as well as in other ways. Modernization reduced infant and child mortality, hence necessitated lower fertility in order not to exceed a given family size; made the upbringing of children more costly and diminished children's economic contributions to the family; increased the economic and social opportunities women had access to with less frequent childbearing; created ways other than family support for providing economic and social support in old age; and increased material aspirations, which could be more easily satisfied if fertility was restricted.

In the awkward language of economics, the process of adjustment was described as substitution of quality for quantity in childbearing and childrearing. Higher "population quality" was of course the avowed objective of the eugenics movement, which had roots in the late nineteenth century and attracted much public attention in the first part of the twentieth. The movement, based on tenuous genetic science and often on plain racist prejudice, sought to discourage births that it considered of inferior social value and tried to promote fertility among those whose offspring could be expected to improve the quality of the human stock, for the benefit of society at large. Despite sporadic successes, notably in the United States and Sweden, with what now look like harebrained schemes—of questionable legality and scant respect for reproductive rights—the demographic impact of the eugenics movement was essentially nil. By midcentury, tainted by Nazi eugenics, the aim of selective breeding was abandoned and Western eugenics transmuted into advocacy of birth control, better prenatal care, and provision of better information on genetic diseases. At the grass-roots level, of course, a kind of eugenics, even if not so labeled, had been an informal mass movement in the West for many decades. Couples restricted their fertility through voluntary birth control and they invested more in the children that they did elect to have. They wanted "higher quality" children but they deemed that they could do so only if they had fewer of them.

Social science analysis was virtually unanimous in its interpretation of this experience. Demand for smaller families was seen as the primary force determining birth rates; the means by which couples regulated their fertility was not unimportant, but was seen as a distinctly secondary factor. If the demand was strong enough, fertility would be low, even if birth control technology was primitive. A transition to low fertility presupposed changing preferences, and such preferences were responses to market signals. It would follow that if policy was to have a role in facilitating fertility decline, it would have to operate primarily through reinforcing those signals.

Four of these signals were particularly relevant, having to do with the direct costs of children to their parents, the opportunity costs of children to parents, the contribution of children's labor services to the family economy, and children's contribution to their parents' old-age security. Fertility decline would occur when shifts in at least some of these components, but preferably in all, made family limitation advantageous to couples, overcoming cultural resistance supporting traditional behavior. Patterns of development generate that effect when at least some (and especially when all) of the following conditions are fulfilled: social expectations and formal institutional arrangements place on parents the major financial responsibility for raising their own children, including a substantial share of the cost of education and health care; women have access to income-earning opportunities in the labor market, including jobs not easily compatible with childbearing and childrearing; social institutions make formal education (primary and early secondary) compulsory and effectively enforce school attendance; child labor is made illegal; effective legal guarantees exist for the security of property rights and for enforcement of private contracts; and the development of public and private insurance and pension schemes provides attractive and comparatively secure alternatives to children as a source of old-age support.

More general social and institutional conditions that made such changes potent generators of fertility decline in the Western experience included emphasis on a person's own economic contribution (rather than, for example, class status or political loyalty) as the primary factor determining earnings, thus providing an incentive for increased investment in human capital; the existence of opportunities for upward social mobility according to merit and corresponding risks of downward mobility; openness to outside influences that create rising expectations with respect to material standards of living; and emphasis not only on the rights but also on the social and economic responsibilities of the individual.

In the West, looking back from the mid-twentieth century to fertility declines already achieved, the broad similarity of various country experiences was unmistakable. At the same time it was evident—and hardly surprising, given the multiplicity of factors that were identified as driving the downward trend in fertility—that there was considerable variation from country to country with respect to the timing of the beginning of the decline and its speed. Within countries, there were also substantial differences in the behavior of various subpopulations, such as those identified by class, religion, or ethnicity. And there were puzzles that did not seem to fit expectations. The core proposition of the theory was that "development"—measured conventionally, if obviously crudely, by such indexes as income per head or proportion urban—generates the transition. But there were exceptions to that rule. To cite only one example, Bulgaria's birth rate was halved during the span of two decades between the World Wars, although Bulgaria was poor and largely agricultural and female literacy was low.

Such seeming exceptions could be readily brought into the same explanatory frame. Decisions leading to lower fertility may originate from two types of individual behavioral response. One is to seize opportunities that open up in the process of development—such as for new consumer goods or new avenues of private investment or for better education and upbringing of children already born. The other behavioral response may be primarily defensive, or even poverty-driven: resistance to a potential lowering of one's own, and one's children's, economic and social status. Either of these responses may be operative, provided the society's institutions allow individuals room to improve or sustain their relative economic position, with the costs of such actions borne by those who directly benefit from them.

Still, even if the conditions of fertility decline were understood, transition theory was not sufficiently predictive to permit gauging the future course of the birth rate in countries where that rate was still high. Answers to the question posed at midcentury about the fertility of less developed countries—when will it start declining? how speedy will the decline turn out to be?—were invariably and necessarily tentative.

There was even skepticism over whether the Western experience with respect to behavioral responses was relevant in non-Western settings. As of midcentury there was no record of any Asian or African developing country exhibiting even early signs of a downward trend in the birth rate. The same was true in Latin America outside the region's southern cone. Even if it were accepted that people everywhere tend to act in accordance with their interests as they best see them, perceptions of those interests might differ. How changes in objective economic and social circumstances are reflected in human consciousness may be affected by hard-to-change cultural factors. Thus, for example, what is judged to be "adequate" shelter, education, or nutrition for one's children (above some critical minimum level)—a judgment that is bound to influence decisions about family size—is contingent on the specific cultural context. Indeed much historical evidence suggested that the response to changes in the pattern of economic opportunities could differ greatly from population to population. Hence there was no reason to expect a close inverse relation between the level of fertility and any particular index of development, such as income per capita, or to assume that attainment of some identifiable threshold values of development would represent a generally valid precondition for the start of a trend toward, and eventual achievement of, low fertility.

Irrespective of these cultural considerations, a slow pace of development—which was expected—would mean a slow or delayed fertility response. This raised the possibility of a vicious circle emerging: lack of development preserving high fertility and hence high rates of population growth, which, in turn, would block economic advance, thus perpetuating poverty but in an increasingly large population. That could eventually create a Malthusian situation of population growth slowing or terminating through a rising death rate.

Policy innovation triumphant

Technological progress has been the main driver in lifting many economies from poverty to material affluence. Such progress, in turn, is the fruit of human inventiveness—of ideas that create something new or that permit people to do things differently and better. In matters that more or less directly serve human needs, the value of new ideas is soon put to a market test. Bad ideas, whether intrinsically so or offering too little value for the effort required, are speedily weeded out. Good ideas triumph and make both the inventors and society richer. Products that were once successful may thus be displaced by new ones that better satisfy human needs. Progress is achieved through creative destruction.

Social arrangements at any given time may also be seen as less conducive to human welfare than some alternative arrangement could be. Politicians and policy entrepreneurs are keenly aware of unsatisfactory features of the economic and social system. This awareness, reinforced by grass-roots dissatisfaction with the status quo, stimulates the search for ideas and solutions that might yield greater satisfaction for the polity, subject to whatever limits may be prescribed by formal constitutional dictate. In the field of politics, the mechanisms of approval and rejection, the weeding out of the bad ideas and the certification of good ones, work far less reliably than in the private economy. For instance, the road to the vast expansion of the functions of government that the last century witnessed everywhere, and especially in the economically advanced countries, was generally paved with good intentions and commanded popular assent but often turned out to have undesired consequences, unforeseen at the outset. Even when this was recognized ex-post, moreover, roll-back was—and is—difficult because groups that benefit from the new state of affairs resolutely defend it. Programs are path-dependent.

International population programs launched in the second half of the last century exemplify this syndrome. Foreign aid, a postwar invention, grew out of emergency reconstruction programs and then, supported by a combination of humanitarianism and self-interest, became a tool in Cold War competition for influence in the third world. Eventually foreign aid came to be accepted as a routine and quasi-permanent function of rich-country governments—a modest extension of a government's domestic redistributive functions into the international arena. With the recognition that population growth might hinder economic progress, political entrepreneurs soon sought to harness some part of the foreign aid program to help moderate high levels of fertility. These efforts at "population control"—as the intent was commonly labeled in the early postwar decades—would serve the material advance of the aid recipients and would also benefit the donor because slowing population growth would contribute to international security. In advancing innovative proposals to help the cause of population control in the developing world, humanitarianism and self-interest thus seemed to be in harmony.

To spell out the essential socioeconomic changes that are necessary for fertility to shift from high to low levels is relatively easy: transition theory performed the task. But assembling the instruments thereby identified into a coherent development strategy of institutional–structural reforms that also promoted fertility decline remained an elusive objective. Not that the search for such a strategy was assiduously pursued. In promoting development, governments in third-world countries, as well as those helping them through foreign aid, came to see their roles as being to organize and support specific goal-oriented categorical programs in performing key developmental tasks. Rather than creating and nurturing institutions that would harness the market and, if only incidentally, stimulate individual initiative, the objective became in effect to replace those markets and limit the scope for that initiative. To be a plausible component of international assistance, population activities needed an instrument around which a tangible program could be built. And to be respectable, a program needed at least a modicum of budgetary heft—foreign aid, by its very conception, meant *spending*—and preferably also a specialized ministry in the recipient's capital to be in charge.

The technology of contraception soon provided the requisite instrument. Starting in the 1950s, as newly developed modern contraceptives became available, concrete proposals for population control programs focused on this technology. It could be reasonably argued that organizing programs that would give access to modern contraception to willing users and help to finance those programs through foreign aid was a natural counterpart of the earlier international transfer of modern technologies of disease control. One kind of program incidentally helped to raise population growth; the other sought to slow it down. Past Western experience and social science theorizing to the contrary, there was, perhaps, a technological fix for the problem of rapid population growth. Many supporters of this idea soon decided that the qualifying "perhaps" could be safely omitted.

Empirical support for this idea was soon provided by surveys in developing countries, sponsored and organized by American foundations and research groups. These surveys identified an unsatisfied "latent demand" for birth control. Lacking access to contraceptives, many people seemed to have more children than they wished for; they were interested in contraception but did not practice it. Markets could not be trusted to help solve this problem: contraceptives were costly and their would-be users were generally poor. But family planning programs could provide free or at least subsidized access to birth control. Thus, in the future, "unwanted" children would be "averted" and birth rates would fall. Such programs would simultaneously serve their clients, who would benefit from the service offered, and would address the macroeconomic problems—and, beyond that, ease the potential menace to international peace and security—posed by rapid population growth.

Initial attempts to stake out a role for the United Nations or for the World Health Organization in population activities foundered because of opposition by Catholic countries to promotion of "artificial birth prevention" and because of the rigid anti-Malthusian ideological stance of the Soviet Union. Initiatives by Swedish development aid, and, even more, by American private organizations, to start pilot programs were necessarily limited in scope. Involvement of the US government was therefore a crucial precondition for more ambitious efforts to set up and support family planning programs in the developing world. This proved to be a protracted process: the proposed activity seemed too peculiar to be a candidate for government support, and the topic was politically highly sensitive.[15] Asked at a December 1959 press conference about a private report that recommended US support for birth control in developing countries, President Eisenhower offered a blunt and unequivocal answer: "I cannot imagine anything more emphatically a subject that is not a proper political or governmental activity or function or responsibility....This government will not, as long as I am here, have a positive political doctrine in its program that has to do with the problem of birth control. That's not our business."[16]

What Eisenhower could not imagine, subsequent US administrations could, just a few years later. Convinced about the high promise of the new technology, the US foreign aid program embraced the goal of providing contraceptives to perhaps hundreds of millions of poor third-world people—living, most of them, in scattered villages or urban shantytowns—through family planning clinics, mobile units, or home visits. By implication and de facto, this indeed became a US "governmental activity, function, and responsibility."

It was not the professed intent. Formally, the responsibility rested with the governments that cooperated in setting up these programs and promised to co-finance them. The United States was merely a donor—providing money, supplies, and advice. But of course the recipient governments were poor and chronically overstretched by the demands of a myriad of other development tasks. Most were glad to accept aid for family planning, and promised coop-eration. The programs provided employment, including government jobs, and earned foreign exchange, since donor financing came partly in hard currency. Inevitably, the donor was destined to bear a disproportionate share of the costs of the program, in return receiving ill-defined spillover benefits.

Advice on how to proceed came entirely free of charge from the do-nor. Had it been much reflected upon, this might have seemed awkward. The West, and especially the United States, had no experience in setting up and operating family planning clinics. In the West fertility decline had to rely on premodern methods of birth control. These were either obtained in the market, with governments paying no attention to the practice—or, more commonly, frowning on it—or else were home-produced, requiring coop-eration between partners but at zero monetary cost. In the United States, even ordinary medical services were predominantly private except services for veterans and some government employees. With its self-assigned in-volvement in worldwide family planning programs, the US government was preparing to become a part-owner of socialized birth control medicine on a grand scale.

By January 1965, an expression of this intent even found its way into President Johnson's State of the Union Message: "I will seek new ways to use our knowledge to help deal with the explosion in world population and the growing scarcity in world resources." And at the twentieth-anniversary celebration of the United Nations in San Francisco, in June 1965, President Johnson was quite specific:

> Let us in all our lands—including this land—face forthrightly the multiplying problems of our multiplying populations and seek the answers to this most profound challenge to the future of all the world. Let us act on the fact that less than five dollars invested in population control is worth a hundred dol-lars invested in economic growth.[17]

For an American couple it was probably not too difficult to divine the underlying rationale of this last bizarre proposition. Contraception is inexpensive. Yet a decision, say, not to have a third child will be a near-certain source of massive savings for that couple in the next 19 or so years—enough, perhaps, to finance the college education of their first two children. By that calculus, their "investment in population control" would have had a remarkably high yield. Of course, millions of such "investments" had been routinely and voluntarily made every year by couples in the West for nearly a century before Johnson spoke, and were being made with increasing frequency among the elites in the developing world. Yet the cultural insensitivity, even deafness, entailed in putting a monetary value on an infant not born in some other country was evident, and was not a good omen for the smooth sailing of the family planning programs to be launched.[18]

Although answers to survey questions about interest in birth control have proven to be unreliable predictors of actual demand for birth control,[19] the existence of a substantial level of unmet need for contraception in high-fertility countries was taken as an axiom. The factors that transition theory considered to be the generators of demand for lower birth rates could therefore be set aside. By the late 1960s, the international population policy debate on the relative importance of the demand for versus supply of contraception was essentially decided in favor of the latter. For the next quarter-century, population policy as seen and promoted by aid donors for the benefit of the developing world became essentially synonymous with family planning programs. Although its mandate was broadly defined, this was true also of the United Nations Fund for Population Activities, which, beginning in 1969, became an increasingly important channel for multilateral population aid. The World Bank also joined in the support of the family planning enterprise, first as a large multilateral lender and later as a donor. Its presidents invariably declared rapid population growth to be one of the Bank's highest priority concerns.[20]

As the Johnsonian statement cited above implied, the cost of birth control technology was, in itself, relatively modest. But building up and sustaining an effective delivery service made significant claims on scarce human and material resources. A prescription offered by Gunnar Myrdal illustrates the magnitude of the task. Myrdal was one of the key actors in expanding the Swedish welfare state in the interwar years and a formulator of Sweden's own population policy; he was also a noted student of the economy of postwar South Asia. He addressed himself squarely to the governments of the countries that operated family planning programs. Unmet needs notwithstanding, he said, any such government should expect the program to meet "very great obstacles among the masses." To carry out an effective birth control policy,

First, it must realize the overwhelming importance for its development planning of bringing down fertility...and it must make *a firm decision to take action by instituting a vigorous policy to spread birth control.*

...the government must, secondly, *build up an administrative apparatus for the purpose....*

Implied in this second requirement is, thirdly, *the need to deploy a large staff of medical and paramedical personnel.* (Myrdal 1970: 156–158. Emphases in original.)

Given its key instrument—birth control services at large—a logical outcome of the basic design of population programs was its medicalization. But medical services were chronically ill-financed and inadequate. Therefore, to provide the requisite priority to birth control, which was seen as not simply catering to individual needs but providing a "merit good"—one with benefits, through reduced population growth, for society at large—it was often necessary to separate family planning services from general health services. They could then be organized as a quasi-autonomous "vertical" program, with its own administration and personnel. Also, by the time family planning programs got organized, foreign aid for medical services proper was evanescent, leaving family planning programs in a specially privileged status—a fact that did not contribute to their local esteem and popularity. But, as was the case with programs in other fields, once a family planning program was organized, its managerial and professional cadres formed a natural advocacy group strongly interested in its sustenance. In this respect, these programs were largely successful.

Although, not surprisingly, people's birth control practice came to rely heavily upon program-provided services, weakness of demand persisted. As late as the early 1990s, by which time fertility levels had been receding for a decade or more in most developing countries outside sub-Saharan Africa, a former Director-General of WHO and head of the International Planned Parenthood Federation laid out the criteria that a program should meet to be successful—a list that would clearly be hard to satisfy. It included such items as "doorstep accessibility of quality services," "broad choice of contraceptive methods," "forceful IEC [information, education, and communication] programs," "sound financing strategies," "sound management with proper logistics," "evaluation systems," "a continuous process of strategic thinking, planning and management," and "staff leadership for program parameters" (Mahler 1992: 5).

The effectiveness of family planning programs in reducing fertility remains a matter of controversy. According to international guidelines, programs recruit their clients on a strictly voluntary basis. By accepting the service voluntarily, the individual "acceptor" (usually a woman) demonstrates that she values that service. But some of the more successful programs, notably in Asia, increased acceptance by heavy-handed methods of persuasion, as was the case most notably in India during the 1975–77 Emergency Period, and, in the especially important instance of China, by outright coercion backed with political, legal, and lately economic sanctions. Where fertility fell in less developed countries with active family planning programs, use of program services has been interpreted as clear proof that fertility reduction was the result of the programs. Yet some less developed countries that lacked government programs also experienced major falls of fertility: Brazil is a conspicuous example. Where a program had seemingly only minor success in reducing fertility, this was taken as evidence that the program was inadequately financed, organized, and managed: greater efforts would have led to better results.

Despite the publicity—and controversy—that surrounded family planning programs from their inception, their weight in development activities at large, and in foreign aid programs in particular, remained relatively modest. In a nearly 400-page report commissioned by the World Bank and IMF in the early 1980s to assess foreign assistance programs and their effectiveness, family planning programs received a three-page commentary (and good marks). The report noted that the programs' share within total development aid thus far was 2.5 percent and that the share had been declining, although the programs could absorb more funds (Cassen and Associates 1986).

A big question but one that cannot be satisfactorily answered is what would have happened to fertility in the countries that received foreign aid for family planning programs had such aid not been forthcoming. Given the rapid social and economic transformation that most of the countries in question experienced, it is a reasonable conjecture that micro-level demand would have emerged naturally (as it had earlier in the West, and later in Japan) and found a way to achieve a desired smaller family size. This might have been possible even in the absence of a domestic program, even with equally strong reliance on modern methods of contraception but obtained in the market. Indeed, if left alone, individual initiative guided by self-interest might have been more readily triggered. John Caldwell, a notably sharp-eyed observer of the great rural transformations in the developing world, once commented that in rural India, the people assume that fertility control cannot be practiced without a government family planning program.[21] This was said in praise of the program, but on the Hippocratic principle such praise, arguably, is its most severe indictment.

A perhaps far more interesting question would probe a different counterfactual: how would governments and lower-level political units have acted in the absence of outside prompting, advice, and financial assistance? The governing elites in the third world in general and in densely populated and rapidly growing countries in particular needed little persuasion that their central goals for their countries—rapid advancement in power and economic strength—would be easier to achieve if population growth were slower. Foreign emphasis on the desirability of that latter objective very likely elicited some degree of backlash, weakening rather than strengthening the domestic resolve for action. More importantly, outside advice on the programmatic model to follow was likely to have short-circuited the search for a distinctly home-rooted approach to population policy. For better or worse, no foreign missions could have gone to China in the 1960s and 1970s offering advice on how to lower fertility. Yet China found a solution, albeit not one that could be recommended for export.[22] Other countries, pursuing their own best interest, might have found equally effective but more humane solutions.

Third-world second thoughts

By the late 1960s the ground for concerted international efforts toward slowing rapid population growth by reducing fertility appeared to be well prepared. Two large scientific population conferences—one in Rome in 1954 and another in Belgrade in 1965—were landmarks of the accumulating analytic work on the nature of contemporary population issues. Rapid population growth came to be seen by many governments and by public opinion as a hindrance, or even as a barrier, to economic development. The willingness of several foreign aid donor countries, most notably the United States, to support family planning programs provided both a financial basis and a model frame for cooperative international action. The time was ripe to give formal recognition and sanction to population programs at a global intergovernmental conference.

Such a conference took place in Bucharest in August 1974.[23] A lengthy and careful preparatory process, led by the United States, yielded a draft population plan of action intended for approval by the conference. This was not to be. The draft plan was conceived as a down-to-earth specialized programmatic guide for the "population sector," setting forth the rationale for and the ends and means of family planning programs. It proposed specific targets for the programs to be launched. The authors of the draft had not been mindful of the fact that this was a time (the early 1970s) when the developing countries were preoccupied with plans of a more ambitious sort: for a "new international economic order" that would give them a stronger voice and greater influence in global affairs and lend a new impetus to their economic growth. The third world, it turned out, had second thoughts about population matters.

After often acrimonious debates, the draft plan was in effect ripped apart and rewritten as a "policy instrument within the broader context of the internationally adopted strategies for national and international progress"—"an instrument of the international community for the promotion of economic development, quality of life, human rights and fundamental freedoms." Echoing social science orthodoxy that family planning programs were supposed to prove obsolete, the new Population Plan of Action declared that the "basis for an effective solution of population problems is, above all, socio-economic transformation."[24] And the most memorable phrase of the conference, uttered by the head of the Indian delegation, proclaimed: "Development is the best contraceptive."

Third-world aversion to the original draft reflected special sensitivity about possible outside interference with policies seen as strictly belonging to countries' internal affairs.[25] In the words of the conference's rewritten Plan of Action:

> The formulation and implementation of population policies is the sovereign right of each nation. This right is to be exercised in accordance with national objectives and needs and without external interference, taking into account universal solidarity in order to improve the quality of life of the peoples of the world. The main responsibility for national population policies and programmes lies with national authorities.

Such strictures were directed primarily to the American delegation—arguably, a sign of failed diplomacy and missed opportunities.

The principle of tying responsibility for population policy to the country concerned was certainly followed in the US's own practice. In the years just prior to the Bucharest conference, America's anxiety about its own rapid population growth in the wake of the postwar baby boom led to the creation, by Congress, of a Commission on Population Growth and the American Future. The Commission submitted its Report in 1972—followed by six weighty volumes of supporting papers, amounting to a painstaking and exemplary evaluation of every aspect of US population trends and their effects on the nation's welfare. The most quoted recommendation of the Report read as follows:

> Recognizing that our population cannot grow indefinitely, and appreciating the advantages of moving now toward the stabilization of population, the Commission recommends that the nation welcome and plan for a stabilized population. (US Commission 1972: 110)

Here was a recipe worthy of emulation and one plausibly to be recommended to other countries: study your situation and determine what is in your own best interest. The outcome of the Bucharest debates, in contrast, were high-sounding but palpably unuseful pronouncements. Thus the Plan of Action (in orotund if insufficiently gender-sensitive language):

Of all things in the world, people are the most precious. Man's knowledge and ability to master himself and his environment will continue to grow. Mankind's future can be made infinitely bright.

The issue that prompted the convening of the Bucharest conference to begin with, rapid population growth and its possibly deleterious effects on economic development, received little attention. "Population is not a problem under socialism" declared, for example, the head of the delegation of the People's Republic of China. In any event, "the primary way of solving the population problem lies in combating the aggression and plunder of the imperialists, colonialists, and neo-colonialists, and particularly the superpowers."

Yet, rhetorical flourishes notwithstanding, the Plan of Action—unanimously adopted at the end of the conference—contained language that could serve as an endorsement of the only operational proposal on the table: family planning programs. The Plan even allowed for the possibility that some countries may elect to set numerical population targets. It acknowledged that "family size may also be affected by incentive and disincentive schemes," while specifying that "if such schemes are adopted or modified it is essential that they should not violate human rights." And on reproductive rights, it made an important if opaquely qualified statement:

All couples and individuals have the basic right to decide freely and responsibly the number and spacing of their children and to have the information, education and means to do so; the responsibility of couples and individuals in the exercise of this right takes into account the needs of their living and future children, and their responsibilities towards the community.

To "have the information, education and means" was an eminently desirable requirement in an ideal world. If "means" meant modern contraceptive technology, the requirement was clearly unsatisfied in the less developed countries, and indeed frequently beyond them. But it could be satisfied, it was readily assumed, by organized, publicly financed family planning programs. How to define "responsibility" in exercising the "basic right" to decide "freely" the number and spacing of children was a more difficult matter. Who decides what is responsible behavior by a couple or an individual toward "living and future children" and "towards the community"? The Plan did not elaborate. By implication, the definition was ceded to the "sovereign right of each nation"—left, in effect, to the discretion of "national authorities."

This gave wide latitude for varying interpretations of reproductive rights, permitting another round of new thinking—yielding great deviations from the Bucharest rhetoric and from the spirit of the Plan. Practices in the world's two most populous countries illustrate the point.

Less than two years after Bucharest, the Indian Government issued a formal statement on national population policy. Brief excerpts suffice to convey its flavor.[26] "If the future of the nation is to be secured...the population problem will have to be treated as a top national priority and commitment.... [I]t is clear that simply to wait for education and economic development to bring about a drop in fertility is not a practical solution. The very increase in population makes economic development slow and more difficult of achievement. The time factor is so pressing, and the population growth so formidable, that we have to get out of the vicious circle through a direct assault upon this problem as a national commitment.... We are of the view that where a state legislature, in the exercise of its own powers, decides that the time is ripe and it is necessary to pass legislation for compulsory sterilization, it may do so."

China's birth rate in 1974—the year of Bucharest—was 28 per 1000, some 10 points below the level that had prevailed just a few years earlier. That spectacular drop was more than the outcome of China's success in combating imperialist aggression and plunder: it reflected the effects of a vigorous family planning program backed by a panoply of social, economic, and political measures. By 1980, the Chinese birth rate had dropped below 18 per 1000. A mild reversal of the trend thereafter was countered by redoubled efforts. In the words of Prime Minister Zhao Ziyang: "Stimulating production and improving the people's living standards both require that we continue to lay special stress on population control. This is our national policy, a policy of fundamental, strategic importance. We must persistently advocate late marriage and one child per couple, strictly control second births, prevent additional births by all means, [and] earnestly carry out effective birth control measures."[27] That policy was in line with Article 25 of China's 1982 Constitution, which declared: "The state promotes family planning so that population growth may fit the plans for economic and social development."

In third-world countries in general, the development-oriented Bucharest rhetoric did not result in a substantial course correction, let alone radical re-thinking of policies aimed at reducing high fertility. Countries that initiated government-organized family planning programs pre-Bucharest sought to continue them with renewed hope, although severe budget constraints and limited managerial and organizational capacities remained major stumbling blocks. More countries joined the pioneers, setting up similar programs. For the diplomats and politicians returning from Bucharest there were other sectoral programs, economic and social, to engage attention, about which large intergovernmental conferences followed one another in steady succession. "Population" was assigned to the care of the health ministry or to an expressly population-dedicated government agency, typically under medical leadership. Surrounding this now-institutionalized government activity was a penumbra of nongovernmental organizations providing complementary or additional services, mostly financed by the government or directly by foreign aid.

Thus, ten years after Bucharest, when national governments met again to discuss population policies, this time in Mexico City, the atmosphere was strikingly different. The 1984 International Conference on Population was essentially a conference of health professionals, hoping for improved family planning programs.[28] A key passage in the conference's Recommendations for the Further Implementation of the World Population Plan of Action complained, with these programs in mind, that "lack of definitive commitment, inadequate resources, [and] ineffective co-ordination and implementation... limited the effectiveness of national Governments in the implementation of their national population policies." But it was not clear how these factors could be changed—and policy effectiveness improved. Political correctness dictated that the principles of the Bucharest Plan of Action be declared valid and reaffirmed. Thus the Mexico City Recommendations, 88 in number, still exuded what might fairly be described as a vision of the omnipresent and omnipotent state, when in truth "overextended" was a more fitting adjective to describe most of the governments concerned. Governments were urged to tackle a virtually endless list of tasks, large and small, feasible or manifestly hopeless, eminently desirable or at best marginally appealing. Relentless repetition of instructions exemplified by the phrase "should give high priority to" only served to emphasize the absence of a sense of priorities. Enumerations of social desiderata were not informed by any philosophy, or by experience-based criteria through which amenability to government intervention could be assessed and calibrated. Nor was any distinction made between government as a doer of things by direct action and government as an organizer and guarantor of a legal-institutional framework for individual action. Governments were to eradicate mass hunger and illiteracy, achieve adequate health and nutrition levels, and eliminate unemployment and underemployment. On a multitude of other tasks covering every facet of demographic change and assorted development objectives they were urged to formulate plans, develop programs, and take concerted action, immediate steps, or remedial measures.[29]

What may have been intended as the most cogent of the Recommendations was addressed to countries "which consider that their population growth rates hinder the attainment of [their] national goals." Such countries were "invited to consider"—this turn of phrase conveyed the most cautious recommendation ventured by the Conference—"pursuing relevant demographic policies, within the framework of socioeconomic development." Such policies, this recommendation went on, should respect "human rights, the religious beliefs, philosophical convictions, cultural values and fundamental rights of each individual and couple, to determine the size of its own family." As at Bucharest, the usefulness of making rights out of things that people find desirable was not considered; neither was the question of what responsibilities should go with the exercise of such rights. People have many desires, often mutually inconsistent. Honoring the "fundamental right" of couples to determine the size of their own family—in effect, their right to multiply as they see fit—may render the realization of other rights impossible. Society then must compromise. There were no a priori reasons why the guarantee of a right to unlimited reproduction should necessarily take precedence over guarantees of other plausible social objectives, whether political, economic, or social.

Proposals for a reassessment of the population policy line that commanded near-consensus at Mexico City came from an unexpected source. The United States, at Bucharest the one unfailing advocate for the overriding importance of family planning programs in solving the problems caused by rapid population growth, appeared at the 1984 conference ready to champion a new approach. It was spelled out in a formal policy statement prepared by the Reagan Administration for the conference. The opening paragraphs gave the rationale for the turn-around:

> For many years, the United States has supported, and helped to finance, programs of family planning, particularly in developing countries. This Administration has continued that support but has placed it within a policy context different from the past. It is sufficiently evident that the current exponential growth in global population cannot continue indefinitely. There is no question of the ultimate need to achieve a condition of population equilibrium. The differences that do exist concern the choice of strategies and methods for the achievement of that goal. The experience of the last two decades not only makes possible but requires a sharper focus for our population policy. It requires a more refined approach to problems which appear today in quite a different light than they did twenty years ago.
>
> First and most important, population growth is, of itself, a neutral phenomenon. It becomes an asset or a problem only in conjunction with other factors, such as economic policy, social constraints, need for manpower, and so forth. The relationship between population growth and economic development is not necessarily a negative one. More people do not necessarily mean less growth. Indeed, in the economic history of many nations, population growth has been an essential element of economic progress.

In the 1960s and 1970s, the American statement went on, there was a "demographic overreaction." Swayed by "extremist scenarios...too many governments pursued population control measures without sound economic policies that create the rise in living standards historically associated with decline in fertility rates. This approach has not worked, primarily because it

has focused on a symptom and neglected the underlying ailments....
[P]opulation programs alone cannot substitute for the economic reforms
that put a society on the road toward growth and, as an aftereffect, toward
slower population increase as well."

This was theorizing cast straight in the Bucharest mold. It harked back
also to the pre-1950s social science consensus.[30] The newfound alignment
of the largest and most active government donor to population programs
with much of the prevailing UN ideology on population policy matters should
have been a cause of rejoicing by the international community gathered in
Mexico City, and especially by its third-world members. But this did not
happen. Along with its espousal of the Bucharest line the United States made
suggestions that the vast majority of other participants at the conference
regarded as inadmissible deviations from orthodoxy. Not only did the United
States endorse the goal of development, it also suggested that international
experience provided guidance on how to achieve rapid economic growth
and how to generate a social transformation most likely to promote a voluntary fertility decline. It inveighed against "economic statism" and government policies that "disrupted economic incentives, rewards, and advancement." Rely more on markets, on entrepreneurial initiative, and on the
aspiration of individuals to improve their lot, the United States urged. "The
postwar experience consistently demonstrated that, as economic decisionmaking was concentrated in the hands of planners and public officials, the
ability of average men and women to work towards a better future was
impaired and sometimes crippled."

The final document that emerged from the Mexico City Conference
was largely uncontaminated by such ideas. The United States was alone in
putting them forward, although mild support came from the Japanese. If
Western European delegations found any merit in the argument, they kept
the thought to themselves. Most likely, they considered the introduction of
policy issues and concepts that were not in line with the UN's programmatic thinking to be divisive, hence unhelpful. The aim was consensus.[31] In
the mid-1980s, few third-world governments considered the American argument palatable or even worthy of second thoughts.

Revisionism ascendant

The realization, early in the postwar period, that the world was entering an
era of extraordinarily rapid population growth, concentrated in the poorer
countries, worried most informed observers. In the nineteenth century, global population growth averaged slightly above one-half of one percent per
year. The first half of the twentieth century saw faster population growth,
but still appreciably below an average of one percent per year. In 1950 the
less developed countries, as they came to be designated, comprised some

1.7 billion people, a number larger than the world's total in 1900. The growth rate of this population in the early 1950s had already passed 2 percent per year and showed signs of increasing further.[32] Obviously, such rates if extrapolated far into the future lead to absurd results. But could they even be sustained in the medium term, such as for the next 50 years?

Some pessimistic postwar forecasts on this score were quickly dismissed by most economists as unfounded. Economic backwardness was a burden, but it had some advantages. There was a large storehouse of technologies, developed elsewhere, that could be drawn on, offering the promise of leapfrogging early stages of technological evolution. For agriculture those technologies had the potential for feeding a much larger population, and feeding it better than ever before. For scarce raw materials, they could point to substitutes or to less resource-intensive production. Shortages of fossil fuels, apart from coal, were seen as a looming problem in the medium term if population size became much larger and more affluent, but even on that score reassurance could be taken from the rosy-eyed forecasts then prevailing about the peaceful use of nuclear energy. In short, Malthusian–Ricardian fears were soon expunged from the dominant postwar economic analyses of the effects of increased population size.

But could economic expansion, and in particular capital accumulation, keep up with the pace of population increase? And if the answer to that question was yes, at least for the medium term, how much of a retarding effect might population growth exert on the rate of economic improvement?

Early answers to those questions were given in a study by Ansley Coale and Edgar Hoover, exploring India's economic prospects under hypothetical alternative scenarios of the future course of demographic change. This indicated that a major and fairly rapid decline of fertility would bring economic advantages, measured as a faster pace of per capita income growth. The advantages derived from a smaller share of savings and investment being absorbed in the sheer maintenance of a larger population; from slowing the expansion of the labor force–age population, hence relieving unemployment and underemployment; and from lessening the public and private burden of a large youthful population, hence freeing up resources that could be used to raise savings rates and improve the health and education of the now smaller youth cohort. In less detail, the study also assessed Mexico's prospects, employing the same model. The conclusions were essentially identical in the two, otherwise very different, economies, suggesting generally applicable results for the developing world at large—as indeed was signaled in the title of the resulting book (Coale and Hoover 1958).

The Coale–Hoover study was highly influential in firming up the economic rationale for what soon became the main public policy response to rapid population growth: family planning programs. Voluntary use of family planning program services would not only directly benefit the clients themselves; it would also have positive effects on economic development at large. But the force of this latter effect remained controversial, and increasingly so as the years passed. The quantitative benefits estimated by the study were surprisingly modest. As Simon Kuznets pointed out in an incisive discussion of the interrelationships between population and economic growth, the gains calculated by Coale and Hoover could be easily matched or surpassed by relatively modest changes in the parameter values of the model, such as savings rates and capital–output ratios, changes that should have been readily achievable in developing countries in the right circumstances. This did not suggest that the economic problem of rapid population growth was not potentially serious, but rather that the Coale–Hoover model's specifications were very sparse, arguably leaving out many of the factors that really matter in sparking economic development, as attested by both historical experience and economic and social theory (Kuznets 1967).

Whatever the analytical shortcomings of the research, to their supporters family planning programs were seen as having a well-established economic rationale. On that basis, donor and recipient governments, initially skeptical, were persuaded to take up an endeavor that was demanding in its claims on both financial and administrative resources. Others, however, recognized that the intellectual underpinnings of the policy as far as the economic case was concerned needed further attention. A report of the US National Academy of Sciences (NAS), prepared in 1963, just two years before the launching of the US Agency for International Development's (USAID) population activities, illustrates this clearly. Addressing the problem of "uncontrolled population growth," which it called "one of the most critical issues of our time," the report in its recommendations focused on the need for better understanding of the problem and for more research. It also called for establishment of an NAS committee to deal with the issue (National Academy of Sciences 1963). Subsequently, the Administrator of USAID asked the NAS to study the questions on which knowledge was found to be deficient.

The results of this multiyear study eventually appeared in a 700-page volume under the title *Rapid Population Growth: Consequences and Implications* (National Academy of Sciences 1971). The bulk of the volume consisted of 17 individual research papers focused on various aspects of the topic. Invariably, these papers came out with guarded appraisals of the nature of the economics of population growth. The first 100 pages, however, were taken up by a report of the Committee (the dozen members of which included only one of the invited contributors, T.W. Schultz), titled "Summary and Recommendations." This was far more assertive and assured in pronouncing on the implications of rapid population growth than were the research papers that followed—a syndrome far from unique in such projects.[33] The report offered a year-2000 global population forecast of 7.5 billion as plausible and 7 billion as "the best estimate now possible." These forecasts, made three decades into the future, need not be seen as egregiously off target, but the direction of their bias—upward—is significant. In retrospect we know that the overall level of fertility in the developing world had already passed its peak when the report was composed. By the year 2000 it had dropped by 50 percent. The report did indeed note fertility declines in many developing countries in the prior decade, but it missed signaling (or even speculating about) the likelihood of a generalized historic turnaround in fertility trends—despite the by then well-recognized pattern of exceptionally rapid economic growth and urbanization, by historical standards, in most developing regions. In the past, similar changes even at far more modest rates invariably generated downturns of birth rates.

The report set out what it saw as the deleterious economic, social, and political effects of rapid population growth and explored the specific consequences of that growth for education, health, welfare and child development, and the environment. Consensus findings on each of these issues were judiciously summarized, highlighting problems caused by population growth but also noting points of disagreement. (Little attention was paid to areas to which population growth made no difference.) Aside from the call for more research on socioeconomic consequences, the report's policy recommendations strongly endorsed family planning programs—"provision of a full range of acceptable, easily used, and effective means of preventing births to be provided by governments to all persons of reproductive age at nominal or no cost." By that time this was of course the common advice to developing countries, backed by international aid. On strategies stimulating grass-roots demand for such services, suspected to be weak or even nonexistent, what little the report had to say lacked conviction and clear articulation—and, unsurprisingly, had no programmatic appeal for those in charge of population policy formulation. There was a recommendation to pursue research on the economics of population change, but no USAID funding for that purpose was forthcoming.

The case for the demand side, however, was taken up by academic researchers. Their writings on the topic, although controversial, tended to be highly critical of—and highly damaging to—the prevailing economic rationale for antinatalist policies. Broadside attacks on the orthodoxy concerning rapid population growth were soon dubbed revisionism. The revisionists included prominent economists: emblematic landmarks were works by Bauer (1981) and Simon (1981).[34] These writings were the main stimulus behind the US population policy line announced at the 1984 Mexico City population conference referred to above. Intellectual preparatory works prompted by that approaching conference date also included other reviews of the economics of population growth, each signaling a far more qualified assessment of the nature and import of that relationship than the orthodox views suggested (World Bank 1984; McNicoll 1984). And, two years after the Mexico City meeting, and based on extensive preparatory studies, the US National Research Council issued a brief policy-oriented report on population and economic development that amounted to a strong confirmation of the revisionist line (National Research Council 1986). This report essentially concluded that in a few areas rapid population growth was not economically advantageous but the adverse effects were not very large. Economies were, or could be made, sufficiently flexible to allow the necessary adjustments to rapid population growth. Some of those adjustments might even lift the economy to a higher level of efficiency and a faster economic growth path. Significantly, the issue of optimal *scale* with respect to population size was not touched on in the report: scale had (and has) little or no place in the standard frame of analysis and tool kit of most economists.

As a result of these developments, the macroeconomic benefits of family planning programs, once their main prop in asking for financial support from governments, began to look quite weak and were less often invoked. References to the programs' impact on aggregate indicators of demographic change, such as birth rates and rates of population growth, similarly became rarer. Emphasis shifted, instead, to pointing to the direct welfare benefits to individual clients, especially women, deriving from subsidized or free services offered by the programs. It is likely, however, that the original rationale persisted in legislators' minds when voting for population budgets: financial support for the programs softened from the 1980s on, but the decline was gradual. The rationale also persisted, or even acquired new life, in the public domain, where alarmist views of the "population problem" were voiced by prestigious observers who appeared to have newly discovered it. Interpretations of the dangers of rapid population growth that would have been understandable at midcentury when made against the background of the lackluster pre–World War II performance of the international economy still fairly regularly surfaced in the 1980s and 1990s—as if the post-1950 decades held no lessons for a different understanding.[35] Political figures also took up the cause, in the United States often coming from widely different points on the ideological spectrum. For some, new ideas about the damaging environmental effects of population growth were given prominence (see, for example, Gore 1992); others discovered the potentially dire geopolitical implications of shifting population numbers and relative economic weights (see, for example, Nixon 1992). Remarkably, however, when turning to the question of how to correct the problem, their solution unfailingly involved better access to contraceptive technology. Belief in what might be called the stupid peasant theory of population change— long abandoned in other parts of development studies—appeared to have remained unshaken: people in some countries or social classes had as many children as they did, not because they wanted them but because they did not know how to prevent births.

What was understandable from a busy politician was less so from scientists. Another 1992 statement—this was during the period leading up to the third intergovernmental world population conference, set for Cairo in 1994—came with the highest scientific imprimatur: issued jointly (the first time this had happened) by the Royal Society of London and the US National Academy of Sciences (Royal Society 1992). Entitled *Population Growth, Resource Consumption, and a Sustainable World*, the statement could certainly be described as an alarmist view of global population growth—a defensible scientific stance. Remarkably, however, the statement made no reference to the 1986 National Research Council report cited above, a widely known and debated document produced by an arm of the NAS and expressing views diametrically opposed in spirit and substance to those of the joint statement. The authors of the latter, coming from the hard sciences, either were unaware of the NRC report or found it so much beyond the pale as not to deserve even dismissive comment.[36] The Joint Statement was more noteworthy still when it turned to matters of population policy—to the ways that might contribute to the solution of the population problem. "Why is population growth rapid?" the statement asked, and answered: because of "large amounts of unwanted childbearing." And what can scientific research do to mitigate the problem? A single answer was given: "development of new generations of safe, easy to use, and effective contraceptive agents and devices." No one could doubt that such "agents and devices" would be a good thing. Yet this diagnosis and this prescription reflected a profound, if perhaps casually arrived at, misreading of the central lessons of the development experience of the now industrialized countries—of the factors that made the West rich and that generated its fertility transition.[37]

The erosion of the developmental rationale for antinatalist population policies under conditions of rapid population growth—whether deservedly so or not—endangered the sustainability of family planning programs. It relegated them to the status of just another social welfare program serving individual client needs. Predictably, in competing with other such programs, notably vital curative health services, family planning could not expect to rank high in priority. Unlike its competitors, it delivered services that could also be home-produced and was dealing with a clientele of predominantly healthy people. But a weakened macroeconomic rationale still could have left intact the notion that such programs have a measurable negative effect on birth rates. In an article which appeared shortly before the Cairo conference, that claim was subjected to a detailed quantitative analysis and found wanting (Pritchett 1994). This was revisionism of a different sort from that epitomized by the 1986 NRC report, but with population policy implications potentially just as important. The article's cogent analysis showed that high fertility closely mirrored desired births and that couples were by and large able to achieve their fertility targets. "[T]he level of contraceptive use, measures of contraceptive availability (such as "unmet need"), and family planning effort have little impact on fertility after controlling for fertility desires." And, as the conclusion: "[S]ince many couples in developing countries currently perceive they are better off with larger families, the best (and perhaps the only palatable) way to reduce fertility is to change the economic and social conditions that make large families desirable." (Ibid.: 2, 41.)[38]

Population programs repositioned

In the lead-up to the 1994 Cairo conference, family planning organizations were confronted with a gradual, if partial and reluctant, acceptance of these revisionist positions. The development rationale for family planning programs was weaker than had been assumed and the programs' effect on fertility slighter. Furthermore, by the early 1990s, the general decline of fertility in much of the developing world had reached a point that seemed clearly to suggest a spreading worldwide convergence of fertility rates to replacement level or even below it. United Nations population projections came to incorporate that assumption into their medium-term forecasts for most developing countries. On the eve of the conference, a commissioned review of population issues, considered highly respectful of the importance of fertility decline for successful economic development, reached the guarded conclusion that the data on the subject "mostly support the view that rapid population growth in poor countries under conditions of high fertility is inimical to many development goals"—with stress on the qualifying words "mostly," "rapid," "high fertility," and "many development goals." Rapid growth was defined as exceeding 2 percent annually (Cassen and Contributors 1994: 13). By that time, among world regions, only sub-Saharan Africa and West Asia had population growth rates meeting that criterion. And in explaining why birth rates were still high in those areas, many observers— by no means only feminists—now pointed less to limitations in family planning access than to poor health conditions, high infant and child mortality, and, especially, women's lack of economic opportunities, their low educational levels, and their unequal legal status.

   Thus, a rethinking of what the conference's subject should be was needed. Population programs had to be repositioned—given a newly articulated raison d'être. As a step in that direction, intended to be symbolic, the conference was renamed: unlike the Bucharest and the Mexico City meetings it was not just a conference on population but on Population and Development. That had a certain irony: there was far less discussion about economic development and its relationship to population at Cairo than at Bucharest or even Mexico City. Among the 179 country delegations at Cairo, economists and demographers were hard to find. "Population" was given a special meaning: it was no longer about numbers. It had to be freed from

crudely quantitative connotations suggesting a concern with aggregate population size, birth rates, or, even worse, population targets. The conference
did not wish to pursue demographic objectives. Its aim, "in the context of
sustained economic growth and sustainable development," was to advocate
programs serving goals that people would value for their own good: education, especially of girls; gender equity and equality; reduction of infant, child,
and maternal mortality; and universal access to broadly construed reproductive health services. Success in these fields would also bear demographic
fruit, but as an almost incidental byproduct, a distinctly subordinate consideration in the corresponding action programs.

Upon closer examination, the spirit of Cairo bore the marks of old-
fashioned thinking about causal chains in the process of development. Technological progress, industrialization, rising incomes, and urbanization were
known to go hand-in-hand with spreading literacy, better education, better
health, low mortality, greater opportunities for women, and, indeed, lower
birth rates. Demographic transition theory was a probing depiction of such
linkages. Population thinking thus came full circle: there was no simple short
cut to the low-fertility–low-mortality balance that the family planners had
envisioned. But there were differences in strategic conceptualization from
the earlier approach. Deferential to historical experience, transition theory
saw no single magic lever that guaranteed progress to individual and social
health and happiness. At Cairo, one factor came close to being elevated to
that status: gender equity.[39] And while causes and effects were intertwined
in the historical experience of development, the primacy of establishing a
growing material base for social progress, and of the institutions that best
support it, was well documented. The Cairo conferees showed scant interest in that task.

Lack of interest in how economic development might come about did
not interfere with the distribution of its fruits. Remarkably, the prescriptions of the Cairo agenda seemed to take for granted the economic foundations of a welfare state. This was a decidedly premature assumption, out of
all proportion to the realistic capacities, financial and administrative, of the
countries concerned. Diverting the already dwindling international aid going to old-fashioned family planning programs in order to finance the much
wider social welfare agenda championed by the Cairo conference could not
hope to suffice; nor could that agenda be fulfilled even if the available resources were substantially increased. The Cairo plan nevertheless was blithely
optimistic on the matter:

> The international community should strive for the fulfilment of the agreed
> target of 0.7 per cent of GNP for overall official development assistance and
> endeavour to increase the share of funding for population and development
> programmes commensurate with the scope and scale of activities required to

achieve the objectives and goals of the present Programme of Action. A crucially urgent challenge to the international donor community is therefore the translation of their commitment to the objectives and quantitative goals of the present Programme of Action into commensurate financial contributions to population programmes in developing countries and countries with economies in transition.

Those commensurate contributions were quite modest, certainly in comparison, say, to private capital flows to developing countries. For the year 2000, for example, the Plan asked for US$6.1 billion (in 1993 dollars)— later scaled down to $5.7 billion. But "population," even in its elaborate new programmatic wrapping (or possibly, in part, because of it), now lacked the appeal of older-style family planning programs. Only about one-third of the envisaged sum was forthcoming.

Cairo-like thinking was influential, however, in shaping the next new effort to invigorate international assistance to less developed countries. This was sparked by the United Nations Millennium Summit in 2000. The Millennium Declaration adopted at that session of the General Assembly set eight goals for the international community over the next 15 years. These eight, known as the Millennium Development Goals, were to eradicate extreme poverty and hunger; to achieve universal primary education; to promote gender equality and empower women; to reduce child mortality; to improve maternal health; to combat HIV/AIDS, malaria, and other diseases; to ensure environmental sustainability; and to develop a global partnership for development. These goals were further broken down into 18 specific targets, some of them quantified, such as "reduce by three-quarters, between 1990 and 2015, the maternal mortality ratio." Like the goals themselves, none of the targets concerned the objectives that preoccupied old-fashioned family planning programs during much of the second half of the twentieth century: assuring people better access to birth control, especially to contraceptives, and reducing "unwanted" fertility. Old-fashioned transition theorists, however, might provide reassurance that meeting the various goals and targets would help in pursuing those ends. Eradicating poverty and hunger, for example, would tend to lower birth rates.

In a 2005 review of progress toward realization of the Millennium Development Goals the Cairo agenda made just two specific appearances. The resolution adopted by the 2005 General Assembly, titled The World Summit Outcome, consists of 178 paragraphs. Paragraph 57(g), part of a section titled *HIV/AIDS, Malaria, Tuberculosis and Other Health Issues*, declares the international community's commitment to:

> Achieving universal access to reproductive health by 2015, as set out at the International Conference on Population and Development, integrating this

goal in strategies to attain the internationally agreed development goals, including those contained in the Millennium Declaration, aimed at reducing maternal mortality, improving maternal health, reducing child mortality, promoting gender equality, combating HIV/AIDS and eradicating poverty.

And Paragraph 58 (c), part of the section *Gender Equality and Empowerment of Women*, reaffirms a commitment to:

Ensuring equal access to reproductive health.

Worry about global population growth had effectively vanished—transmuted here, in the form of reproductive health, to a walk-on part as an "other health issue" or as an incidental component of women's empowerment. Whatever the millennium goals might do to help the world's poor, they can be read as a requiem for the international family planning enterprise of the twentieth century.

Population problems recrudescent

By 2000, the ending of global population expansion was not yet at hand but was clearly foretold. Even those academics who disdained transition theory qua theory accepted the long-range population forecasts based upon it, showing a tailing-off in growth over coming decades. Premature though the sentiment might have been in many respects, the "population problem" of the early postwar period tended to be seen as something that had now been dealt with—a twentieth-century matter that need no longer engage policy attention and required only routine further policy action. The era when terms like crisis or explosion seemed applicable had long passed.

But people, like the poor but in even greater numbers, are always with us; population issues are inescapable. That is obviously true at the country level: any country, like any society, must necessarily be concerned with how its membership roll changes over time and with the rules and practices, open or tacit, that influence those changes. It is also true at the global level, where differential demographic change bears on the relations between states. In particular, the successive transformations of national demographic regimes seen over the second half of the twentieth century, together with the shifts in relative population sizes that accompanied them, began to create new problems for the international system. Two such problems, emerging late last century, were of particular significance; they are connected in various ways and both seem bound to stay high on the public policy agenda in the years ahead. One is the issue of very low fertility; the other, international migration.

Fertility at levels below that required for population replacement had been experienced in many Western countries early in the twentieth century, eliciting much hand-wringing and gloom. As the depression years ended, however, there was a demographic as well as an economic recovery—and, after World War II, a baby boom. Perhaps in part because of that experience, the return of low fertility later in the century was met mostly with equanimity. Only as evidence mounted against the likelihood of a renewed upturn, particularly in Europe and Japan, and as the declines spread to countries or regions that had been supposedly protected by cultural and religious tradition, like Italy and Spain or Quebec, did low fertility come to be considered a problem. There were potentially serious domestic implications—in particular, for the financial base of the welfare state; the forecast actual shrinkage of population, perhaps both drastic and long-lasting, suggested international repercussions as well. Even so, for ideological reasons having to do with rights of privacy (like those earlier expressed by President Eisenhower, as noted above) and awareness of the unappealing pronatalist measures taken in the past by totalitarian states, there was little support for efforts at remedy.[40] And on the financial side, certainly, birth subsidies at levels likely to have much effect could hardly have been affordable amid all the other transfers that the welfare state had established and was seeing burgeoning.

International migration, the second emerging issue, also had an important prehistory. In the major destination country, the United States, the proportion foreign-born had been steadily declining over the first two-thirds of the twentieth century, from around 14 percent to below 5 percent. A low point of 4.7 percent was recorded in the 1970 census.[41] After that, the proportion began edging up again, reaching just over 12 percent by 2000.

Europe had of course been the scene of major population displacements associated with its twentieth-century wars and revolutions and with the Cold War, and received a trickle of migrants from its former colonies. What was novel in late-century migration was the scale of the inflow from the developing world—a good part of it making use of the asylum framework that had been established to deal with earlier intra-European flows. Foreign-born population shares in various European countries moved sharply higher, and now included significant "visible minorities" from Asia and Africa.[42] In both the European Union and the United States, public debate on immigration brought out disparate voices, including strongly nativist views and others welcoming potential workers. Welcome or not, the press of would-be migrants was clearly growing, with many entering illegally— supporting a fair-sized black economy of human traffickers.

While these problems had their origin in the twentieth century, the development of policy responses to them will largely be a matter for the twenty-first. They are discussed further in several chapters in this volume, and together make up the main theme of the final chapter.

The 50-year record

Thus far this chapter has been mainly concerned with recounting how the developed countries over half a century witnessed and responded to changing demographic regimes in the rest of the world. We conclude with a brief review of the actual demographic and developmental outcomes over the period, however large or small the policy input to them may have been.

The second half of the twentieth century was not exempt from international conflict, even protracted wars; from economic hardship, even mass famine; and from ill health, even a devastating epidemic. But its overall record compared to the first half of the century was shining. By 2000, the globe accommodated 3.6 billion more people than the 2.5 billion that inhabited it 50 years earlier—itself a kind of accomplishment. At the same time, economic development made great headway, major wars were avoided, political freedom increased in many countries and spread to some that did not have it before, literacy and access to information expanded, and most people enjoyed greater health and lived longer. The more crowded planet and emergence of new and large industrializing economies created often severe environmental problems, but most of these were, if not successfully coped with, at least kept on the economic sidelines—or kicked forward for possible remedy at some future time. And the pace of demographic expansion, after peaking in the 1960s, steadily lessened. (At the turn of the century, however, the momentum deriving from a youthful age distribution was still generating a net global addition of some 76 million persons per year.)

By 2000, a few erstwhile third-world countries[43] had successfully caught up with the advanced industrial countries; more of them had at least surpassed the average income levels enjoyed by the West 50 years earlier. Many other countries, of course, lagged far behind, but despite widening absolute income gaps within the international system, even the poorest countries provided better conditions of life than they did 50 years earlier.

The comparative experience with respect to population change and change in aggregate and per capita income is summarized in Table 1 and Figure 1, drawing on the consistent data set constructed by Maddison (2003). In the 11 units (that distinguish four countries and seven regional/continental groups) shown in Table 1, population growth between 1950 and 2001 ranged between an increase of 29 percent (in Western Europe) and 261 percent (in Africa).[44] In between these extreme values, growth has been very rapid in Latin America (220 percent) and in Asia outside Japan, China, and India (213 percent). It was also substantial in the two demographic giants, with India's population growing by 185 percent and China's by 133 percent. At the lower end, Eastern Europe's growth, at 38 percent, exceeded Western Europe's only modestly. Japan's population growth registered at 51 percent, that of the United States, fueled also by immigration, at 87 percent.

**TABLE 1   Population, gross domestic product, and GDP per head in the
United States, Japan, China, and India and in world regions, 1950 and 2001**

	Population (millions)			GDP (billion dollars)			GDP per head (dollars)		
	1950	2001	2001/ 1950	1950	2001	2001/ 1950	1950	2001	2001/ 1950
Western Europe	304.9	392.1	1.3	1,396	7,550	5.4	4,579	19,256	4.2
Eastern Europe	87.6	120.9	1.4	185	729	3.9	2,111	6,027	2.9
Former Soviet Union	179.6	290.3	1.6	510	1,343	2.6	2,841	4,626	1.6
United States	152.3	285.0	1.9	1,456	7,966	5.5	9,561	27,948	2.9
Other Western offshoots	24.2	54.8	2.3	180	1,190	6.6	7,425	21,718	2.9
Latin America	165.9	531.2	3.2	416	3,087	7.4	2,506	5,811	2.3
Japan	83.8	126.9	1.5	161	2,625	16.3	1,921	20,683	10.8
China	546.8	1,275	2.3	240	4,570	19.0	439	3,583	8.2
India	359.0	1,024	2.9	222	2,003	9.0	619	1,957	3.2
Other Asia	392.8	1,228	3.1	364	4,908	13.5	926	3,998	4.3
Africa	227.3	821.1	3.6	203	1,223	6.0	894	1,489	1.7
World	2,524.3	6,149.0	2.4	5,330	37,194	7.0	2,111	6,049	2.8

NOTE: GDP and GDP per head measured in 1990 international dollars.
SOURCE: Maddison 2003: Tables 8a, 8b, and 8c.

For all the attention these remarkable figures of population change richly deserve in their own right, they need to be seen in the larger context of the economic growth experience highlighted in Table 1 over the period.[45] With the exception of the former Soviet Union and of Eastern Europe, aggregate gross domestic product at least quintupled in each of the units shown. GDP grew 19-fold in China, 16-fold in Japan, and 9-fold in India. In the rest of Asia GDP registered a 13-fold increase. Latin America's increase was only slightly above the 7-fold increase of the global total; Africa's, with a 6-fold increase was below that average. In combination with population growth, this expansion of aggregate GDP meant that only the former Soviet Union and Africa fell short of at least doubling real income per head. Among developing regions Asia was by far the strongest performer, including—wholly unforeseen at midcentury—its giants, though with China, where income per head grew roughly 8-fold, far outpacing India, where that indicator merely tripled. The star performer, however, was Japan, with income per head growing nearly 11-fold. Latin America, always somewhat anomalous as part of the less developed world given its major "settler economy" components that have much in common with North America and Australia, had, especially in comparison to Asia, a disappointing economic record: its improvement in income per capita was below the world average and well below that registered in Western Europe. As a matter of sheer arith-

FIGURE 1   Growth of populations and incomes, 1950–2000: Selected regions and countries

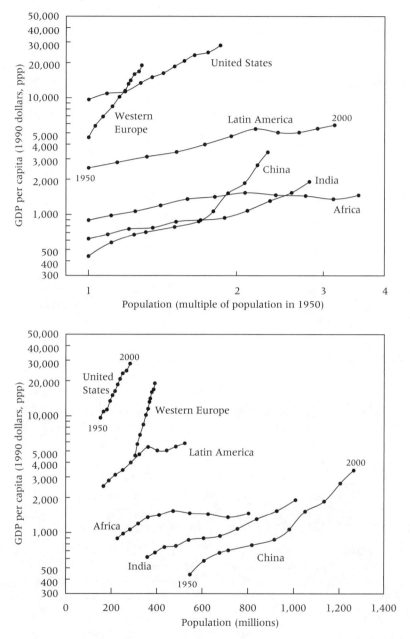

NOTE: Data points mark 5-year intervals between 1950 and 2000.
SOURCE OF DATA: Maddison (2003).

metic, demography played a role in shaping that performance. Although Latin America, and indeed also Africa, recorded quite impressive aggregate growth of GDP, large shares of that growth went toward accommodating greatly expanded populations.

Slower aggregate GDP growth in combination with relatively moderate expansion of population numbers still yielded quite rapid income gains in the older industrial countries. Per capita income, for example, more than quadrupled in Western Europe and nearly tripled in the United States. And the start from a relatively high GDP base and relatively slow population growth meant that despite slower rates of aggregate income growth, the developed-country group had a share of that growth disproportionate to its population increase. As is implicit in Table 1, world population grew between 1950 and 2001 by some 3.6 billion persons and some 12 percent of that growth represented population increase in the more developed countries. World GDP grew in the same period by some 31.9 trillion dollars. Of that increase, 54 percent accrued to the more developed countries.

The charts in Figure 1 provide two graphical depictions of this experience for a subset of the countries and regions identified in the table. The top panel plots trajectories of growth in population and per capita income over 1950–2000 on a double log scale, the data points identifying five-year intervals. The long horizontal trajectories of Latin America, India, and Africa reflect the large demographic expansion in those regions. The divergence of China and India, starting at the midpoint of the period, is a striking feature, as China's economy took off and its birth rate plummeted. In the United States a near doubling of population went with a trebling of per capita income.

In the bottom panel, the horizontal axis simply records population size, so the horizontal positions of the trajectories depict relative population weights in the world and the changes in those weights over the 50 years. The demographic marginalization of the United States and Europe is apparent. Africa's demographic weight increased substantially, although the bigger change is to come in the next half-century when its population is projected to surpass both China's and India's.

The growth record of the second half of the twentieth century is concisely recapitulated in Table 2 in terms of average annual percentage rates of change. The table also distinguishes two periods within the full 51-year span: 1950–73 and 1973–2001, the year of the first oil shock providing the mark that separates the full time period into two nearly equal segments. As to population, the rate of growth decreases from the first to the second period in 10 of the 11 units shown. Africa is the sole outlier in this regard: there, the annual rate of population growth goes from 2.4 percent to 2.7 percent. The demographic slow-down in the second period is marked in 8 of the 10 units that show decreases, but it is very small in India (from 2.11 percent to 2.05 percent) and elsewhere in Asia outside Japan and China. (Some countries in that residual category of course experienced rapid de-

TABLE 2   Average annual rates of growth (percent) of population, GDP, and GDP per head in the United States, Japan, China, and India and in world regions, 1950–73, 1973–2001, and 1950–2001

	Population			GDP			GDP per head		
	1950–1973	1973–2001	1950–2001	1950–1973	1973–2001	1950–2001	1950–1973	1973–2001	1950–2001
Western Europe	0.7	0.3	0.5	4.8	2.2	3.3	4.1	1.9	2.8
Eastern Europe	1.0	0.3	0.6	4.9	1.0	2.7	3.8	0.7	2.1
Former Soviet Union	1.4	0.5	0.9	4.8	–0.4	1.9	3.4	–1.0	1.0
United States	1.5	1.1	1.2	3.9	2.9	3.3	2.5	1.9	2.1
Other Western offshoots	2.1	1.2	1.6	4.8	3.0	3.7	2.6	1.7	2.1
Latin America	2.7	2.0	2.3	5.4	2.9	3.9	2.6	0.9	1.7
Japan	1.1	0.6	0.8	9.3	2.7	5.5	8.1	2.1	4.7
China	2.1	1.3	1.7	5.0	6.7	5.8	2.9	5.3	4.1
India	2.1	2.1	2.1	3.5	5.1	4.3	1.4	3.0	2.3
Other Asia	2.4	2.2	2.2	6.0	4.6	5.1	3.5	2.4	2.9
Africa	2.4	2.7	2.5	4.4	2.9	3.5	2.0	0.2	1.0
World	1.9	1.6	1.8	4.9	3.1	3.8	2.9	1.4	2.1

SOURCE: Maddison 2003: Tables 8a, 8b, and 8c.

celeration of demographic growth—South Korea, for example.) Globally, despite the slow-down, the average annual rate of population expansion between 1950 and 2001 was 1.8 percent: a speed unprecedented in any comparable period in modern demographic history. By the turn of the millennium the rate is estimated as 1.25 percent.

Population growth, however, was matched by even faster expansion of aggregate GDP. In this regard the period 1950–73 stands out. Annual GDP growth ranged between 3.5 percent (in India) and 9.3 percent (in Japan). In combination with population change this meant that with the exception of India, per capita annual income growth was 2 percent or higher in all the units shown. This golden period of growth brought rates of per capita annual enrichment of 8.1 percent in Japan and 4.1 percent in Western Europe, but respectably high rates also elsewhere. (The "Hindu rate of growth" registered in India was 1.4 percent.)

The 1973–2001 period saw not only decelerating rates of population growth but also substantial, and more marked, decreases in aggregate income growth. Rates of improvement in terms of income per capita thus dropped substantially. In Latin America, growth fell below 1 percent; in Africa stagnation ensued; in the former Soviet Union income per capita regressed. Japan's rate dropped to 2.1 percent per year; elsewhere in the developed world the rates achieved were appreciably below 2 percent. The big exceptions to this somber picture—somber in comparison to the early postwar decades—were Asia's two demographic giants. China's annual rate of per capita income growth shot up to 5.3 percent and India's more than doubled to 3.0 percent. The average of these varied changes worked out globally as a 50 percent drop from the first period to the second in the rate of growth of per capita income. Still, for the full 51-year period the average annual global rate was 2.1 percent, a stellar achievement without precedent in modern economic history for a comparably long stretch of time.

Differential growth rates in population and in aggregate income produce shifts in the relative size of countries and regions with respect to those characteristics. Similarly, their combined effect on income per capita may result in changes in the comparative standing of countries and regions with respect to that crude but important indicator of material well-being. Such shifts, as observed in the second half of the twentieth century, are concisely depicted in Figure 1. Table 3 provides a more detailed numerical elaboration of the changing relative shares of population size and of aggregate GDP of countries and regions within the global total. And the last three columns of the table characterize per capita income levels in comparison to income per capita in the United States in 1950, 1973, and 2001.

A growth rate in a given country or region slower than the rate of global growth brings about a decreasing share within the global total and vice versa. The period covered by the table exhibits marked relative shifts with respect to both population size and aggregate income. Changing rela-

TABLE 3   Percentage share of world population and world GDP, and GDP per head relative to GDP per head in the United States: United States, Japan, China, and India and world regions, 1950, 1973, and 2001

	Population			GDP			GDP per head: US = 100		
	1950	1973	2001	1950	1973	2001	1950	1973	2001
Western Europe	12.1	9.2	6.4	26.2	25.6	20.3	47.9	68.4	68.9
Eastern Europe	3.5	2.8	2.0	3.5	3.4	2.0	22.1	29.9	21.6
Former Soviet Union	7.1	6.4	4.7	9.6	9.4	3.6	29.7	36.3	16.6
United States	6.0	5.4	4.6	27.3	22.1	21.4	100.0	100.0	100.0
Other Western offshoots	1.0	1.0	0.9	3.4	3.3	3.2	77.7	80.3	77.7
Latin America	6.6	7.9	8.6	7.8	8.7	8.3	26.2	27.0	20.8
Japan	3.3	2.8	2.1	3.0	7.8	7.1	20.1	68.5	74.0
China	21.7	22.5	20.7	4.5	4.6	12.3	4.6	5.0	12.8
India	14.2	14.8	16.6	4.2	3.1	5.4	6.5	5.1	7.0
Other Asia	15.6	17.3	20.0	6.8	8.7	13.2	9.7	12.3	14.3
Africa	9.0	10.0	13.4	3.8	3.4	3.3	9.4	8.4	5.3
World	100.0	100.0	100.0	100.0	100.0	100.0	22.1	24.5	21.6

SOURCE: Maddison 2003: Tables 8a, 8b, and 8c.

tive levels of average income per head are also in evidence, although to a lesser degree. Thus Western Europe's share in the global population went from its 1950 level of 12.1 percent to 9.2 percent in 1973 and 6.4 percent in 2001. The progressive demographic marginalization of the rest of the developed world is echoing that of Western Europe but to an attenuated degree. Regions and countries of the developing world, in contrast, have steadily increased their relative population shares, with the exception of China in the last quarter of the century. Income shares also show marked changes. For example, Japan went from 3.0 percent to 7.8 percent from 1950 to 1973 but then dropped back to 7.1 percent by 2001. Between 1973 and 2001, Western Europe went from 25.6 percent to 20.3 percent; the former Soviet Union from 9.4 percent to 3.6 percent, and China from 4.6 percent to 12.3 percent. And with respect to income per capita levels there were also some substantial shifts. Thus between 1950 and 2001 Japan went from income per capita representing one-fifth of the US level to three-quarters of that level. Western Europe also narrowed the gap, going from less than half of the US GDP per head in 1950 to more than two-thirds of that level in 2001. From 1973 to 2001 China climbed from one-twentieth to one-eighth of the prevailing US income per capita level. During the same time span Latin America and Africa lost ground: going from 27.0 percent to 20.8 percent and from 8.4 percent to 5.3 percent, respectively.

The dynamics of population numbers and income are intertwined in complex relationships to one another. Population growth stimulates economic growth yet may retard gains in per capita terms, and economic growth affects demographic behavior. These linkages and their outcomes are conditioned by numerous characteristics of the surrounding economic and social systems. Exploration of these dynamics was beyond the scope of the present discussion. We probed, however, a less ambitious question. Would the variegated outcomes of these relationships have looked any different—better in their effects on human welfare—had the Western world arrived at different understandings of the roots of economic growth and demographic transition? A proper modesty might suggest a negative answer. Foreign aid flows were decided in large measure by strategic considerations rather than through calculations of need or economic return to the recipient. A very small part of that aid went to population programs. But while modesty on that score may be appropriate, it is not a complete answer. If anything should have been transferred from rich to poor countries, it was surely the lessons of how to organize a society to foster economic growth and slow the expansion of population—lessons derived from past experience, hard-learned and evident mainly in retrospect. In the event, that did not happen in any concerted way. Whether deficiencies in demand for institutional innovation would have defeated that sharing of experience anyway is impossible to say. It should at least have been tried.

Notes

1 Population estimates here and, unless otherwise specified, below are drawn from United Nations 2005.

2 Population size, or rather the size of the population fit for military service and for participation in the labor force, may have become less relevant for determining military strength, but it remains far from negligible. World War II demonstrated that point: Hitler's plans for a unified Europe under German overlordship could not have been defeated by the combined forces of, say, Switzerland and Sweden.

3 With the demise of the Soviet Union in December 1991, its seat in the Security Council was inherited by the Russian Federation, which had a population slightly less than half that of the Soviet Union.

4 The godfather for the term "third world" was, incidentally, Alfred Sauvy—an obscure reference borrowed from eighteenth-century French history that few ever understood outside France.

5 Japan was an exception in this regard; its fertility dropped rapidly in the early postwar years. Using a narrow definition of the West, Japan was the first non-Western country to experience a radical transition from high to low fertility.

6 China, first a follower of the Soviet model, was the major exception to this rule: after lurching beginnings, it found its special path to rapid development, combining authoritarian party rule with market capitalism. It is a recipe that is unlikely to be sustainable. Its application, however, had important consequences for China's demographic makeup and dynamics.

7 During the interwar years, the League of Nations did much to gather and analyze international statistics, including population statistics. But the League was essentially a European club, and the focus of these activities was almost entirely on Europe.

8 Underestimation of the coming growth also affected the population numbers projected for the more developed areas, reflecting the assumption of continued very low fertility in these lands and conservative estimates of the improvement in survival and of the extent of net immigration. Thus, for example, the projected 2000 population of North America (the United States and Canada combined) was 176 million, or just 56 percent of the population size actually achieved at the turn of the millennium (Notestein 1945). Five years later Notestein published another article that discussed the future growth of the world's population. In this he no longer offered numerical estimates, emphasizing instead the great uncertainty of long-term population trends (Notestein 1950).

9 Later projection by the United Nations (and also by the World Bank, which published separate sets of population projections) failed to fully allow for future fertility declines, hence tended to acquire an upward bias—they overestimated future population growth.

10 Widely read and influential examples of the literature conveying that interpretation were Vogt 1948, Paddock and Paddock 1967, Ehrlich 1968, and Hardin 1968.

11 For example, in Asia, containing the great bulk of the developing world's population, economic growth barely kept up with population. According to Angus Maddison's estimates, Asia's population (excluding Japan) grew from 926 million in 1913 to 1,299 million in 1950, or by 40 percent. Aggregate GDP, measured in 1990 international dollars, grew during the same period from $609 billion to $823 billion, or by 35 percent. Thus, over a period of nearly four decades, real per capita income went from $658 to $634 (Maddison 2003: Tables 8a, b, and c).

12 The group consisted of five economists, one each from Chile, India, Lebanon, Britain, and the United States. The last two of these were later recipients of the Nobel Prize in economics: Arthur Lewis, then with the University of Manchester, and Theodore W. Schultz, of the University of Chicago.

13 For instance, in the late nineteenth century, John Billings, an American physician, who served as the chief librarian of the New York Public Library, reviewed what he considered the causes of the decline of the US birth rate. His account enumerates all the basic factors, including the change in the status of women, that later theorists agreed led to the

desire for fewer children and hence the voluntary restriction of fertility (Billings 1893).

14 For a concise early statement, see Kirk 1943. That article also presents cogent comments on the potential geopolitical implications of the shifting balances of population size and power that the demographic transition may eventually create within the world system.

15 For chronicles of the beginnings of US government involvement in international population assistance, see Piotrow 1973 and Donaldson 1990.

16 Cited by Piotrow 1973, p. 45.

17 Cited by Piotrow 1973, pp. 89 and 90.

18 The calculation apparently originated in the work of Stephen Enke, a well-known economist at that time, whose genuine interest in enlisting economic analysis to help the progress of poor countries is evident in all his writings. He calculated the "value of permanently preventing a birth" based on "conditions representative of some undeveloped countries" and taking into account the "future consumption and production" of a representative infant. He found the value to be negative, specifically $–127. A small investment in contraception that would avert a birth could then eliminate this net loss. Enke, however, unlike most early advocates of family planning programs in less developed countries, was pessimistic about the prospect that contraceptives and related services would find ready takers if offered free. But the high value (relative to average income levels) of an "averted birth" indicated to him that the government could afford to provide substantial incentives to attract clients for the program. (His attempt to delineate the intricacies of how such incentives might be designed betrays some extraordinary illusions about the societies concerned.) See Enke 1963, Chapter 20.

19 For a vigorous criticism of these surveys, see Mamdani 1972.

20 To Robert McNamara (1977: 2), "Short of thermonuclear war itself, it is the gravest issue the world faces over the decades immediately ahead."

21 See Caldwell (1993: 309).

22 Ironically, there *was* a Western influence behind China's population policy, although probably neither sufficient nor necessary to explain the actions that were eventually

taken in controlling the birth rate. The Chinese studied Western research reports concerned with "limits to growth," offering analysis of questionable merit but which they found scientific, hence compelling (Greenhalgh 2003). The books must have cost them a few dollars. That was an investment with even greater yield than the one identified by President Johnson.

23 Bucharest was seen as an astute choice of location. It manifested the global character of the conference by ensuring Soviet bloc participation. It was also expected to help attenuate the sharp ideological conflict between Western and Communist views on population issues. At the same time, having Nicolae Ceausescu, the Romanian head of state and Communist Party leader—self-designated Genius of the Carpathians—as host to the conference was rather awkward. In the annals of national population policies Ceausescu had made a unique mark. In 1967, he abruptly outlawed abortion (which, as in other Soviet bloc states, was by far the major method of birth control) and imposed draconian punishments for violators. As intended, this measure raised—indeed for a brief period doubled—the Romanian birth rate, but, as might have been predicted, the effect quickly waned: people found other ways to limit their families. The effects on women's health and on child welfare, however, were both dire and lasting.

24 This section of the text in part draws on Demeny 1985. For a discussion of the background and substance of the Bucharest conference see Finkle and Crane 1975. A detailed comparison of the draft Plan of Action and the document eventually adopted by the conference is given in Berelson 1975. For the text of the finally adopted Plan see «http://www.un.org/popin/icpd/conference/bkg/wppa.html».

25 Some observers at the meeting shared the sentiment. Writing from Bucharest on the eve of the conference, Alfred Sauvy commented (in *Le Monde*, 14 August 1974): "This political gathering will be led, kept in motion, directed and controlled by the United States.... At Bucharest a world population plan of action will be proposed that will take aim, whatever may be said to disguise it, at the sovereignty of nations." The "plan of action proposed by the Americans," he continued, talks about reducing the birth rate of the less

developed countries by 10 per 1000. "If the matter would not have also its overtones of tragedy, one would be tempted to speak of childish games."

26 The full statement is reprinted in *Population and Development Review* 2 (2): 309–312.

27 Speech delivered at the Sixth National People's Congress, 16 April 1976.

28 On the eve of the Conference, however, an impressive compendium of statements by 92 world leaders—heads of state or government, the large majority from developing countries—was assembled and published by UNFPA. Most of these leaders gave ringing endorsement to family planning programs as a tool for moderating population growth (UNFPA 1984).

29 The Mexico City Recommendations also employed a veritable thesaurus of exhortative action words. Governments were to achieve, improve, formulate, accelerate, increase, lower, strive, restore, maintain, redress, implement, expedite, create, ensure, provide, and foster. And they referred readers to similarly adorned recommendations in the plans of action drafted by numerous other world conferences, ranging from Agrarian Reform and Ageing, through Basic Needs, Habitat, and Labour, to Water, and Women.

30 The statement also insisted that the US was not abandoning its support for family planning programs—then amounting to 10 percent of US foreign assistance. Qualifying that promise was the statement's enunciation of what became known as the US Government's "Mexico City policy." Invoking the United Nations Declaration of the Rights of the Child (1959), "which calls for protection of children before birth as well as after birth," the statement declared: "In keeping with this obligation, the United States does not consider abortion an acceptable element of family planning programs and will no longer contribute to those of which it is a part. Accordingly, when dealing with nations which support abortion with funds not provided by the United States Government, the United States will contribute to such nations through segregated accounts which cannot be used for abortion. Moreover, the United States will no longer contribute to separate nongovernmental organizations which perform or actively promote

abortion as a method of family planning in other nations. With regard to the United Nations Fund for Population Activities (UNFPA), the U.S. will insist that no part of its contribution be used for abortion. The U.S. will also call for concrete assurances that the UNFPA is not engaged in, or does not provide funding for, abortion or coercive family planning programs; if such assurances are not forthcoming, the U.S. will redirect the amount of its contribution to other, non-UNFPA, family planning programs." The policy was withdrawn immediately after the inauguration of the Clinton Administration in 1993, and reinstated immediately after the inauguration of the Bush Administration in 2001.

31 The "refined" Plan of Action *was* adopted by consensus, with the Vatican as the lone dissenter.

32 The UN estimates that the peak population growth rate of the less developed countries was reached in the 1965–70 quinquennium, at the average annual rate of 2.51 percent.

33 The dissonances, here and elsewhere, are compellingly chronicled by Kelley 2001.

34 See also the arguments in Hayek's *Collected Works* (1988).

35 To cite one example, the noted Yale historian Paul Kennedy declared in 1993 that "The population explosion (combined with limited resources) is the greatest problem facing developing regions" (Kennedy 1993: 124).

36 Mutual isolation or disdain seems to be a feature of the various academic communities concerned with population matters. Demographers do not read what biologists and ecologists write about population change, and conversely. Anthropologists, political scientists, historians, and ethicists seldom publish in population journals, nor do demographers appear in theirs. Mainstream economists tend to dismiss their disciplinary renegades who call themselves ecological economists, a sentiment that is reciprocated.

37 On a more mundane level, the authors of the Joint Statement might have noticed that by 1992 fertility had been declining steadily in most of the world's population for decades; that a large part of the world's population already had below-replacement fertility; that in numerous countries in Europe and elsewhere

prevailing fertility levels, if maintained, would lead to precipitous population decline; that such a level was achieved in Japan without modern contraceptives such as the pill; and that product-development lead times for new contraceptives make it extremely unlikely that devices other than those in the already existing armamentarium of birth control would make an appreciable contribution to achieving low fertility levels worldwide.

38 The article grew out of a World Bank study, coauthored by Lawrence H. Summers, then Chief Economist, and Lant H. Pritchett, Senior Economist, and circulated as a Bank working paper. Summers, by then a senior US government official as undersecretary of the Department of Treasury for international affairs (he was later Treasury Secretary, then president of Harvard), withdrew his name from the published version at the last moment, under pressure from the Department of State which was at that time preparing for the Cairo conference. The article was viewed as damaging to the US policy position to be taken at the conference.

39 Historical transitions, in fact, have taken place under a broad range of degrees of deficiency in gender equity.

40 Some East Asian countries—Singapore most famously—did adopt strongly activist policies to boost low birth rates, with unimpressive results.

41 See Gibson and Lennon 1999.

42 Foreign-born proportions were still somewhat below those in the US, but nearing 10 percent in Germany, Austria, Belgium, and probably France (OECD data). Proportions in Australia and Canada were substantially higher: 23 percent and 18 percent.

43 By that time of course the term was entirely obsolete, if only because the "second world" had disappeared—either having melted, post-1989, into the former third world or, at least nominally, having rejoined the "first world."

44 For clarity, Figure 1 selects only six of the 11 units.

45 Comparing incomes of economies at differing levels of development is notoriously difficult. Money values of GDP expressed in a common metric, such as dollars, are apt to give misleading results if calculated by using currency exchange rates: they underestimate real income levels in less developed economies. This is because non-tradeable services and products are cheaper in lower-income countries than in more advanced economies. The dollar values shown in Tables 1–3 and in Figure 1 are corrected for this problem, however imperfectly, by providing purchasing power parity estimates, expressed in 1990 US dollars.

References

Balfour, Marshall C. et al. 1950. *Public Health and Demography in the Far East.* New York: The Rockefeller Foundation.

Bauer, Peter. 1981. *Equality, the Third World and Economic Delusions.* Cambridge, MA: Harvard University Press.

Berelson, Bernard. 1975. "The World Population Plan of Action: Where now?," *Population and Development Review* 1: 115–145.

Billings, John. 1893. "The diminished birth-rate in the United States," *The Forum* 15(4): 467–477.

Brown, Harrison. 1954. *The Challenge of Man's Future.* New York: Viking Press.

Caldwell, John C. 1993. "The Asian fertility revolution: Its implications for transition theories," in Richard Leete and Iqbal Alam (eds.), *The Revolution in Asian Fertility: Dimension, Causes, and Implications.* Oxford: Clarendon Press.

Cassen, Robert and Associates. 1986. *Does Aid Work? Report to an Intergovernmental Task Force.* Oxford: Clarendon Press.

Cassen, Robert and Contributors. 1994. *Population and Development: Old Debates, New Conclusions.* Washington, DC: Overseas Development Council.

Coale, Ansley J. and Edgar M. Hoover. 1958. *Population Growth and Economic Development in Low-Income Countries.* Princeton: Princeton University Press.

Davis, Kingsley. 1951. *The Population of India and Pakistan.* Princeton: Princeton University Press.

Demeny, Paul. 1985. "Bucharest, Mexico City, and beyond," *European Journal of Population* 1: 131–140.

Donaldson, Peter J. 1990. *Nature Against Us: The United States and the World Population Crisis, 1965–1980.* Chapel Hill: University of North Carolina Press.

Ehrlich, Paul R. 1968. *The Population Bomb.* New York: Ballantine Books.

Enke, Stephen. 1963. *Economics for Development.* Englewood Cliffs, NJ: Prentice-Hall.

Finkle, Jason L. and Barbara B. Crane. 1975. "The politics of Bucharest: Population, development, and the new international economic order," *Population and Development Review* 1: 87–114.

Gibson, Campbell J. and Emily Lennon. 1999. *Historical Census Statistics on the Foreign-born Population of the United States: 1850–1990.* Washington, DC: Population Division, Bureau of the Census.

Gore, Al. 1992. *Earth in the Balance: Ecology and the Human Spirit.* New York: Houghton Mifflin.

Greenhalgh, Susan. 2003. "Science, modernity, and the making of China's one-child policy," *Population and Development Review* 29: 163–196.

Hardin, Garrett. 1968. "The tragedy of the commons," *Science* 162: 1243–1248.

Hayek, F. A. 1988. *The Fatal Conceit: The Errors of Socialism. Collected Works of F. A. Hayek, Volume 1.* Chicago: University of Chicago Press.

Kelley, Allen C. 2001. "The population debate in historical perspective: Revisionism revisited," in Nancy Birdsall, Allen C. Kelley, and Steven W. Sinding (eds.), *Population Matters: Demographic Change, Economic Growth, and Poverty in the Developing World.* New York: Oxford University Press.

Kennedy, Paul. 1993. *Preparing for the Twenty-First Century.* New York: Random House.

Kirk, Dudley. 1943. "Population changes and the postwar world," *American Sociological Review* 9(1): 28–35.

Kuznets, Simon. 1967. "Population and economic growth," *Proceedings of the American Philosophical Society* 111(3): 170–193.

Maddison, Angus. 2003. *The World Economy: Historical Statistics.* Paris: OECD.

Mahler, Halfdan. 1992. "Our next forty years," *People* 19: 3–6.

Mamdani, Mahmood. 1972. *The Myth of Population Control: Family, Class, and Caste in an Indian Village.* New York: Monthly Review Press.

McNamara, Robert S. 1977. "Accelerating population stabilization through social and economic progress," Overseas Development Council, Washington, DC. Development Paper no. 24.

McNicoll, Geoffrey. 1984. "Consequences of rapid population growth: An overview and assessment," *Population and Development Review* 10(2): 177–240.

Myrdal, Gunnar. 1970. *The Challenge of World Poverty.* New York: Pantheon Books.

National Academy of Sciences. 1963. *The Growth of World Population.* Washington, DC: National Research Council.

———. 1971. *Rapid Population Growth: Consequences and Policy Implications.* Baltimore: Johns Hopkins Press.

National Research Council. 1986. *Population Growth and Economic Development: Policy Questions.* Washington, DC: National Academy Press.

Nixon, Richard M. 1992. *Seize the Moment.* New York: Simon and Schuster.

Notestein, Frank W. 1945. "Population—The long view," in Theodore W. Schulz (ed.), *Food for the World.* Chicago: University of Chicago Press, pp. 36–57.

———. 1950. "The population of the world in 2000," *Journal of the American Statistical Association* 25(251): 335–345.

Paddock, William and Paul Paddock. 1967. *Famine—1975!* Boston: Little, Brown.

Piotrow, Phyllis Tilson. 1973. *World Population Crisis: The United States Response.* New York: Praeger Publishers.

Pritchett, Lant H. 1994. "Desired fertility and the impact of population policies," *Population and Development Review* 20(1): 1–55.

Royal Society [of London and the US National Academy of Sciences]. 1992. *Population Growth, Resource Consumption, and a Sustainable World.* London and Washington.

Sauvy, Alfred. 1949. "Le 'faux problème' de la population mondiale," *Population* 4(3). (English translation in *Population and Development Review* 16(4), December 1990, pp. 759–774.)

Schumacher, E. F. 1955. "Population in relation to the development of energy from coal," *Proceedings of the World Population Conference, 1954,* vol. V. pp. 149–164.

Simon, Julian L. 1981. *The Ultimate Resource.* Princeton: Princeton University Press.

UNFPA. 1984. *Population Perspectives: Statements by World Leaders.* New York: United Nations Fund for Population Activities.

United Nations. 1951. *Measures for the Economic Development of Under-Developed Countries.* Report by a group of experts appointed by the Secretary-General of the United Nations. Department of Economic Affairs. New York.

———. 1955. "Framework for future population estimates, 1950–1980, by world region," *Proceedings of the World Population Conference, 1954,* vol. III, pp. 283–328.

———. 1958. *The Future Growth of World Population.* Department of Economic and Social Affairs. New York.

———. 2005. *World Population Prospects, The 2004 Revision. Volume I: Comprehensive Tables.* Department of Economic and Social Affairs. New York.

US Commission. 1972. *Report of the U.S. Commission on Population Growth and the American Future.* Washington, DC: Government Printing Office.

Vogt, William. 1948. *Road to Survival.* New York: William Sloane Associates.

World Bank. 1984. *World Development Report 1984.* New York: Oxford University Press.

Europe's Demographic Future: Determinants, Dimensions, and Challenges

DAVID COLEMAN

Europe shares, to a varying degree in different countries, common demographic processes with the rest of the post-transitional world. These are the familiar characteristics of developed societies: fewer babies, longer lives, older populations, diverse households, more immigrants. These trends differ in important ways from those across the Atlantic. In Europe fertility is lower than in the United States despite more pervasive welfare programs in the former. In parts of Eastern Europe and the former Soviet Union numbers have been heading down, not up. Europe's 40-odd countries are diverse, not unified or even convergent. Current patterns and trends preserve or accentuate demographic diversity and its challenges, despite the influence of the European Union and of the allegedly pervasive effects of "globalization."

A brief pause is needed to consider the definition of Europe to be used here. Endless geo-political fun can be had in debating the merits of various cultural, political, racial, and geographical definitions of Europe: who is in, and who is out (Huntington 1997; van de Kaa 1999: 24). For the sake of simplicity Europe will be considered within its traditional geographical boundaries: that is, from Iceland to Russia. Most emphasis will be given to Western Europe, where, in a less crisis-laden atmosphere than further East, it is easier to make demographic generalizations. The temptations offered by institutions such as the Eurovision Song Contest, the Council of Europe, and the United Nations Economic Commission for Europe to include more exotic additions to the European population (e.g., Israel, Turkey, Kazakhstan) will be resisted.

The shadow of the past

In all countries and regions the past casts a shadow over the future, nowhere more so than in Europe. There, ancient history, the events of the calamitous twentieth century, and postwar reactions to them have created the European populations that now face the twenty-first century and have formed and constrained the responses available to meet its challenges. Europe's demographic story to the end of the twentieth century will not be described systematically here. For that we need merely turn to luminaries such as Livi Bacci (2000) and to Bardet, Dupâquier, and their colleagues (1999) and to numerous technical analyses by, for example, Sardon (1990), Frejka and Calot (2001), Vallin et al. (2002), and Frejka and Sardon (2004).

Europe's divisions

Europe's divisions have an ancient history and deep roots. The Emperor Diocletian may have much to answer for separating, in AD 287, the Eastern from the Western parts of the Roman Empire in modern Slovenia, not far from Trieste. That division nudged the two parts of Europe to different fates. Constantinople, unlike Rome, withstood assault for a further millennium. The division may simply have reinforced existing differences in family, society, and inheritance between the Greek/Slavic and Latin/Teutonic worlds. But the significance of that geographical divide was inherited and emphasized by the Christian church in its later ascendancy, once its Roman and Eastern branches diverged in language, devotional emphasis, and relations with the state, even if the fundamentals of belief remained the same. Arab, later Seljuk and Ottoman conquest of all the former Eastern Empire reinforced a divergence that has persisted to the present and destroyed the former unity of the civilized Mediterranean world. It is surely no coincidence that the southern end of Hajnal's line (one drawn between Trieste and St. Petersburg), the divide between Pope and Patriarch, and the North-Western limits of the high water mark of permanent Ottoman occupation, not to mention the Iron Curtain, roughly coincided with Diocletian's division.

Hajnal's line separated statistically, in a rough and ready sort of way, a Western Europe of (mostly) nuclear families, where women often married late or not at all, from an Eastern Europe where households could be complex and where marriage was usually early and universal (Hajnal 1965, 1982; Coale and Watkins 1986). That distinction remained valid at least until the 1990s and is still apparent, though diminishing, in the first decade of the twenty-first century. The Russian succession to Byzantinism in the North, and the Ottoman succession to the South, insulated much of Eastern Europe and the Balkans from Renaissance, Reformation, and Enlightenment influences. These latter influences, according to Lesthaeghe (1995), van de Kaa (1999), and others, were seedbeds for the individualism and personal autonomy (of which Eastern Europe has been a late recipient) that lie behind both the first and the second demographic transitions.

That "second transition" in individualistic attitudes, the retreat of marriage, and the adoption of new family forms is still most unevenly distributed over Europe, separating in different ways North-Western Europe both from the Catholic South and from the East. The pattern of the transition in Eastern Europe is much modified by the disorderly and anomic social situation in part of that region (Philipov 2003; Philipov et al. 2005), and some of the empirical trends may even be better understood in those terms rather than in terms of "postmaterialism" as usually understood. The North/South division, roughly coincident with the boundary at which the Reformation was halted, separates a Southern "familist" Europe from the rest, characterized by different patterns of living arrangements and lower fertility compared with their Northern neighbors (Reher 1998). Familist attitudes, however, cut across religious lines in the South, being shared with Orthodox Greece and the Balkans, including its Muslim populations.

The inheritance of age structure

The twentieth century has bequeathed to the twenty-first a set of population age structures that guarantee population aging, further distorted by the baby boom in the West and wartime damage and more erratic changes in fertility in the East. (For an illustrative example, depicting the age structure of the Russian Federation, see Figure 1.) Births from previous decades

FIGURE 1   Population of the Russian Federation, by age and sex, 2000

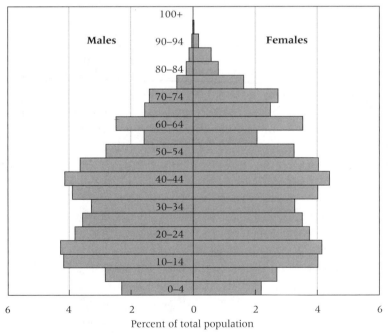

Percent of total population

SOURCE: United Nations (2005).

determine the numbers of mothers today and thereby constrain, or inflate, the numbers of current births. Thanks to population momentum, many European populations still maintain (slow and diminishing) levels of growth through natural increase despite nearly 30 years of below-replacement fertility rates. That positive momentum is nearly exhausted (Calot and Sardon 1999). In the lowest-fertility countries (Austria, Italy, Germany, Greece) and in the East with no baby boom but high death rates, the natural growth rate has become negative. In the East, deaths already exceed births in almost all countries except Poland and Slovakia. In some of these countries, decades of low fertility have built up a reverse momentum for the future. Net immigration apart, even a rapid return to replacement fertility could not now of itself prevent such countries, especially Germany where low fertility is of long standing, from experiencing substantial population decline before stabilizing at a new, lower level.

Substantial future population aging is now set in stone for Europe. Current age structures are nonstable—not a product of current vital rates but of those of the previous century. During the twentieth century they served us well, providing until recently an unusually favorable overall dependency ratio: a demographic bonus now enjoyed by many developing-world populations that have experienced falling birth rates (Bloom and Williamson 1998). In the developed world, as future population age structures acquire a more stable form in keeping with the lower vital rates of the present, a much more top-heavy population will unfold. Its more burdensome form will become a permanent characteristic of developed societies from then onward, especially in low-fertility countries of Europe. Details are considered later.

Distorted transitions and demographic damage

The demographic damage—the excess deaths, missing births, and displaced populations of the wars and revolutions of the twentieth century—is an inheritance of a different kind. The period 1914–48 was in demographic terms surely the worst 34 years in Europe's history since the Black Death and, although strictly outside our period, had enduring effects on age structure, population size, and population distribution. The 140 million violent deaths during 1914–45 particularly afflicted the populations of Central, Germany, Serbia, and Poland, while Ukraine and the Baltic States, notably Estonia, suffered additional heavy losses through Soviet deportations (DellaPergola 1996; Courtois et al. 1999). As a result the population of Central and Eastern Europe lost ground compared with the West. Poland suffered badly in both World Wars. Its population in 1950 on present boundaries was 23 percent less than in 1940 (Kosinski 1970: 16). The failure of the Eastern European countries to follow a "normal" mortality transition in peacetime has caused further demographic damage (Meslé et al. 1996; Daróczi 2003). Had Russia experienced a normal demographic transition starting from its total population of 71 million in 1900, then it could have ended the twentieth century with some 120 million more people than it has today—269 million rather than 148 million. By any standards, that is a big change in the potential balance of power (Vishnevsky 1997: Table 1.2).

The shifting of people and boundaries in Europe is hardly new but proceeded at an unprecedented scale and frequency in the twentieth century. Instabilities released by the retreat of the Ottoman domain and later meddling with the map at Versailles replaced old minority problems with new ones (e.g., Hungarians in Slovakia and Romania; see Courbage 1998) still salient in the twenty-first century and introduced a fragmented political instability that contributed to future population change. World War II displaced about 30 million people (Kosinski 1970) although some were eventually repatriated. The postwar settlement moved Poland westward by about 200 miles as part of the Soviet Union's incorporation of 7 percent of Europe's area and 5 percent of its people. Old problems have reemerged as the tide of Communism receded in 1989, stranding numerous minority populations formerly forced, enabled, or even encouraged to diffuse and migrate by the Soviet system outside their original "homeland." Twenty-four million Russians suddenly found themselves in "foreign" countries of the "near abroad" in 1992, in newly independent former Soviet republics such as Ukraine, Kazakhstan, Latvia, and Uzbekistan, keen to assert the primacy of languages and of ethnic identities long marginalized. Their return migration turned Russia into the biggest "immigration" country in Europe in the mid-1990s. In Bosnia between 1992 and 1995 about 103,000 persons may have died from war-related causes, and 2.6 million have been displaced, some permanently to the West, with the dissolution of the post–World War I creation of Yugoslavia. Earlier estimates of war-related deaths in 1992–95 ranged from 156,000 to 329,000 (see Tabeau and Bijak 2005). The consequences of the failure to deliver the Kurdish homeland promised at Sèvres in 1923 manifest themselves today by the boatload in Italian ports and at airports throughout Europe. Ethnic return migration of German *Aussiedler* and of "Pontic" Greeks from the former Soviet Union continues, although at a diminishing rate, and the continued (but finite) exodus of Russian Jews to Israel provides one element of the latter country's demographic salvation, for the time being.

The state socialist demographic regime

The division of Eastern and Western Europe into opposed political and military camps was one of the defining themes of the second half of the twentieth century, and its demographic, political, and social legacy will endure well into the twenty-first. That divide continued, indeed accentuated, existing demographic divergence into the latter part of the twentieth century (Meslé and Hertrich 1997). Eastern Europe's unique political system forced the region into aberrant patterns of mortality and fertility, distorting the course of the demographic transition into some highly distinctive patterns. It more or less brought international migration to a halt, ending the East-to-West movements that had contributed to Europe's economic development in the first half of the twentieth century and before. By contrast, Western Europe, North America, and the English-speaking world overseas developed in a less constrained, yet parallel fashion generally considered to be "normal," with its baby boom associated with a unique economic resurgence in the postwar decades (Crafts and Mills 1995). This pattern does not need further attention here. Instead, we concern ourselves with the unusual pattern in the East and its recent demise.

The Soviet state and its satellites arrogated to themselves most resources, often including the allocation of housing and employment, bringing most institutions outside the family and most decisionmaking under the umbrella of the state. Soviet policies, whether through intended or unintended effects, determined the rationality of choices made by citizens—in living arrangements and family formation, as well as the unavoidable risks of mortality. It is not surprising that a characteristic demographic regime arose distinct from that of the free market economies. It was partly the result of muddle, contradiction, and unintended consequences: for example, pronatalist ideology was not compatible with the need to maximize female labor force participation in the absence of market pricing methods to improve productivity.

For ideological and practical reasons, access to abortion was usually easy while modern contraception was frowned on as a capitalist error and was in any case undeliverable, like many other consumer goods (see DaVanzo and Grammich 2001). Cramped housing with shared facilities arising from forced urbanization and industrialization, and labor-intensive living characterized by queues rather than domestic appliances, tended early on to depress fertility, notably in Hungary and Romania. Such unacceptably disloyal fertility trends provoked temporarily effective pronatalist welfare measures and tightening of the valve of abortion to encourage a higher rate of production of babies, most brutally in Romania. The regularities and security of state socialism, however, did sustain a stable, if stagnant, economy and society (Sobotka 2003a). By the 1970s, the birth rates of the Communist societies, most of which (except Poland) missed the baby boom of the free market economies, were still sustaining a total fertility rate of around 2, somewhat higher than in the West: the time series of the birth rates of the two regions are correlated negatively up to the 1990s (Coleman 1993). The net result has bequeathed a less exuberant age structure to the twenty-first century than in the West, almost a complementary one to that of the West up to the 1990s. Fertility, already in decline, collapsed once central control and state subsidies disintegrated from 1989 to 1992 (Macura 1999), leading to the small cohorts of the post-1989 period. Partly because of weak population momentum, Eastern age structures were unable to stave off natural decrease in the 1990s. Immigration moderated population decline in Russia (Vassin 1997), but emigration has reinforced it in most of the other former Communist states (Salt 2003).

The Communist system paradoxically preserved and accentuated the old Eastern European pattern of early and universal marriage. All European countries enjoyed a marriage boom up to the early 1970s. But only in the Communist states did mean age at marriage and childbearing continue to fall, or at least remain low, throughout the period up to about 1990—including in those states annexed to the East (the Czech lands, East Germany, and the Baltic States), which formerly had a Western marriage and household pattern. The Red Army tilted the northern part of Hajnal's line about 200 miles westward in 1945. Marriage remained, or became, universal: popular, indeed necessary, as a key to state housing and as the only private personal institution remaining in a state monopoly of institutions (Mozny and Katrnak 2005). Even in 2004, mean age at marriage remained considerably lower than in Western countries.

The disintegration of the Communist system from 1989 onward impoverished perhaps 25 percent of the population of Eastern Europe (Ellman 2000) and not surprisingly depressed fertility and survival, accelerated changes in marriage patterns, and promoted some migration (although on nothing remotely resembling the scale of 1917–22). The extent to which these changes were due to a "crisis response" to those years, rather than an adaptation to a new regime, remains controversial (Conrad et al. 1996; Cornia and Paniccia 1998; Kennedy et al. 1998). Substantial economic recovery is now underway but the demographic future remains unclear. Are depressed levels of nuptiality and fertility crisis responses (implying reversibility) or adjustments to new and more normal conditions—essentially a delayed convergence to the Western pattern (as suggested by Kharkova and Andreev 2000)? Quantum reductions in fertility predominate in worse-affected countries such as Russia and Bulgaria (Avdeev 2001), while tempo effects (that is, postponement rather than cancellation) predominate in Hungary and Poland (Philipov and Kohler 2001). If it is adjustment, then Hajnal's line has had its day. It is important to remember that, despite the crises, Russia's fertility transition has proceeded, if somewhat behind the West's. Fertility in all female generations born from 1920 to 1960 has been no more than replacement level or even below it, taking the higher mortality into account (Scherbov and van Vianen 2001), although recent trends seem likely to take fertility to much lower levels (Avdeev 2001).

While improvement in survival continues at a brisk pace in the West at almost all ages, in the East progress ground to a halt about 40 years ago, after approximate parity with the West had been achieved in the 1960s. Formerly, rapid advances could be made against infectious disease through mass vaccinations and other processes requiring organization and authority. The ironically named "diseases of affluence" are more refractory. Negligible public health information, poorly paid and trained medical personnel, the high priority given to military projects, low priority given to industrial safety and environmental protection, the state monopoly of alcohol, and traditional diet and drinking habits have all been blamed (Andreev, Scherbov, and Willekens 1992; Bobadilla et al. 1997). Less emphasis has been placed on tobacco use, although smoking accounts for perhaps half of cancer deaths in the former Soviet Union (Lopez 1997). As smoking among men is near-universal, socially acceptable, and not countered by any government publicity (Prokhorov 1997)—as was also true in the West until the 1960s—this practice is likely to impose a burden on adult male mortality well into the twenty-first century.

These "proximate" factors of high mortality comprise a syndrome that may be considered to have common origins in the fundamental non-democratic features of the former Communist political system: the absence of public information or market signals, the forced urbanization and industrialization, the disruption of ordinary social links in collectives, and mass urban housing. Some of these factors worsened temporarily in the early 1990s as medical infrastructure fell apart and stressful circumstances increased (Shapiro 1997). Expectation of life has risen again in most Eastern countries: fastest in those that have most speedily restructured politically and economically. However, despite aggregate GDP growth in the former Communist bloc of 6 percent in 2000 (UNECE 2001a: 9), only four economies had regained by 2000 the material position they had enjoyed in 1990, and the average was then 40 percent less than in 1990 (UNECE 2001b). Since 2000, however, real GDP growth has for the most part remained impressive: about 7 percent in Russia in 2003 and 2004, and even higher in Belarus and Ukraine.

Future demographic change, particularly improved survival, must be dependent in part on further economic, social, and political restructuring. EU membership and subsidies will help those countries that joined in May 2004 (Czech Republic, Hungary, Poland, Slovakia, Estonia, Latvia, Lithuania, Slovenia), although the cost in unemployment (e.g., to older industrial areas and agricultural populations) is likely to be high. The future of fertility is perhaps less affected by economic recovery; even in the more successful states, period fertility showed little sign of increase up to 2004. If the timing of births is being delayed to Western levels, there is still a long way to go and depressed period fertility rates will persist for some years. Some calculations for estimating a value for total period fertility "corrected" for postponement, always a controversial procedure, have suggested that co-hort fertility in the Central European countries may hardly be depressed at all (Philipov and Kohler 2001). It appears too early to decide how far the spread of new ideas associated with the second demographic transition is serving to depress fertility, and how far adverse economic circumstances are responsible. Some studies on Central European populations (Sobotka et al. 2003) suggest that ideational shift toward "postmaterialist" attitudes may indeed be an important factor in recent demographic evolution; while fur-ther East, social malaise of a less uplifting kind in impoverished and "anomic" parts of society may be a more prominent factor. A line from Dubrovnik to St. Petersburg, which roughly divides the Orthodox East from the Roman Center, also separates the less successful from the more successful coun-tries (Philipov 2001). In Russia, it may be that the economic transforma-tions have "instigated the transition to a one-child family model," or at least that the trends cannot be reduced to a temporary adaptation of the old two-child system to a new social environment (Avdeev 2001).

Economics apart, more equal relations between the sexes in the do-mestic sphere may be a further prerequisite for future higher fertility in the East, as they are in the South, in order to restore some symmetry to gender equity in the private as well as the public realm. Soviet women may have been hero workers (labor force participation rates of women aged 30–39 in 1989 were 95 percent) but also had to be hero queuers, baby washers, flat cleaners, and dinner cooks, without labor-saving appliances, without much help from husbands, and increasingly without a babushka. Domestic, as op-posed to public, gender equity is low; its asymmetrical nature, expressed also in the repressed sexuality of the Soviet era (Stern and Stern 1981), while it prevails, may preserve low fertility (see McDonald 2000). This po-tential obstacle to higher birth rates is by no means confined to Russia (Muszynska 2004) and may even be growing, if Eastern European societies are becoming more "masculinized" as a reaction to the "top-down egalitari-anism" of the Communist period (Mateeva and Wallace 2005).

In the short run, however, this depressing outlook has some advantages. High death rates in later life mean lower future pension burdens (Vishnevsky 1999). In the late 1990s, the Russian percent of elderly was the lowest in Europe except for Serbia and Albania, followed by most of the other Eastern bloc countries (Vassin 1997). Pensions in Russia used to be high in relation to industrial wages, but no longer. The breakup of the Soviet Union has wors-ened Russian pay-as-you-go pension problems by reducing demographic bur-den-sharing with younger republics (DaVanzo and Grammich 2001: 67), as well as reducing the value of pensions through inflation. After 2010, many people born in the 1950s will retire (conventionally at age 60), but for a short time that will be matched by an echo boom of young people in the workforce.

Small birth cohorts from the 1990s will also keep overall dependency rates low in the short run. Restricted labor supply may help to force a solution to low productivity and 15 percent unemployment.

Moral and political reactions

The twentieth century has given to the twenty-first an enduring set of attitudes in reaction to its disasters and problems, with considerable effect upon European demography and society. The pressure for European unification is one example. Among the many motivations behind the drive for European unity and harmonization, some with unilateral precedents, one is quite explicit: the desire to avoid further conflict. Even though no EU Directives on family size have yet been issued (Gesano 1999), explicit social harmonization is an ambition of the Commission, and demographic indicators are a measure of it. Greater demographic homogeneity might in any case be an unintended consequence of the "harmonized" tax, welfare, and economic arrangements desired by the Commission and by the less competitive member states.

In revulsion at the repression of the twentieth century, European governments have endorsed open-ended principles of asylum, initially intended to help clear up the sequelae of World War II, and comprehensive declarations of human rights. These promises have now been taken up by over 6 million asylum claimants coming to European countries since 1980. The revolutions in rights, communication, and transport (Freeman 1994) that have facilitated this inflow were unimaginable in the 1950s. Those commitments now sustain an apparently unstoppable flow of asylum seekers and illegal migrants to Europe, the biggest such inflow in its history. Removing the majority with ill-founded claims has proved difficult. Even if claims could be limited to genuine cases of state persecution, the potential flow from developing-world totalitarian states and autocracies would be very large. European countries will find it very difficult to unravel or modify these commitments, even if they could decide they wanted to, especially when their powers to take unilateral action are overridden by broadening EU "competences."

Features and processes of Europe's demography

Fewer babies

A specter is haunting Europe and, according to the latest thinking from the United Nations, will haunt the whole world later this century—that of below-replacement fertility. Low fertility—a two-child family or less—was first achieved in Europe in the 1930s. Its persistence over two generations since has been obscured by the transient distraction of the baby boom. Few cohorts born in Europe since the 1930s have replaced themselves. To the question whether low fertility is here to stay, the almost invariable expert answer is yes; it only depends "how low?," to which no convincing answer can yet be given (Golini 1998; Namboodiri and Wei 1998). Nevertheless, one cannot be certain that fertility will not exceed the replacement rate again (it did so in the United States in 2000 when total fertility reached 2.06, and was 2.04 in 2003). The exact level of fertility matters. Differences in period fertility that appear small eventually have powerful effects on population size, on natural change, and on the dependency level in the medium to long term.

Part of the problem with making sensible comments about fertility levels and their future implications is the difficulty—perhaps impossibility—of making a definite statement as to the actual level of contemporary fertility. This is not the place to describe the index wars over which so much ink has been spilled. The essential problem is that delays—postponements or "tempo" changes—in the timing of births depress statistically the value of the usual period fertility indicator, the total fertility rate (TFR). Various approaches, all disputed, have attempted to show the "true" figure without tempo changes (Bongaarts and Feeney 1998; Kohler and Philipov 2001; van Imhoff and Keilman 2000; Sobotka 2003b). A frequent result of such adjustments is to elevate the TFR by 0.2–0.4 births; thus the catastrophic Italian TFR of 1.2 becomes a merely disastrous 1.4 or 1.6. Analysis of unfolding cohort patterns of births suggests that remarkable and unprecedented levels of fertility would be needed among women in their 30s if the completed fertility of current cohorts of women were not to fall in the short to medium term (Lesthaeghe 2002; Frejka and Sardon 2004).

Most of the evidence therefore points to persistent below-replacement fertility (Demeny 1997). However, optimists point out that for 30 years most women have stated consistently that they want to have at least two children (Cuyvers 2001). The discrepancy between preferred and actual fertility suggests an "unmet need," which family welfare policy could address (Bongaarts 2001: Table 1). Fertility will recuperate in some countries as births postponed in earlier life are at least partly compensated by higher birth rates later in life. Hence fertility can go up as well as down: TFR has been rising for some years in France (1.94 in 2005), the Netherlands (1.74), and Denmark (1.8) and remains high in New Zealand (2.0) and Norway (1.85). Recuperation is scarcely evident in Southern and Eastern Europe, however; indeed it is conceptually very difficult to distinguish postponement from mere delay (Ní Bhrolcháin and Toulemon 2002). Bongaarts (2001: 278) claims that "one fairly robust conclusion" of his analysis is that "the total fertility rate is likely to rise in the not too distant future in countries where the age at childbearing is now rising rapidly." High ethnic minority fertility can be important here, but in the United States white non-Hispanic fertility alone is 1.85. Unplanned fertility, however, remains high in the United States Frejka and Kingcade 2001), and if the desire for at least one child of each sex could be satisfied, large families would become even scarcer and fertility could fall further.

Evolutionary biological models propose a general need to nurture offspring (Foster 2000; Morgan and King 2001) but so far can offer no specific reasons why that need should not be satisfied with only one child. In their models, economists assume that demand for children is axiomatic, children being desired for the various "child services" (mostly psychological nowadays, or even illusory) that they are held to provide. On this view, once the contraceptive revolution is complete a positive relationship will emerge between income or social status and fertility. Such a relationship has already become apparent in some societies with respect to education.

Most population projections incorporate some fertility increase into their models, although not always for well-considered reasons. But few if any now project future fertility in developed countries to rise to replacement level. The UN Population Division, which in the late 1990s introduced declining global population into its scenarios for the first time, has since 2002 adopted a below-replacement target (1.85) in its medium projection for world population growth. The Eurostat projections of 2004 even envisage (rather pessimistically) lower fertility in some European countries than the actual current level.

The retreat of mortality

In the Western world, mortality has fallen, at first almost imperceptibly, then with increased vigor, from the late eighteenth century onward. Its decline is primarily responsible for the quadrupling of Europe's population between 1800 (180 million) and 2000 (730 million). When mortality was high, improvements in survival gave more years of life to babies, children, and younger adults, making population younger. Thanks to the near-elimination of deaths from infectious disease, male babies now have a 93 percent chance of survival to age 50 years and female babies a 96 percent chance. Further improvements in survival mostly benefit the older population, making the population itself older. In the 1960s it appeared that improvement in survival had ground to a halt, as mortality rates among middle-aged and older men ceased improving or even deteriorated in Western and Eastern Europe and overseas. The newer major causes of death—chronic age-related diseases such as cancers and circulatory disease—were believed to have become inevitable diseases of affluence.

In the West, however, these have been driven further into retreat. The improvements in lifestyles, material conditions, and medical science, and notably the passing of the effects of the smoking epidemic among males in the 1970s, all played a part. The chronic diseases of affluence have become diseases of poverty, early deaths from which are now more prevalent among poorer sections of Western society and in the former Communist states of Eastern Europe, where the 1960s stagnation in survival has persisted. Economic success, freedom of information, and government responsiveness to health concerns have clearly contributed to the difference between the failure of Eastern countries and the success elsewhere in adapting to industrial and postindustrial society.

Western Europe entered the twenty-first century with age-specific mortality rates falling between 1 and 2 percent per year for most age groups except for young adults aged 15–30 years, especially males. The persisting levels of young adult mortality rates are due to accidents and violence and, among the "older young," to AIDS. The gap between the sexes is narrowing somewhat as male survival improves and that of females is hampered as belated adoption of smoking exacts a belated penalty of mortality (Vallin et al. 2002). Most striking, the "oldest-old" (aged 85 and older) have shared almost equally in these improvements. Evidence is accumulating that the pace at which mortality rates worsen with age, once defined by Gompertz as a rigid mathematical inevitability, is moderated at extreme old age, making maximum life span difficult if not impossible to define (Robine et al. 2006).

The consequences of these trends will be worked out in the twenty-first century. There are two major questions: (1) What are the limits to human lifespan? and (2) How many of the extra years of life thereby gained will be active, disability-free, working years of life? The crucial consequences for population aging will be considered in a subsequent section.

While no scientist believes that man can live forever, there is otherwise little agreement between optimists and pessimists. The optimists note that recent trends in death rates show no sign of abating and that the oldest maximum observed age keeps increasing; some suggest averages exceeding 100 years (Wilmoth and Lundstrom 1996; Vaupel 2001). "There is no limit to what is possible," claim Caselli and Vallin (2001: 61), offering a "conservative" hypothesis of 150 years. Those who take a more cautious view envisage the extraordinary practical difficulty of making large improvements in the burden from specific causes of death that could permit an average expectation of life of much more than 85 years, which is the limit assumed in the UN projections (Olshansky and Carnes 1996); some suggest that even a reversal of the trend might be possible (Olshansky 2005). Genetic modification of the duration of life, if it could be shown to be possible, would be hard to resist, and might really upset the aging applecart.

If the future of the survival curve is to become rectangular, then we can look forward to a delay of mortality—and morbidity—until a maximum age is reached, at which time an increasing proportion of deaths—eventually almost all—will occur. The curves of disability-free and disease-free life will then increasingly coincide with the survival curve. But in fact the whole survival curve is still moving to the right. The average age at death is rising but its variance is not tending to zero, ensuring a continuing variety of old-age life experience. However, the right-hand side of the distribution around that average is being narrowed "as though it were meeting an invisible wall... offering stiffer resistance to further progress but without setting any definite limit to it" (Kannisto 2001: 169). The assumption that old people have to be in bad health also appears to be wrong. Evidence is not unequivocal, but against some pessimistic views (Dunnell and Dix 2000) US cohort studies suggest that disability-free life expectation in the West accounts for an increasing proportion of the gain in years of life (Manton and Land 2000). If so, this is hopeful news when confronting the future problems of population aging discussed below.

Migration

Postwar migration to and within Europe had novel and enduring features: the scale of migration from the fringes of (mostly Southern) Europe into areas of rapid economic growth; the first-ever peaceful large-scale migration from outside Europe's boundaries; and the absence, thanks to the Iron Curtain, of the large-scale movement from Eastern Europe that had provided workers for Germany's industry before World War I. Most European countries have at various times wanted workers but almost always wished to restrict foreign population. In most countries the guestworkers of the 1960s were intended, insofar as any thought was given to the matter, to be short term. Many of the earlier immigrants from Southern Europe have indeed returned, as their native economies grew to par with the rest of the European Union. But few things are more permanent than temporary foreign workers from poor countries (Martin and Widgren 1996); those from developing countries, whether organized or irregular, have tended to stay. Most European governments lacked the will or the means to enforce return (Kubat 1984; Freeman 1994).

Immigration of relatives and dependents continues, establishing ethnic minority populations now continuously reinforced and diversified by migration of all kinds, with migration for arranged marriages and asylum-claiming now particularly prominent. Few flows from the developing world, once established, have ever stopped; transnational populations of immigrant origin develop their own autonomous life and momentum, constantly tending to increase through the process of "cumulative causation" (Massey and Zenteno 1999). Parallel development of the postwar revolutions in rights, information, and transport has made further immigration difficult to resist even when Europe was minded to do so. Recent, more positive consideration of migration, fueled by fears of specific skill shortages and of more general supposed workforce and demographic deficits, and by the apparent hopelessness of stopping flows, has prompted more receptive attitudes on the part of some European governments and the EU. The picture is further complicated by the recent salience of security and integration problems. Such problems, along with sluggish economies and truculent electorates, have, for example, at least temporarily barred free movement of labor from the new Central European members to most other EU countries and promoted further restrictions in Denmark and the Netherlands. Whatever happens, the demographic, economic, and security pressures surrounding migration will endure for most of the century. The demographic and economic disparity between the developed world and large parts of the rest is if anything widening.

In terms of numbers, since the mid-1980s over a million international migrants on average have moved to Western Europe each year, creating a net legal inflow of about 600,000 annually. Illegal immigration has been estimated to bring in another 350,000. In the exceptional year of 1992, total gross inflow was estimated to be 2.7 million (Widgren 1994). Immigration can go up as well as down—flows have since declined and risen again (see Figure 2). Since the 1950s Germany has been Europe's chief importer

FIGURE 2   Annual net foreign immigration to EU-15 countries, 1960–2003 (thousands)

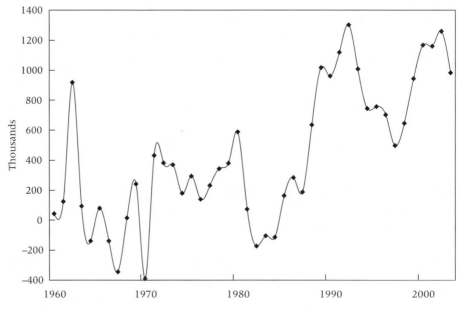

SOURCE: Eurostat, various years.

of legal immigrants and—until overtaken recently by Britain—of asylum claimants as well. More foreigners left Germany than entered it in 1998 and 1999, however, thanks to high levels of return migration, despite the arrival of large numbers of new labor migrants. These inflows have greatly increased the foreign-origin populations in Western European countries and, more recently, in Central Europe as well. Conventional published statistics usually present the "foreign citizen" population (Table 1). Although impressive, these numbers substantially understate the foreign immigrant population as a result of the rapid pace of naturalization in many countries (e.g., France, Netherlands, Sweden; see Table 2). The reasons for this inflow to Europe and its increase are complex and are only partly connected with labor demand or economic trends. For decades, most immigrants to most European countries have not been workers: most are dependents, new spouses through arranged marriage, students, and overstayers. An exception, possibly temporary, arose in Britain after 2004 with the very large inflow of people from the new EU accession countries.

Political developments in sending and receiving countries—instability and expulsions on the one hand, the trend of relaxation, the hope of amnesties, or toughening of control on the other—together with economic changes in the sending countries, are also important. The end of Soviet Communism opened the novel prospect of flows from Eastern Europe and increasingly also through it and to it from the developing world. Behind all of this are the great disparities in population growth, economic level, security, and welfare between the developing world and Europe. Insofar

TABLE 1   Resident foreign citizen population in selected European countries 1971–2001 (thousands)

	1971	1976	1981	1986	1991	1995	2001
Austria	195	271	288	304	468	674	705
Belgium	663	835	861	847	905	910	847
Denmark	100	91	102	117	161	223	267
Finland		12	13	17	26	69	99
France		3,442	3,714	3,594	3,608		3,263
Germany	3,054	4,567	4,453	4,379	5,343	7,174	7,319
Italy	122		211	319	566	991	1,363
Netherlands	247	351	521	553	692	725	690
Portugal	32	32	458	80	108	168	239
Spain	148	165	183	242	279	500	1,109
Sweden	411	422	422	389	484	532	476
Britain			1,638	1,785	1,892	1,948	2,587

NOTE: Totals for foreign citizens can be about one-half or one-third of the foreign immigrant total, because of naturalization (France, Netherlands). See Table 2 below.
SOURCE: Council of Europe.

TABLE 2   Numbers of foreign-born and non-citizens compared to native-born and citizens in selected European countries, c. 2000/2001 (thousands)

	Native-born		Foreign-born		All native-born	All foreign-born	All non-citizens
	Citizens	Non-citizens	Citizens	Non-citizens			
Austria	6,914	116	408	593	7,029	1,002	709
Belgium	9,001	194	448	651	9,196	1,098	845
Denmark	4,939	43	146	215	4,982	361	258
Finland	5,032	13	54	76	5,045	130	89
France	52,143	510	3,115	2,754	52,652	5,868	3,263
Germany					71,973	10,256	
Netherlands	14,269	103	1,051	565	14,372	1,615	668
Portugal	9,692	12	431	220	9,704	651	232
Spain	38,604	71	672	1,501	38,675	2,172	1,572
Sweden	7,826	71	673	405	7,898	1,078	476
Britain					53,924	4,866	

NOTE: Persons of undeclared status excluded. Data for Italy not available in this form.
SOURCE: Dumont and Lemaitre 2005, Annex 2, p. 34.

as these underlie pressures to migrate, migration will persist for most of the twenty-first century. Despite the more rapid fertility decline in North Africa forecast by Courbage (1999) and endorsed for the rest of the developing world by the United Nations at its Expert Group Meeting of March 2002, substantial population growth will continue. Population will be further mobilized by economic restructuring. Economic disparities show few signs of diminishing generally; overseas aid makes little impact—none at all, it would appear, in sub-Saharan Africa. The flow of information and the ease of movement can hardly be curtailed. Only entitlement to enter is within the control of governments. It takes unusually tough-minded governments to curtail such rights. The governments of Denmark and the Netherlands have shown that effective action can be taken when electorates are sufficiently provoked.

Asylum claims and illegal immigration

The huge growth of asylum claiming took Europe by surprise. Encouraged during the Cold War when the flow was modest and most claims were seen as justified and politically useful, no one imagined it would lead to mass migration and settlement from elsewhere. Once discovered and available, asylum has proved to be an easy way of gaining settlement by evading the processes whereby European countries attempt—with uncertain success— to regulate entry. European countries have outflanked their own controls by surrendering sovereignty to broadly phrased international treaties, often even more broadly interpreted by their courts. Most claims are nonetheless rejected but most claimants stay; asylum has become a settlement process rather than a protection process. Temporary protection, of course, has been offered on a large scale, outside the strict definitions of asylum, to the victims of war in Yugoslavia and elsewhere. Asylum overlaps closely with illegal immigration, a flow linked with the black economy and with existing immigrant communities. Immigration has become one of the biggest international businesses (Salt 2001) and one in which international criminal organizations are heavily involved (Salt 2000; NCIS 2003).

In their scale, legal and illegal movement from Eastern Europe and the former Soviet Union, although substantial from Poland and Romania, had not lived up to the fears expressed in the early 1990s—until Britain became the only major country to allow free entry from the new EU members starting in May 2004. By March 2006, 392,000 persons had registered for work in Britain, nearly 30 times the government's estimate and by far the largest single inflow in the country's history. It is not known how many have returned. Minorities (*Aussiedler*, Jews, Gypsies, Kosovans) still make up an important proportion of inflows to the EU-15. Eastern Europe has itself begun to receive immigrants in large numbers, forming the nuclei of novel developing-world minorities: those attempting transit to the West and others who stay. And, as mentioned earlier, Russia unexpectedly became the biggest country of immigration in Europe for a time around 1992.

Economic, political, and environmental consequences for Europe

Population aging

Population aging is perhaps the most salient problem facing Europe today. The higher birth and death rates that created a young population throughout history have vanished. Their reduction was a prerequisite for the improvement of human welfare and a sign of a vastly improved mastery over the conditions of life. Most of tomorrow's population aging is already built into today's age structure. While population in the developed world is aging, the process will markedly slow down by approximately midcentury when all cohorts will be the product of a moderate or low fertility regime. Once fertility rates have stabilized, although at a low level, population aging arising from low fertility (aging from the base) will eventually cease. By that time a new stable but older population structure will have time to emerge.

Thereafter, further population aging will be entirely due to any additional increases in survival (aging at the summit), which seem set to continue. Differences in the proportions of old persons within the total population in different Western countries, however, will be due more to their divergent birth rates, which now and in the recent past vary much more than their death rates. In the West, but not in the East, the retirement of the baby boom cohorts will accelerate population aging from about 2020 until about 2070, just as the low birth rates of the 1930s are currently retarding it. In Eastern Europe, in the absence of much mortality improvement, and where sharp fertility reduction is much more recent, aging will continue for longer to be driven by low birth rates. In France, mortality decline was the more important contributor to population aging during 1946–95. From the end of the last century until the middle of the twenty-first, the effects of fertility change will predominate (Calot and Sardon 1999). In the long run, if decades of stability or even modest increase in birth rates can be assumed, any continued mortality decline later in the century will become the sole agent of population aging (aside from any effects of migration).

Major differences in age structure are likely to emerge among the countries of Europe by 2050 (see Figure 3). Southern European countries are likely to end up with at least 33 percent of their population aged over 65 years. By contrast, about 24 percent of Northern Europeans would be over that age. Eastern Europe begins with fewer elderly than in any other major European region (12.9 percent) but ends up with about 26 percent. There, higher mortality moderates aging at the summit of the age pyramid but is somewhat counteracted by low fertility accentuating aging at the base. This 26 percent figure assumes considerable recovery in both birth rates and survival in the UN projections, optimistic assumptions not shared in those prepared by Andreev et al. (1997). In the case of Britain, official national projections, which take actual, higher migration into account, reach more favorable conclusions than the United Nations (Coleman 2000; Shaw 2001), but UN data will be used here for the sake of consistency.

Concerns about population aging have inspired a lively debate in the media, bringing "demographics" to every breakfast table, with excited headlines about "population implosions" and "demographic timebombs." The reasons for concern are well known: the threat to the solvency of pension systems, especially unfunded pay-as-you-go state systems; and the expenditure of resources for the medical and physical care of a growing elderly population, with a correspondingly diminishing relative or even absolute size of the workforce. As usual, demographers bring bad news about a problem that it is then the business of economists to resolve.

Particular attention has been given to future trends in the "potential support ratio" (PSR), that is, the ratio of the number of persons in the nominal active age groups (conventionally 15–64 years) to the number of persons in the elderly population (conventionally aged 65 and older). This indicator is shown for selected countries in Figure 4.

In most European countries, the PSR today is around 4; Russia's is unusually favorable (5.6) owing to its high death rate. Death rate trends in Western countries are expected to resemble one another, but if differences in birth rates remain these populations will end up with very different lev-

FIGURE 3   Current and projected population by age and sex, Northern and Southern Europe, 2004 and 2050 (millions)

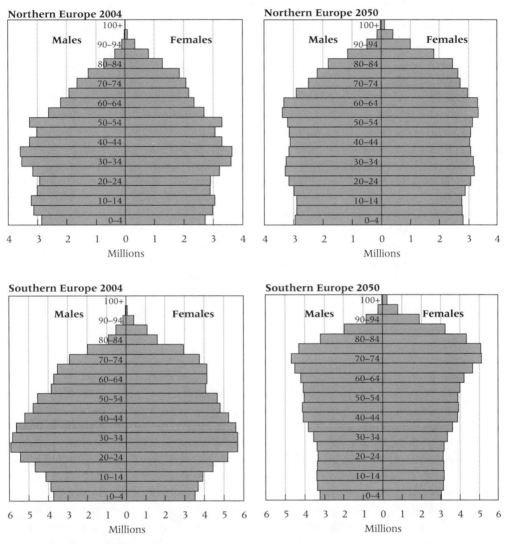

SOURCE: United Nations 2005 (medium variant).

els of PSR: 1.4 in Southern Europe and over 2 in North-Western Europe. Projection of population over a period of 45 years is naturally subject to substantial error. However, the 2004-based Eurostat baseline projections tell essentially the same story, although the suspiciously high British PSR projected by the United Nations (2.63) for 2050 is moderated to a more plausible 2.21 in the Eurostat scenario, still just ahead of that of France (2.13). The other Eurostat PSR projections are 1.79 for Germany, 1.52 for Italy, and 1.48 for Spain.

**FIGURE 4   Potential old-age support ratios (number of persons aged
15–64 divided by number of persons aged 65 and older), selected
countries, 2000 and 2050**

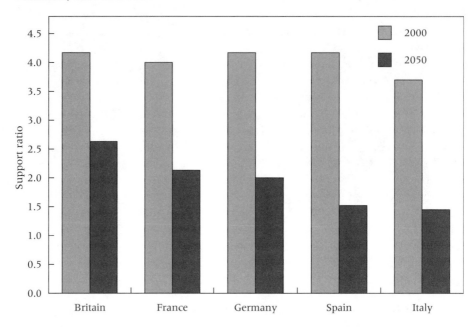

SOURCE: United Nations 2005 (medium variant).

Demographic solutions to population aging

In many Western countries, the search for appropriate responses to manage future population aging and population decline has directed attention
to international migration. It seemed reasonable to some that international
migrants, mostly of young working age, could make up for population deficits created by low birth rates, protect European society from the economic
costs of elderly dependency, provide a workforce to care for the elderly,
and save European populations from the trouble of reproducing themselves.
On this view, past European resistance to migration pressures is misguided;
both sides can get what they want and live happily ever after. Particular
prominence was given to this option through the publicity attendant upon
a report from the UN Population Division (2000) on "replacement migration," which has been widely reported and widely misunderstood (as detailed by Teitelbaum 2004).

Immigration can prevent population decline and does indeed moderate
population aging, as immigrants tend to be younger than the populations
into which they move. But the effect is not great, and immigration can only
fully prevent population aging at unprecedented and unsustainable levels of

inflow, which would generate rapid population growth and quickly displace the original population from its majority position—"replacement migration" indeed. For example, in the case of the European population, migration to preserve the present potential support ratio would need to increase to about 25 million every year on average and would treble Europe's population by 2050 from 754 million to 2.35 billion, and so on at an accelerating rate. The "Korea syndrome" is the *reductio ad absurdum* of this option: the entire world population would have to migrate to Korea to preserve its PSR just up to 2050. Furthermore, all inflows would have to be highly variable in order to preserve a constant ratio from one period of time to the next. Under these "demographic engineering" solutions, the receiving societies would rapidly cease to exist in any recognizable form.

Fertility is more efficient than migration at improving PSR (i.e., it has equivalent effects on aging at the cost of lower levels of population growth). But even with replacement-level fertility, PSR in Europe would still fall from about 4 today to under 3 in 2050. To preserve current PSR, the TFR would need to rise to about 3.5, thereby increasing population size although less spectacularly than the immigration option would do (Calot and Sardon 1999; Shaw 2001). There are, therefore, no demographic solutions to population aging, although both processes can ameliorate it. While the effect of migration is not dismissed, more attention is nowadays paid to the effects of higher fertility and of adjustments to labor markets, pension systems, and retirement age (United Nations 2001; European Commission 2005).

Workforce size can be conserved with more modest immigration, although at the cost of considerable population increase. Here too sharp fluctuations in inflow would be needed (e.g., Shaw 2001): immigration is always easier to start than to stop. Population totals in Italy, Germany, and some other countries, which are in a state of natural decline, are now maintained by immigration. In the case of Germany, migration has been so substantial that the rate of population growth increased sharply in recent years, as it has in Britain, Norway, and Sweden.

The projected future decline of the working-age population has attracted much interest, often misinterpreted by the media as an actual decline today. However, the population of working age is expected to rise by about 5 million in North and West Europe from 1995 to 2010, and by 4 million in Eastern Europe, and to decline by about 1 million in the South—in all cases accompanied by an older age structure. After 2010, numbers are expected to decline overall, and more severely after 2025 unless there is an upturn in fertility. Projected totals of the working-age population and of entrants to working age vary greatly between different European populations, a fact to which EU proposals for a common European migration policy (European Commission 2000) pay insufficient attention. Given the level of youth unemployment in many European countries, especially among immigrants themselves, moderation of supply might seem welcome in the short run. As Pearce and Punch note, there is only a "weak link between demographic factors and the labor market in Europe," arising from widespread underutilization of labor and productive capacity. An immediate general labor shortage in Europe looks unlikely given unemployment levels and productivity gains (Pearce and Punch 2000: 10–15). In the longer run it is clear that some countries can expect a decline in their working-age populations, inevitable given their recent low birth rates. Figure 5 shows the expected changes up to 2050. These projected figures in part are affected by assumed net immigration.

Numbers of workforce entrants are scheduled to diverge considerably—in the cases of Norway, France, and Netherlands increasing in the next 15 years and then declining only modestly, if at all, up to midcentury. Germany and above all Italy and Spain show more serious falls on present trends especially after 2025. The fall to the 2000 level looks impressive when measured from the troublesome height of the baby boom generation and the curse of youth unemployment that accompanied it, less so in longer perspective. Moreover, if projected changes in the size of workforce-entry generations are allied to moderate projected increases in workforce participation rates, the numbers of projected young workers increase in most

FIGURE 5   Projected changes in the population aged 20–24 in selected European countries, 2000–2050 (population in 2000 = 100)

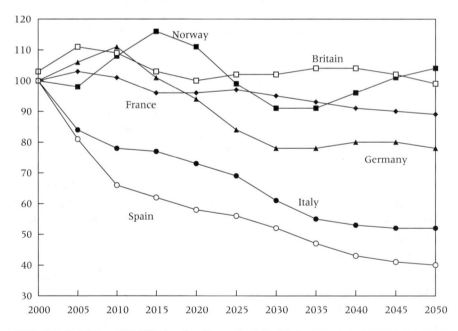

SOURCE: United Nations 2004 (2002-based medium variant); for Britain: Government Actuary's Department 2005.

countries and do not return to their 2000 level until about 2020, and in some cases much later. Only Italy shows a substantial imminent shortfall on this basis (Feld 2005). McDonald and Kippen (2001), however, come to less optimistic conclusions.

For many decades labor migration for specific jobs from foreign countries, or from outside the EU, has been regulated in accord with economic needs through work permit systems. Most legal entrants have been highly skilled. Since the late 1990s, rising demand for information technology specialists unmet from Europe's own resources, fears of general labor shortage, and a more positive reevaluation of migration by current EU governments have fired enthusiasm for labor migration as a means of promoting EU economic efficiency. The economic superiority of the United States is attributed to its high migration rate, and EU countries are seen as competitors in an international sellers' market for skills. The current government consensus for a common EU migration policy, otherwise hardly justified in view of the highly divergent needs in different EU countries, arises from these considerations. The general merits of skilled labor migration are not in doubt, but the idea that migration can be Europe's economic salvation is deluded (Coleman and Rowthorn 2004), putting cart before horse in its analysis of US economic advantage and distracting attention from Europe's need to reform its own labor markets.

Nondemographic responses to population aging

In the absence of demographic "solutions," the question arises whether the effects of aging can be moderated in other ways. In financial and actuarial circles, attention tends to be focused upon fiscal, economic, and workforce adjustments (e.g., McMorrow and Roeger 2004; Turner 2005), often in relatively optimistic terms. What matters ultimately is whether the economy can manage the changed pattern of consumption and investment and still deliver acceptable economic growth or at the very least maintain standards, and whether public opinion will permit labor markets and pension systems to be adjusted to allow the economy to do so. Some cost in growth is hardly avoidable, however—the twentieth-century demographic bonus is over. Estimates based on relatively benign demographic regimes such as those of the United States conclude that population aging will reduce base-rate annual economic growth by about 0.5 percentage points, that is, by about one-fifth. Most opinion suggests that growth can be managed, albeit with some pain, if birth rates remain reasonably favorable or, in the case of Southern and Eastern Europe, become so (see, e.g., Weil 1997; Gillion 1999; World Bank 1994; Daykin and Lewis 1999; Dunnell 2001). However, European countries not only differ substantially in the demographically defined problem of aging that they confront; they also face a variety of nondemographic problems in terms of unreformed labor markets, retirement systems, and pension indebtedness. And the countries that are worst off demographically also tend to be those facing the biggest institutional challenges (Jackson and Howe 2003). Accordingly, "management" involves a combination of responses, divided here into three broad categories.

(1) Improving the real, as opposed to the potential, support ratio   Low levels of female workforce participation, early retirement, extended tertiary education, and unemployment all mean that actual workforces in European countries are considerably smaller than the population of working age: just 62 percent overall in the EU. Hence the real support ratio of taxpayers to pension recipients is already much lower than the demographic abstraction known as the potential support ratio. For example, in Britain today the real support ratio of workers to pensioners is about 3.2 to 1, not the "demographic" 4.1 to 1; and the real support ratio of actual workers to all nonworkers over age 15 is just 1.67 to 1, a ratio evidently still capable of supporting national life. Elsewhere in Europe, where the figures are mostly worse, there is much scope for increasing workforce participation: retraining the unemployed, discouraging early retirement, reducing obstacles to internal labor mobility (Fuchs and Schmidt 2000), and above all making it easier for women to combine work with childcare. The Scandinavian countries have been the most successful in reducing the incompatibilities between childcare and work: North-Western Europe has the highest levels of female workforce participation and also the highest fertility in Europe.

An increase of workforce participation to Danish levels would mobilize considerable demographic reserves of labor and increase the EU workforce by over 30 million—much more than the expected demographic shortfall for the next 25 years (see Figure 6). This is a one-off, if large, bonus: such measures cannot be effective much beyond that time period as participation rates cannot exceed, or even approach, 100 percent (Lesthaeghe 2002). Nor will such reforms be easy. Existing labor protection laws discourage recruitment and in 2005 helped to keep unemployment at 9 percent in the Euro zone and 12 percent in Italy and Spain: immigrant and foreign populations may suffer double that figure or more. European higher education systems, until they were recently reformed, helped to keep young people out of the market until their late 20s or even 30s, notably in Germany. European bureaucracies keep hundreds of thousands occupied in unproductive regulatory activities and form-filling, notably in Southern Europe. This encourages black market working (about 4 percent of GDP in Denmark, affecting 26 percent of adults, and supposedly much more elsewhere: Mogensen et al. 1995) and the recruitment of illegal immigrant labor. Illegal labor, although gratifying to employers, does not contribute to tax or pension systems. Continental European workers and unions have displayed an impressive determination to pursue unsustainable policies favoring early retirement (e.g., French railway

**FIGURE 6   Potential increase in millions in the size of the EU-15
workforce, by sex, 1999, assuming Danish participation rates**

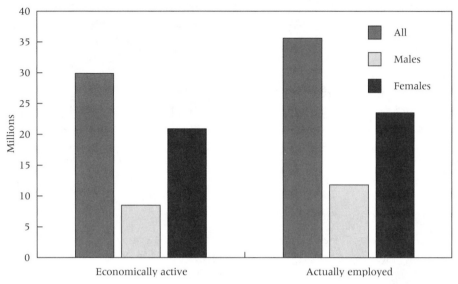

SOURCE: Eurostat 2000: Tables 1 and 4.

workers in 2000) and job protection. In the early 2000s, the then leaders of
the four biggest EU countries (Chirac, Berlusconi, Schröder, Blair) each saw
his reform plans rebuffed or severely weakened. EU institutions struggle between promoting welfare and social protection, on one hand, and economic
efficiency, on the other.

Labor mobility within and between EU-15 countries, despite freedom
of movement, remains modest. Frictions of various kinds will always allow
unemployment to coexist with labor migration. But the plans of the German
government passed by the Bundesrat in March 2002, to open borders to even
more immigrant workers while 4.3 million Germans remained unemployed,
show how easy an option immigration may seem compared with the political minefield of fundamental domestic reform. In Southern Europe a more
radical version of the same strategy proposes the acceptance of permanent
lowest-low fertility, exploitation of the economic and educational benefits of
very small families, and supplying the labor force deficit by expanded large-
scale immigration from North Africa and elsewhere (Dalla-Zuanna 2006).

In the longer run, increasing the average age of retirement is more effective. It would, at least in theory, transfer individuals from dependency into
economic activity, thus improving both the numerator and denominator of
the dependency ratio. Steps to raise pension entitlement age and to remove
tax disincentives for working pensioners and employment barriers imposed
solely on grounds of age are already variously in train in the United States,

Italy, and Japan. The Institute of Public Policy Research, linked to the ruling Labour Party in Britain, recently advocated an increase in the retirement age in Britain to 67, as did the authoritative Turner Report (Turner 2005). Already, male and female retirement ages will be unified at 65 between 2010 and 2020 from their present 65 and 60. In order fully to maintain today's support ratios, most scenarios envisage a universal retirement age rising to between 72 and 75 and varying from one country to another, depending mostly on the birth rate. Even with continued extension of active life, this seems severe. However, Europe is not starting from a real retirement age of 65. In reality, actual retirement age is about 59. If maintaining the potential support ratio involves a longer nominal working life of 7 years (72 – 65), then maintaining the real support ratio means an increase in normal retirement age from, roughly, 59 to 66 (59 + 7). The European Commission (1996) came to a similar conclusion: average real age at retirement would have to rise to 66 from the then EU average of 60.

(2) Moderating the financial burden. State pay-as you-go pension schemes, on which almost all European pension systems are based, are subverted demographically by the evolution of older population structures. The populations for which they were created have ceased to exist. These schemes build up formidable future indebtedness, exceeding annual GDP in some countries, unless contribution rates are greatly increased or pensions cut. (Britain did this in the 1980s by linking state pensions to prices, not incomes. But that reform is coming under attack, as occupational and private funded schemes suffer from weak market returns, underestimated survival, and misguided tax policies.) For this and other reasons the World Bank and others have emphasized the importance of diverse sources of old-age support through "second and third pillar" occupational and private funded pension schemes. These may have the additional advantage of improving the savings rate for investment (World Bank 1994; Daykin and Lewis 1999). Over 70 percent of Britain's population is already covered by such schemes (European Federation for Retirement Provision 1999; Stein 1997). However, funded pensions cannot escape adverse demographic effects. Their value still depends on the output of the economy, in which the size of workforce plays an important role (Chand and Jaeger 1996). Low interest rates and longer lives can weaken their solvency. The "defined contribution" schemes now favored in an era of uncertain investment returns also transfer risk to the employee and pensioner. Again, while EU policy is to diversify pensions, addiction to social protection leads to contradictory policies, for example, the current draft Directive intended to oblige pension funds to take responsibility for all risk. The transitional economies of Eastern Europe show even less inclination for reforms of this kind. Former state pensions were adequate in relation to the standard of living. Free market systems are still developing and little trusted.

(3) Capital investment to improve worker productivity. Such investment is a desirable step in its own right, to improve Europe's poor international competitiveness, and one that would naturally follow from the pressure of higher wages arising from any labor shortage as long as it were not alleviated by higher migration inflows. Productivity growth per capita required to cover all increased old-age dependency would amount to about 0.5 percent per year by 2020, resulting in 2.5 percent growth compared with normal annual growth of up to 3 percent per year. In the EU specifically, productivity would have to rise by about 0.8 percentage points per year if that were the sole means to meet the need for extra resources arising from population aging (European Commission 1996: 36–39). That is a very substantial increase. In the majority of European countries a multiple response should be feasible to make the problems of population aging manageable. However, the extreme low-fertility countries, especially Italy, face in the long run an apparently unsustainable burden unless their birth rate increases.

The problem of population decline and lower population size

In the medium to longer run, many European countries face population decline, some small, others substantial (see Figure 7). National population decline has often been regarded as a symptom as well as a cause of national decline relative to neighbors in a competitive and hostile world (Teitelbaum and Winter 1985; Teitelbaum 1999). This concern, nearly universal in the mercantilist climate of previous eras, dates from the beginnings of states themselves. The merits of large populations, and the corresponding fear of their decline, have been taken as axiomatic when population was the prime factor of production, the guarantor of revenues and of national security. Population decline followed war and plague. The mercantilism of Colbert, Bodin, and the physiocrats (van de Kaa 1999) found more recent expression among European governments of the 1930s, among the postwar Communist rulers of Eastern Germany, and even among some free-market economists today, notably in North America. On the other hand, some economic historians describe the medieval post-plague era, when population was reduced by a third, as a "golden age of the peasant" with real wages and technical innovation rising in response to labor shortage, giving the coup de grâce to feudal exploitation (Postan 1972).

The UN report on replacement migration (2000) inherited the assumption that population decline is ipso facto undesirable. However, these notions nowadays reflect trans-Atlantic rather than universal Western concerns; population stabilization or reduction may be contrary to the American dream, but mixed opinions can be found elsewhere. It is true that Malthusian views have never found favor in French political, public, or demographic

FIGURE 7   Population growth and decline, projections for selected European countries, 2004–2051

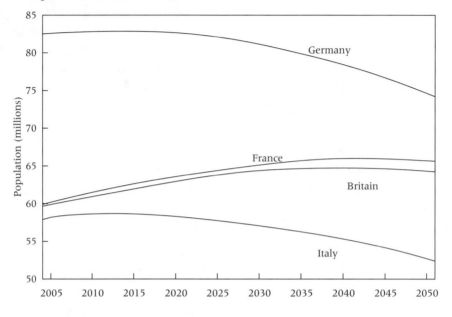

NOTE: According to latest national projections, 2051 totals for France and Britain are underestimated here by about 5 million.
SOURCE: Eurostat medium projection, 2004-based.

opinion—as the works of Sauvy (1969), Chesnais (1995), and others so eloquently testify. But, for example, even in the 1930s while demographers presented alarming projections of population decline, some European economists took a more sanguine view, seeing some advantages in a population no longer increasing or even declining (Keynes 1936; Reddaway 1939). The UK Royal Commission on Population (1949: 60, 61; 1950: 58) welcomed the end of population growth as a relief from balance-of-payments problems, unproductive housebuilding, and pressure on land, environment, and natural products (opposite lessons about housebuilding have been voiced recently in the United States) while also noting adverse consequences for pensions and fears for employment owing to shortfalls in demand. This concern too is nowadays reversed. The last official report on population in Britain (Population Panel 1973) considered that the end to growth in a crowded island facilitated the solving of social and economic problems. Official comments in Germany (Höhn 1990) have discussed the management of population decline with apparent equanimity. The government of the Netherlands has long welcomed the end of growth, noting in 1983 that "Continuing population growth will have an adverse effect on the well-being of the nation," a view repeated in more nuanced fashion in 1998 (Government of the Netherlands 1998: 9).

Can we then face declining or at least lower population with equanimity, apart from the specific problems of aging mentioned above? The answer does not seem to be entirely obvious either way. However, the effects of a smaller stable population must be distinguished from the problems associated with the population decline that must occur before we reach that position.

As regards numbers, there is no cross-sectional relationship in Western Europe between population size or population growth and GDP per head or economic growth rates. Over the last half-century, European countries with the oldest and most slowly growing populations (e.g., Sweden) have been the richest. In a global economy enjoying free trade, where export markets may be dominant and where rates of population increase or decline can only be low, the effect of domestic population size on markets may be minimal. While mercantilist demographic concern about the ability to project military force still has relevance today, old potential enemies have cohorts of military age declining in step, and new ones pose very different kinds of threat. Concerns about the relative population growth rates across the Mediterranean, the "biggest demographic and economic fault line in the world" (Chesnais 1995), can only be resolved by the improvement of the situation to the South, hardly by renewed population growth in the North. The declining proportion of the Western world in global population must eventually weaken this aspect of power, as it has done in the more peaceful aspects of representative world governance (McNicoll 1999). But that is a very long-term affair, quite overshadowed by more immediate considerations, about which Western countries can in any case do little.

Enthusiasts for population growth (e.g., Simon 1981) point to the counter-inflationary effects of workforce growth and the guarantee provided by growing numbers of consumers in underwriting productive investment and promoting innovation, and they fear decline for the reverse reasons. Some of these effects, often cited and often taken to be axiomatic by economists and in business circles, chime with common sense but lack empirical evidence.

Unemployment and labor shortage have been contradictory concerns in many Western countries. There is now little concern about insufficient demand, which Keynes feared, except in savings-mad Japan or in Germany, and in neither case is population to blame. In a modern economy, increased productivity per head leading to higher competitiveness is the key to economic growth. That involves higher capital inputs, in some cases removing workers from production altogether. Few now believe that technology creates unemployment. If labor is in short supply, then the incentives for capital substitution and productivity gain become stronger, while at the bottom of the social scale higher demand for labor may help resolve problems of low wages. Some activities that cannot be made profitable by any means can be run down or exported to places where labor is cheaper, as so many already have been—to everyone's benefit.

Polls indicate that public opinion often fears overpopulation, with issues of land, overcrowding, and environmental amenity much to the fore, although they are far down the scale of most people's political priorities. Such views were cited prominently in the reasons for leaving the Netherlands in a recent survey of emigrants (ter Bekke 2005). Both the Netherlands and Britain have experienced sharp upturns in population growth in the last decade, primarily through immigration, and in both countries citizens have been departing in unusual numbers. At the local level, popular dislike of population growth is general, contrary to the views of business interests. Governments waver on this issue. In Britain most local authorities in growth areas oppose new housebuilding; those in areas of decline look for development. Cities used to be regarded as unhealthily overcrowded, and decentralization was encouraged. But when urban population decline does occur, this tends not to be regarded as a rational readjustment of population from declining rust-belts to economic growth areas, but instead as a problem requiring intervention.

Environmental concerns, including countryside and wildlife protection, have become prominent in the Western world, creating new Green parties and forcing governments and others to change their agendas—especially in Western Europe, less in Eastern Europe. Attitudes to population, however, have been equivocal. Britain's Green Party has advocated a halving of British population to 30 million but was equivocal about linking the issue of population growth to migration. The German Greens, with a more radical political agenda, favor immigration. While such activists—and many others unconnected with a political movement—may favor a population lower than the present one, the concept of "optimum" population has so far eluded generally accepted scientific or economic definitions, despite heroic efforts. In the developed world, faith in the need for growth is stronger in countries outside Europe with more space than history.

Shacking up and breaking up: The second demographic transition

The first demographic transition has left an enduring legacy in the form of aging populations in the twenty-first century. Radical changes in living arrangements, sexual habits, and marriage, under the label of the second demographic transition, have bequeathed to this century a diversity of household and living arrangements hitherto unknown. These radical changes have upset the centuries-old pattern in much of Western Europe since the 1960s and since the 1980s have spread to some Eastern European countries as well. Divorce and abortion are nearly universally legalized and in most cases made readily accessible. Welfare arrangements and law have abolished the former distinction between legitimate and illegitimate births. Sexual activity begins at younger ages and is nearly universal before marriage. Cohabitation before marriage is regarded as normal in many countries, with the popularity of marriage falling as its mean age rises to levels not seen since the 1930s. Up to 40 percent of marriages end in divorce.

This second demographic transition, it is claimed, reflects a new primacy of enlightened postmaterialist individual aspiration over traditional restraints and obligations to a wider society (Lesthaeghe 1995; Lesthaeghe and Surkyn 2004; van de Kaa 1987), promoted by universal education and made possible by prosperity and the blanket of welfare. The prevalence of this behavior and of the underlying ideational change in some countries is not in doubt, although their real novelty is disputed (Cliquet 1991) and the theory of postmaterialism has not gone unchallenged (Wilensky 2002). The theory itself combines empirical data with testable hypotheses in a way that is absent from the theory of the first demographic transition. But the rates at which different populations have embraced these novelties have differed greatly, and this has created a renewed diversity within and between Europe's populations (Kuijsten 1996). Further falls in the birth rate are also claimed as part of this postmaterialist syndrome, although that claim seems to fit the facts less well—the populations most enthusiastic for these behaviors (those in North-Western Europe and the English-speaking world overseas) tend to have higher, not lower birth rates.

Despite general supporting trends, it remains unclear whether this second transition will follow the first in becoming universal in the developed world, or remain in its present half-complete state. So far only in Scandinavia have any of these behaviors become the lifetime experience of the majority (cohabitation, birth outside marriage). In some other countries, they have made little headway. Not all cultural revolutions become universal. The Reformation, seen as quite progressive at the time, stopped at more or less its present boundaries in the seventeenth century, boundaries perhaps not coincidentally similar to those that now interest us.

It may also be asked whether the second demographic transition is sustainable in all respects. Some postmaterialist demographic manifestations of postmodernism rest upon a cushion of welfare, especially in Britain and the United States, which may be considered aberrant in this regard. Modern societies do not permit their citizens to remain in abject poverty, regardless of their behavior. Mothers are free to divorce and move into free or subsidized housing, single parents can depend on welfare payments provided by others to stay at home to raise children and not work. This does not provide luxury; standards of living still decline after these personal transitions. But as van de Kaa has noted, "Whenever externalities result, they are borne by the state or the community" (1999: 31). That fact may limit the extent to which this diversity can be afforded, insofar as it tends to impoverish families and make them dependent on welfare, especially when public finances are also challenged by population aging. Some modern alternatives may have no such implications—for example, children being brought up by their two parents whether married or not.

No one has estimated the full cost of the second demographic transition, but some of its manifestations have already provoked governments to act against it, implicitly if not explicitly. Thus attempts have been made (e.g., in Britain and America) to oblige absent males to support their offspring. In both those countries, government programs aim to reduce the high rate of teenage childbearing and to persuade single mothers to enter the workforce. These responses, however, spurred by fear of the growth of an unemployed welfare-dependent underclass (Murray 1990), may be to problems more typical of Anglo-Saxon societies rather than those of Continental Europe, where, for example, teenage and single unsupported motherhood is much less common.

On the other hand, many women may be prepared to contemplate motherhood only if they can do it their way, and have at least some of those babies in a loose, unconstrained relationship. In the industrial world, populations with primarily marital fertility suffer low birth rates. Many women, it seems, want to have children more than they want a firm commitment to any partner (Kravdal 1997).

Immigration and population replacement

International migration may bring, in the long run, the most dramatic changes of all in the social, cultural, political, and racial characteristics of European and other developed countries. If immigration persists at current levels it will transform Europe's ethnic and racial composition. Foreign population in the EU is now about 24 million, of whom about 14 million are from non-European countries. That total, based on citizenship, considerably understates—perhaps by up to one-quarter—the number of foreign immigrants, because of the rapid pace of naturalization. In France over the last 20 years, naturalization has turned foreigners into citizens faster than they arrive by immigration.

These populations grow both by immigration and by natural increase, the level of the latter depending on the countries of origin of immigrants and their degree of acculturation. European foreign residents in other European countries often have lower birth rates than the national average, whereas residents from non-European countries often have rates that are higher. In Britain, for example, the TFR of the Bangladeshi population is about 3—not lower, at least, than among Bangladeshis in Bangladesh itself. The overall British ethnic minority population increased by 1 million during the 1990s, growing at 5 percent per year, 15 times faster than the white population. A number of local authorities of major cities have officially projected a non-European ethnic majority in ten years, and also in the medium term in London, where many boroughs (with a population of about 180,000) already have nonwhite majorities. In 2001 there was media speculation that the whole of Britain might have a nonwhite majority by the end of the century, an unlikely conjecture, however, not supported by any population projection. (The relative decline into minority status of the US white non-Hispanic population by the end of the century has been projected officially for a decade—US Census Bureau 2000.)

Few European countries have attempted projections of their immigrant populations. In the Netherlands, official projections point to a foreign-descent population of 6 million by 2050, one-third of the projected national total of 18 million. Of the 6 million, one-half (still projected to be increasing in 2050) are expected to be of non-European origin, the rest, declining in number, of European or other Western origin. The definition of "foreign origin" extends only to those born abroad, or with parents born abroad (Alders 2005). Projections of "immigrants and descendants" in Denmark use a similarly restricted definition of foreign origin. According to the Think Tank on Integration in Denmark (2002), from 2001 to 2021 the immigrant-origin population is projected to increase by 88 percent (compared with 6 percent for the whole population), growing from 350,000 (7.4 percent) to 746,000 (13 percent), of whom 60 percent will be from the developing world. The pace of change in all these projections is dependent primarily upon the level of immigration, not on the level of fertility of the foreign-origin populations. The size of these populations is therefore at least in theory responsive to public policy and sometimes in practice. For example, the flow of foreign citizens and the projections of their future number have declined sharply since a more restrictive policy was introduced in 2002. A more modest reduction in flows and in projections is also seen in the Netherlands for the same reason.

The political response in Europe to the presence of substantial non-European populations has been mixed. Until recently in Germany and Austria economic integration was encouraged, but the foreign-born populations were in some ways kept at arms length from local citizens. The distinctive French approach still stresses the indivisible equality of citizenship, encouraging naturalization while not recognizing ethnic or religious groups. Dual nationality is increasingly widely accepted. Britain and, from 1980–92, the Netherlands moved toward various kinds of official or unofficial multiculturalism. None of these approaches has been conspicuously successful; all the countries named above have experienced serious socioeconomic and security difficulties associated with immigrant minorities—especially with Muslim minorities, who comprise the largest component and whose religion and culture are most seriously challenged by living in a minority status. It is not yet clear whether multicultural societies with multiple identities and loyalties can succeed in European democracies. The British government, for example, now speaks in favor of a "diversity" that would earlier have been seen as a problem. Concrete practical advantages of such diversity beyond increased choice of restaurants, an improved ability to speak the languages of developing-world trading partners, and cultural vibrancy in popular music still await detailed exposition.

Until recently there has been little disposition among European elites to address issues of social and cultural integrity. Problems that go beyond simple economic models have tended to be ignored. For example, recent publications from Britain's Home Office illustrate the fiscal benefits of immigration but explicitly assume that no additional costs arise in relation to education, health, and crime except on an age-related basis (Glover et al. 2001). The additional costs arising from security problems and terrorist activities by minority groups, and of race relations programs, were not mentioned, nor were the more difficult noneconomic problems of cultural or religious conflicts of interest or values. These are very difficult to discuss without embarrassment or censure. They include the disproportionate involvement of immigrant or minority populations in some categories of crime, both opportunistic and organized; the connections with and indebtedness to traffickers; the importation to Europe of overseas disputes involving, for example, Kurdistan and the Punjab; and more recently involvement in and sympathy for terrorist activities. Only in the last few years has discussion begun on how to resolve issues of contrasting attitudes on the status of women, on the tolerance appropriate to sexual minorities and to the critics of religion or those who reject it, and on the separation of the powers and influence of church and state. Most crucially, the growth of minorities raises the issues of who should be expected to make an accommodation to whose values and how the "national interest" is defined given the globalized concerns of transnational minorities (Rowthorn 2003; Goodhart 2004). If the new demographic emphasis upon the role of culture and of ideas tells us anything, it is that the postwar new diversity is likely to be a much more important feature of European society in the future than any economic disparities. How these issues are managed will be highly significant for the future of the continent.

Conclusions

Europe or at least the European Union faces several possible futures. One, rather unlikely, is to become a superpower to rival the United States and to become, in the aim of the EU Lisbon summit, "the most productive economic unit in the world" by 2010. The EU's persistent failure, as in Barcelona 2002, to make much progress on liberalization of markets in food, financial services, and airlines, for example, points to a more pessimistic view. That alternative outcome, given present trends, is to remain an inferior and diminishing rival or ally to the United States, with less growth, continued divisions, more social protection, less self-confidence, and less common identity. Europe may be set on a path emphasizing welfare and rights, rather than production and power. Europe's political systems find it difficult to choose between episodic bids for economic reform from national governments and the EU Commission, attempting to increase productivity and mobilize labor resources, and equally powerful preferences for protection of employment, welfare support, and the rights and entitlements to benefits. The tendency toward harmonization in the EU furthermore may tend to make economic arrangements fit the lowest common denominator and make radical change less likely.

Demographic processes, however, are not likely to have a determining role in the outcome. In countries with reasonably robust birth rates, there seems to be no reason why workforce, retirement, and pension adjustments should not cope with inevitable population aging, albeit with some diminution of rates of economic growth. Longer lives, increasingly the sole driver of future population aging, will partly bring their own solution in the form of longer active life. Replacement migration is clearly irrelevant in this context, although a return to birth rates closer to replacement would help considerably. However, if fertility in any European countries persists at a very low level up to the midpoint of the current century, the excess dependency and deficient workforces could present grave difficulties. That of course can be seen coming a long way off, and institutional and attitudinal change may by that time have responded by, for example, making it easier for women to have the children they say they want. Difficult to envisage now, but it would have been difficult to foresee the Europe of 2000 in 1950. Feedbacks form no explicit part of projections.

If a pessimistic long-term view is taken, continued low productivity and failure to mobilize the economically inactive population will exacerbate future labor shortages in some Mediterranean countries and make more unavoidable their demand for additional immigrant labor (which is then free, of course, to move elsewhere in the EU). The priority given to a particular interpretation of "rights" has until recently made it unlikely that European governments will reform or renegotiate the open-ended promises made to the world 50 years ago, under very different circumstances, to guarantee political asylum. If that is the case, Europe will be locked into its present contradictions of trying to prevent illegal entry into the EU but then, if entry succeeds, rewarding some entrants with attractive entitlements.

On the other hand, the same tendency to extend welfare rights may eventually improve the position of women in the low-fertility countries of Europe. While it is notoriously difficult to detect intended or unintended

effects of government policy on birth rates through international comparisons, it seems obvious that both social and welfare arrangements and the
domestic attitudes in North-Western Europe are more favorable to childbearing than those in Southern Europe. In Southern and Eastern Europe
the equality of women's opportunities remains asymmetric. While many
now work, at home they face domestic duties unassisted, including more
care of elderly parents than is normal in North-Western Europe. Hence childbearing is minimal. If Southern Europe is to regain some equilibrium in its
future population, it may have to move toward new policies and attitudes.
The latter are likely to change only slowly. If they did, would that also imply an acceptance by Southern Europe of the levels of cohabitation, extra-
marital births, and divorce found in Northern Europe? Can measures to
support the family be afforded when the demands of a rapidly aging population sustained by pay-as-you-go systems are growing at the same time?
Could population be absorbed into a demographic black hole driven, paradoxically, by its attraction to "familism"?

Europe will clearly include a diverse set of demographic systems for
decades to come, but its economic and demographic divisions may move
further East. The countries of Central Europe, part of a broader Western
world before 1945, and the Baltic States—now part of the EU—seem likely
to recover their economic strength and political stability before the rest of
the former Communist world. Survival rates are already back on track to a
more normal level, and total fertility may increase in time once postponement of births has run its course. Further East, all these processes seem to
proceed much more slowly. Perhaps the most significant aspect of Europe's
diversity, however, is the relative growth of populations of foreign origin,
with the prospect of achieving a completely novel and permanent transformation of the nature of European societies that may render the populations of 2100 unrecognizably different from those of 2000. How far that
comes to pass will depend primarily on policies on immigration and the
perception of immigration as a response to other aspects of demographic
change and economic challenges.

In low-fertility countries, however, even a revival of fertility to something close to replacement level cannot now prevent considerable population decline for 20 years or so, before it would stabilize at a lower level.
While the process of decline may be inconvenient, smaller final populations, if decline eventually halts, may bring some advantages, not least to
the environment. Reliance on large-scale homoeostatic mechanisms for
population regulation has found little favor with contemporary demographers. However, we are moving into an unknown post-transitional world,
and opinion may be changing (Lutz and Qiang 2002). It is possible to imagine, for example, that some effects of smaller population size might actually
encourage family building.

References

Alders, M. 2005. "Allochtonenprognose 2004–2050: belangrijkste uitkomsten" (Projections of the foreign-origin population), *Bevolkingstrends* 53(1st quarter): 32–41.

Andreev, E., S. Scherbov, and W. Willekens. 1992. "Mortality in the former Soviet Union," in *Population of the former USSR in the 21st Century*. Amsterdam: Royal Netherlands Academy of Arts and Sciences.

———. 1997. *The Population of Russia: Fewer and Older. Demographic Scenarios for Russia and Its Regions*. Groningen: University of Groningen, Faculty of Spatial Sciences.

Avdeev, A. 2001. "The extent of the fertility decline in Russia: Is the one-child family here to stay?," presented at the IUSSP seminar on "International Perspectives on Low Fertility: Trends, Theories and Policies," Tokyo. Liège: IUSSP.

Bardet, J.-P. and J. Dupâquier (eds.). 1999. *Histoire des populations de l'Europe III. Les temps incertains 1914–1998*. Paris: Fayard.

Bloom, D. E. and J. G. Williamson. 1998. "Demographic transitions and economic miracles in emerging Asia," *World Bank Economic Review* 12(3): 419–455.

Bobadilla, J. L., C. A. Costello, and F. Mitchell (eds.). 1997. *Premature Death in the Newly Independent States*. Washington, DC: National Academy of Sciences Press.

Bongaarts, J. 2001. "Fertility and reproductive preferences in post-transitional societies," in R. A. Bulatao and J. B. Casterline (eds.), *Global Fertility Transition*. New York: Population Council, Supplement to *Population and Development Review*, Vol. 27, pp. 260–281.

Bongaarts, J. and G. Feeney. 1998. "On the quantum and tempo of fertility," *Population and Development Review* 24(2): 271–291.

Calot, G. and J.-P. Sardon. 1999. "Les facteurs du vieillissement démographique," *Population* 54(3): 509–552.

Caselli, G. and J. Vallin. 2001. "Demographic trends: Beyond the limits?," *Population: An English Selection. Demographic Perspectives on Human Longevity* 13(1): 41–72.

Chand, S. K. and A. Jaeger. 1996. "Aging populations and public pension schemes," Occasional Paper No. 147. Washington, DC: International Monetary Fund.

Chesnais, J.-C. 1995. *La crépuscule de l'Occident: dénatalité, condition de femmes et immigration*. Paris: Robert Laffont.

Cliquet, R. L. 1991. "The second demographic transition: Fact or fiction?," Population Studies No. 23. Strasbourg: Council of Europe.

Coale, A. J. and S. C. Watkins (eds.). 1986. *The Decline of Fertility in Europe*. Princeton: Princeton University Press.

Coleman, D. A. 1993. "Contrasting age structures of Western Europe and of Eastern Europe and the former Soviet Union: Demographic curiosity or labor resource?," *Population and Development Review* 19(3): 523–555.

———. 2000. "Who's afraid of low support ratios? An unofficial response to the UN Population Division Report on Replacement Migration," *Population Bulletin of the United Nations Special Issue: Expert Group Meeting on Policy Responses to Population Aging and Population Decline* (44/45): 288–329.

Coleman, D. A. and R. Rowthorn. 2004. "The economic effects of immigration into the United Kingdom," *Population and Development Review* 30(4): 579–624.

Conrad, C. et al. 1996. "East German fertility after unification. Crisis or adaptation?," *Population and Development Review* 22(2): 331–358.

Cornia, G. A. and R. Paniccia. 1998. "The transition's population crisis: Nuptiality, fertility and mortality changes in severely distressed economies," in M. Livi-Bacci and G. De Santis (eds.), *Population and Poverty in Developing Countries*. Oxford: Clarendon Press, pp. 217–249.

Courbage, Y. 1998. "Demographic characteristics of national minorities in Hungary, Romania and Slovakia," in W. Haug, Y. Courbage, and P. Compton (eds.), *The Demographic*

Characteristics of National Minorities in Certain European States, Volume 1. *Population Studies* 30: 123–158. Strasbourg: Council of Europe.

———. 1999. *Nouveaux horizons démographiques en Méditerranée.* Paris: INED.

Courtois, S. et al. 1999. *The Black Book of Communism.* Cambridge, MA: Harvard University Press.

Crafts, N. F. R. and T. C. Mills. 1995. "Europe's golden age: An econometric investigation of changing trend rates of growth," Discussion Paper No. 1087. London: Centre for Economic Policy Research.

Cuyvers, P. 2001 "Toet Mem," in *Samenleven: nieuwe feiten over relaties en gizinnen.* Den Haag: Centraal Bureau voor de Statistieck pp. 199–209.

Dalla-Zuanna, G. 2006. "Population replacement, social mobility, and development in Italy during the twentieth century," *Journal of Modern Italian Studies* 11(2): 188–208.

Daróczi, E. 2003. "Deviation from epidemiological transition," in I. E. Kotowska and J. Jozwiak (eds.), *The Case of Hungary, 2003.* Warsaw: Statistical Publishing Establishment, pp. 351–368.

DaVanzo, J. and C. Grammich. 2001. *Dire Demographics: Population Trends in the Russian Federation.* Santa Monica, CA: RAND Corporation.

Daykin, C. D. and D. Lewis. 1999. "A crisis of longer life: Reforming pension systems," *British Actuarial Journal,* 5, Part 1(21), 55–113.

DellaPergola, S. 1996. "Between science and fiction: Notes on the demography of the Holocaust," *Holocaust Genocide Studies* 10(1): 34–51.

Demeny, P. 1997. "Replacement-level fertility: The implausible endpoint of the demographic transition," in G. W. Jones, R. M. Douglas, J. C. Caldwell, and R. M. D'Souza (eds.), *The Continuing Demographic Transition.* Oxford: Clarendon Press.

Dumont, J.-C. and G. Lemaître. 2005. "Counting immigrants and expatriates in OECD countries: A new perspective," OECD Social, Employment and Migration Working Paper No. 25. Paris: OECD.

Dunnell, K. 2001. "Policy responses to population ageing and population decline in the United Kingdom," *Population Trends* (103): 47–52.

Dunnell, K. and D. Dix. 2000. "Are we looking forward to a longer and healthier retirement?," *Health Statistics Quarterly* 6: 18–25.

Ellman, M. 2000. "The social costs and consequences of the transformation process," in UNECE, *Economic Survey of Europe 2000* No. 2/3, pp. 125–145. New York and Geneva: United Nations.

European Commission. 1996. *The Demographic Situation in the European Union 1995.* Luxembourg: Office for Official Publications of the European Communities.

———. 2000. *On a Community Immigration Policy.* Communication from the Commission to the Council and the European Parliament. COM(2000) 757 Final. Brussels: Commission of the European Communities.

———. 2005. *Confronting Demographic Change: A New Solidarity Between the Generations.* Brussels: European Commission.

European Federation for Retirement Provision. 1999. *European Pensions: The New Challenges.* London: Royal Institute of International Affairs.

Eurostat. 2000. *Labour Force Survey Results 1999.* Luxembourg: Office for the Official Publications of the European Union.

Feld, S. 2005. "Labor force trends and immigration in Europe," *International Migration Review* 39(3): 637–662.

Foster, C. 2000. "The limits to low fertility: A biosocial approach," *Population and Development Review* 26(2): 209–234.

Freeman, G. S. 1994. "Can liberal states control unwanted migration?," *Annals of the American Association for Political and Social Sciences* (534): 17–30.

Frejka, T. and G. Calot. 2001. "Cohort reproductive patterns in low-fertility countries," *Population and Development Review* 27(1): 103–132.

Frejka, T., and W. Kingcade. 2001. "Why is American fertility so high?," Proceedings of the Conference of the US Bureau of the Census, "The Direction of Fertility in the United States," Alexandria, Virginia.

Frejka, T. and J.-P. Sardon. 2004. *Childbearing Trends and Prospects in Low-Fertility Countries: A Cohort Analysis*. Dordrecht: Kluwer.

Fuchs, J. and D. Schmidt. 2000. "The hidden labour force in the United Kingdom—A contribution to the quantification of underemployment in international comparisons," *IAB Labour Market Research Topics* 39.

Gesano, G. 1999. "Maastricht requirements for European populations?," *Demotrends— quadrimestrale sulla realtà demografica italiana* 1999(1): 1.

Gillion, C. 1999. "The macroeconomics of pension reform," in UNECE, *Economic Survey of Europe 1999* No. 3, pp. 62–64. New York: United Nations.

Glover, S. et al. 2001. "Migration: An economic and social analysis," Home Office Research and Development Directorate Occasional Paper No 67. London: Home Office.

Golini, A. 1998. "How low can fertility be? An empirical exploration," *Population and Development Review* 24(1): 59–73.

Goodhart, D. 2004. "Too diverse? Is Britain becoming too diverse to sustain the mutual obligations behind a good society and the welfare state?," *Prospect* (95).

Government of the Netherlands. 1998. National Report submitted by the Government of the Netherlands to the Regional Population Meeting, Budapest 1998.

Hajnal, J. 1965. "European marriage patterns in perspective," in D. V. Glass and D. E. C. Eversley (eds.), *Population in History*. London: Edward Arnold.

———. 1982. "Two kinds of preindustrial household formation system," *Population and Development Review* 8(3): 449–494.

Höhn, C. 1990. "International transmission of population policy experience in Western Europe," in United Nations, *International Transmission of Population Policy Experiences: Proceedings of the Expert Group Meeting*. New York: United Nations, pp. 145–158.

Huntington, S. P. 1997. *The Clash of Civilisations and the Remaking of World Order*. London: Touchstone Books.

Jackson, R. and N. Howe. 2003. *The 2003 Aging Vulnerability Index*. Washington, DC: Center for Strategic and International Studies and Watson Wyatt Worldwide.

Kannisto, V. 2001. "Mode and dispersion of the length of life," *Population—An English Selection. Biodemographic Perspectives on Human Longevity* 13(1): 159–172.

Kennedy, B. P. et al. 1998. "The role of social capital in the Russian mortality crisis," *World Development* 26(11): 2029–2043.

Keynes, J. M. 1936. "The economic consequences of a declining population," *Eugenics Review* 29: 13–17.

Kharkova, T. L. and E. M. Andreev. 2000. "Did the economic crisis cause the fertility decline in Russia? Evidence from the 1994 microcensus," *European Journal of Population* 16(3): 211–233.

Kohler, H.-P. and D. Philipov. 2001. "Variance effects in the Bongaarts–Feeney formula," *Demography* 38(1): 1–16.

Kosinski, L. 1970. *The Population of Europe: A Geographical Perspective*. London: Longman.

Kravdal, Ø. 1997. "Wanting a child without a firm commitment to the partner: Interpretations and implications of a common behaviour pattern among Norwegian cohabitants," *European Journal of Population* 13(3): 269–298.

Kuijsten, A. C. 1996. "Changing family patterns in Europe: A case of divergence?," *European Journal of Population* 12: 115–143.

Kubat, D. 1984. *The Politics of Return: International Return Migration in Europe*. New York: Center for Migration Studies.

Lesthaeghe, R. 1995. "The second demographic transition in Western countries: An interpretation," in K. O. Mason and A.-M. Jensen (eds.), *Gender and Family Change in Industrialized Countries*. Oxford: Clarendon Press, pp. 17–62.

————. 2002. "Europe's demographic issues: Fertility, household formation and replacement migration," *Population Bulletin of the United Nations*. Special issue. *Policy Responses to Population Ageing and Decline* (44/45): 385–423.

Lesthaeghe, R. and J. Surkyn. 2004. *When History Moves On: The Foundations and Diffusion of a Second Demographic Transition*. Brussels: Interface Demography, Free University of Brussels.

Livi Bacci, M. 2000. *The Population of Europe: A History* (translated by C. de Narden Ipsen and C. Ipsen). Oxford: Blackwell.

Lopez, A. D. 1997. "Mortality from tobacco in the new independent states," in J. L. Bobadilla, C. A. Costello, and F. Mitchell (eds.), *Premature Death in the Newly Independent States*. Washington, DC: National Academy of Sciences Press, pp. 262–274.

Lutz, W. and R. Qiang. 2002. "Determinants of human population growth," *Philosophical Transactions of the Royal Society B* 357(1425): 1197–1210.

Macura, M. 1999. "Fertility decline in the transition economies 1982–1997: Political, economic and social factors," in UNECE, *Economic Survey of Europe*. New York and Geneva: United Nations, pp. 181–194.

Manton, K. G. and K. C. Land. 2000. "Active life expectancy estimates for the US elderly population: A multidimensional continuous-mixture model of functional change applied to completed cohorts 1982–1996," *Demography* 37(3): 253–265.

Martin, P. and W. Widgren. 1996. "International migration: A global challenge," *Population Bulletin* 51(1).

Massey, D. and R. Zenteno. 1999. "The dynamics of mass migration," *Proceedings of the National Academy of Sciences* 96: 5328–5235.

Mateeva, L. and C. Wallace. 2005. "Attitudes to gender equality in East-Central Europe," International Conference on Central and Eastern Europe: A feminist dialogue on transition and EU-enlargement, Budapest.

McDonald, P. 2000. "Gender equity in theories of fertility transition," *Population and Development Review* 26(3): 427–439.

McDonald, P. and R. Kippen. 2001. "Labor supply prospects in 16 developed countries, 2000–2050," *Population and Development Review* 27(1): 1–32.

McMorrow, K. and W. Roeger. 2004. *The Economic and Financial Market Consequences of Global Ageing*. Berlin: Springer.

McNicoll, G. 1999. "Population weights in the international order," *Population and Development Review* 25(3): 411–442.

Meslé, F. et al. 1996. *Tendances récentes de la mortalité par cause en Russie 1965–1994*. Paris: INED.

Meslé, F. and V. Hertrich. 1997. *Evolution de la mortalité en Europe: la divergence s'accentue entre l'Est et l'Ouest*. International Population Conference Beijing 1997, International Union for the Scientific Study of Population.

Mogensen, G. V., H. K. Kvist, E. Körmendi, and S. Pedersen. 1995. *The Shadow Economy in Denmark 1994: Measurement and Results*. Copenhagen: Rockwool Foundation Research Unit.

Morgan, S. P. and R. B. King. 2001. "Why have children in the 21st century? Biological predisposition, social coercion, rational choice," *European Journal of Population* 17: 3–20.

Mozny, I. and T. Katrnak. 2005. "The Czech family," in B. N. Adams and J. Trost (eds.), *Handbook of World Families*. Thousand Oaks, CA: Sage, pp. 235–261.

Murray, C. 1990. *The Emerging British Underclass*. London: Institute of Economic Affairs Health and Welfare Unit.

Muszynska, M. 2004. "Family models in Europe in the context of women's status," Working Papers on Population, Family and Welfare No. 6. Budapest: Hungarian Central Statistical Office.

Namboodiri, K. and L. Wei. 1998. "Fertility theories and their implications regarding how low can low fertility be?," *Genus* 54(1–2): 37–55.

National Criminal Intelligence Service (NCIS). 2003. *UK Threat Assessment of Serious and Organised Crime 2003. 4. Organised Immigration Crime*. London: NCIS.

Ní Bhrolcháin, M. and L. Toulemon. 2002. "The trend to later childbearing: Is there evidence of postponement?," SSRI Applications and Policy Working Papers, A03/10. Southampton: Southampton Statistical Sciences Research Institute.

Olshansky, S. J. 2005. "A potential decline in life expectancy in the United States in the 21st century," *New England Journal of Medicine* 352(11): 1138–1145.

Olshansky, J. and B. A. Carnes. 1996. "Prospects for extended survival: A critical review of the biological evidence," in G. Caselli and A. D. Lopez (eds.), *Health and Mortality among Elderly Populations*. Oxford: Clarendon Press, pp. 39–58.

Pearce, D. L. and A. Punch (eds.). 2000. *Europe's Population and Labour Market Beyond 2000*. Volume 1. *Population Studies* No. 33. Strasbourg: Council of Europe.

Philipov, D. 2001. "Low fertility in Central and Eastern Europe: Culture or economy?," presented at the IUSSP Seminar on International Perspectives on Low Fertility: Trends, Theories and Policies, Tokyo, 2001. Liège: IUSSP.

———. 2003. "Fertility in times of discontinuous societal change," in I. E. Kotowska and J. Jozwiak (eds.), *Population of Central and Eastern Europe: Challenges and Opportunities*. Warsaw: Statistical Publishing Department, pp. 665–690.

Philipov, D. and H.-P. Kohler. 2001. "Tempo effects in the fertility decline in Eastern Europe: Evidence from Bulgaria, the Czech Republic, Hungary, Poland and Russia," *European Journal of Population* 17(1): 37–60.

Philipov, D. et al. 2005. "Now or later? Fertility intentions in Bulgaria and Hungary and the impact of anomie and social capital," Vienna Institute of Demography Working papers 08/2005.

Population Panel. 1973. Report. Cmnd. 5258. London: HMSO.

Postan, M. 1972. *The Mediaeval Economy and Society*. London: Weidenfeld and Nicholson.

Prokhorov, A. V. 1997. "Cigarette smoking and priorities for tobacco control," in J. L. Bobadilla, C. A. Costello, and F. Mitchell (eds.), *Premature Death in the New Independent States*. Washington, DC: National Academy of Sciences Press, pp. 275–286.

Reddaway, W. B. 1939. *The Economics of a Declining Population*. London: Allen and Unwin.

Reher, D. S. 1998. "Family ties in Western Europe: Persistent contrasts," *Population and Development Review* 24(2): 203–234.

Robine, J.-M., E. M. Crimmins, S. Horiuchi, and Y. Zeng (eds.). 2006. *Human Longevity, Individual Life Duration and the Growth of the Oldest-Old Population*. International Studies in Population. Vol. 4. Dordrecht: Springer for the International Union for the Scientific Study of Population (in press).

Rowthorn, R. 2003. "Development and distribution in an open world economy: The moral dilemmas of immigration policy," in H. Disney (ed.), *Work in Progress: Migration, Integration and the European Labour Market*. London: Institute for the Study of Civil Society (Civitas), pp. 40–53.

Royal Commission on Population. 1949. Report. Cmd. 7695. London: HMSO.

———. 1950. Papers of the Royal Commission on Population. Volume III. Report of the Economics Committee. London: HMSO.

Salt, J. 2000. "Trafficking and human smuggling: A European perspective," *International Migration* 38(3): 31–56.

———. 2001. "The business of international migration," in M. A. B. Siddique (ed.), *International Migration into the 21st Century: Essays in Honour of Reginald Appleyard*. Cheltenham: Edward Elgar, pp. 86–108.

———. 2003. *Current Trends in International Migration in Europe*. Strasbourg: Council of Europe.

Sardon, J.-P. 1990. "Le remplacement des générations en Europe depuis le début du siècle," *Population* 45(6): 947–968.

Sauvy, A. 1969. *General Theory of Population*. London: Weidenfeld and Nicholson.

Scherbov, S. and H. van Vianen. 2001. "Marriage and fertility in Russia of women born between 1900 and 1960: A cohort analysis," *European Journal of Population* 17(3): 281–294.

Shapiro, J. 1997. "The hypothesis of stress as a leading explanatory variable," in *International Population Conference Beijing 1997,* Vol. 3. Liège: International Union for the Scientific Study of Population, pp. 529–554.

Shaw, C. 2001. "United Kingdom population trends in the 21st century," *Population Trends* 103: 37–46.

Simon, J. 1981. *The Ultimate Resource.* Princeton: Princeton University Press.

Sobotka, T. 2003a. "Understanding lower and later fertility in Central and Eastern Europe," in I. E. Kotowska and J. Jozwiak (eds.), *Population of Central and Eastern Europe: Challenges and Opportunities.* Warsaw: Statistical Publishing Establishment, pp. 691–724.

———. 2003b. "Tempo-quantum and period-cohort interplay in fertility changes in Europe," *Demographic Research* 8(6): 152–214.

Sobotka, T. et al. 2003. "Demographic shifts in the Czech Republic after 1989: A second demographic transition view," *European Journal of Population* 19(3): 249–277.

Stein, G. 1997. "Mounting debts: The coming European pensions crisis," Policy Series No. 4. London: Politeia.

Stern, M. and A. Stern. 1981. *Sex in the Soviet Union* (translated by M. E. Heine). London: W.H. Allen.

Tabeau, E. and J. Bijak. 2005. "Deaths in the 1992–1995 armed conflicts in Bosnia and Herzegovina," *European Journal of Population* 21(2–3): 131–144.

Teitelbaum, M. S. 1999. "Sustained below-replacement fertility: Realities and responses," *Population Bulletin of the United Nations* Special Issue Nos. 40/41, pp. 161–193.

———. 2004. "The media marketplace for garbled demography," *Population and Development Review* 30(2): 317–327.

Teitelbaum, M. S. and J. M. Winter. 1985. *Fear of Population Decline.* Orlando: Academic Press.

ter Bekke, S. 2005. *Emigration Motives, Intentions and Expectations in the Netherlands.* Groningen: Population Research Centre.

Think Tank on Integration in Denmark. 2002. *Population Development 2001–2021: Possible Developments* (translated by Charlotte Moshø). Copenhagen: Ministry of Refugee, Immigration and Integration Affairs «http://www.imm.dk».

Turner, A. 2005. *A New Pension Settlement for the 21st Century: The Second Report of the Pensions Commission.* London: The Stationery Office.

United Nations. 2000. *Replacement Migration: Is It a Solution to Declining and Ageing Populations?* New York: United Nations.

———. 2001. *United Nations Expert Group Meeting on Policy Responses to Population Ageing and Population Decline, New York 16–18 October.* New York: United Nations.

United Nations, Economic Commission for Europe (UNECE). 2001a. *Economic Survey of Europe 2001,* No. 1. New York and Geneva: United Nations.

———. 2003b. *Economic Survey of Europe 2001,* No. 2. New York and Geneva: United Nations.

———. 2005. *World Population Prospects: The 2004 Revision.* New York: United Nations.

United Nations, Population Division. 2000. "Future expectations for below-replacement fertility," *Population Bulletin of the United Nations* Special Issue Nos. 40/41, *Below Replacement Fertility,* pp. 137–160.

US Census Bureau. 2000. *Population Projections of the United States by Age, Sex, Race, Hispanic Origin and Nativity, 1999–2100.* Washington, DC: US Census Bureau.

Vallin, J. et al. 2002. "A new estimate of Ukrainian population losses during the crises of the 1930s and the 1940s," *Population Studies* 56(3): 249–264.

Vallin, J., F. Meslé, and T. Valkonen. 2002. *Trends in Mortality and Differential Mortality.* Strasbourg: Council of Europe. Population Studies No. 36.

van de Kaa, D. J. 1987. "Europe's second demographic transition," *Population Bulletin* 42(1).

———. 1999. "Europe and its population: The long view," in D. J. van de Kaa, H. Leridon, G. Gesano, and M. Okolski (eds.), *European Populations: Unity in Diversity.* Dordrecht: Kluwer, pp. 1–49.

van Imhoff, E. and N. Keilman. 2000. "On the quantum and tempo of fertility: Comment," *Population and Development Review* 26(3): 549–553.

Vassin, S. A. 1997. "The determinants and implications of an aging population in Russia," in J. DaVanzo (ed.), *Russia's Demographic Crisis.* Santa Monica: Rand Corporation.

Vaupel, J. 2001. "Demographic insights into longevity," *Population—An English Selection. Biodemographic Perspectives on Human Longevity* 13(1): 245–260.

Vishnevsky, A. G. 1997. *Naselenye Rossii 1996* [Population of Russia 1996]. Moscow: Tsentr Demographii i Ekologii Cheloveka [Centre for Population and Human Ecology].

———. 1999. "The demographic potential of Russia" (translated by R. Valliere), *Russian Social Science Review* 40(4): 4–29.

Weil, D. N. 1997. "The economics of population ageing," in M. R. Rosenzweig and O. Stark (eds.), *Handbook of Population and Family Economics* Volume 1B. Amsterdam: Elsevier, pp. 967–1014.

Widgren, J. 1994. *The Key to Europe: A Comparative Analysis of Entry and Asylum Policies in Western Countries.* Stockholm: Fritzes.

Wilensky, H. L. 2002. *Rich Democracies, Political Economy, Public Policy and Performance.* Berkeley: University of California Press.

Wilmoth, J. R. and H. Lundström. 1996. "Extreme longevity in five countries: Presentation of trends with special attention to issues of data quality," *European Journal of Population* 12(1): 63–93.

World Bank. 1994. *Averting the Old Age Crisis.* Oxford: Oxford University Press.

The Political Economy
of African Population
Change

CHRISTOPHER CLAPHAM

Sub-Saharan Africa stands firmly at one end of the demographic and development continuum. Demographically, it ranks highest in the world in its recent level of population increase, at 2.5 percent per annum over the period 1990–2003, though this marks a decrease from the 2.9 percent of the previous decade. The region combines this growth with by far the lowest life expectancy at birth of any part of the world, at 46 years in 2002, or 17 years below the next lowest, South Asia; alarmingly, life expectancy has fallen by six years between 1995 and 2003, a drop to be explained almost entirely by the impact of HIV/AIDS (World Bank 2004: Table 1).[1]

Economically, Africa's estimated gross national income per capita of $490 in 2003 was likewise the lowest among world regions, just below South Asia at $510, although in purchasing power parity terms the discrepancy was much greater, giving Africans only two-thirds the effective income of their South Asian counterparts (ibid.). Africa's recent political record has been uneven, with a significant number of countries showing signs of improvement in their previous levels of stability, multi-party democracy, and good governance, set against several of the world's worst cases of state failure and political collapse. Its economic growth rate has also moved sharply upward in recent years, largely as a result of the boom in primary product prices driven by China's industrialization. All in all, however, it is depressingly hard to disagree with the common conceptualization of the continent as an economic, political, and humanitarian "problem," even though it may be going too far to condemn it roundly as a "failure."

Any attempt to explore the demographic elements of this problem, let alone to prognosticate the likely future of the continent, must be pursued under the shadow of deep uncertainties. One basic difficulty is the sheer inadequacy of the statistical base. Demography depends on the collection of numbers, and the collection of numbers in turn depends on a stable state structure within which the necessary data can be gathered and recorded.

One of the fundamental underlying problems of Africa is that it lacked such a state structure until fairly recently, and in many areas has lost it again. Figures for African populations for any period prior to the mid-twentieth century can be no more than speculative, while, for much of Africa, the totals confidently published in such standard sources as the World Bank's annual *World Development Report* are little more than educated guesswork. The same goes for the population figures published by the Population Division of the United Nations. It follows that population and economic statistics, such as those cited above, are subject to a wide level of uncertainty: the actual levels, could one but know them, may be significantly higher or lower than those that are assumed here.

Although the confident projections of future population trends that demographers characteristically provide are in any event a complete mystery to a nondemographer such as myself, in Africa there are particular reasons for approaching the future with caution. The most obvious and significant of these is AIDS, which affects the continent far more deeply than any other part of the world and has led to notable revisions in population projections; in Botswana—by far the most successful African state in developmental terms—life expectancy has been reduced from 71 years to 38 years (Stanecki 2000; World Bank 2004: Table 1). Because of the way in which it principally affects distinct sectors of the population, AIDS also has particularly important developmental implications. The effects of AIDS are especially difficult to estimate, not only because of uncertainties about the future development, availability, and application of medical treatment, but also because the epidemic may bring about changes in social behavior—especially in sexual activity and gender relations—that are difficult to predict. I address these issues later in this chapter.

In addition, African demography is deeply affected by factors that go beyond the simple extrapolation of figures for fertility and mortality that provide the staple ingredients of population projections. For example, the exceptional levels of increase in African populations over the last century can be ascribed to an essentially external political development: the imposition of colonial rule and the at least relatively settled structures of government that came with it. Some of the recent uncertainties correspondingly result from political failure, both in its most dramatic form of complete state collapse or continuing serious violence, as in Somalia or the Democratic Republic of the Congo, and more insidiously through the much more widespread decay of state services, not least medical services, across the continent as a whole. Africa's development record, likewise, is deeply affected by political considerations, one indicator of which has been the World Bank's recent concern for issues such as the sources of political violence, which would until recently have been regarded as falling entirely outside its remit.[2] Much of Africa's demographic and economic future thus turns on whether it is possible to reverse its extremely disappointing political record, and likewise on the role of the outside world as a source of investment, aid, and humanitarian assistance and, at least to some degree, a refuge for Africa's emigrants.

Despite these caveats, demography has been so central to the African experience that we must tackle it as best we can. John Iliffe, in his outstanding general history of the continent, identifies demography as the key element around which the history of Africa must be constructed, and in the process he singles out a number of distinctive features of this experience that will be noted shortly (Iliffe 1995: ch. 1). Analogously, in what must likewise be reckoned the single most important recent attempt to analyze the problems of African governance, Jeffrey Herbst notes that "the fundamental problem facing state-builders in Africa ... has been to project authority over inhospitable territories that contain relatively low densities of people" (Herbst 2000: 11). I have no doubt that the story of Africa's population provides the essential starting point for an understanding of its past and for any attempt to puzzle out its likely future.

Historical features of Africa's demography

Although human beings had their origin in Africa, this has also been a continent in which it has been particularly difficult for them to survive and multiply. Its soils are generally poor; its rainfall is both uneven and uncertain, concentrated over much of the continent into brief periods of intense deluge that scours gullies and washes off topsoil, interspersed with long periods of drought; its people are exceptionally vulnerable to disease, a fact that Iliffe ascribes to Africa's long history of human evolution, which "made its disease environment exceptionally rich and diverse" (1995: 10). As a result, its historical population densities were both low and exceptionally uneven, with relatively dense populations concentrated in a few isolated areas of the continent, notably the Ethiopian highlands (which alone sustained grain-growing plough agriculture of a kind broadly familiar to Europeans); the Great Lakes region now occupied by Burundi, Rwanda, southern Uganda, and eastern Congo; the West African forest belt between what are now southern Ghana and Nigeria; and the southern highlands that gave rise to Great Zimbabwe. Elsewhere, although only parts of the Sahara and the Kalahari were completely uninhabited, people were for the most part very sparsely spread across huge tracts of forest and savannah. Rates of population increase in the precolonial era were correspondingly low, and overall densities are estimated to have risen only from 1.9 persons per square kilometer in 1500 to 2.7 in 1750 and 4.4 in 1900.[3]

Social values and political organization largely corresponded to the demographic imperative. Organizations broadly recognizable as "states" were for the most part restricted to areas of comparatively dense population already identified, together with a few places where surpluses could be extracted from long-distance trade, whether by sea or across the desert. High levels of population movement, continuing into modern times, left many if not most African peoples with a folk memory of migration and helped to consolidate the idea of descent, rather than attachment to territory or political obedience, as the primary form of social solidarity. Human reproduction was very highly valued—as witnessed by Africa's extraordinarily rich tradition of figurative sculpture, much of which has fertility as its basic motif—and was encouraged by polygamy, fostering, and other mechanisms designed to ensure that precious offspring were not lost. Social constraints on sexual activity were correspondingly slight by comparison with many other areas of the world, a fact that would have a significant influence on the spread of HIV/AIDS, while infertility was a major stigma.[4]

The impact of the outside world initially reduced rather than augmented Africa's limited population: it was, as Iliffe remarks, brutally ironic that the slave trade should seek to repopulate the New World by raiding an already underpopulated continent (1995: 3). The demographic picture of the early colonial period was mixed. In some areas, most notoriously King Leopold's Congo, there was massive population loss, and in much of equatorial Africa population decline may have continued into the 1930s (ibid.: 241). Over a longer period, nonetheless, colonization helped to end the worst forms of external exploitation and to create the conditions in which rapid population growth could occur. Africans, unlike native Americans, had had ample opportunity to build up immunities to whatever diseases foreign conquerors brought with them—it was instead the Europeans who suffered from the African diseases that they encountered. And the ending of the slave trade, stable administration, greatly improved communications, and the introduction of Western medicine all helped to lay the foundations for population growth exceeding 40 percent between 1920 and the late 1940s (ibid.).

The role of this population growth in fueling anticolonial nationalism is difficult to assess, but changes in population *distribution* were clearly important. Although nationalism was far from being solely an urban phenomenon, rapid urbanization certainly created the strategically placed concentrations of people that were needed to organize an effective challenge to colonial rule. Critical to the political economy of population change, however, was the fact that the major sources of export production remained in the countryside, whether in zones of cash crop agriculture or in mining enclaves. Although Africa's economies for the most part grew rapidly during the later colonial era, they were heavily dependent on the export of primary products to industrial states—a form of production that not only left them highly vulnerable to unpredictable changes in price (and generally declining terms of trade), but also created major sources of domestic political cleavage. These circumstances were exacerbated by the fact that descent remained the major source of social and political identity: the high levels of population movement that were fostered both by stable government and by changing economic conditions helped to intensify, rather than to blur, social division on the basis of ethnicity.

In short, the continent's precolonial history and the experience of colonial rule bequeathed to the newly independent African states that emerged around 1960 a peculiar demographic and economic legacy: population levels remained low, but were increasing very rapidly, a trend that accelerated after independence; population distribution, always uneven, became still more so with rapid urbanization and high levels of migration to restricted zones of export production. This production, moreover, was highly dependent on global markets and incapable of absorbing more than a very limited proportion of the increased population, many of whom took refuge in urban areas, where industrialization was slight and opportunities for productive employment were low. Despite rapid economic growth in the period leading to independence, it was not a happy inheritance.

The political economy of population change

Some basic data

During the second half of the twentieth century, rates of population increase in sub-Saharan Africa reached what will almost certainly prove to be their highest level. On United Nations Population Division figures, growth rates rose from 2.18 percent per annum in 1950–55 to a peak of 2.93 percent in 1980–85, before starting to drop quite steadily to 2.48 by the end of the millennium, with further falls in growth rates (which, of course, would bring about a continuing increase in the total population) projected beyond 2000. Total numbers rose from 180 million in 1950 to 670 million in 2000, an increase of 272 percent (United Nations 2005). This growth, despite variations between states, was broadly consistent across the continent as a whole, with Western, Central, and Eastern Africa all registering increases between 271 percent and 282 percent, and only Southern Africa coming in rather lower at 240 percent. This dramatic rate of increase appears to have been fueled not only by reductions in death rates (especially of babies and young children), which accounted for the rise in population before 1950, but also by increases in birth rates, which at their peak in Kenya in the late 1970s reached an average total fertility rate of 8 births per woman (Iliffe 1995: 243–246).[5]

The most recent UN figures on population and fertility changes in the continent as a whole over each of the five decades show that levels of fertility (and not simply of population growth, which have been heavily affected by death rates, and notably AIDS) have started to decline sharply, especially in the southern tip of Africa. The continental figures indicate that the total fertility rate peaked at 6.86 children per woman in 1960–65, falling slowly to 6.45 in 1980–85; in the following two decades, the rate of decline rapidly accelerated, to 4.97 in 2000–05. UN projections assume this rate of decline will be maintained until the mid-twenty-first century, by which time total fertility is projected to be 2.52 (United Nations 2005). In Zimbabwe, Botswana, South Africa, and Lesotho, significant declines in childbearing have reduced the total fertility rate to 3–4 children by 1995–2000, representing a decline of some 40–50 percent from the peak level in the 1960s. In Zimbabwe, the rate dropped from 6.7 children per woman in 1962 to 3.8 in 1997.[6] Elsewhere in Southern Africa, the decline has not been nearly so significant, and in Angola and Malawi the total fertility rate remains between 6 and 7. The sharpest decline anywhere in the continent (and possibly in the world) has taken place in Kenya, where the total fertility rate by 1998 had fallen to 4.7, but the likelihood is that in most of Africa high fertility continues.[7] Even so, when the rapid increase in death rates resulting from AIDS is taken into account, there is a considerable prospect that Africa will move, over a very short period of time, from a demographic profile characterized by rapid population increase to one characterized by slow increase, stability, or even in some areas decline. Even though the 2004 revision of the UN's *World Population Prospects* projects continuing very high levels of population growth for such countries as Niger, where estimated total fertility in 2000–05 remained as high as 7.9, the implications of such a shift are clearly profound.

Every bit as significant as the changes in total population over the last half-century have been changes in population distribution, especially between rural and urban areas. While total levels of urbanization remain relatively low, at 34 percent in 1995, the 5.0 percent growth rate of the African urban population between 1980 and 1995 was the highest in the world.[8] Unlike the high levels of urbanization in South and East Asia, however, this has not been accompanied by any equivalent increase in urban production or employment opportunities. On the contrary, annual average growth rates in industry rose only from a thoroughly inadequate 1.2 percent per annum between 1980 and 1990 to 1.5 percent between 1990 and 1999, in sharp contrast to 9.5 and 9.8 percent industrial growth rates over the same two periods in East Asia, and 6.8 and 6.3 percent growth rates in South Asia (World Bank 2001: Table 11). The proportion of the labor force employed in industry remained at 9 percent between 1980 and 1990, by far the lowest in the world (World Bank 1997: Table 4).

These basic indicators enable us to identify a number of key demographic issues in the political economy of modern Africa. First, the high levels of population growth and urbanization, coupled with the low level of growth in urban production, emphasize the critical role of urban youth, who have emerged as a major source of violence in cities and the country-side. Second, the high historical mobility of African populations, coupled with demographic change, political crisis, and the incorporation of Africa into a globalized economy, has made migration—both voluntary and invol-untary—a topic of particular concern. Third, the impact of AIDS and of other changes in fertility and mortality that are related to the epidemic calls into question many of the assumptions that have hitherto guided projections for Africa's development, and raises the need for a comprehensive reassess-ment of the continent's demographic, economic, and political future.

Urbanization and the politics of youth

To a greater degree than cities in other parts of the developing world, Afri-can cities present a paradox of governability. On the one hand, cities need, and in one form or another will almost necessarily acquire, some kind of government. Dense agglomerations of humans require mechanisms that en-able them to live reasonably peacefully with one another, since the costs of extensive violence are too great to be supportable for more than a short pe-riod. These mechanisms may well be hand-to-mouth affairs, dependent on people of related ethnic origin clustering together for protection, or on tac-itly accepting the protection rackets established by urban gangs, rather than providing any ordered form of municipal administration. Africans, like other peoples forced into large cities, have been extremely adept at developing the means required for survival, and the cases of complete urban breakdown—Brazzaville, Freetown, Mogadishu—have been few and usually brief.

On the other hand, cities—especially those in which productive op-portunities do not begin to approach the levels needed to sustain a decent life for most of their inhabitants—are breeding grounds of crime and social decay. Although one should not assume that the African countryside is the locus of "traditional stability," it is in the cities that the most intense effects of rapid population increase, a young age structure, and economic decline are concentrated. Already in the colonial era, the authorities were concerned about the threat presented by urban growth, and nationalist leaders mobi-lized disaffected urban youth to give impetus to their demands for indepen-dence. The "verandah boys" (so-called because they slept outside on veran-dahs, rather than having homes of their own) who rallied to Kwame Nkrumah's Convention People's Party in 1950s Ghana provide a classic ex-ample (Austin 1964: 77).

African cities accordingly provide a source for what could in Marxist terms be described as a lumpenproletariat: a deprived, unemployed, and quasi-criminal urban class that lacks the organization and values imposed by regular industrial employment, and that Marx regarded with deep sus-picion. "Lumpens" acquire their own local names—*tsotsis* in South Africa, for example, *kiyaye* in Uganda, *hittistes* in Algeria—and have proliferated from Algiers to the Cape.[9] Expelled from the countryside by the lack of employment opportunities or simply a reluctance to engage in the back-breaking physical labor that African farming requires, and attracted to (but unable to enjoy) the Western lifestyle associated with the towns, they form a permanently disaffected backdrop to the politics of the continent. Characteristically organized into gangs, they range from the straightforwardly criminal to the partisans of ethnic causes or of religious movements that offer some relief (on earth or in the afterlife) to the poor and oppressed.

In the early decades after independence, the urban mob was for the most part contained, however tenuously, within political patronage networks, occasionally turning out in riots that helped to oust one regime and install another, before subsiding into uneasy acquiescence. Over time, however, as urban conditions continued to deteriorate and politicians failed to deliver, levels of crime increased, together with alienation from the political system as a whole. One important precipitant was the price of food, a factor critical to urban populations for whom finding the next meal was the key to survival. The postindependence decline in per capita African food production, in sharp contrast to the picture in much of Asia, resulted from a combination of rapid population increase and the failure to generate significant improvement in agricultural productivity. By the late 1970s and early 1980s, the stagnation of African agriculture was being ascribed to the "urban bias" of African governments,[10] the solution to which was to be found in the application of the principles of market economics, and notably by providing farmers with the price incentives that would encourage them to increase production.[11] Price increases for producers, of course, resulted in price increases for consumers, and—especially in places where the political structure was in any case vulnerable—led to "rice riots" such as those in Monrovia in July 1979 that precipitated the collapse of the True Whig Party government in Liberia.

The processes by which such alienated groups may, given propitious conditions, be mobilized in search of radical political alternatives have been most intensively analyzed in Sierra Leone, a small West African country that provides a case study in political collapse.[12] There, the Revolutionary United Front (RUF), which gained a merited reputation in the 1990s as one of the most violent and destructive of African insurgencies, originated in an association between the dispossessed of Freetown and university or high school students and dropouts who, despairing of achieving their goals through incorporation into the "system" represented by a corrupt and failing single-party regime, turned instead to the "potes," or drinking dens of the city for an alternative revolutionary strategy. Although it benefited from external aid, in the form of military training provided by Qaddafi in Libya, and the opportunity to operate across the frontier, provided by Charles Taylor, then president of neighboring Liberia, the RUF was in essence a product of the Freetown slums. It was characteristically lumpenproletarian in its hatred of the system that had engendered it, its propensity to extreme forms of violence (among which the penchant for chopping off people's hands attracted particular attention), its lack of discipline, and its failure to develop any plausible alternative to the state that it wanted to destroy. In recent years, the growth of ethnically related violence in Nigeria has also gained attention, justifiably enough given Nigeria's massive population, heavily ethnic focus of political organization, and centrality to the political stability of a large part of the continent.[13]

In an important contribution, Thandika Mkandawire argues that the extreme brutality of many modern African insurgencies derives from their origins in the lumpenproletariat (Mkandawire 2002). Essentially urban in nature, they cannot effectively pursue their goals in the city, where the state can still muster enough force to suppress any overt challenge to its power, and are therefore compelled to retreat to the countryside. Unlike the classic Maoist people's war, where the insurgents seek to swim among the population like fishes in the sea and accordingly take up peasant demands (notably the demand for control over their own major means of production, land), rebels like those of the RUF have nothing in common with the peasantry, whose interests they are in no position to serve. Instead, they can survive only by intimidating it, and have few inhibitions in engaging in the violence needed for the purpose. However, Mkandawire's analysis does not apply to the whole continent, and in some countries, including Liberia and Mozambique, appalling levels of violence have occurred in movements of largely rural origin. In some countries, including Sierra Leone, significant lumpen elements are already found in the countryside itself, resulting in this case from alluvial diamond mining, and this helps to provide urban insurgencies with local allies, who have a basic knowledge of the terrain in which they have to operate.

The politics of migration

The politics of population can no longer be constrained within the borders of states.[14] Most African states have extremely porous frontiers, externally imposed by colonial rule, that have never posed much of a barrier to people who seek to cross them. Few African states, in any event, can be described as "sovereign" in anything but a purely technical sense of the word, and they maintain little control over their populations or indeed anything else. All of them are embedded in a globalized world order, in which not only their economies but their cultures and their social policies are deeply affected by developments beyond their own territories.

One important respect in which development in particular is affected by migration derives from the mobility of skilled labor within the global system, and the very different rewards accruing to it in different parts of that system. At one extreme, star African football players can earn salaries in Europe that are barely conceivable at home.[15] More broadly and more damagingly, African professionals—most obviously medical doctors and other health workers, but also lawyers, accountants, engineers, teachers, and academics—can earn considerably greater salaries and live in vastly more secure and satisfying conditions if they move to the industrialized world. While erecting barriers against unqualified immigrants, moreover, the industrialized states are generally only too happy to welcome the highly qualified.[16] Perhaps the critical factor in Africa's extremely disappointing development record has been the shift in the modern global economy from natural resources toward human skills as the key element in the creation of wealth— a shift which, among other things, is reflected in the generally declining terms of trade for the producers of primary commodities, despite a recent upsurge triggered by China's rapid industrialization. Africa's comparative disadvantage, as the continent with by far the lowest level of human skills, can only be exacerbated when those who possess such skills are disproportionately likely to move elsewhere.

As in many other parts of the developing world, the overwhelming desire of a large number of the teeming youth in African cities is to escape them. City life, with its access to Western popular culture, offers them the picture of a world dramatically different from anything they know. Many African societies, as already noted, have a history of migration, and the bonds of family and descent that provide most Africans with their major source of identity are independent of geographical location and are maintained across great distances. Somali pastoralists may readily be found, satellite telephone in hand, speaking directly from their camels to relatives in Abu Dhabi or Toronto. Mouride traders hawk their wares throughout the world, guided by the same hierarchical organization and discipline as their groundnut-growing parents in central Senegal. Even peoples without a historical tradition of migration, such as highland Ethiopians, now have a significant diaspora in Europe and the United States, and those who remain at home are keenly aware of the lifestyles available in societies vastly richer than their own. In a world of unrestricted population movement, there would be a massive shift of people from Africa and other parts of the developing world into Europe and North America, resulting in a corresponding level of social globalization and the incorporation into their cities of the issues that affect African cities, with a corresponding easing of pressures within Africa itself. While such movement has, of course, been heavily restricted, one must recognize that the (at least partial) insulation of the industrialized world from the problems of African demography rests on imposition of the political power of the West. The attempt to maintain this insulation is likely to be intensified in the aftermath of the terrorist attacks of September 11, 2001, which can at one level be ascribed to the ability of alienated youth from developing countries to gain access to the Western technologies needed to assault the cities of the West itself.

The impact of HIV/AIDS

Any attempt to project the political economy of African population change over the next half-century depends vastly more on assessing the impact of HIV/AIDS than on any other factor. This in itself alerts us to the uncertainties of the exercise: a similar projection attempt 25 years ago would certainly have taken some account of the problems of urban youth and of migration (especially the problem of refugees), which have been on the agenda for several decades, but could scarcely have been expected to take account of AIDS. The next 25 to 50 years may bring similar shocks, for better or for worse, and they will certainly provide a far better perspective from which to appraise the importance of AIDS. Although a vast amount has now been written about the subject, much consists in generalized prognostications of doom or, at the other extreme, in localized and limited studies from which it is difficult to draw broader conclusions. It is clear, too, that there are considerable variations across the continent, and indeed even within states and particular societies. On this inadequate basis, however, I endorse the conclusion of the United Nations General Assembly document that assessments of the socioeconomic impact of HIV/AIDS by development experts and policymakers have been extremely limited (*Population and Development Review* 2001). For an example of the almost willful failure of development analysts to confront the problem, I cite the most relevant passage from a considered attempt by the World Bank, the global organization most immediately concerned with African development issues, to assess the continent's economic prospects on the eve of the millennium:

> Then there is the HIV/AIDS pandemic. With 70 percent of the world's cases in Africa, AIDS has already had an enormous impact on life expectancy in the countries most affected. It is projected to reduce life expectancy by up to 20 years from today's modest levels—more than erasing the gains since the 1950s. AIDS orphans already make up 11 percent of the population in the most afflicted countries. This could rise to more than 16 percent in the next 25 years, with disastrous implications for traditional social structures. The ultimate economic impact of AIDS, not yet fully known, promises to be devastating.

> Unless action is taken, the scale of these problems will only increase. Population growth continues to be faster than in other regions, so primary school cohorts will continue to grow rather than shrink as in most parts of the world. For every potential worker between 15 and 64, Africa now has almost one dependent, almost all of them young. Even with a progressive demographic transition, Africa's dependency rates will fall only gradually through the next century. (World Bank 2000: 11)

The problems with this analysis lie not so much in the outline of the scale of the crisis, which is broadly in keeping with other assessments, as in the failure to examine the implications of the data for development. Remarkably, the discussion goes on to assume that population growth will remain the major demographic problem facing Africa, whereas AIDS has already had a substantial impact precisely in this area. It then treats dependency rates (the ratio of working to nonworking populations) in terms of assumed continued high fertility, and postulates the occurrence of a "progressive demographic transition," whereas dependency rates have already been dramatically affected by AIDS itself, and the kind of demographic transition to which AIDS is leading in Africa is very different from the type of transition to which we have become accustomed in states with successful economic development. Finally, the policy implications of the epidemic are reduced to the flabby "unless action is taken," which assumes that it is within the capacity of African and other states and international organizations to take measures to remove or at least stabilize the development problems that AIDS brings with it. This assumption, given the extent of state decay in much of Africa and the limited ability of any state to change basic patterns of reproductive behavior, is highly questionable. The broader implications of HIV/AIDS for the economic policies that the Bank is promoting elsewhere in the document are nowhere considered. Faced with this level of professional failure by the organization that should be most responsible for offering solutions to the problem, the ability to apply effective policy responses to the impact of HIV/AIDS on development is severely handicapped.

For a start, in some areas of Africa, notably the more highly developed southern part of the continent, population growth now appears to have virtually stopped, and *declines* in population are likely in the near future. Population growth has been sharply reduced throughout Southern Africa (except possibly for Angola and Mozambique, where the data are in any event inadequate). One 2001 study projected that Botswana, South Africa, and Zimbabwe would experience population loss by 2003, with population growth likely to sink to near zero in other Southern African states by 2010.[17] This decline results from a combination of the lower fertility levels already noted and high levels of HIV prevalence and AIDS mortality. In states to the north, where fertility levels (although declining) remain high, population growth is likely to continue, though at a reduced rate.[18] While it is too soon to state that levels of infection in West and West-Central Africa will not reach those found in the major areas of incidence from South Africa and Botswana north to Ethiopia, it is at least hopeful that this spread has not yet occurred.[19]

Equally important, AIDS appears to have a significant effect in reducing fertility. To some extent, this is simply the result of women dying before bearing the number of children they would otherwise have had; one estimate puts the number of children born to HIV-positive mothers at 20 percent fewer than they would have had otherwise (Baylies 2001). In addi-

tion, about one-third of children born to HIV-positive mothers are themselves infected and are likely to die within a few years of birth. There are
also indications that women in HIV-affected areas are choosing to have fewer
children, in sharp contrast to the historically observed tendency for couples
to rapidly compensate for population losses due to factors such as war and
famine by increased fertility.[20] To the extent that contraceptive use increases
in order to prevent HIV transmission, fertility will be further reduced. The
negative impact of AIDS on fertility in sub-Saharan Africa can only be enhanced by the fact that more women than men are HIV-positive; some 55
percent of HIV incidence in the continent is among women, who also tend
to be infected at a younger age than men (Stanecki 2000). One study of a
Kenyan city where the epidemic had reached a relatively mature stage
showed HIV prevalence rates of 20 percent among men aged 15–49, as
against 30 percent for women (Hargreaves et al. 2002). Although women
in every society tend to be younger than their partners, this discrepancy
also results from men seeking sex with younger girls, in the belief that they
are less likely to be infected, or even that forced sex with underage girls
may actually cure the disease.

The effect of HIV/AIDS on the population age structure is dramatic,
and several studies have reported the emergence of a population distribution in which, instead of the usual pyramid, the population bulge at the
lower ages is topped by a relatively narrow chimney, evident from the early
40s onward, of individuals who have escaped AIDS and are likely to live to
a normal age (Stanecki 2000; Baylies 2001). This situation is likely to affect
economic development in a number of ways, all of them negative. For a
start, it is not the large number of children, but the small number of adults
that creates the high dependency rates noted by the World Bank. Despite
the strongly felt obligation in many parts of Africa to take in the children of
deceased relatives, fostered children are likely to be less well cared for than
they would have been by their parents. They are likely to be put to work at
a younger age to compensate for labor shortages due to AIDS and to care
for sick parents and other relatives, rather than attending schools that themselves are suffering from a shortage of teachers (Baylies 2001). A further
significant developmental effect of AIDS in Africa is that at least in the early
stages of the epidemic, HIV/AIDS appears to be most prevalent among the
relatively wealthy and well educated, although this distinction dissolves as
the disease spreads, with low-status women ultimately becoming the worst-
affected section of the population (Hargreaves et al. 2002). A high incidence
among certain occupational groups such as soldiers and long-distance lorry
drivers is also not unexpected.

Government action can certainly make at least some impression on HIV/
AIDS levels, and countries such as Senegal and Uganda have been singled
out for their successful efforts to restrict the disease. On the other hand, the

deep reluctance of South African President Thabo Mbeki to acknowledge that HIV and AIDS are related, allied to a belief that AIDS is due principally to poverty and even Western conspiracy, has had a disastrous effect on its incidence in that country. South Africa's government has even been prepared to go to court to prevent HIV-positive pregnant women from gaining access to antiretroviral drugs that might stop the virus from being passed on to their babies. International action also has a potentially critical role in enabling African states to overcome the financial and organizational constraints on the provision of effective treatment. On the whole, however, the impact of AIDS is likely to be affected less by official action, and more by behavioral changes within the afflicted societies, and by the tendency of any epidemic illness to stabilize over time at a level at which it continues to debilitate the population, without having the apocalyptic impact that could be extrapolated from its rate of growth over the first few years.[21]

The broad conclusion to be drawn from the HIV/AIDS trajectory is that the problems associated with population *increase* in Africa are likely to be significantly less than has commonly been assumed, whereas the problems associated with population *distribution* and economic development are likely to be significantly greater. The common pattern of population change, to which we have become accustomed in countries experiencing economic development, is one in which increasing wealth and (especially female) education lead to rapidly declining fertility and the stabilization of population with high levels of skills and welfare. There is no indication that sub-Saharan Africa will follow a similar transition. Instead, population growth is already slowing, and overall populations may even stabilize, but under conditions of low skills and welfare and with a high dependency rate induced by the need for a relatively small number of working adults to care for a large number of children, many of them orphans. It is an alarming prospect.

Conclusion

External perceptions of African demography have been heavily dominated by Malthusian scenarios, in which rapidly rising populations place unsustainable pressures on already scarce resources, leading to environmental degradation and death by famine. The two great Ethiopian famines of 1973/74 and 1984/85 gave added force to these predictions and helped to create a popular impression of the continent that is dominated by images of starving children. This scenario continues to have considerable resonance, reinforced by figures such as those provided by the UN's *World Population Prospects*, which projects very rapid population increases in a number of African states, including Uganda and Niger.[22]

This chapter suggests a much more nuanced picture. Certainly there are areas of the continent, such as the highlands of Ethiopia and Eritrea, that have proved chronically unable to achieve food self-sufficiency even for their present populations, let alone for their projected future ones. Even here, however, there are important issues of governance, in that both peace and agricultural policies more suited to the needs of peasant producers might permit increases in agricultural productivity of the kind that have transformed Malthusian perspectives in other parts of the world (Abegaz 2004). In much of the continent, moreover, problems of food sufficiency have been directly driven by political failure, with the collapse of Zimbabwe from being a food exporter to a position of heavy food dependence as the most striking example. Nor is it the case that increased population densities necessarily lead to environmental decay and food shortages. On the contrary, there are well-documented cases in which high population density both enforces and enables changes in agricultural production systems, promoting a shift from extensive farming methods appropriate to sparse populations, in which land is freely available and its maintenance is of little concern, to more intensive systems in which it becomes economically efficient to invest in soil, tree, and water conservation.[23]

Rather than the simple quantity of Africa's population, its quality emerges from this survey as the issue of main concern. Demographic transition in both Europe and East Asia has classically followed, often very rapidly, from improvement in the quality of life resulting from economic development, and it can correspondingly be argued that Africa's rapid population growth and low quality of life are the consequences rather than the causes of its lack of development (Kiribige 1997). It appears to be the case, certainly, that birth rates have fallen most rapidly in those African states, such as Botswana, Kenya, and Zimbabwe, in which infant mortality has dropped below 7 percent, while high levels of education for girls also have a significant impact (Caldwell, Orubuloye, and Caldwell 1992). Lacking, however, is the sustained economic transformation without which these indicators may prove to be only temporary improvements. Declining female education is indeed one of the evident effects of the AIDS epidemic, which has likewise had a deeply depressing effect on human skills in the most affected parts of the continent, ranging from the loss of qualified staff in key sectors to the decline in primary education provision.[24] Equally, while the emigration of many of Africa's most highly skilled workers produces remittances that help to sustain the people whom they have left behind, it contributes little to the development of the continent itself; the "reverse migration" that has done much to promote the development of a country such as India is in Africa confined to a relatively small number of personally committed individuals, whose often heroic efforts pale in relation to the problems of the continent as a whole.

The one mitigating thought that I can contribute to this dismal scenario is that human beings are capable of adapting, often in unpredictable ways, and of deriving some benefit even from situations that appear to have nothing to offer. By far the single greatest demographic disaster to have struck Europe, for example, was the mid-fourteenth-century Black Death, in the course of which about one-third of the population died (Tuchman 1979: ch. 5). In retrospect, this appalling tragedy may be seen to have helped Europe's subsequent development, by reducing pressure on agricultural land, assisting the shift toward wage labor, and inducing the introduction of capital to increase productivity under conditions of labor shortage. I do not wish to propose any equivalent scenario for twenty-first-century Africa, even though important social changes are already afoot, in areas ranging from religious belief and practice to changing sexual moralities. I seek only to raise the possibility—and the hope—that this disaster-ridden continent may be able to surprise future generations for the better rather than the worse.

Notes

1 One of the problems of Africa's weak statistical base is that divergent figures derive from different sources and are impossible to reconcile with one another, while recourse to only a single source is prevented by the fact that no source provides all the information that is of interest to a study such as this. Where possible, I have taken figures from the annual volumes of the *World Development Report* and from United Nations (2005), but at several points it has been necessary to draw on other sources.

2 The work of Paul Collier and his associates at the World Bank has been particularly important in this respect. See, for example, Collier and Hoeffler (1999) and Collier, Elbadawi, and Sambanis (2000). Over the last two decades, there have been dramatic shifts in orthodox thinking on the sources of Africa's development problems, as represented by the World Bank, from an emphasis on markets as the critical factor throughout most of the 1980s, to one on "governance" through most of the 1990s, and one on conflict since the late 1990s.

3 Durand (1977: 259), cited and adapted in Herbst (2000: 16).

4 As Iliffe puts it (1995: 240), "Infertile women were colonial Africa's chief reservoir of misery." Potts and Marks (2001) note that the fear of infertility remains widespread, despite significant changes in Southern African fertility indicators in recent years.

5 The total fertility rate is the number of live births that a woman could expect to have if she were to bear children throughout her childbearing years at the prevailing age-specific rates.

6 These country figures are taken from Potts and Marks (2001), the introductory summary and discussion for a special issue of the *Journal of Southern African Studies* on fertility in Southern Africa. The decline for Zimbabwe given by United Nations (2005) is even steeper, from 7.65 in 1965–70 to 3.56 in 2000–05.

7 Ibid. The United Nations (2005) figures for Kenya are 8.12 in 1965–70 and 5.00 in 2000–05.

8 World Bank (2001: Table 2) and (1997: Table 9); equivalent figures are not reported in the most recent editions of the *World Development Report*.

9 See El-Kenz (1996) for a somber analysis that concentrates on francophone North and West Africa.

10 Notably in Lipton (1978).

11 See Bates (1981). This proposed solution in turn informed the "structural adjustment programs" instituted by the World Bank from the early 1980s.

12 See Abdullah and Muana (1998) and Abdullah (1998).

13 See, for example, Harnischfeger (2003); Nolte (2004); and Adebanwi (2005).

14 I disagree with Paul Demeny's comment that their international dimensions represent "a relatively small subset of the issues that would be involved in a comprehensive discussion of population policies in the contemporary world" (Demeny 1982: 206). From the viewpoint of modern Africa, these dimensions loom extremely large.

15 George Weah, the Liberian footballer and one-time "Footballer of the Year," was able to equip a Liberian national football team to take part in an international competition, entirely from his own resources, at a time when Liberia as a state could barely be said to exist and the country was embroiled in a murderous civil war; in the 2005 election, he was the second-placed candidate for the presidency of Liberia.

16 The British government was strongly criticized for its campaign to recruit teachers in postapartheid South Africa, a country with a far greater need for them than the United Kingdom, and desisted (officially at least) following an appeal from Nelson Mandela; the recruitment of medical professionals has been the subject of a campaign in *The Lancet* to discourage the practice.

17 Stanecki (2000). These projections are based on US Census Bureau figures. The United Nations (2005) projects population loss in Botswana after 2005, and continuing but very low population increase in South Africa.

18 Some studies, on the other hand, suggest that AIDS is likely to have only a marginal effect on population growth rates. Bongaarts (1996) projects an annual average growth rate decline from 2.77 percent without AIDS to 2.63 percent with AIDS. This is supported by a case study of a district in Uganda where growth rates remained high despite high levels of AIDS infection. Critically, however, this study assumed that birth rates would remain constant, despite a finding that 87 percent of deaths in the 20–39 age range were due to AIDS. This assumption is simply unsustainable: given that the population group most heavily afflicted by AIDS is women of childbearing age, a significant number of prospective mothers would be dead.

19 See Commission for Africa (2005: 201) for a map showing the relative incidence of HIV prevalence, which however only distinguishes between areas of high, intermediate, and low incidence, without providing any percentages for the levels concerned.

20 This tendency to have fewer children has been found in two studies of which I am aware: Grieser et al. (2001) and Baylies (2000). Similar findings have been reported orally from HIV/AIDS clinics in South Africa.

21 For a study of social responses to AIDS, see Watkins (2004).

22 See, for example, Alexandratos (2005) and Cleland and Sinding (2005).

23 An extensive critical literature on the African environment challenges the crude Malthusian assumptions that apparently continue to hold sway among demographers; see Boserup (1965); Tiffen, Mortimore, and Gichuki (1994); and Leach and Mearns (1996). For a general history of the African environment, see McCann (1999).

24 Barrett and Whiteside (2002: 279). This book is strongly recommended as the clearest available survey of current research on AIDS and its consequences, with particular attention to Africa.

References

Abdullah, Ibrahim. 1998. "Bush path to destruction: The origin and character of the Revolutionary United Front/Sierra Leone," *Journal of Modern African Studies* 36(2): 203–235.

Abdullah, Ibrahim and Patrick Muana. 1998. "The Revolutionary United Front in Sierra Leone: A revolt of the lumpenproletariat," in C. Clapham (ed.), *African Guerrillas*. Oxford: James Currey.

Abegaz, Berhanu. 2004. "Escaping Ethiopia's poverty trap: The case for a second agrarian reform," *Journal of Modern African Studies* 42(3): 313–342.

Adebanwi, Wale. 2005. "The carpenter's revolt: Youth, violence and the reinvention of culture in Nigeria," *Journal of Modern African Studies* 43(3): 339–365.

Alexandratos, Nikos. 2005. "Countries with rapid population growth and resource constraints: Issues of food, agriculture, and development," *Population and Development Review* 31(2): 237–258.

Austin, Dennis. 1964. *Politics in Ghana 1946–1960*. London: Oxford University Press.

Barrett, Tony and Alan Whiteside. 2002. *AIDS in the Twenty-First Century: Disease and Globalization*. Basingstoke: Palgrave Macmillan.

Bates, Robert H. 1981. *Markets and States in Tropical Africa: The Political Basis of Agricultural Policies*. Berkeley, CA: University of California Press.

Baylies, Carolyn. 2000. "The impact of HIV on family size preference in Zambia," *Reproductive Health Matters* 8(15): 77–86.

———. 2001. "Precarious futures—The new demography of AIDS in Africa," paper presented at the Conference on Africa's Young Majority: Meanings, Victims, Actors, Centre of African Studies, Edinburgh University, May.

Bongaarts, John. 1996. "Global trends in AIDS mortality," *Population and Development Review* 22(1): 21–45.

Boserup, Ester. 1965. *The Conditions of Agricultural Growth: The Economics of Agrarian Change under Population Pressure*. Chicago: Aldine.

Caldwell, J. C., I. O. Orubuloye, and P. Caldwell. 1992. "Fertility decline in Africa: A new type of transition?," *Population and Development Review* 18(2): 211–242.

Cleland, John and Steven Sinding. 2005. "What would Malthus say about AIDS in Africa?," *The Lancet* 366(9500): 1899–1901.

Collier, Paul and Anke Hoeffler. 1999. "Loot-seeking and justice-seeking in civil war," Washington, DC: World Bank, Development Research Group.

Collier, Paul, Ibrahim Elbadawi, and Nicholas Sambanis. 2000. "Why are there so many civil wars in Africa?," Washington, DC: World Bank, Development Research Group.

Commission for Africa. 2005. *Our Common Interest: Report of the Commission for Africa*. London.

Demeny, Paul. 1982. "Population policies," in Just Faaland (ed.), *Population and the World Economy in the 21st Century*. New York: St. Martin's Press, pp. 206–228.

Durand, John D. 1977. "Historical estimates of world population: An evaluation," *Population and Development Review* 3(3): 253–296.

El-Kenz, Ali. 1996. "Youth and violence," in Stephen Ellis (ed.), *Africa Now: People, Policies, Institutions*. London: James Currey.

Grieser, Mira et al. 2001. "Reproductive decision making and the HIV/AIDS epidemic in Zimbabwe," *Journal of Southern African Studies* 27(2): 225–243.

Hargreaves, J. R. et al. 2002. "Socioeconomic status and risk of HIV infection in an urban population in Kenya," *Tropical Medicine and International Health* 7(9): 793–802.

Harnischfeger, Johannes. 2003. "The Bakassi boys: Fighting crime in Nigeria," *Journal of Modern African Studies* 41(1): 23–49.

Herbst, Jeffrey. 2000. *States and Power in Africa: Comparative Lessons in Authority and Control*. Princeton, NJ: Princeton University Press.

Iliffe, John. 1995. *Africans: The History of a Continent*. Cambridge: Cambridge University Press.

Kiribige, Joachim S. 1997. "Population growth, poverty and health," *Social Science and Medicine* 45(2): 247–259.

Leach, Melissa and Robin Mearns (eds.). 1996. *The Lie of the Land: Challenging Received Wisdom on the African Environment*. Oxford: James Currey.

Lipton, Michael. 1978. *Why Poor People Stay Poor: A Study of Urban Bias in World Development*. London: Maurice Temple Smith.

McCann, James C. 1999. *Green Land, Brown Land, Black Land: An Environmental History of Africa, 1800–1990*. Oxford: James Currey.

Mkandawire, Thandika. 2002. "The terrible toll of post-colonial 'rebel movements' in Africa: Toward an explanation of the violence against the peasantry," *Journal of Modern African Studies* 40(2): 181–215.

Nolte, Insa. 2004. "Identity and violence: The politics of youth in Ijebu-Remo, Nigeria," *Journal of Modern African Studies* 42(1): 51–89.

Population and Development Review. 2001. "On the socioeconomic impact of the HIV/AIDS epidemic," *PDR* 27(3): 619–624.

Potts, Deborah and Shula Marks. 2001. "Fertility in Southern Africa: The quiet revolution," *Journal of Southern African Studies* 27(2): 189–205.

Stanecki, Karen A. 2000. "The AIDS pandemic in the 21st century: The demographic impact in developing countries," paper prepared for the XIII International AIDS Conference, Durban, July.

Tiffen, M., M. Mortimore, and F. Gichuki. 1994. *More People, Less Erosion: Environmental Recovery in Kenya.* Chichester: Wiley.

Tuchman, Barbara. 1979. *A Distant Mirror: The Calamitous 14th Century.* London: Macmillan.

United Nations, Department of Economic and Social Affairs, Population Division. 2005. *World Population Prospects: The 2004 Revision.* «http://esa.un.org/unpp/».

Watkins, Susan Cotts. 2004. "Navigating the AIDS epidemic in rural Malawi," *Population and Development Review* 30(4): 673–705.

World Bank. 1997. *World Development Report 1997.* New York: Oxford University Press.

———. 2000. *Can Africa Claim the 21st Century?* Washington, DC: World Bank.

———. 2001. *World Development Report 2000/2001.* New York: Oxford University Press.

———. 2004. *World Development Report 2005.* New York: Oxford University Press.

Demographic Dimensions of China's Development

EDUARD B. VERMEER

From time immemorial, China has been the most populous country in the world. The rise of China after 1949 was a political event and since 1980 also an economic event. Neither one had much to do with the growth of its population. If the country's present below-replacement fertility continues, its population of 1.29 billion in 2005 (exclusive of 7 million people in Hongkong and Macao and 23 million people in Taiwan) may reach a maximum of about 1.4 billion around 2030 and decline thereafter. By 2050 China's share of world population is likely to have dropped from 21 percent to 15 percent. Yet China looms large in pessimistic projections of world resource shortages and atmospheric pollution, in part, no doubt, because its (and India's) rapid economic growth threatens the dominant position of the West—a contemporary version of the Yellow Peril. Owing to the continuous inflow of cheap semi-skilled labor from rural areas and its millions of university graduates, China has become "the factory of the world" with the help of foreign companies and to the benefit of Western consumers. Why has export-led growth worked so well for China? The answer lies partly in its social institutions, universal primary education, the global reduction of trade barriers since the 1990s, and priority placed on economic improvement.

In spite of its huge size, growing differences in economic development between coastal and interior areas, a persistent rural–urban income gap, and low level of urbanization, many of China's demographic characteristics and tendencies are rather uniform throughout the country. The general patterns are universal marriage, nuclear households, preference for sons, fertility decline, reduced infant mortality, and rising life expectancy, traits that hold also among most non-Han ethnic minorities. While some of these characteristics should be attributed to a rapid improvement in living standards over the past 25 years, three factors appear to be mainly responsible: cultural homogeneity, the key socioeconomic role of the family, and forceful government intervention—most notably through the one-child policy. Cultural homogeneity is preserved by the vast masses of China's society, in spite of widening differentials in income and development. The family rather than the state still has to meet most social security needs (and in the case of education and health care, increasingly pay for the cost directly), even as households become smaller and smaller. Strict birth control (one child for urbanites, two for farmers, and something in between for the most developed rural regions) still rests on a widely held belief that China is overpopulated. It is remarkable that even as the Chinese people became more affluent and resource constraints eased, birth planning policies became stricter. In 2002, finally they were anchored in law.

The 2004 population age structure of China has comparatively few people under age 15 years (21 percent) and very few above age 64 (8 percent). Under full employment policies, the ratio of workers to dependents has been very favorable. Official estimates are that between 1982 and 2000, the improvement of the ratio to 4.3:1 has accelerated China's economic growth by 2.3 percent per year, that is, it contributed to over one-quarter of China's economic growth (www. chinapop.gov.cn/20051008). Nationwide, 76 percent of the population over 15 years old are economically active; in the cities alone, because of continued education, this is 64 percent (Guojia tongjiju 2005). As a result of the traditions of Chinese farming and socialist attention to gender equality, at the end of 2004 women accounted for 45 percent of the employed in China, and for 44 percent of the professionals and technicians in state-owned enterprises and state organizations. Even if urban women usually quit their jobs earlier than urban men (because of their legal retirement age of 55—for males it is 60 years—and gender-selective pressure of employers or family members), they make up 38 percent of the more than 100 million employees of larger urban work units and almost one-half of the other 150 million urban workers. Rural women retain their jobs and do their utmost to combine jobs (with or without grandmotherly assistance) with maternal child care (Short et al. 2002). Many women guide the education of their children and run a farm or business. There is a lesson here for those economically stagnant countries that for religious or cultural reasons do not develop and use the potential of women.

In 2004–05, unemployment stabilized,[1] but it remains high in old industrial regions, and most rural laborers are underemployed on their tiny farms of less than a hectare that are less and less capable of providing adequate income because of rising expectations that reflect urban income improvements. Agriculture now employs half of the labor force, whereas one-quarter would be quite sufficient. Creating employment for those who leave farming—some 10 million people every year—will remain a major challenge for at least the next three decades. As long as the economy grows by 9 percent per year, as it has done in the past quarter-century, almost any economic problem (unemployment, regional poverty, ailing state enterprises, polluting rural industries) may be kept within manageable proportions.

Population aging will become serious, but only after 2025. By 2035–40, about 20 percent of the population will be over age 64. For these reasons, the present time is a temporary window of opportunity for creating a framework of rural social security and pension schemes. Caught between increasingly self-centered capitalist trends of society, fast-rising incomes, a lack of confidence in future entitlements, and a weak rural presence, government efforts to date have not been very successful.

Since the 1980s, increasingly formal restrictions on population movements and migration have been lifted. The pace of urbanization has accelerated. The result has been a loss (or at least shift) of social and political controls. The premodern settlement pattern, which was continued and even reinforced by the institution of the people's communes and collective villages, has begun to change. With such rapid and widespread economic, social, and institutional changes, it is hard to predict how long China's present antinatalist policies will last. So far, the highly efficient administration of the birth planning policy, with its severe sanctions both for parents and for lax officials, has not faltered. Increasingly, policies call for raising people's "quality" through education and health care. Acceptance levels of the one-child policy (for rural areas, actually a two-child policy) seem to have increased, but the evidence is tainted by the political sensitivity of the subject.

Present policies have singled out China's roughly 140 million mostly rural-to-urban migrants (in 2005) as a major social problem, whether in the enforcement of birth control, in guaranteeing their children's access to education and health care, or in social discrimination and crime. Solutions are largely in the hands of municipal governments. Many migrants are ruthlessly exploited and work and live under appalling conditions, which they accept for the time being. But local governments provide little support. They have swung away from socialism and collectivism, which for three decades failed to provide income growth and individual freedom. Central government protection against the negative effects of the free market and capitalism extends only to the unemployed in the formal urban workforce and the most disadvantaged regions. Although it is widely agreed that "market socialism" is just a slogan, few care about ideological correctness or economic orthodoxy as long as China's economy continues to perform extremely well. The trickle-down effect has worked, even if not for everyone, and the Chinese remain proud of their socioeconomic achievements and optimistic about the future.

Population growth: Mortality, fertility, and migration

Once the war and revolution in China were over, improvements in food supply, more equitable distribution of income, and public health programs rapidly lowered the crude death rate. Infant mortality rates fell from 200 per thousand live births in 1949 to 100 in 1959 and 50 in the early 1970s. They continued to drop more slowly thereafter. Crude death rates shot up during the Great Leap Forward in 1959–61, to around 15, 25, and 14 per thousand, with total excess deaths estimated as between 17 and 30 million (23 million according to Peng Xizhe) and a total fertility loss of some 25 million (Peng 1987).[2] The famine struck very unevenly, most deaths occurring in rural and remote areas where the government had requisitioned (and zealous local cadres offered to deliver) too much grain.[3] The failure of the Great Leap and the resulting famine had lasting political and economic effects. The Communist Party and collective production gradually lost their credibility in the eyes of the peasantry. Most new urban immigrants were sent back to their villages. The fear of another famine prompted the Party leadership to pursue a policy of expanded grain production and local self-reliance in food production at all costs, even after China had become glutted with grain at the end of the 1990s. In the 1960s, crude death rates fell to around 10 per thousand, and then declined below 8 in 1970 and to a low of 6.3 in 1980. Reflecting changes in age composition, they have fluctuated between 6.5 and 7 since then.

Whatever its drawbacks, the rural collective framework made the delivery of free health and basic education much easier, and in these fields as in some others Communist village leaders were effective agents of modernization and social welfare programs. Since 1980, age-specific mortality rates have improved further for those aged 0–15 years, primarily because of more extensive immunization programs and improvements in diet, water supply and other sanitary conditions, and health care. Between the early 1990s and 2000, infant and child mortality (<5 years) rates dropped from 47 and 61 per 1,000 to 32 and 40 (Lin et al. 1996). Substantial further decline is expected. In the 1990s, death rates began to fall also in the age group over 65, but rose for males aged 20–30 years. Probably because of differences in life style, smoking habits (in 2005, only 2.8 percent of Chinese women were smokers, as against 24 percent of the general population: *Chinaview* 12/1/2006), and risks associated with labor and transport, mortality dropped less for males than for females (Banister 1998). By 2000, life expectancy at birth had increased to 69.6 years for men and 73.3 for women, more than two years higher than a decade earlier. This is already close to levels of advanced industrialized countries. Regional differences narrowed but remained substantial, varying from 76–78 years in Beijing and Shanghai to 64–66 years in southwest China and Tibet.

Several periods of changing fertility rates in China may be distinguished. Traditional high rates of about 6 births per woman continued until 1959. The Great Leap famine caused a steep drop and was followed by compensatory childbearing with high TFRs of well above 6 in rural areas, but much lower rates in urban areas. During the 1970s fertility declined rapidly, reaching 2.8 in 1979, and the TFR fluctuated around 2.5 for some years thereafter. Finally, in the 1990s it declined further to a below-replacement level of around 1.8, and urban and rural fertility started to converge. The present pattern of fertility is early, universal, and highly concentrated first births, relatively early and common second births, and a low and late incidence of third births (Tu Ping in Peng Xizhe and Guo Zhigang 2000: 23–25). In 2002, first births were concentrated around the mother's age of 22–26 years and second births at 29–32 years (Guojia 2003: 52). Between 2000 and 2004, China's rate of natural increase fell from 8.7 to 5.9 per thousand, attributable to decreasing numbers of women of childbearing age, a continuing rise in average age at first marriage (from 20.8 years in 1970 to 22.3 in 1995 and 23.6 in 1999), urbanization, and (partly related) increasing coverage of the one-child policy requirements (SFPC 2001; Ma 2005).

Weighting the many factors behind China's rapid fertility decline during 1950–90 is difficult because of political sensitivity and the dearth of demographic studies before 1980. As elsewhere in the world, changes in the household economy, labor opportunities, costs of raising children, perceptions of the family, women's liberation and education, decreases in child mortality, and greater availability and knowledge of contraceptive methods played important roles. Specific for China were, and remain, its draconian measures, heavy penalties, and collective pressures, and also the different policies for urban and rural areas. The resulting urban and rural population structures have diverged. Suburban and industrialized villages, where birth control policies and practices largely followed those of urban areas, now have an age structure with fewer children and more elderly than rural areas in general.

Distribution by province has changed only slightly. Natural population increase is lower in the east and in the cities. However, primarily because of migration to the coastal region and higher-than-average natural increase in minority areas,[4] between 1990 and 2000 total population increased fastest in the provinces of Guangdong and Fujian (38 and 16 percent), the cities of Beijing and Shanghai (28 and 26 percent), and in the "autonomous regions" of Xinjiang and Tibet (27 and 19 percent). The increase was slowest (5 to 6 percent) in provinces with few economic opportunities, namely Heilongjiang, Hunan, and Guangxi. Most rural migrants, whether male or female, are married and eventually return to their home villages.[5] The percentage of urban population (including residents of towns) has risen from 21 in 1982 and 26 in 1990 to 36 in 2000. The minority population increased to 106 million, or 8.4 percent of China's total population. Between 1990 and 2000, it increased by 16.7 percent as against 11.2 percent for the Han, mainly because of lower urbanization rates and less restrictive birth control policies for minorities.

International migration has been a minor factor in China's population development, apart from the southern provinces of Guangdong and Fujian with their tradition of overseas trade and export of coolie labor. The overseas Chinese population (not including Taiwan) numbered 11 million in 1950 (2 million of whom had fled the Communist revolution), 20 million in 1972, and about 40 million in the early 1990s. Almost all live in Southeast Asia, but the percentage living in the United States is rising (Poston et al. 1990). Migration became more substantial beginning in the 1990s. Since then, larger numbers of Chinese students go abroad and often continue to live in Europe and America; foreign expatriates live for some years in China's metropoles; and Hongkong and Taiwanese businessmen make frequent visits to mainland China, where some maintain a "second wife." International tourism is also on the rise.

Concerns over population growth

During much of the second half of the twentieth century China's leaders saw the relation between population and development as a negative one and considered China to be overpopulated. Only in border regions was Han Chinese expansion encouraged for strategic and developmental reasons. Posthumously, Mao Zedong has been blamed for brushing aside the concerns of China's foremost demographer, Ma Yinchu, in the late 1950s, and for viewing people (if organized well) as productive assets rather than as consumers; his conviction delayed the adoption of national birth planning policies until the early 1970s. It took time and great effort before central government concerns about population growth were transmitted to village households. Under the leadership of the Communist Party, collective villages, urban work units, and neighborhood committees played essential roles in policy implementation. Since 1956, these intermediary institutions have controlled the economic and social conditions of most Chinese. For half a century, rural Chinese have depended on village governments for renting farmland, jobs in local factories, permits for other gainful employment, and welfare.

In rural areas, the village collective felt population pressure mainly because of shrinking farm size and insufficient alternative sources of income. Income growth was stunted by state restrictions on rural economic activities, particularly trade and manufacturing. Many of the dry, mountainous areas in west and central China have insufficient agricultural resources and limited economic prospects. Population pressure in these areas was exacerbated by continuous restrictions on mobility, whereby peasants were forced to make a living within the confines of their collective village. Some of this pressure has been alleviated by the outflow of rural migrants since the 1980s. Differences in employment opportunities induced by regional economic disparities have been the main cause of migration (Li Ling

2001). However, most of the poor, elderly, uneducated, and minorities are not in a position to find work elsewhere. These groups have been targeted by poverty alleviation policies with some degree of success.

In the cities, the migrant influxes in the late 1950s and again in the 1980s and 1990s were keenly felt. Under tight government control, living conditions were cramped. Only four square meters of living space were available per resident in 1978. A quarter-century later, this has tripled, in urban as well as rural areas. Yet the perception of crowded urban living conditions has not changed, now that every household needs space for a sofa, television, and refrigerator, a separate kitchen and bathroom, and often a desk with computer for a child.

The revisionist idea that population growth is a neutral factor with respect to economic development, or even beneficial to it, has not found any acceptance by Chinese officials or scholars. Even at the household level, few Chinese farmers or urban businessmen favor having more than one or two children. Rather, in spite of China's formidable economic growth over the past two decades, Chinese officials have continued to argue that population and economic growth are negatively associated. Birth planning, they contend, should be extended and intensified; together with the improvement of population quality, it remains an integral part of development policies.[6]

China's economic growth has been promoted by a highly favorable age structure. However, one might well argue that growth has been fueled by the rapid increase in demand after liberalization in the 1980s, prior to improvements in technology, efficiency, and factor markets. Moreover, growth of production and income has been fastest in the most densely populated eastern areas. A high concentration of population lowers transport and transaction costs and contributes to well-functioning markets for labor and capital. Only very recently have some Chinese scholars begun to point out some negative effects of the one-child policy: it restricts births in urban areas where social and health conditions for child development are best and skilled labor is most needed; it creates an unbalanced population structure; and it contributes to sex-selective abortions.

Before 2000, environmental concerns about China's population growth did not extend much beyond traditional Malthusian concerns over limited natural resources, particularly farmland, water, and food grain. In the 1990s the concept of "sustainable development" slowly gained recognition[7] (Zhou 2000) and it became a professed basic principle in the eleventh five-year plan (2006–10). Severe drinking water shortages, numerous pollution accidents, the Yangzi river floods, preparations for the 2008 Olympic games, urban traffic congestion, high technological standards required for export goods, international treaties, and an increasing dependency on imports of crude oil are some of the many factors that have raised the environmental awareness of government and parts of society. China is being forced to become less wasteful and more energy-efficient. Yet fast economic growth remains its paramount goal. It is a paradox that China's present policies aim at stimulating expansion of domestic consumption and foreign exports, while restricting population growth. Having more urban children seems a great way to boost consumption.

Political and institutional factors behind declining fertility

An assessment of the relation between economic development and declining fertility requires a definition of "modern" development. If it means development within the framework of a modern state willing and able to mobilize substantial resources and regulate people's economic behavior, then both urban and rural China entered the modern stage during the 1950s. However, by other standards such as level of urbanization, increase of household income, and technological progress, China moved only slowly until 1978. It built an extensive Soviet-style industry and rural infrastructure, but with backward technologies. Real urban wages did not increase, and the modest income increase was entirely due to higher labor force participation and laborer–dependent ratios (resulting from a decreasing number of children).

The decline of fertility rates in rural areas preceded modern agricultural development. The improved status of women, the disappearance of the extended family, increased economic value of human time, and the collective framework of rural work and life appear to be have been the most influential factors, together with effective institutions capable of delivering services in health care, education, and birth control. While in traditional China family wealth and status were associated with having many children (for some, by more than one wife), after the revolution distinctions of class and education were much reduced.

Family life under Communism became an object of state regulation in many ways. The 1954 constitution affirmed the traditional obligation that "adult children have the duty to support and assist their parents," a lifelong financial and social responsibility that does not change after setting up a separate household. Children may be imprisoned for neglecting their parents. The 1950 marriage law introduced the rights of free marriage and divorce for women. Cohabitation became a legal offense. The revised law of 2001 stresses gender equality and forbids domestic violence. But in China the law carries less weight than do Party policies or social norms. As a rule urban marriages need prior approval by employers and local authorities (who also control housing allocation), which is generally not given before age 25 years. Birth control regulations and sanctions (including forced abortions), which have frequently struck foreign observers as extremely harsh, were based on Party policies and were part of widely imposed social controls over family life. The 1995 eugenics law, later renamed, requires health approvals before marriage in order to protect the health of marriage partners and reduce the number of children with genetic defects. Such invasions of private life fit within a long-standing Chinese tradition of social responsibility (Dikötter 1998). The family planning law promulgated in December 2001 severely restricts couples' reproductive rights, while extending legal protection and good quality health services to mothers and infants who abide by the law. Its prohibitions against coercion in birth control and sex identification for abortion are mainly cosmetic.

In the mid-1950s, the Chinese government started promoting the use of contraception and recognized that "a due measure of birth control" was desirable. In 1964 a Family Planning Office was set up, with branches in all cities, but the Cultural Revolution interrupted its work. It was resumed with great vigor in 1971 under the slogan "later-longer-fewer." Local authorities could set their own standards for "later" marriages; "longer" meant about four years' spacing between children; and "fewer" meant two children at first and some years later "at most two, best only one." Policy measures became very strict, supported by law and rigorously enforced. The 1978 constitution declared that "the state advocates and encourages birth control," and thereupon the State Council introduced the "only one child per couple" rule, backed up by a "one-child certificate." The policy had been designed by a leading missile scientist, as a "scientific" solution to population growth that, based on studies paralleling the work of the Club of Rome, was portrayed as a threat to China's national survival and economic development. The ideal population size target for 2080 was 650 to 700 million (Greenhalgh 2005). The new marriage law of 1980 stipulated minimum marriage ages of 22 for men and 20 for women. As these were well below the then current policy, many young couples took advantage of the law to marry (10.4 million in 1981, as against 7.2 million the previous year), and birth rates jumped. In reaction, control over births and marriages was tightened still further and pronounced "fundamental state policy," and extremely harsh implementation methods with forced sterilizations and abortions spread throughout the country (Greenhalgh and Winckler 2005).

Present policies were first set in 1988. According to a Party document, "State cadres and employees and urban residents should have only one child per couple (except under special circumstances). In rural areas a one-child policy is promoted, but if people really have difficulty and demand two children, after permission this can be arranged in a planned way. Minority people may have two children and in some cases three." Provincial governments set more specific policies in order to achieve imposed targets.[8] Municipal governments formulate detailed rules for implementation and also decide on bonuses and fines. Every township has a birth control office, which over-sees faithful implementation of birth plans by village governments. In 2000, the Communist Party reaffirmed that strict birth control policies should be maintained "for at least another decade." Unless both parents are single chil-dren, couples in urban and a growing number of rural areas can have only one child. Many rural areas allow farmers to have a second child only if the first child was a girl and only after payment of a high license fee. Admit-tedly, the traditions of patrilocal marriages and continuation of the family line are hard to change.

The cost of second and third children born "out of the plan" has kept rising. In 1992, the fine in rural areas for the first offense against planned births averaged more than 40 percent of the annual income of a laborer (Yang Tao and Elroy 2000). Rich and daring farmers may have a second child anyway, and then pay very stiff fines or bribes to corrupt cadres. Be-cause liberalization has weakened state control over jobs, wages, housing, and people's movements, in recent years the government has increasingly sought to supplement its "carrot and stick" approach with indirect mea-sures in the areas of women's liberation, education, and economic develop-ment. Nevertheless, administrative measures and force are still needed. Achievement of birth control targets (municipal governments receive an-nual quotas of the maximum number of births allowed) has become a main, if not *the* main criterion for evaluating the performance of local officials, and lax officials have been fired or their salaries withheld. The family plan-ning law that took effect in 2002 stipulates that parents who violate the one-child rule have to pay "social expenses of raising a child"—the amount of which is to be determined by the local authorities. The 2002 law gives unlimited powers to local governments to impose sanctions on offending couples.

After rural areas were collectivized in 1956, households lost most of their productive functions (except for the private plot) but continued as units of consumption. This changed the economic rationale of having chil-dren. The abolition of family farms reduced the need for households to have male offspring for future farm labor. The collective guaranteed a basic in-come for all members, young and old. Moreover, the social position of women was enhanced and their labor value increased because of their in-dependent contribution to and earnings from collectively organized labor. Because collective income was distributed mainly on a per capita basis, most of the costs of having children (including education, health care, and creat-ing employment) were borne not by the household but by the collective (a group of 30 to 50 households) and the village. The increasing collective burden helps explain why at the village level cadres strongly supported a reduction in the number of children, while ordinary farmers did not. But the great dependence of villagers on their collective leaders, and the severity of sanctions, made it difficult to resist birth control measures and policies. In the cities, dependence on the work unit was even greater.

Some have argued that the temporary rise of total fertility in the early 1980s was due to the reintroduction of family farming, which increased the need for male labor (e.g., Yang Zihui in Chang 1993: 118). However, it also made having and raising children more costly. A better explanation may be found in the drop in average marriage age. The distribution of farmland to households gave an incentive to set up separate households as early as possible. Average female age at first marriage dropped suddenly from 21.9 in 1979 to 20.5 in 1984, and for males from 22.6 to 21.2. This led to a significant increase in the number of marriages and first births. Also, the abolition of collective production and people's communes meant a temporary slip of party and village control over people's reproductive behavior. Some Chinese observers feared that the family farm had brought a return of "feudal" marriage and childrearing practices (Yang Zihui in Chang 1993: 119–120). However, the drop in marriage age and the increase in fertility were only temporary.

A similar drop in marriage age occurred in cities, for which other reasons have been identified, notably liberalization of government controls in this period and the 1980 revision of the marriage law. Although this law raised the legal marriage age by two years, its short-term effect was to undermine the legality of government regulations that had imposed much higher minimum age requirements. These institutional changes coincided with the small birth cohorts of 1959 through 1961 reaching marriage age. In the 1990s, the average female age at first marriage rose again, reaching 22.6 by 2000.

In the 1970s, the percentage of women of reproductive age practicing birth control rose rapidly to over 80 percent, and it increased further thereafter. IUDs were most commonly used, particularly by urban and young women, and were used by one-half of all couples in the 1970s and by 40 to 45 percent in the 1990s. Prevalence of female sterilization, preferred mainly by older and rural women, rose from around 12 percent to 40 percent in the 1990s, and male sterilization remained around 10 percent. The young, minorities, and the illiterate were least inclined to practice birth control.

Cooney and Li (1994) demonstrated that compliance with the one-child policy was related to five main factors: 1) acceptance of the "one-child certificate," a contract with considerable financial benefits, but severe penalties if broken; 2) sex of the first child; 3) urban or rural household registration; 4) educational level of the wife; and 5) coresidence with parents, which increases pressure to conform to traditional family norms and facilitates child care. Economic sanctions for urban couples include loss of subsidized services for the child, pay-backs of individual and collective bonuses received on the basis of compliance with the one-child policy, loss of access to cheap housing and subsidized education, possible loss of employment or chances for promotion, and the like. Taken together, costs are so high as to be prohibitive. For that reason it is difficult to estimate the effect on births of other factors commonly associated with fertility decline, such as rise of income, female education, and urbanization. Reportedly, the number of births "outside the plan" decreased from 12 percent in 1995 to 6 percent in 1999, most unauthorized births occurring in the richest provinces and minority regions.[9]

Sex preference for children

China has a long tradition of gender discrimination. Sons continue the family line, whereas daughters leave the family and home after marriage. Successive marriage laws and other regulations (including those on inheritance and rural land contracting in 2003) have stipulated gender equality, and the official position is that women's rights should be promoted through all means. In rural areas, almost as many women are engaged in economic activities as men, but until recently they constituted less than one-third of rural high school graduates (National Agricultural Census 1998). The female wage averages about two-thirds of the male wage (Vermeer 2003). Between 1980 and 2000, the percentage of female students in tertiary education almost doubled, to 40 percent. In spite of such progress, cultural preference for males has persisted.

Coale and Banister (1994) noted a large excess of female mortality for cohorts born in the 1930s and 1940s, and again for female children during the 1960 famine. Female infanticide declined, but was not eliminated. Since the 1970s birth control led to a cessation of fertility after the birth of a wanted son. The proportion of "missing" girls (after deduction of selective underreporting) may have been 3 percent around 1980, but after ultrasound scans became widely available, sex-selective abortion escalated, leading to very high sex ratios at birth. For third- and fourth-order births, the ratio rose from 108 males per 100 females in the cohorts born in 1977–81 to 123 per 100 for the 1985–89 cohorts. Because of an even higher rise in Korea, Coale and Banister argued that the sex-selective abortions should not be attributed to Communism, compulsory family planning, or the one-child policy. Rather, once prenatal sex determination became available, parents in both countries with a preference for males used it. Yet it seems likely that if more children were allowed, sex-selective abortions would decrease. China's minorities have much lower sex ratios than the Han. In 1990, the Han ratio was 111.9, but it was 106.5 for Mongols and Hui, 103.9 for Tibetans, and 103.4 for Uighurs (Zhongguo guojia tongjiju 1994: 180–181).

Fetal sex determination for selective abortion is officially forbidden, but its practice in hospitals and private clinics is condoned. A recent rural survey showed that 61 percent of only children were male; among couples with two children, 22 percent had two boys and 5 percent two girls (Chu 2000). The 1990 and 2000 censuses showed an overall infant sex ratio rising from 111.3 to 116.9. The ratio remained close to normal for first-order children (at 105.2 and 107.1) but leapt for second-order children (from 121.0 to 151.9) and third- and higher-order children (from 127.0 to 159.4). The rise occurred mainly in rural areas and small towns, where ratios increased from 112 to 117–118, but urban rates also rose, from 109 in 1990 to 113 in 2000. Figures were highest in the southern provinces of Hainan (136) and Guangdong (131) (Stats.gov.cn/tjfx/jdfx/2002/05090129). Moreover, the probability of death among infants is slanted: 41/1,000 for girls and 30/1,000 for boys (SFPC 1996: 483), which suggests sex-selective infanticide or death by neglect of around 1.5 percent of all female births. The resulting marriage squeeze will become serious once the generations born after 1990 reach marriage age. Chinese officials predict that "after 2030 some 30 million young men will be unable to find a marriage partner" and proposed policies that should restore a normal sex ratio at birth by 2015 (Deng and Guo 1999; Fan Yi and Cai Fei, *Guangming ribao* 21/12/2005). The problem is not unique to China, but exists in India and Korea as well. Some Chinese fear the dire consequences for society and family values of so many unmarried young men, but one might also argue that it will relieve some of the pressure on male bachelors (including homosexuals, a legally and socially repressed group) to enter into marriage. An optimistic economic prediction would be that as girls become scarce, their economic value increases, so parents will want to have more of them, and in the long term gender balance will be restored.

Fertility preferences, past and future

Traditionally, married Chinese women practiced birth control with some degree of effectiveness. Women born between 1914 and 1930 and living in rural areas in 1982 with primary education or less had married on average at age 18.6, had their first birth at 21.8, their last birth at 38.2, and a total of 5.9 births. Only 3.5 percent never had a child. This is a moderate level of marital fertility. Birth intervals show conscious planning by couples: those with only daughters had the shortest intervals, and those with both sons and daughters the longest (Zhao 1997).

In rural China collective production had deep and long-lasting effects on family circumstances, noticeably on the liberation of women and the young. It is less clear to what extent traditional preferences favoring larger and extended families living under one roof might have reasserted themselves if given the chance, once the family farm was reinstated in a more capitalist setting after 1980. Growing opportunities for alternative employment outside the farm and the village, and almost universal education (compulsory since 1986), reduced the hold of parents over their children, of men over women, and of the old over the young. These weakened the traditional structure of the family farm as the dominant form of economic (and social) life. By 1997, 60 percent of China's 215 million rural households were still engaged solely in agriculture, and 23 percent had their main or entire income from nonagricultural work (National Agricultural Census and FAO 1998: 16). Particularly for those with little education, farming is the main source of income, and it guarantees employment of and income from their children and their own social security (Vermeer 2004). The tiny size of the farms (on average less than 0.5 hectare) allows for having only one son; because of the custom of patrilocal marriage, girls are of little economic relevance.

For an understanding of Chinese fertility changes at the household level, a framework of perceived and actual economic costs and benefits of children has limited use. We lack scientific survey data showing how decisions about fertility were taken.[10] Economic perspectives differed greatly between rural and urban areas, and between regions, yet trends in fertility changes were rather uniform. Often, economic prospects were uncertain because of policy shifts with regard to employment, income distribution, housing, cost of education and health care, sanctions against having more children, and so on. While households might calculate the short-term economic costs of having an unauthorized child, such an estimate would be rather uncertain because the punishments for an extra child are not spelled out. The social and psychological "cost" to the household that decides to defy the authorities is likely to differ greatly between households and between communities. A perceived lack of direct control of the household over its economic future, in combination with the idea that government would provide some kind of minimal social security, may have contributed to an acceptance of China's birth control and late marriage policies.

Some Chinese scholars[11] contend that preference for the number of children changed from two or three in the early 1980s to one or two by 2000, and conclude that therefore resistance to birth control regulations is much less now than it was in the 1980s. A recent survey showed 43 percent of unmarried women to prefer two children, four-fifths of whom wanted a boy and a girl (*SFPC Bulletin*, 3 March 2002). Indeed, preference for two is common, a boy for economic reasons and a girl for social reasons. Only recently have official Chinese planners lowered the level of the TFR underlying their population projections from 2.0 to 1.8, under the assumption of a continuation of current restrictive measures.

Chinese officials associate having more children with backwardness. "In rural areas, university graduates have only one child... high school graduates three, primary school graduates four, illiterates five."[12] Actual differences are not nearly as large. In 1992, cumulative fertility at ages 35 and 45, respectively, was 2.5 and 3.5 for illiterate rural women, 2.3 and 3.4 for primary school graduates, and 2.1 and 2.6 for high school graduates. For urban women, fertility at age 45 in these three educational categories was 3.4, 2.7, and 2.0 (SFPC 1995: 456–457). Numbers have gone down in all categories since then. Several reasons may be suggested for higher fertility among the uneducated and poor. First, the official economic sanctions on having unauthorized children have less effect. The poor and uneducated do not draw wages from factories or urban organizations, so forfeits and paybacks of bonuses, housing subsidies, and the like do not apply. Second, they are less vulnerable to political and social sanctions, being at the bottom of society already. Third, the labor time of women in this category has less economic value. Many are underemployed. In the absence of satisfaction from outside labor, gratification from raising children becomes more attractive. Finally, lack of education may be more readily used as an excuse, and often rightly so because of a lesser comprehension of birth control techniques.

In the government drive to develop the backward western regions of China, propaganda related to birth control (e.g., through mobile birth clinics) and stricter measures have been given a prominent place. The rapid improvement of literacy since the introduction of compulsory education in 1986 (the illiteracy rate dropped from 34 percent of those aged 13 and above in 1964 and 23 percent of those aged 15 and above in 1982 to 7 percent in 2000) has benefited mountainous areas in particular. Their access to health care and receptiveness to birth control programs have been greatly increased.

Population distribution and urbanization

China's population is mainly concentrated in the lowlands in the east, in areas with high agricultural productivity, and in industrialized areas. From 1950 to 1980, changes in distribution were mainly due to government-supported industrialization in the border regions in west and northeast China, with an active policy of settlement of Han Chinese. Thus, population became somewhat more evenly distributed. Improving health conditions and poverty alleviation programs have led to higher birth rates and lower death rates, which have increased the population in minority and mountainous areas at a higher than average rate, in spite of limited economic opportunities. The population may be close to or even exceed the land's carrying capacity in the southwest and hilly areas in central China. High population density in areas without adequate resources has been exacerbated by government restrictions on population movements and the institutional arrangement of collective ownership of farmland. Only recently have such restrictions been loosened.

Urbanization in China started rather late. In 1958, household registration rules were adopted that required rural migrants to urban areas to have urban work or school permits, or settlement permits from urban authorities. This started the formal separation of rural and urban households. Strict urban rationing of food, cloth, and housing and strict controls on population movement succeeded in stemming the rural-to-urban flow. In the 1970s about 20 million urban youths were sent to countryside—for "reeducation" according to the Communist Party, although the real reason was primarily to relieve the cities from housing and employment burdens. As a result, during the 1960s and 1970s only about 15 percent of the population lived in cities. In an effort to gain popular support, in 1979 the new regime allowed some 30 million "sent-down" people to move back from rural areas. After the people's communes were abolished in 1984, some 50,000 rural towns were redefined as urban areas. During the 1990s the urban/rural distinction became more vague because of large-scale migration, relaxation of controls, introduction of new categories of urban residents, and redefinition of towns as urban areas. Since 1998, infants have been entitled to urban residence status if either parent is urban.

Between 1978 and 2000, the urban population doubled from 18 percent to 36 percent of the total population. This still rather low percentage can be mainly explained by three factors: the institutional and economic links of rural residents with their villages, strict government control of urban settlement, and rural industrialization. Traditionally, Chinese municipalities have administrative control over vast agricultural areas. The phenomenal growth of township and village enterprises, stimulated by their low costs of land and labor, resulted in 130 million nonfarm jobs for rural residents by 1995.

Present urbanization policies call for a liberalization of settlement of rural people in some 20,000 towns. Restrictions will be slightly relaxed for small and medium-size cities. However, strict control will be maintained over immigration into large cities. Since 2000, the annual urbanization rate has been well above one percentage point, and it is expected that between 2000 and 2020 about 300 million people will move into urban areas. The growing rate of urbanization will facilitate government control over births and accelerate cultural acceptance of the one-child policy. Moreover, it will lead to later marriages.

Regional and urban/rural differentials and labor migration

China has some 748,000 administrative villages with an average size of 1,200 people, and 16,000 rural towns with an average population of 4,500. Because of the country's collective past, most have important economic functions in renting out land or operating industries and services. Suburban villages have become rich and developed. Other villages (particularly the 200,000 in mountainous areas) are poor and lack access to modern amenities. As of c.

2000, 12 percent of the administrative villages (in mountainous areas 25 percent) have difficulty accessing drinking water, and only 17 percent have tap water. Thirteen percent are not accessible by road, and 34 percent are more than 20 kilometers from a bus station. Thirty-eight percent do not have a primary school, and 23 percent do not have a rural doctor. Forty-eight percent have no telephone connection, and 71 percent rely mainly on firewood for their fuel (National Agricultural Census 2000: 97–100). Nevertheless, rural poverty has been considerably reduced and services improved since the 1980s through generally effective poverty alleviation programs. At present, these programs target 150,000 villages and 80 million poor people. Increasingly, resettlement is becoming an acceptable solution for those living in the ecologically most vulnerable and economically least productive areas. The example of the changing resettlement plans for almost a million people from the future location of the Sanxia Reservoir shows that ecology and nonagricultural employment have become important considerations.

Net urban income per capita is over three times as high as rural income, and rural income in the richest provinces averages three to four times that in the poorest provinces. The urban/rural gap has widened for two decades and now is very high by international standards. The richest province (Shanghai) has 12 times the average per capita net income of the poorest province (Guizhou). Of urban households in 2004, the per capita disposable income of the richest 10 percent (25,400 yuan) was nine times as high as that of the poorest 10 percent, and 20 percent of the population owns 80 percent of all assets. Neither fiscal nor economic policies succeeded in mitigating these growing differentials, with the exception of those policies targeting the very poorest. Since 2000, the political goal of reducing "the peasant burden," by forbidding all kinds of village and township government levies and fees and abolishing the agricultural tax, has shifted some burdens to companies and higher levels of government. The other solution has been to demand greater private contributions to health care, education, and other services. One way or another, local services, infrastructure, and cadres' salaries must be paid for, and in agricultural areas this burden falls on farmers.

Officially allowed only since 1984, labor migration has helped to reduce income differentials. Its direction is rural to urban, from inland to coastal areas, and from backward to developed areas. In 1997, 13 percent of the rural labor force worked outside their township (27 million), county (21 million), or province (24 million) (National Agricultural Census 1998). Migrants were mostly married and predominantly male, but women dominated in short-distance migration; most migrants were young and comparatively well educated.

Male and female migrants worked in industry, building, trades, and catering, but held on to their farms, which were cultivated by their relatives; and most eventually returned to their villages (Yang Zihui 1997;

Murphy 2002). Migrants' numbers and their movements' geographical scope declined in the late 1990s because of higher migration costs, such as management fees, permits and train tickets, over-capacity and restrictions on urban labor markets (CASS 1999: 305), but increased again between 2002 and 2004, to an estimated 140 million people. Migrants' most common initial motives are a lack of opportunities for gainful employment on the farm or locally, a negative attitude toward farming, the poverty of rural life, and the prospect of higher income in the city. After some time, migrants also become accustomed to their new life and their higher income (Wang Chunguang in Li Peilin 2003).

In recent years, more and more migrants have opted to stay in the cities, and very few want to return to their village to set up a new business there. This means that the new urban dwellers will have to "re-socialize" (Bai Nansheng in Li Peilin 2003). The rights of urban in-migrants are limited and not well defined. Without permanent residence status, they are excluded from certain branches of work and from social security, and often their children do not have access to subsidized education and health care. Since 2000, the central government and several large cities have passed regulations to improve migrants' rights and access to social amenities. At the same time, they are targeted for birth control and anti-crime measures. Discrimination, withholding of wages, and arrears in wage payments have given rise to violent social protests, which local governments have found hard to handle. In-migrants are the new underclass in China's cities, living at worksites and in (sometimes self-organized) shantytowns.[13] So far, the rural traditions of work and family still hold this group in check, but government and urban society are suspicious and watchful.

Minorities

Reviving a Qing tradition, in the 1950s and again in the 1970s China sent millions of Han Chinese soldiers and young people to its western and border regions, in order to settle among the minorities and reinforce political and economic control. The 55 officially recognized minority peoples constituted almost 6 percent of the total population in the 1960s, increasing to 6.6 percent in 1982, 8 percent in 1990, and 8.4 percent (106 million) in 2000. The rapid increase of the 1980s was partly due to a 26 percent higher annual birth rate among minorities than among Han Chinese, but mostly to the fact that 14 million Han changed their ethnic registration in order to profit from more liberal birth control regulations. This loophole was closed in 1989 (CASS 2000: 132).

Between 1964 and 1990, minorities increased at twice the rate of the Han. Manchus increased from 2.7 million to 9.9 million, Miao by 165 percent to 7.4 million, Mongols by 144 percent to 4.8 million, Muslims and Yi by about 95 percent to 8.6 million and 2.7 million, respectively. Tibetans and Uighurs, having high birth rates but almost no changes in ethnic registration, increased by 80–85 percent to 4.6 million and 7.2 million, respectively. The Zhuang, hardly distinguishable from the Han and subject to the same birth control policy, grew by 85 percent to 6.7 million over this period. In 1990, there were 16 million mixed households with 73 million people (Zhongguo guojia 1994).

In the 1990s, the minority population increased further by 17 percent, as against 11 percent for the Han, mainly because of more liberal birth control policies for minorities. These were part of a general policy of positive discrimination. Combined with strict political control (with some autonomy), subsidized government services, and poverty alleviation programs, this policy has fostered integration and helped prevent serious ethnic conflicts. However, in many minority regions, cities and industries are increasingly dominated by the Han who settled there in the 1950s and 1970s. This is a continuing process. Between 1990 and 2000, the Han population of Xinjiang increased at twice the rate of the Uighurs and other minorities, to 7.5 million or 40 percent of the region's population. Only Tibet has attracted few Han Chinese other than temporary military or civil government personnel;[14] that will change now that the railroad has reached Lhasa.

China has successfully managed to include its persecution of ethnic separatist movements as part of the international war on terrorism. But the main thrust of central government actions in the western regions has been economic. Concerns about political and social stability were a major reason for starting the Open Up the West campaign in 2000, a gigantic investment project of development of infrastructure, energy resources, industries, and services in 12 provinces and minority regions. The project also includes central government funding for education, health care, and subsidies for the social cost of closing many state-owned enterprises that are unable to compete with companies from the east on a commercial basis. Dubbed exploitative and colonialist by some, the campaign has proven to be an effective mechanism of marketization, economic integration, and national strengthening, and it has temporarily boosted local government services. Long-term economic prospects for most western regions are poor, however, and what their opening-up will do to ethnic and regional identities and acceptance of Han dominance remains unknown (Goodman 2004).

Household size, marriage, and children

A substantial reduction in average household size took place after 1949 as a result of land reform. The Communist rejection of the traditional family, and the practice of land redistribution on a per capita basis, irrespective of age and sex, meant that extended families were divided up and small families mushroomed. In 1947, an official report put the nation's total households at 87 million; by 1953 it had rocketed to 136 million. Average family size fell to 4.3 in 1953, rose to 4.9 in 1959, dropped again because of the Great Leap Forward, and then returned to 4.8 in the 1970s (Tuan Chi-hsien et al. 1990). There has been a steady decline since then: 4.4 in 1982, 4.0 in 1990, and 3.4 (3.6 in rural and 3.1 in urban areas) in 2004. The tendency toward smaller households continues as the population ages.

Between 1999 and 2004, the proportion of households with two generations dropped from 62 to 56 percent of all households, and those with three generations from 19 to 17 percent. Single-person households (mostly widows) rose from 6 to 8 percent (Guojia tongjiju 2005). These trends reflect the rapid shrinking of household sizes. Even so, grandparents may have an important role in child care and household chores while parents are at work. From 1949, Chinese Communist leaders have adhered to the ethic of self-reliance and family responsibility. The promotion of "utilitarian familism" has been a major building block of China's welfare system. In rural areas, elderly parents in need of support move in with their eldest son's family or rotate between sons, rather than move into a home for the elderly. In the absence of adequate pensions, both urban and rural families provide material support and social care for their elderly.

Marriage is still nearly universal, and so is having a child. A rising percentage, now approaching 10 percent, of marriages are second marriages. Moreover, because of high minimum age at marriage requirements, cohabitation has become more common since the 1980s (Zhang 1993). The registered early marriage rate (below the legal limit of 22 years for men and 20 for women) fell below one percent in 1999, but was 5–15 percent in minority regions such as Tibet, Qinghai, and Yunnan. The late marriage rate (conforming to the government-set rule of at least 25 years of age for men and 23 for women) was 60 percent of all marriages. It varied greatly between provinces, probably because of different local regulations and quality of registration; it was 99 percent in Shandong, but 50 percent in Hebei province, 86 percent in Beijing, and 64 percent in Shanghai. In 2000, average female age at first marriage was 22.6 and the first birth occurred at 24.1. The average spacing between the first and second child increased from three years in 1990 to 5.7 years in 2000 (*SFPC Bulletin*, 3 March 2002).

China's divorce rate doubled between 1985 and 2000 to 2 percent or 1.2 million cases a year. Divorcees—in rural areas primarily men, as most women remarry—made up only 1.5 and 0.8 percent, respectively, of the urban and rural population in 2004 (Guojia Tongjiju 2005). The high labor participation rate and relatively strong legal position of women should make divorce easier, but traditional social values and institutional pressures to maintain the household remain very strong. There is little acceptance of alternative lifestyles. Nevertheless, among young people traditional attitudes about sex before marriage and homosexuality are changing. A survey among college students found that 60 percent felt homosexuality should be permitted openly, 62 percent rejected chastity before marriage as a "suppression of human nature," and 71 percent did not object to marrying someone who had prior sexual relations with others. Condom machines are accepted on campuses (www.sfpc.gov.cn/EN/enews20020131).

In 2000, a website for reproductive health was opened with emphasis on sexual education and AIDS prevention. China was estimated to have 225,000 HIV/AIDS patients in 1998 and 840,000 in 2003. The government aims to keep infected cases under 1.5 million by 2010; UNAIDS, however, has estimated the 2010 number might reach 10 to 20 million (CASS 1999: 306; Zhang 2002; www.avert. org/aidschina.htm). Because of the association of HIV with illegal drug abuse and prostitution, and unwillingness to report infection for fear of discrimination, actual numbers are highly uncertain.

The reforms of the 1980s reestablished the family farm as the primary unit of production. Some traits of the traditional family were revived, particularly the division of labor between household members. But increased mobility and diversification of labor, higher income, urbanization, fewer children, compulsory education, television, and other factors introduced new and modern patterns. In rural areas, the practice of patrilocal and exogenous marriage did not change. For egalitarian reasons, in spite of the law most villages periodically redistributed their farmland leases on the basis of changes in the size and labor availability of village households, which gave an incentive for household division (Vermeer 2004). But nowadays in suburban areas and many regions, households derive less income from crop cultivation than from employment in factories and services or migrant labor in distant cities, and family ties have loosened because of this diversification.

Differentials in development and income have widened, and more room has been given for developing cultural identities, whether regional, subethnic such as Cantonese or Hakka, or linked to youth, profession, or religion. It is too early to tell whether the present substantial provincial differences in rural late marriage rates, fertility, gender preference, household size, labor migration, and other practices (such as acknowledging female heads of household) are due to different local regulations and levels of economic development, or already reflect different cultural preferences. When two rich coastal provinces show very different average household sizes, both urban and rural (3.4 and 4.0 in Guangdong, 2.9 and 3.1 in Zhejiang), one has to look for cultural as well as institutional explanations.

Projections for 2050

Births, deaths, migration

It is difficult to forecast the future size and distribution of China's population. The problem does not lie with death rates, unless the avian flu turns pandemic—China is densely populated, with large numbers of migrants, and the risks of new viruses and epidemic diseases are enhanced by the close interaction of man with pigs, fowl, and other species of farm animals, and numerous markets with mixed live animals. Absent such a disaster— and even worse scenarios such as a nuclear war—death rates will move closer to advanced-world levels. That goes for the main causes of death, too. Traffic accidents kill over 100,000 per year, and obesity has begun to afflict the urban fast-food generation. However, it appears that few Chinese women have taken up the habit of smoking.

Somewhat more difficult to predict are the effects of globalization on transnational migration. Although one would expect only a marginal influence on China's huge population size, the number of Chinese studying and working overseas is turning from a trickle into a steady flow of hundreds of thousands a year. In 2001, then President Jiang Zemin declared that China should focus its economic policies on human resource development. Chinese universities are starting to turn out millions of well-educated young people, and Chinese and foreign companies are expanding their highly qualified work force. These young Chinese will be increasingly welcome in the aging European countries, the United States, and global companies. Because many are female, the demographic impact might become appreciable. If, say around 2020–25, political frustration, economic stagnation, and heavy social obligations (these are single children with two parents to care for) make living in China less and less attractive, many may decide to emigrate. That happened in Taiwan during the 1970s, and a reverse flow occurred two decades later after Taiwan had become an open and democratic society. The UN Population Division's projections of an average net outmigration of only 320,000 to 350,000 per year through 2050 seem much too low. Still, such emigration is more likely to be a qualitative loss than a quantitative one.

Future birth rates are hardest to predict, because the present rates reflect past and present political intervention, and lifestyles and family circumstances are likely to change more rapidly and become more diverse than before. With the advance of so many young women into tertiary education and professional careers, late marriage will become the preferred individual choice instead of a political imposition. Also, the universality of marriage will change. At present, China's fertility is in the transitional stage in rural areas and in the post-transitional stage in urban areas, but neither reflects free choice. In the short term, one may see an upward trend in fertility among the urban and suburban population, and a continuing downward trend in rural areas. The 2004 UN Population Division's medium scenario forecasts a fall in the TFR to a low of 1.7 in 2001–05, then a gradual rise to a constant 1.85 from 2015 until 2050, but in the light of China's rapid social (and possibly also political) changes, fertility rates will probably show greater variations over the years.

Maybe because of both traditional and Communist beliefs in the malleability of man as a social animal, so far Chinese scholars have given little thought to innate behavioral predispositions affecting family and fertility. The wish for multiple children is considered to be a cultural, not a biological phenomenon, and individual urges are expected to be subordinated to common social interests. Chinese citizens have openly worried about the one-child policy's effect on the ability of single children to support their parents in their old age, and sometimes also about the present and future social behavior of these "Little Emperors." Private desires for having more children and resistance to forced abortions have remained subdued or have been harshly suppressed. However, pressures for change are likely to build. It is highly doubtful that even 30 years of propaganda could have permanently instilled the idea in Chinese couples that having just one child is ideal. Rather, once given the choice, they will follow other modern societies in preferring two or three children, or even none. If one out of every five women decides not to have children, and the others have an average of two, the resulting total fertility rate would be 1.6, well below replacement. Relaxation of political controls over timing and spacing of births may have little impact, as social tendencies are moving toward later births.

An uncertain factor is the timing of the eventual relaxation of political control over marriages and births. This will not be a democratic decision, reflecting changing values in society, but a technocratic decision by the Party leadership five or ten years from now. Most likely, it will be based on actual birth rates, economic growth targets, perceptions of "quality" of people and shortage of resources, environmental carrying capacity, and the like. The most interesting question is whether the leadership will devise a uniform policy for all Chinese or will introduce new rural/urban or regional distinctions (other than the present one for minorities). China has a strong tradition of social engineering, and if the above-mentioned criteria are applied, rich municipalities and regions should have more children and resource-poor (or just poor) municipalities should have fewer. In such a scenario, birth policies would become a local responsibility, not just in their implementation but also in setting targets. Because municipalities are already responsible for unemployment, housing, settling of migrants, education, and other social expenditure, why not shift the basic burden of population planning to them as well? However, China's past experience has shown that favorable treatment granted to some areas was quickly demanded by other areas, and with success. Eventually, the devolution of central birth control policies to the local level might result in their demise.

Urbanization: Sectoral productivity, village functions, and treatment of migrants

With continuous annual urbanization rates of around one percentage point, by 2050 three-quarters of all Chinese will live in urban areas. Without going into problems of definition (China uses criteria of administrative control or nonagricultural occupation, but not density), one may point out three main determinants of the pace of urbanization: future levels of productivity of farming, industry, and services; changes in the socioeconomic function of the collective village; and policies toward migrants. The actual location of urban expansion will continue to be influenced by state policies that have been devised to absorb as much rural surplus labor as possible in small towns; but their effect critically depends on the ability of small towns throughout China to generate local employment, which may suffer from the present tendencies of concentration of manufacturing, economies of scale, and lower transport costs in large cities.

Industrial labor productivity has increased at three or four times the rate in agriculture (8 percent and more as against 2 or 3 percent), and this differential is likely to continue for at least another two decades. Assuming that half of productivity gains in industry will accrue to labor in the form of wage and social security improvements, by 2025 industrial workers' income will have tripled, but farmers' incomes will have increased by only about two-thirds. As in other countries, the growing income differential will push people from the farm to the city. Reducing agricultural employment by one-half would stabilize the present income differential, but will be impossible to realize within just 20 years. The present emphasis of the Party on constructing a "new socialist countryside" before 2010, with more state support, improved living conditions, institutional reform of townships, and increasing subsidies for farmers, reflects the efforts to keep the outflow of Chinese farmers within manageable levels, below 10 million a year.

As noted above, China's villages have the unique responsibility of providing income and social security to their residents from their collective resources of land, industry, and other assets. This remnant of the period of forced collectivization cannot last forever, as it discriminates against rural residents and produces unjust inequalities between villages with different factor endowments. So far, little progress has been made toward a nationwide social security system, or toward freeing the markets in land and labor, or toward substantial interregional budgetary transfers. Yet all these have been mentioned as political goals for the medium and long term. A realization of these goals will change the Chinese social landscape beyond recognition. We could see hundreds of millions of villagers in the interior vote with their feet and flock to the east and south.

Current policies related to the treatment of migrant laborers call for "establishing minimum wages, providing guarantees that wages will be paid fully and in time, enforcing labor contracts, removing discriminatory and unreasonable restrictions, solving their social security needs, granting access to urban public services and improving their dwelling conditions, and helping sur-

plus rural laborers to find jobs in local cities." Their goal is "safeguarding social equity and justice and maintaining social harmony and stability" (State
Council guidelines passed 18 January 2006, www.chinaview.cn 20060119).
Almost all these lofty goals depend on the ability and willingness of local
government, companies, and society to adopt practical measures and develop
new attitudes among the privileged urbanites. Beijing municipality has promised to build 11 satellite towns to accommodate 5.7 million mostly immigrant residents within a few years; Shanghai has built such towns already;
but not many municipalities have the political and economic resources to
expand their urban area in a planned and controlled manner. Their treatment of migrant laborers and their children, recognition of their rights to
education, health care, and social security, granting equal rights in the local
labor market, eventual allocation of social or commercial housing, and getting official permission to stay permanently and become an accepted part of
urban society: all these will greatly influence migrants' ability and willingness to stay. Those who argue that urban economies and export industries in
eastern China have become so dependent on migrant laborers that the migrants' continued residence there is guaranteed could be proven wrong.
China's authoritarian government has a tradition of forced resettlement and
is quite capable of harsh measures against its own residents and even more
so against migrant laborers. The present building and investment boom may
be over within a decade, economic growth rates may fall back to 5 percent or
less, and, once urban unemployment rises, migrant laborers will be the first
to be dismissed. China is not a European welfare state, and unemployed migrants will not be entitled to social welfare and will probably be forced to
leave. The Department of Labor and Social Security listed 21.5 million urban
job seekers in 2006, of which 2.6 million are former rural residents with registered permanent urban residence status,[15] but the Department does not accept any responsibility for laborers with a rural status, and there are no signs
that will change in the near future. Under these circumstances, in municipalities where boom goes to bust and employment falls, the goal of building a
"harmonious society" will become an unrealistic dream, torn by social strife,
police brutality, and migrant resistance.

Aging and population projections

From 2025 onward, a rapid aging of the population will transform the present
age structure. The final phase of the demographic transition will affect China
and its urban economy with double force. A smaller percentage of children
and fewer households will tend to moderate demand, while a high percentage of elderly will require large investments, financially and in labor, in
mostly non-paid care. This projection has elicited the political promise that
in the future, marriage partners who are both single children will be al-

lowed to have two children. Whether this promise will be kept is uncertain; clearly it would create great discrimination in the future marriage market. Economically, single-child couples will be in a difficult position because they have to support four elderly parents and two children of their own, on both counts twice the burden of other couples. Aging will affect the cities first, but the resulting urban labor shortage will be filled by an accelerated influx of mostly superfluous, well-educated rural youths, so the economic impact will remain limited.

At the end of the 1990s, based on different TFRs, Chinese demographers gave three scenarios for population growth until 2050. 1) TFR drops to 1.62 in 2010 and stays at that level (which corresponds to present birth policies); 2) TFR remains at about 1.8 (the level of the late 1990s); and 3) TFR increases from 1.8 in 2000 to 2.1 in 2010 and remains at that level (based on more liberal policies of two children per couple after 2010). An increase in life expectancy at birth was expected from 68.8 for men and 73.1 for women to 73.1 and 79.1 in 2050. The resulting population figures in 2050 for the three scenarios were 1272, 1369, or 1544 million people (*SFPC Bulletin*, 3 March 2002).

Around 2000, forecasts by the State Family Planning Commission, based on TFRs of 1.8 or 2.0, had peaks of 1.47 billion in 2033 or 1.57 billion in 2043, with total population declining to 1.41 billion and 1.56 billion, respectively, in 2050. Even the low forecast seems too high now, and a recent report by CASS predicted that China's population would peak between 2025 and 2030 at a level between 1.39 and 1.45 billion (*People's Daily Online*, 8 December 2005). The UN Population Division's 2004 revision (medium projection) sees a peak at 1.45 billion after 2030, followed by a decline to 1.39 billion by 2050. However, possibly under Chinese political pressure the UN has continued to use unrealistically low sex ratios at birth of 110 and 109 instead of the current 120 for its projections, so its computations should be revised downward. If the present infant sex ratio at birth of more than 120 persists, one needs TFRs greater than 2.3, not 2.1, for replacement of the current population.

Regional developments will differ. One may expect higher than average population growth in east China, primarily because of migration, and a loss of population, particularly the young and skilled, in the mountainous and hill areas in the interior. Many rural people will leave agriculture and move into small towns. In contrast, because of the current age structures of different provinces, future natural population increases will be highest in minority and border regions such as Tibet, Guizhou, Ningxia, Hainan, Gansu, Yunnan, and Guangxi (where the population under age 15 ranges from 26 percent to 31 percent), and lowest in Shanghai, Beijing, and Tianjin and in Heilongjiang, Jilin, and Liaoning (where the under-15 percentage is below 20). These opposing tendencies will partly offset each other.

Stabilizing the present low birth rate still depends on continued strong government efforts. Farmers demand sons to run the farm, the social security system is still in the making, and children still have an irreplaceable function in increasing family income and supporting the elderly. In cities, recent social developments have made birth control more problematic: the increase of unemployment, the privatization of enterprises and reorganization of service units, and the increase of the floating population and separation of migrants from home all provide conditions and opportunities for having more children than permitted (Zeng Peiyan 2001: 241–244). Also the general increase in wealth, privatization of housing, and relaxation of controls over the labor market have increased individual freedom of action. However, it is hard to predict where these changes will lead.

Apart from the above-mentioned questions, a fundamental unknown is how long we can expect continued acceptance by the populace of the legitimacy of government and its birth control regulations. Unpopular policies may be pursued and enforced for a longer period in China than would be possible in democratic countries. At the same time sudden policy shifts, whether impositions from above or concessions to popular demand, cannot be excluded. The expected moderate growth of China's population, when compared with most other developing countries, provides an extra argument why China is unwilling to sacrifice economic growth and increased consumption in response to global concerns about limited resources and environmental deterioration. China still has a long way to go before it reaches American and European levels of squandering global resources. One should worry not about the size of China's population, but rather about its social and economic institutions and people's attitudes toward those institutions and toward future generations. For better and worse, China is becoming a major actor on the world stage.

Notes

1 According to the official very narrow definition (that excludes people over 50, non-residents, and several other categories), urban unemployment was 4 to 5 percent; a more realistic figure would be 10 percent.

2 These official figures were released only after two decades.

3 Heavy requisitioning, wasteful consumption, and inadequate regional distribution all were due to unchecked Party policies, which were corrected only in 1961. Peng Xizhe (1987) noted that abnormally low monthly births occurred in some provinces in late 1958 and again in many in mid-1959.
He attributes these to the irrigation construction campaign, the 1958 communalization movement, and large-scale rural-to-urban migration, all of which interrupted peasant family life. Grain production shortages occurred only later.

4 Between 1990 and 2000, 76 percent of the 40 million interprovincial migrants moved to an eastern province, 62 percent of them originating from central and west China. Only 14 and 10 percent, respectively, went to a western or central province. As a result, Guangdong, Hainan, Xinjiang, and Ningxia provinces and Beijing and Shanghai had the

highest population increases, while Heilong-jiang, Liaoning, and Sichuan had the lowest.

5 A 2001 survey of interprovincial migrants between 15 and 50 years of age in 15 municipalities with large migrant populations showed that 87 percent were married (as against 82 percent in the 1997 survey of the general population). Anhui, Sichuan, Jiangxi, Henan, and Hubei were the most common provinces of origin (www.sfpc.gov.cn/cn/news2011126-1 and 20011204-1.htm).

6 White Paper of the Chinese Government, December 2000; "The Central Government recognizes that the conflict between population and development is acute," State Council Bulletin, Renmin Ribao 20/12/2000.

7 There is less concern over the effect of population growth on pollution, on climate change, and on other global problems. See, e.g., Shen Yimin, president of the China Population and Environment Society, in China Population and Environment Society (ed.), China Population and Environment, pp. 48–58.

8 For instance, the Fujian provincial government had stipulated that only areas where rural households had more than 3.3 hectares of farmland per household could have two children, and that miners were also allowed a second child (because of their high rate of accidental death). See Huang Shu-min (1998).

9 Unauthorized births were highest but also declining in Hainan (from 40 percent to 25 percent), Guangdong (24 percent to 14 percent), Guizhou (18 percent to 12 percent), and Ningxia (28 percent to 10 percent). The proportion of such births rose only in Shanxi (from 12 percent to 16 percent). Liaoning, Shandong, Tibet, and Inner Mongolia reported less than one percent of unauthorized births. (sfpcdata, 14/11/01).

10 Chinese respondents tend to give (and interviewers accept) the politically correct answer. For example, a survey of rural couples concluded "their main motives for birth control were 'responding to the call of the state' and 'becoming wealthy faster.' Only an extremely small number answered to be afraid of fines, which proves that birth control is spontaneous self-motivated behavior" and "man and wife usually agreed; those preferring one child did not have a clear gender preference." Renkou yu jingji 1998: 6.

11 For example, Lu Hongping, head of the Hebei University Population Research Institute, Renkou yanjiu 25(2001)4: 34.

12 Shi Hailong, vice-director of the State Family Planning Commission Propaganda Bureau, in Renkou yanjiu 25(2001)4: 28.

13 See, e.g., Li Zhang (2001) for a description of life in "Zhejiang village" near Beijing.

14 Melvyn Goldstein et al. (2002) found no evidence of enforcement of the three-child policy adopted for Tibet.

15 The other job seekers are 4 million and 2.7 million graduates, respectively, from colleges and secondary vocational schools, 2.1 million graduates from middle and high schools, 700,000 ex-servicemen, 1 million laid-off workers from state-owned enterprises, and 8.4 million registered unemployed people (Xinhuanet 1 January 2006).

References

Banister, J. 1998. "Population, public health and the environment in China," The China Quarterly 156: 986–1015.

CASS Institute of Population Studies. 1997–2000. Zhongguo renkou nianjian 1997, 1998, 1999, 2000 (Almanac of China's Population). Beijing: Zhongguo minhang chubanshe (1997) and CASS (subsequent years).

Chang Chongxuan (ed.). 1993. Zhongguo shengyu jieyu chouxiang diaocha Beijing guoji yantaohui lunwenji (Collection of articles of the Beijing Conference on the sample survey of fertility and birth control in China). Beijing: Zhongguo renkou chubanshe.

China Population and Environment Society (ed.). 1996. China Population and Environment. Beijing: China Environmental Science Press.

Chu Junhong. 2000. "Zhongguo nongcun chanqian xingbie xuanzedi jueding yinsu fenxi" (Determinants of prenatal sex selection in rural China), Zhongguo renkou kexue (China population science) 1: 61–66.

Coale, A. J. and J. Banister. 1994. "Five decades of missing females in China," *Demography* 31(3): 459–479.

Cooney, R. S. and Jiali Li. 1994. "Household registration type and compliance with the "one child" policy in China, 1979–1988," *Demography* 31(1): 21–32.

Deng Guosheng and Guo Zhigang. 1999. "Hunyin yongji yanjiu" (On marriage squeeze), in *Zhongguo renkou nianjian* (Population Yearbook of China). Beijing: CASS Institute of Population Studies, pp. 92–128.

Dikötter, F. 1998. *Imperfect Conceptions: Medical Knowledge, Birth Defects and Eugenics in China.* London: Hurst.

Goldstein, M. C., B. Jiao (Benjor), C.. M. Beall, and P. Tsering. 2002. "Fertility and family planning in rural Tibet," *The China Journal* 47: 19–39.

Goodman, D. (ed.). 2004. *China's Campaign to "Open Up the West": National, Provincial and Local Perspectives.* New York: Cambridge University Press.

Greenhalgh, S. 2005. "Population science, missile science: The origins of China's one-child policy," *The China Quarterly* 182: 253–276.

Greenhalgh, S. and E. A. Winckler. 2005. *Governing China's Population: From Leninist to Neoliberal Biopolitics.* Stanford: Stanford University Press.

Guojia tongjiju (State Statistical Bureau) (comp.). 2000–2003. *Zhongguo renkou tongji nianjian 2000–2003* (China population statistics yearbook 2000–2003). Beijing: China Statistics Press.

———. 2005. *2005 Zhongguo fazhan baogao* (2005 China Development Report). Beijing: China Statistics Press.

Huang Shu-min. 1998. *The Spiral Road: Change in a Chinese Village Through the Eyes of a Communist Party Leader.* Boulder: Westview Press, p. 179.

Li Baihua. 1999. "Guanyu funü shengzhi jiankang zhuangkuangdi diaocha baogao" (Report of a survey about reproductive health of women), *Zhongguo renkou nianjian 1999*: 159–184.

Li Ling. 2001. "Gaige gaifang yilai Zhongguo guonei renkou qianyi jiqi yanjiu" (Internal population migration in China since the reforms and opening-up: a review), *Dili yanjiu* (Geographical research) 20(4) 453–462.

Li Peilin (ed.). 2003. *Nongmingong: Zhongguo jincheng nongmingongdi jingji shehui fenxi* (Rural migrant workers: an analysis of the economy and society of Chinese rural workers entering the cities). Beijing: Shehui kexue wenjian chubanshe.

Li Zhang. 2001. *Strangers in the City: Reconfigurations of Space, Power and Social Networks within China's Floating Population.* Stanford: Stanford University Press.

Lin Liangmin et al. 1996. "1991–1993-nian Zhongguo ying'er, 5 sui yixia ertong siwang shuiping ji qushi fenxi" (Mortality levels in infants and children below 5 and trends in China, 1991–1993), *Renkou yanjiu* (Population research) 4: 50–56.

Ma Kai. 2005. *2005-nian Zhongguo guomin jingji he shehui fazhan baogao* (Report on China's national economic and social development for 2005). Beijing: China Statistics Press.

Murphy, Rachel. 2002. *How Migrant Labour is Changing Rural China.* New York: Cambridge University Press.

National Agricultural Census Office of China and FAO Statistics Centre (comp.). 1998. *Abstract of the First National Agricultural Census in China.* Beijing: China Statistics Press.

———. 2000. *Abstract of the First National Agricultural Census in China (supplementary tables).* Beijing: China Statistics Press.

Peng Xizhe. 1987. "Demographic consequences of the great leap forward in China's provinces," *Population and Development Review* 13(4): 639–670.

Peng Xizhe and Guo Zhigang. 2000. *The Changing Population of China.* Oxford: Blackwell Publishers.

Poston, D. L., Jr. et al. 1990. "The distribution of overseas Chinese in the contemporary world," *International Migration Review* 24(3): 480–506.

Renkou yu huanjing shehuixue yanjiuhui (Population and environment research society) (ed.). 1998. *Zhongguo renkou yu huanjing (China's population and environment)*. Vol. 4. Beijing: China Environmental Sciences Press.

Short, Susan et al. 2002. "Maternal work and child care in China," Population *and Development Review* 28(1) 31–35.

State Family Planning Commission (SFPC). 1995, 1996. *Zhongguo jihua shengyu nianjian 1995, 1996*. (State Family Planning Yearbook 1995, 1996) Beijing: SFPC Press
———. 2001. *Bulletin of Birth Planning Statistics* 1, July 19.

Tuan Chi-hsien et al. 1990. "The size of family and household in China: An analysis based on the 1982 census," in Zeng Yi et al., pp. 22–57.

Vermeer, Eduard B. 2004. "Egalitarianism and the land question in China," *China Information* 18(1) 107–140.

———. 2003. "Determinants of income from wages in rural Wuxi and Baoding: a survey of 22 villages," *The Journal of Peasant Studies* 30(3/4): 93–120.

Yang Tao and Marjorie Elroy. 2000. "Zhongguo renkou zhengce dui shengyu di yingxiang" (The influence of China's population policy on the birth rate), *Zhongguo renkou kexue* (China population science) 3.

Yang Zihui. 1997. "Zhongguo liudong renkou yu chengshihua yanjiu," (Research on China's floating population and urbanization) in *Zhongguo renkou nianjian 1997*, pp. 111–118.

Zeng Peiyan (ed.). 2001. *2001-nian Zhongguo guomin jingji he shehui fazhan baogao* (Report on China's national economic and social development for 2001). Beijing: Zhongguo jihua chubanshe, pp. 241–244.

Zeng Yi et al. (eds.). 1990. *Changing Family Structure and Population Aging in China*. Beijing: Peking University Press.

Zhang Hanxiang. 2002. "Statement on Agenda Item 4 at the 35th Session of the UNPDC," www.sfpc.go.cn/EN/enews20020402-1.htm.

Zhang Pin. 1993. "Zhongguo weifa hunyin xianzhuang yu fenxi," (The situation of illegal marriages in China and an analysis) *Shehuixue yanjiu* (Sociological research) 5: 89–91.

Zhao Zhongwei. 1997. "Deliberate birth control under a high fertility regime: Reproductive behaviour in China before 1970," *Population and Development Review* 23(4) 729–767.

Zhongguo guojia tongjiju. 1994. *Zhongguo minzu renkou ziliao—1990 renkou pucha* (Tabulation on China's Nationality—The 1990 Census). Beijing: China Statistics Press.

Zhonghua renmin gongheguo guowuyuan xinwen bangongshi. 2000. "Zhongguo ershiyi shiji renkou yu fazhan" (Population and development of China in the 21st century), in *Renmin ribao* Dec. 12. Also by Foreign Languages Press, *White Papers of the Chinese Government (3)*, Beijing 2002.

Zhou Guangzhao (ed.). 2000. *Zhongguo kezhixu fazhan zhanlüe: lingdao ganbu tuben* (A strategy for China's sustainable development: a reader for leading cadres) Beijing: Xiyuan chubanshe.

India: Population Change and Its Consequences

Deepak Lal

In the 1980s I wrote two books—*The Poverty of "Development Economics"* (1983/2000) and *The Hindu Equilibrium* (1988/2005).[1] The first questioned the intellectual consensus on dirigiste trade and development policies; the second, the view that India's age-old poverty was due to over-population. These repudiated views on which I was brought up in the early 1960s at Oxford. I know the first of these works of revisionism has had some effect in changing perceptions on the appropriateness of "outward-looking" policies for development. But I had not realized the once heretical view that the "population problem" is not a problem (except in the very short run, and only if appropriate policies are not in place) is also now very much the consensus view (see Kelley 2001). My late friend Julian Simon, who was universally reviled by mainstream economists for his view that a large population is a country's ultimate resource, is now seen to have been proved right by a burgeoning body of research. During the mid-1970s to mid-1980s I was also associated with the World Bank's research establishment. The sheaf of old memos in my files from those days demonstrates how entrenched was the old dirigiste consensus in an institution that is now seen as having been in the vanguard of the new revisionist consensus on population and development.[2] So, returning in this essay to the issues discussed in the first edition of *The Hindu Equilibrium*, I feel rather like the old lady who went to see *King Lear* and found it full of quotations!

I will first review what is now known of the economic effects of population growth over the last century in India, including the emerging concerns that have been expressed by the environmental movement and why their attempts to legislate their "habits of the heart" pose real dangers for the welfare of the poor in India.[3] I then examine the social and political consequences of this population growth.

Economic effects of population growth

Many people find the Malthusian fear, that in a country with limited land and natural resources excessive human breeding will lead to the continuing immiserization of labor, intuitively obvious. At its crudest, this fear is based on the law of diminishing returns from increases in only one factor of production, and on the simple arithmetic of calculating per capita income as a ratio of gross national product to population. Thus if an infant is born to a cow, per capita income goes up, but if an infant is born to a human it goes down. But there is also an emotional response, expressed for instance by Paul Ehrlich, who in his famous book *The Population Bomb* writes: "I came to understand [the population explosion] emotionally one stinking hot night in Delhi.... The streets seemed alive with people. People eating, people washing, people sleeping. People visiting, arguing, and screaming. People thrusting their hands through the taxi window, begging. People defecating and urinating. People clinging to buses. People herding animals. People, people, people, people" (Ehrlich 1968: 15). Many Westernized Indians share this emotional response as well as the crude intellectualizing of the "population problem." So it is not surprising that Sanjay Gandhi believed that India's problems of poverty could be solved by coercive sterilization of the poor. The resulting civil resistance provoked by the mass sterilization camps and by the Emergency declared by his mother, Prime Minister Indira Gandhi, in the mid-1970s led to the virtual abandonment of family planning programs in India.

Yet, as economic historians and many eminent economists have known, Malthus had been overtaken by the "demographic transition," first in the West, then in East Asia, and by the time Sanjay Gandhi began his sterilization campaign, also in India. This can be seen from the relevant demographic data for the twentieth century in India, summarized in Table 1. As is well known from the new household economics (see Becker 1981, 1991) and the economic history of the industrial world, a decline in mortality, particularly infant mortality, due to better sanitation, vaccination, and other means of controlling infectious diseases, is followed with a lag by a decline in birth rates as families seeking the same completed family size adjust their childbearing habits to the new mortality regime. Furthermore, if economic progress raises the opportunity costs of the time spent in rearing children, parents will substitute quality for the quantity of children in their childbearing choices.

This path has been validated for India, which except for the brief period of the Emergency had an exhortative and informative rather than coercive family planning program. It is debatable whether India's family planning program had much effect in reducing fertility (see Mamdani 1972). India's demographic transition would have proceeded more rapidly if more

TABLE 1   Demographic and economic change in India, census years, 1901–2001

	Annual percentage growth rate of population	Birth rate	Death rate	Growth rate of GDP	Infant mortality rate	Life expectancy		Growth rate of per capita GDP
						Female	Male	
1901	0.30	49.2	42.6		210			
1911	0.56	48.1	47.2	2.1	204	23.3	22.6	1.5
1921	−0.03	46.2	36.3	−0.8	219	20.9	19.4	−0.9
1931	1.06	45.2	31.2	2.3	174	26.6	26.9	1.3
1941	1.34	39.9	27.4	0.8	161	31.4	32.1	−0.6
1951	1.26	40.9	22.8	−0.5	146	31.7	32.4	−1.7
1961	1.98	40.0	17.6	3.7	129	40.6	41.9	1.8
1971	2.20	37.8	15.4	3.3	110	44.7	46.4	1.0
1981	2.22	34.0	13.0	3.5	92	54.7	54.1	1.2
1991	2.14	30.0	10.0	5.4	75	60.9	59.7	3.1
2001	1.93	26.0	9.0	6.2	70	61.8	60.4	4.3

SOURCE: Lal (2005).

intensive public health measures had been taken to reduce infant mortality and if the country's economic growth rate had been increased by an earlier abandonment of the dirigiste Nehruvian model of development.

The most sophisticated argument for public action to limit fertility was based on the purported "market failure" attributable to technological (not pecuniary) externalities, which caused a discrepancy between the private and public costs of childrearing.[4] The empirical study by Lee and Miller (1990) found positive or no Pareto-relevant economic external effects from childbearing, and the negative externalities they did find for India (and Saudi Arabia) were entirely due to the presumed dilution by a larger population of the average claim on the country's mineral wealth, mainly coal. But this is a factor of little relevance in a globalized world, where a country's wealth no longer depends directly on its location-specific mineral resources. Moreover, as Lee and Miller note, "if we take the plausible view that Indian coal reserves have low value, then India would…[have] net externalities close to zero" (p. 290). Hence their conclusion in favor of a laissez-faire population policy that does not "go beyond assisting well-informed parents to attain the family size goals they seek" (p. 296).

Demographic trends

Figure 1 charts the crude birth and death rates for India during the past century from the censuses,[5] while Figure 2 charts the growth rates of population, per capita GDP, and GDP.[6] The decline in the death rate, as demographic transition theory predicts, has been faster than the fall in the birth rate, so that the population growth rate continued to rise until 1981. Since

FIGURE 1   India: Birth and death rates 1901–2001

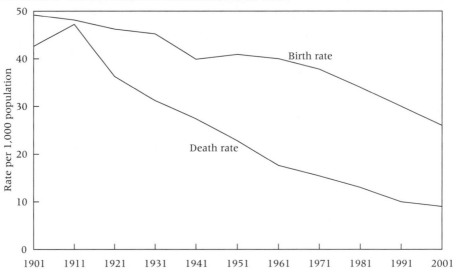

then the birth rate has been declining faster than the death rate. Figure 3 charts the birth rate and the infant mortality rate.[7]

There has been a rise in the mean age at marriage and a decline in the age-specific marital fertility rate, the latter attributable to the spread of contraceptive practices. But, as Visaria (1987) noted, "it is futile to discuss

FIGURE 2   Growth rates of population, GDP, per capita GDP, India 1901–2001

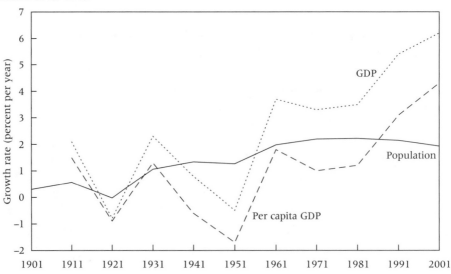

FIGURE 3 Birth rates and infant mortality rates, India 1901–2001

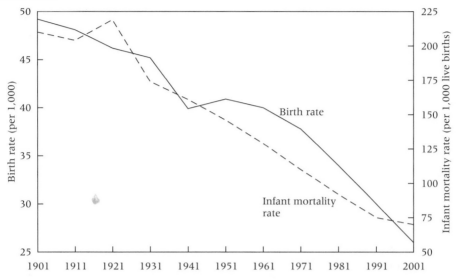

whether the increase in the level of contraception should be attributed wholly or only in part to the official program to promote family planning" (p. 140). The sex ratio of the population rose from 1029 males per 1000 females in 1901 to 1079 in 1991 and then fell slightly to 1071 in 2001.[8]

The masculinity of the Indian population has spawned a large litera-ture attempting to explain the male sex bias, particularly in the northern as compared with the southern states (see Mayer 1999 for a succinct survey). But as Mayer rightly argues, given the historical sex bias in favor of males in India, particularly in the north, the rise in the sex ratio still needs to be explained. If it is to be explained as purely due to the anti-female bias of Indians, this bias would have to be increasing to yield the trends in increas-ing masculinity over the twentieth century. But, as can be seen from Figure 4, which charts the sex ratios and the life expectancy at birth for males and females, female life expectancy has been rising along with the rising sex ratio, so there could not have been a rising sex bias against females—what Mayer labels the "mortality paradox." This question is resolved by observ-ing from Figure 4 that life expectancy for females did not catch up with and surpass that for males until 1981. The lag in the decline of female mortality as compared with that for males is sufficient to explain the rising sex ratio. For "if successive cohorts of children born in the intervals between decen-nial censuses experience higher rates of survival than those that have pre-ceded them, then those cohorts will be correspondingly larger. If the boys in each of those new cohorts experience slightly greater improvement than the girls, then we might well find that while all children gain in survival,

FIGURE 4   Sex ratio (M/F) and life expectancy at birth for males and females, India 1901–2001

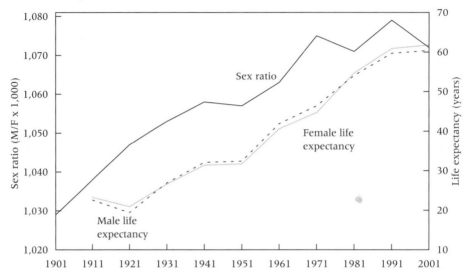

during the period of population transition the number of males would become larger than the number of females (Mayer 1999: 334–335).

China, too, has the growing problem of a highly distorted sex ratio. It has been suggested (Oster 2005; Barro 2005) that the problem of the missing women (Sen 1990) in both India and China is caused by the prevalence of hepatitis B in women, which leads to their giving birth to a higher proportion of male children than the norm. But, in a recent examination of this biological thesis, Das Gupta (2005) convincingly shows, by examining the sex ratios for different birth orders, that for both India and China the sex ratio is "closely related to the sex composition of the children already born in the family" (p. 533). Hence biological factors cannot provide the dominant explanation, and the main causes for the overall sex bias appear to be sex-selective abortion and neglect of female infants, based on the cultural preference for males in certain regions in both countries.

These aggregate trends, of course, conceal very large regional variations in a vast country with a great variety of ecological conditions, which as we know (see Lal 1998; Goody 1990, 1996) influence family patterns and "heirship strategies" in premodern agrarian societies and, thence, demographic trends. Mari Bhat's (1998) mapping of fertility regimes in the districts of India from the census data for 1981 and 1991 shows the north–south divide and the decline in fertility moving inward from the coast. His multivariate analysis of the data shows that the case for patriarchy and female autonomy as causes of regional variations in fertility has been overstated, and that differences in social structure (rather than structural factors) and ideational factors (mainly due to differences in exposure to the mass media) are the major variables explaining the differences in fertility across districts. But, as Dyson (2001) notes there is evidence from the 2001 census that while in most states the rise in the male sex ratio is fairly modest, in Punjab, Haryana, Maharashtra, and Gujarat there has been a marked rise in the male child sex ratio since 1991, which is due to sex-selective abortions (Das Gupta and Bhat 1999). Explaining this in terms of the new household economics should be a fruitful topic for future research.

Even anthropologists (see Goody 1990) argue that divergences in the domestic domain are conditioned by differences in ecological regimes, forms of social stratification, differing needs for insurance (see Rosenzweig 1988), and heirship strategies. Two examples will have to suffice. Numerous observers have commented favorably on the balanced sex ratio in the state of Kerala, along with its positive social indicators despite low economic growth. It is not often noted, however, that polygyny, which is uncommon among human populations (see Kuper 1994), arose among the Nairs of Kerala. Particular historical circumstances led Nair men to specialize as mercenary soldiers, who were absent for long periods, which led to the female-based family arrangements, which in turn made this way of life possible. When, after annexing Malabar, the British in 1792 suppressed the military system that had underwritten this domestic system, polyandry also died out. But the enhanced status of women and its social and economic correlates cast a long shadow on the social performance of Kerala. In the context of the relationship of population growth and various social indicators to be discussed below, it should be noted that, despite these better social indicators, the level of malnutrition in Kerala is among the highest in India (see Kumar 1993). This is probably because of "the weaknesses in real economic performance [which] have arguably played a crucial role in restraining the capacity of the economy to stimulate employment conditions, increase incomes and nutritional levels, and thereby raise long-term living standards" (ibid.: 337). This underlines the importance of economic growth in the sustainable alleviation of poverty (see Lal and Myint 1996).

The second example is the study by Monica Das Gupta (1998) of fertility decline in 11 villages of Ludhiana district that were originally part of the famous Khanna study (Wyon and Gordon 1971). As she notes, fertility decline started in this area when the "society was overwhelmingly agrarian, illiterate, had infant mortality well above 150 per thousand livebirths, and was without modern contraceptive technology" (p. 91). She finds that historically, as in Europe, joint families tried to keep a balance between population and available resources through regulating marriage and through permanent celibacy to avoid subdivision of land, given the system of partible inheritance. These traditional means of dealing with fluctuations in population were inadequate when sustained mortality decline began in the 1920s. This then led to a concerted effort at fertility reduction, so that "By the time Mamdani visited this area and concluded that for these people reducing fertility would mean 'courting economic disaster,' the total fertility rate had already fallen by nearly 40 per cent, and all the socioeconomic groups in these villages were engaged in rapid fertility decline" (p. 92).

The major conclusion we can derive from these noneconomic perspectives is that, at the micro level, there is likely to be a complex pattern of fertility decline as well as changes in the sex ratio. But households are still responding to the underlying forces determining the macro picture—the decline in infant mortality rates, followed by a decline in birth rates—and even at the micro level the material factors—the relationship of population to available resources, the nature of localized risks, and heirship strategies—are all best studied as part of the new household economics.

It is instructive to compare India's more laissez-faire approach to population control with the coercive policies adopted by China through its draconian one-child policy. These coercive policies undoubtedly accelerated China's demographic transition, but they have bred serious problems for the future. The most important is the premature aging of its population, which is projected to begin in 2010, with the ratio of the working-age population to retirees falling from 6 today to 2 in 2040 (UN 2002), when even with its current spectacular economic growth rate China will confront the problems of caring for the old currently facing most developed countries but with possibly a lower per capita income. Equally serious is the social stress likely to be caused with the ending of the Maoist "iron rice bowl" and the privatization of health, education, and housing, along with the emergence of the "4-2-1" phenomenon: four grandparents and two only-child parents being supported by one child. Finally, and perhaps most important is the welfare loss the Chinese have suffered as a result of having their preferences for children (and the joy they bring) being overruled by a coercive state.

By contrast India, with its more natural demographic transition, will not see an aging of its population until after mid-century. This, of course, implies that India's population is expected to stabilize at a much higher level (1.6 billion) than China's (1.4 billion). But with its traditional family systems still secure (see Lal 2006), India should be able to cope better than China with the eventual aging of its population, particularly if it completes its economic reforms and continues growing at its potential rate of growth of about 8 percent per annum for the next few decades.

Employment, poverty, and population growth

This leads us to the effects of population growth on employment and wages and thus on poverty. The main fear underlying the population problem was that all these indicators of socioeconomic performance would be worsened by rapid population growth. As I noted in *The Hindu Equilibrium* (1989, vol. 2: 10–11), these fears seemed to ignore the most simple outcomes of an open economy. As the well-known Rybczynski and Stolper–Samuelson theorems of trade theory show, in an open economy the effect on the real wage of a population expansion depends upon what happens to the relative world price of the labor-intensive goods whose production will expand with the expansion of the labor supply. If there is no change in this relative price, there will be no change in the real wage. Also, of course, without any barriers to employment in such a model, there is no need for any of the additional labor to be unemployed. Thus there is no necessity of any increase in unemployment or poverty caused by declining wages following a population increase in an efficient open economy.[9]

These predictions have been borne out for India (Lal 1989, vol. 2). Despite the large increase in population, the National Sample Survey (NSS) data indicate that "rates of unemployment in India have not only (a) been low between 1972–73 and 1987–88, but also (b) have declined between 1983 and 1987–88, and that (c) this decline does not seem to have been at the cost of an increase in visible unemployment" (Visaria and Minhas 1991/ 1993: 149). Nor has there been any decline in labor force participation rates, which according to the NSS have been stable since the 1960s at "around 41–42 percent" (ibid.: 139).

This is so despite the slow growth of employment in the formal organized sector at the rate of 1.6 percent per annum between 1979 and 1989 (ibid.: 142). During the era of partial reform, organized-sector employment rose from 26.4 million in 1990 to 28.1 million in 1999, that is, at the rate of only 0.65 percent a year. This reflects the capital-intensive bias of Indian industrialization, which goes back to the implicit tax on labor that was instituted in the late nineteenth century by the various labor laws introduced by the British Raj and maintained to this day by the government of India (see Lal 1988, vol. 1: 208–209, 260–264; also see Visaria and Minhas 1991/ 1993: 152).

Much of the increase in employment has been in the service and construction sectors. Thus, from NSS data it appears that, between 1972 and 1988, while agriculture's share in the industrial distribution of increments to the male workforce declined from 40 percent to 12 percent and while that of mining and manufacturing was stable at around 19–20 percent, construction's share rose from 3.4 to 19.6 percent and that of trade and restaurants from 18 to 23 percent, and of other services from 9 to 14 percent (Visaria and Minhas 1991/1993: Table A3). Banking and insurance grew at the rate of 13.1 percent per annum between 1980 and 2000, while communications (which includes the information technology sector) has grown at the rate of 16.6 percent per annum since the reforms of 1991. There has been a large increase in public administration and defense, whose relative share in GDP has risen from 3.1 percent in 1950–51 to 7.8 percent in 1999–2000 (Sivasubramonian 2000: 601, 604).

Nor, as had been feared, has the eight-fold increase in high school and college graduates from 1961 to the late 1980s led to a worsening of unemployment among the educated (see Blaug, Layard, and Woodhall 1969). The data from the three NSS surveys of 1977–78, 1983, and 1987–88 "show a clear decline in the unemployment rates for the matriculates and the higher educated" (Visaria and Minhas 1991/1993: 147). Much of the increase in employment of the educated has been in self-employment. The rise in the rate of unemployment as measured by the employment exchange registrations is not a true measure of educated unemployment, as there is no requirement for those on the register to be unemployed. As outlined in Lal (1989, vol. 2), the numbers on these registers reflect the excess demand for public sector jobs, which usually pay a higher wage with security of tenure than equivalent private sector jobs, and to get these jobs the applicant has to be on the register. So, as I showed in Lal (1988a, 1989), the numbers on the unemployment register can be explained in terms of a variant of the well-known Harris–Todaro migration model, as depending upon the changing public–private sector wage differential.

The most enduring myth about the relationship of population growth, wages, and poverty was the belief in the existence of vast pools of surplus labor in India. Following on from the models of Lewis (1954) and Fei and Ranis (1964), it was believed that, because of overpopulation, there was a perfectly elastic supply of rural labor available at a given institutional wage. This implied that until the surplus was absorbed through increases in the demand for labor greater than the increments in supply, there would be no rise in wages (whether rural or industrial) for the mass of Indian workers, and hence no alleviation of India's age-old poverty. In *The Hindu Equilibrium* I argued against this Malthusian view and showed how the alternative Boserupian perspective better described the changing fortunes of the rural countryside.

As is well known, Boserup (1965) argued that population pressure both induces and facilitates the adoption of more intensive forms of agriculture. She identifies the differing input-per-hectare requirements of different agrarian systems by the frequency with which a particular piece of land is cropped. Thus settled agriculture is more labor- and capital-intensive than nomadic pastoralism, which in turn is more intensive in these inputs than hunting and gathering or the slash and burn agriculture practiced until recently in parts of Africa and the tribal regions of India. Contrary to Malthusian presumptions, she argues that population growth leads to the adoption of more advanced techniques that raise yields per hectare. Because these new techniques require increased labor effort, they will not be adopted until rising population reduces the per capita food output that can be produced with existing techniques and forces a change.[10]

Boserup's theory is of considerable interest in explaining India's long-run agricultural growth performance. In *The Hindu Equilibrium* I provided some tentative and imperfect evidence that the population of the subcontinent in times of peace and stability remained relatively constant between 100 and 140 million from about 320 BC until the late eighteenth century. There was a mild expansion of about 0.45 percent per annum in the nineteenth century and the early part of the twentieth. From the 1920s, as we have seen, population has increased steadily because of the dramatic reductions in mortality. Because of the time it takes humans to reach adulthood, however, the population bulge did not affect the rural labor supply until the 1950s. Thus the Malthusian fear of the immiserization of labor could be expected to be most potent in the period after Independence.

Indian agriculture grew relatively slowly until 1946, at about 0.94 percent per annum between 1878 and 1900, and at 0.62 percent per annum between 1900 and 1946. But since Independence from 1950–51 to 1983–84 growth accelerated to 2.18 percent. This improved agricultural performance was responsible for the modest growth in per capita income of about 1.39 percent per annum from 1950–51 until the early 1980s. From 1980–81 until 1999–2000, agriculture grew at the rate of 3.2 percent per annum, which exceeds the population growth rate of 2 percent per annum over the period, while per capita income has grown at the rate of 3.1 percent per annum between 1980 and 1991 and at the rate of 4.3 percent since the reforms of 1991. Thus, looked at in the broad sweep of history, population growth and agricultural growth have gone hand in hand in India. There is evidence that this was due to the Boserupian process.

First, until recently Indian agriculture was faced with a shortage of labor. Thus, for instance, even in 1965–70 total agricultural area per inhabitant in India was 0.33 hectares compared with 0.06 for Japan. Until about 1921, the modest expansion of population was accommodated by extending the land frontier, with relatively unchanged technology and cropping patterns. Thereafter, more intensive methods of cultivation were called for. Comparing the period 1901 to 1940–41 with 1950–51 to 1970–71 (see Table 2), we see a rise in the output/labor ratio. This was achieved by a more rapid extension of both the net sown area and the double-cropped area, so that the total cropped area increased between 1950 and 1971 in rough proportion to the rural work force. More remarkable was the change in the rate of capital formation in agriculture in the two periods, with the capital/labor ratio being stagnant in the first period, and rising by over 30 percent between 1950 and 1970. Part of this increased capital formation was of the land-saving variety (mainly in the form of irrigation, which permits multiple cropping). Clearly in this second period, as compared with the first, capital was being used to

TABLE 2 Agricultural ratios and elasticities

	1901–41	1950–70	1970–2000
Percent change			
Output/labor	16.8	35.3	28.2
Output/capital	na	3.8	4.9
Capital/labor	0	31.1	21.6
Capital/land			
Net sown area	na	39.2	102.3
Total sown area	na	30.7	82.3
Land/labor			
Net sown area	−8.7	−6.1	−39.8
Total sown area	−6.7	0.8	−33.6
Elasticities			
Output/labor	2.5	2.7	1.7
Land/labor			
Net sown area	0.22	0.71	0.02
Total sown area	0.36	1.03	0.18
Output/land			
Net sown area	11.29	3.85	83.0
Total sown area	7.02	2.71	9.2
Capital/labor	na	2.54	1.53

SOURCE: Lal (1988, 2005: Table 7,4) and derived from official statistics.

substitute for land, which was becoming scarce, as is evident from the steady decline in the land/labor ratio over the 70-year period.

Various elasticity estimates derived in Table 2 bear out the role of population growth in driving these changes. The elasticity or responsiveness of output with respect to labor supply remained relatively constant over the two periods—a cornerstone of Boserup's hypothesis. But the responses to the differing growth rates of labor supply were markedly different in the two periods. The elasticity of land and capital with respect to labor increased greatly from the pre-Independence period when labor supply growth was low, to the post-Independence period when it was more rapid. The elasticity of double-cropped land with respect to labor supply rose to unity, through the increase both in new land and in multiple cropping. But the most important factor keeping the elasticity of output with respect to labor constant has been the marked rise in the capital/labor supply elasticity. Because much of this capital formation is labor intensive, we can assume, following Boserup, that it is more likely the increased labor supply induced this increased capital formation than the other way around.

Since 1970, there has been virtually no increase in the net sown area, but a 12 percent increase in the gross sown area between 1970 and 1990. This increase is largely due to the increase in the percentage of the net sown area that is irrigated, which has risen by 115 percent between 1970 and 1990 (see Lal 2005: Ch. 11.4). Output per laborer was virtually stagnant between 1970 and 1980, but rose by 18.3 percent from 1980 to 1990 and 18.4 percent between 1990 and 2000. This reflects the spread of the Green Revolution, with the fraction of the total cropped area under high-yielding varieties rising from 15.1 percent in 1970–71 to 66.6 percent in 1993–94.

Two other pieces of evidence support Boserup's thesis. First is the near constancy of per capita net domestic product in agriculture from 1950–51 to 1984–85 (see Dandekar 1988). But it has risen by 21 percent between the mid-1980s and 2001. So, I would conjecture that after the mid-1980s the Boserupian process has ended, with agricultural growth becoming dependent on shifts in the production function associated with technical change rather than on the increasing labor intensity of production induced by population expansion.

Second, what I have called the Ishikawa curve for the Indian states for 1970–71 also supports the Boserup hypothesis for Indian agriculture. Ishikawa (1967) argues that in the traditional subsistence cultivation of rice, the relationship between land productivity and per farm holding of cultivated land is a rectangular hyperbola, so that, roughly speaking, increases in total output keep pace with rural labor supply (which is the force reducing farm size). Figure 5 shows the Ishikawa curve for the Indian states in 1970–71. Because Punjab and Haryana had already begun their Green Revolutions, moving them out of the traditional subsistence agricultural process, they were excluded from the statistical estimation. As Figure 5 shows, apart from these two states, the others were taking part in the Boserup process—

FIGURE 5   Ishikawa curve for 1970–71

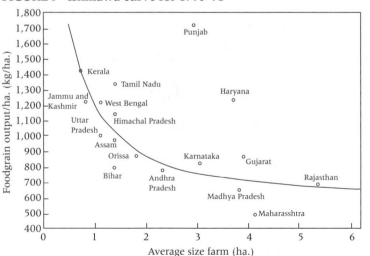

crawling up the Ishikawa curve with population expansion. Since then, many other states have moved away from the Ishikawa curve thanks to the Green Revolution (see Lal 2005: Figure 11.4(b)).

If the Boserupian process applies to India, one of the basic assumptions underlying the surplus labor view would be invalid. Surplus labor in India has been estimated as the amount of surplus labor time that is available from some given norm of working hours per day (see Mehra 1966). But in an economy undergoing a Boserupian transformation, the surplus of labor time would be very high in the least labor-intensive form of agriculture because the labor input required to obtain the necessary food output would be very low. This surplus of labor time would then decrease as we looked at more and more intensive agricultural systems with their increasing labor input required to keep per capita food output constant. This transformation would not tell us anything about the supply price of rural labor in these systems. Once we take account of the wage at which people are willing to work, taking account of the leisure-versus-income choice facing rural labor, then, even in overpopulated countries (as Sen 1966 showed), surplus labor in the sense of a constant (perfectly elastic) supply of labor at a given wage would imply that leisure was an inferior good.

That this is not so is borne out by various studies which have estimated wage elasticities for rural labor in India (see Lal 1989, vol. 2; Bardhan 1979, 1984; Rosenzweig 1978, 1980; Evenson and Binswanger 1984). They provide powerful evidence against the hypothesis of a horizontal supply curve of rural labor supply. They find that the wage elasticities of both rural labor demand and supply are low. Therefore, far from increases in demand not increasing rural wages, one can expect, ceteris paribus, a substantial increase.

In terms of the Boserupian process, over a long historical time scale we would expect that with population expansion the supply curve for labor would shift rightward with an accompanying rightward shift in the demand curve to maintain a relatively constant per capita level of living (implicit rural wage). Around this long-term trend, however, there would be large short-term shifts (in both directions) in the labor demand curve due to variations in the climate, which, given the low wage elasticities, would lead to large short-term movements in real agricultural wages around a nearly constant trend. This is what the historical record shows to have been true of rural wages, until the recent Green Revolution led to a massive increase in the demand for labor and thence a marked rise in rural real wages (see Lal 1989, vol. 2).

Because the surplus labor hypothesis is invalid, so is its corollary that mass poverty would not be alleviated until the rural labor surplus is removed. This can be seen from Table 3, which gives data on the poverty ratios for rural and urban India from the NSS and the National Council of Applied Economic Research (NCAER) household survey data. Of these, for

TABLE 3   Poverty headcount ratios: India (percent)

	Planning Commission (NSS)		NCAER	
	Rural	Urban	Rural	Urban
1970–71	57.33	45.89		
1983	45.6	40.79		
1987–88	39.09	38.2	39.09	38.02
1993–94	37.27	32.36	30.86	24.37
1997–98	38.5	34	17.98	12.63

SOURCE: Tendulkar (1998); Lal, Mohan, and Natarajan (2001).

the reasons explained in Lal, Mohan, and Natarajan (2001), the NCAER series is the more reliable. It is by now a well-established stylized fact that the only cure for mass structural poverty is rapid income growth, with poverty ratios falling as soon as countries' per capita incomes are growing above about 2.5 percent per annum (Lal and Myint 1996). Not until the 1980s, when Indian per capita income growth rose above what had been termed the "Hindu rate of growth" of about 1.5 percent, did poverty ratios start falling, and the fall accelerated with the boost to the GDP growth rate given by the partial liberalization of the economy in the wake of the economic reforms in 1991.

Table 4 summarizes Sivasubramonian's (2000) estimates of the sources of growth for the pre-Independence period (1900–01 to 1946–47) and for the period 1950–51 to 1997–98. There is no evidence that the increase in the population growth rate has adversely affected GDP growth. In fact, in the period of high population growth following Independence, total factor

TABLE 4   Sources of growth of real GDP: India 1901–97/98

Rates of growth	Undivided India 1900–01 to 1946–47			India 1950–51 to 1997–98		
	Agriculture	Non-agriculture	Total	Agriculture	Non-agriculture	Total
GDP	0.44	1.69	0.92	2.6	5.1	4
Persons employed	0.4	0.42	0.41	1.5	2.1	1.7
Capital stock including land	0.45	3.02	1.13	2.5	4.5	4
Combined factor inputs	0.41	1.12	0.56	1.69	2.74	2.22
Increase in output per unit of input	0.03	0.57	0.36	0.91	2.36	1.78

SOURCE: Sivasubramonian (2000: Tables 7.21 and 9.34.).

productivity growth accelerated in both agriculture and nonagriculture. Thus population growth, far from damaging, has probably helped economic performance, and fears concerning the effects on wages, employment, and poverty have proved to be misplaced. It is owing to India's failure—until the 1990s—to accelerate its growth rate, because of the inward-looking dirigiste economic policies it adopted in the post-Independence Nehruvian era, that performance on these fronts has not been even better.[11]

Demographic transition, dependency, savings, and growth

One of the inimical effects of population growth was supposed to manifest itself through rising dependency ratios, which depressed savings and thus damaged economic growth. This conventional channel has now been turned on its head as a result of the work of Jeffrey Williamson and his colleagues (Williamson 2001). They argue that the effect of demographic change on economic performance depends on what happens to the age distribution. Thus, per capita income growth is thwarted in the early stages of the demographic transition as the dependency ratio rises: smaller shares of the population of working age mean fewer savers and workers. But over time, as the transition proceeds, the youth dependency ratio falls as the share of working-age adults rises, leading to more workers and savers and hence higher per capita income growth. This higher share of adult workers becomes an economic gift—assuming it is efficiently used. The gift fades with the end of the transition and a rise in the share of the elderly.

Figure 6 charts the population growth rate and the share of workers in the population for the past century. The share of workers declined until 1971 but, as population growth slowed, has been rising since then. Figure 7 charts the savings rate (which is only available for the period since 1951) and the share of workers in the population. As can be seen there is no relationship at present of the sort postulated by Williamson.

In fact, Williamson's view is an adaptation of the well-known life cycle/permanent income (LC-PI) theories of savings. These theories posit a relationship between savings and growth through life-cycle "hump savings" (Harrod 1948). Savings are independent of the level of permanent income and also of the distribution of income (Modigliani 1970). But, as Summers and Carroll (1989) note, the positive empirical relationship between savings and growth, if it is due to the life cycle, should show up in differences in the age-consumption profiles of countries with differing growth rates. This is not so for comparisons of Japan, Canada, and the United States. Deaton (1990) also finds that it is not so for comparisons of the Ivory Coast, Hong Kong, rural Indonesia, urban Korea, and Thailand.

Furthermore, for individual developing countries, as Deaton (1990) notes, the key prediction of the life-cycle hypothesis of a unitary elasticity of

FIGURE 6 Population growth rate and share of workers, India 1901–2001

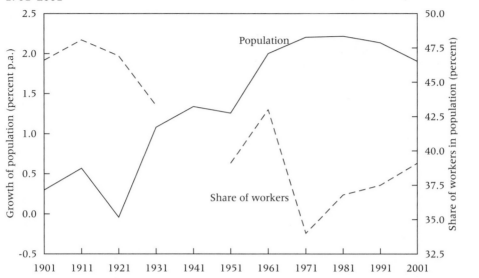

consumption with respect to permanent income has been uniformly rejected. For India, Bhalla (1979, 1980) finds it is less than unity—so savings are not independent of the level of income. This, of course, is the assumption underlying the Keyensian consumption function, where average savings rates increase with income. Moreover, in Kaldor's version (Kaldor 1955–56), the distribution of income between capitalists and workers with differing propensities to save is an important determinant of the overall savings rate.

FIGURE 7 Savings rate and share of workers in population, India 1901–2001

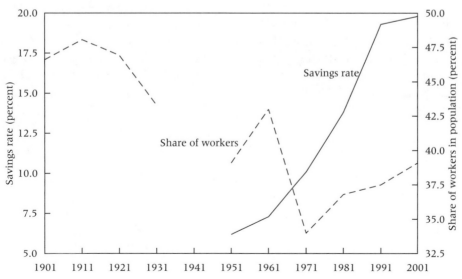

Bhalla (1980) provides the most robust study of savings behavior in rural India based on NCAER's three-year longitudinal sample survey data for 1968–70. This savings function behaves in Keynesian fashion during the middle-income range and then at higher income levels asymptotically approaches a savings rate that is constant and independent of permanent income in line with the life-cycle hypothesis. This savings function can be rationalized in terms of a model that combines the hump savings underlying the life-cycle model with a model of "precautionary savings" developed by Deaton (1990) in which, in poor agrarian economies subject to climatic risk, savings are motivated by the desire to smooth consumption between good and bad years.

This discussion provides a link between the distribution of households by different income levels and aggregate savings. With savings rising with assets and thus with permanent income, the effects of growth on savings will be mediated through the effects on the income–asset levels of different households. One robust finding of the Lal–Myint (1996) study is that growth trickles down—and as we have seen, this is also the case for India—with the poverty ratio declining faster the more rapid per capita income growth. Because the savings propensity increases with the household's income level, growth shifts households of the low (or zero and negative) income–savings classes into higher (and positive) income–savings classes, thereby raising the aggregate savings level. This "distributionally" mediated effect of growth on savings is different from that postulated by the life-cycle theories relying on the dependency ratio—for which there is no empirical confirmation for India. It provides a more plausible explanation of the virtuous circle whereby rapid growth, by moving low income–savings households into higher income–savings brackets, raises the aggregate savings rate, which in turn fuels rapid growth. The rise in labor supply during the demographic transition would of course still affect the "natural rate" of growth in the standard neoclassical growth framework, while the rise in the savings rate would lead to a higher rate of growth along the "traverse" as the economy moves from an initial low savings steady-state path to one with a higher savings and hence higher steady-state capital/labor ratio. This model was used in Lal and Natarajan (2001) to explain the aggregate savings rate for India during 1955–95 and performed well.

The future

Whether one believes in Williamson's demographic gift or the Lal–Natarajan view of the distributionally mediated determinants of savings, it is clear that, as long as India completes the reform process, including the rescinding of its century-old and deeply inefficient labor laws, there is no reason why, given a rising savings rate, India could not be growing at 8–10 percent per annum for the foreseeable future. Because population growth has begun to slow, this should provide a double hammer to deal with India's age-old scourge of structural poverty. Although there are signs that agricultural growth has slowed, largely because much of the potential irrigable area is already utilized and most of the cropped area suitable for high-yield varieties is already under this new technology, one sees both hope for more efficiency gains from the old "new" technology and the promise of a newer technology in the form of genetic modification (see Lal 2000). On the former point it is worth noting that efficiency gains are to be had from removing the continuing discrimination against agriculture in even the liberalized post-1991 trade regime (see Gulati 1998) as well as gains from exploiting India's comparative advantage, if the various barriers to world trade in agricultural goods are finally tackled by the World Trade Organization. On the latter, apart from offering various nutritive additions to traditional crops as in the "golden rice" that has been developed, genetic modification technology also promises to reduce the crop losses due to pests as with genetically modified cotton, while reducing the potential environmental damage from pesticides.

The most serious problems relate to the provision of infrastructure. Apart from the reforms needed in irrigation subsidies and power tariffs to improve the efficient use of existing infrastructure, there is also the need for massive investment in providing transport and power (see Ahluwalia 1998). The remedies for these planners' headaches exacerbated by population growth are well known.

There is a view current in India that with the explosive growth of services, particularly in information technology beginning in the 1990s, India can skip the usual stages of development, whereby agriculture is replaced by manufacturing industry as the leading sector and then by services, as in the post-industrial economies of the West. But given the size of the Indian population and the fact that, though literacy rates have risen, the educational levels (particularly in rural areas) of the majority are insufficient to allow them to participate in the human-capital-intensive services sector, India still needs to exploit its comparative advantage in labor-intensive manufacturing. This requires removing the remaining barriers to efficient industrialization, the most important of which remain the colonial industrial labor laws that have discouraged the use of labor in industry, and the set-asides for labor-intensive small-scale industry that prevent the exploiting of economies of scale.

The environment

The use of genetic modification technology in agriculture and the continuing need to expand labor-intensive manufacturing raise the specter that haunts environmentalists: the threats they see arising from India's burgeoning population. Economic historians (see Wrigley 1988) have established that the Industrial Revolution, which launched the era of modern intensive growth, was based on the transformation of an organic agrarian economy whose growth was ultimately bounded by a fixed factor, land, to a mineral-energy-using economy where the supply of energy from fossil fuels was for all practical purposes unbounded. This removed the constraints to a sustained rise in per capita income. Mass structural poverty need no longer be the inevitable fate of humankind. This process of transforming an organic into a mineral-energy-using economy, which India has fitfully engaged in, has already lifted millions out of poverty. For a full elimination of this ancient scourge India will have to consume even more energy from fossil fuels, which we are told will lead to global warming. I remain deeply skeptical (as do many others) about the underlying science and the dire effects predicted about global warming (see Lal 2006). But if India is forced to limit its greenhouse emissions from burning fossil fuels, it will indubitably condemn millions of poor Indians to perpetual poverty (see Lal 1995, 1997, 2006).

The attempt by environmental nongovernmental organizations like Greenpeace to push their agenda on a host of issues—including genetically modified foods, DDT, and trading in waste under the Basle treaty—also threatens the livelihood and welfare of millions of Indians (Lal 2000). India needs to beat off these threats to its poor as it has done to threats from the dirigiste planners of the Nehruvian era.

Nevertheless, there will be environmental problems associated with the rising per capita incomes of over a billion people. But as Panayotou (1994) rightly notes, most of these are best dealt with by setting up the right systems of incentives and disincentives. These include systems of property rights for hitherto common resources, proper pricing policies, and (where necessary) regulation to internalize externalities associated with the use of natural resources. The problems of deforestation, soil erosion, salinity, air pollution, and other forms of environmental degradation are due to the omissions and commissions of public policy "with price policies, taxes and subsidies encouraging environmentally destructive behavior" (Panayotou 1994: 177). These include corrupt logging contracts in the foothills of the Himalayas; irrigation, fertilizer, and power subsidies to the rural sector; and the failure to prescribe or enforce pollution standards for motor vehicles. In a dramatic example, when the Supreme Court, which is located in the capital, New Delhi, issued an order that by a certain date the government had to enforce various pollution standards (including the conversion of all diesel-powered public vehicles to the use of an alternative fuel), there was a remarkable improvement in the air quality in Delhi, which had been the second most polluted city in the world after Xian in China. There is thus no necessary conflict between the policies for efficient development and preserving the environment.

Social and political effects of population growth

India, like most other great Eurasian agrarian civilizations, was until recently a labor-scarce and land-abundant economy. As Domar (1970) demonstrated in a sadly neglected essay, in such economies free labor, free land, and a nonworking population cannot coexist. Only two out of the three will be found together. For instance, if there are free peasants and abundant land then the marginal and average product of labor will be nearly the same. Hence no surplus will be available to support a nonworking population of soldiers and priests. All the great Eurasian agrarian civilizations were created by obtaining a surplus for use in the towns (civitas, being the emblem of civilization). This predatory purpose required that peasants in these land-abundant civilizations be tied down to the land: to provide the required labor for the intensive processes of plough agriculture and to allow the extraction of a surplus over subsistence to support the wielders of the pen and the sword in the towns.

The swordsmen were necessary, as these riverine Eurasian civilizations were sandwiched between two major areas of nomadic pastoralism—the grasslands of the great steppe regions to the north and the semi-desert of the Arabian peninsula to the south. The nomads of these regions had maintained many of the war-like organizations and violent habits of big game hunters characteristic of their hunter-gatherer ancestors. They constantly preyed on the more numerous but sedentary populations of the agrarian civilizations. In the subsequent collision between farmers and pastoralists, the inherent military advantages the latter enjoyed made the sword wielders among the farmers essential in preventing the pastoralists from conquering and exploiting them (see McNeill 1979: 23–25). There were thus important external exigencies for obtaining a surplus to support specialists in wielding the sword, commanded by some form of monarch. Moreover, this nomadic threat also induced the creation of empires in order to acquire more natural and easily defensible borders against the barbarians (see Lal 2004).

Caste society

The means used to tie down labor to land to extract the surplus—the caste system in India, various forms of serfdom in Europe and China, slavery in many civilizations—were determined more by ecology than ideology. But in many cases (like caste in India) an ideology or, as I prefer to call it, a set of cosmological beliefs (Lal 1998) became an essential element in maintaining the necessary social control.

In India, as I argued in *The Hindu Equilibrium*, Hindu civilization developed on the vast Indo-Gangetic plain. This geographical feature meant that, with the existing means of transportation and communication, the ancient Indian polity was marked by grave instability among numerous feuding monarchies, none of which could successfully establish hegemony over the vast plain for any sustained period. This political instability ruled out those forms of tying labor to land that required some means of political control. The ancient Hindus found in the caste system an apolitical decentralized system to tie labor down whose survival did not require any overall (and larger) political community, and ensured that any attempt to start new settlements outside its framework would be difficult if not impossible. The division of labor by caste and its enforcement by local social ostracism were central to the schema.

The endogamous specialization of the complementary services required as inputs in the functioning of a viable settlement, and the social sanctions against the imparting of these complementary skills to other castes, meant that it would be virtually impossible to organize caste-breaking coalitions (see Akerlof 1976; Lal 1988). Moreover, through the process of "preference falsification" (see Kuran 1995), the system could continue even in the presence of hidden dissent and led to a climate of opinion where even the oppressed internalized its hierarchical cosmology.

The resilience of the caste system is shown by the fact of its survival, even though since AD 1000 India has been ruled by foreigners whose egalitarian ideology would have been expected to undermine the hierarchical caste system. The system even had some success in converting its conquerors, who in the personal domain adopted many aspects of the caste system (see Lal 1988). Recently, a revisionist school of historians claimed that caste is a colonial construction reflecting the Orientalism denounced by Edward Said (see Chaturvedi 2000; Inden 1990). But, as I briefly discuss in the preface to Lal (2005), their case is unconvincing. Caste (particularly the pollution barrier it embodies) has played and continues to play a major role in Indian society and politics (see Srinivas 1996).

In keeping with my materialist explanation for the origins of the caste system, I would have expected its erosion with the ending of the scarcity of labor relative to land following the twentieth-century population expansion. This has not happened, for two reasons. First, as I noted in *Unintended Consequences* (Lal 1998), there is an important distinction between the material and the cosmological beliefs of civilizations. The former are beliefs relating to the material world and ways of making a living. They can change fairly rapidly with changes in the material environment. The latter are related to understanding the world around us and mankind's place in it, which determines how people view their lives in terms of purpose, meaning, and relationship to others. There is considerable cross-cultural evidence that cosmological beliefs are less malleable than material beliefs. Cosmological beliefs are determined more by the language group from which the culture arose than by the environment, and there is considerable hysterisis in these beliefs on how, in Plato's words, "one should live" (see Hallpike 1986). So these cosmological beliefs can persist even if the original ecological circumstances that gave rise to them change, or if the relevant group migrates to another location.

This means that, even though the material bases for the origins of the caste system have been eroded, the set of cosmological beliefs, which were part and parcel of the system of social control it embodied, continue to resonate in modern India. Although officially caste has been abolished, it remains the bedrock of political competition in the country. Its continuing hold on social attitudes is neatly captured by Susan Bayly's description of the 1997 inauguration of the first untouchable President of the country. She notes the amalgam of symbols from the Raj, the dharmic kingdom of Hindu maharajas, and the symbols of Kshatriya martial races at the inauguration of President K. R. Narayanan: " both the staging of the event and its media representations took for granted the existence of caste as a potent reality of Indian life, at least in the past as well as the immediate present, if not necessarily for the future" (Bayly 1999: 381). Given the resilience of cosmological beliefs, I would demur with her prognostications about the future.

The second reason for the resilience of caste is that the democratic system has inadvertently given it a fillip. This is best discussed in the context of the reasons for the survival of democracy in India when it has manifestly failed to secure any sort of resilient foothold in the rest of the developing world.

Politics

One of the critical consequences of the apolitical and decentralized caste system established in ancient India was that, by making war the trade of endogamously specialized professionals, the mass of the population was spared from being inducted into the deadly disputes of its changing rulers. At the same time, the ancient tradition of paying a customary share of village output as revenue to the current overlord meant that the victor had little incentive to disturb the daily business of his newly acquired subjects. The democratic practices gradually introduced by the British in the late nineteenth century fit these ancient habits like a glove. The ballot box has replaced the battlefield for the hurly-burly of continuing "aristocratic" conflict, while the populace accepts with ancient resignation that its rulers will, through various forms of "rent-seeking," take a certain share of output to feather their own nests. These age-old cosmological beliefs, in my view, explain why, unlike in so many other developing countries, democracy has thrived in such a vast, diverse, and poor country, and taken deep root—as was shown by Indira Gandhi's aborted attempt to stifle it during the Emergency.

In the ensuing democratic political competition, caste affiliations remain of paramount importance, as witness the continuing attempt by successful political parties to constitute caste blocs. The higher ("twice born") castes have feared that relatively more rapid population growth among the lower castes and among the Muslim population would reduce their own political power. But this fear has remained unfounded. As Jeffery and Jeffery (1997) note, although there are differences in fertility rates between caste Hindus, Scheduled castes, and Muslims, with those for the first being the lowest, the differences can be explained in terms of income, education, child mortality, and age at marriage—the traditional socioeconomic variables—and not by caste or religion. Thus Cassen (1978: 57) rightly predicted that, ceteris paribus, the decline in Muslim fertility rates was about ten years behind that of Hindus, and that, even assuming the Muslim birth rates remain above Hindu rates, it is unlikely the Muslim proportion of the Indian population will rise to as much as 15 percent by 2021.

Nor has the achievement of political power by the untouchables (Dalits)—heralded by the rise of their party, the Bahujan Samaj Party, and the temporary elevation of its leader to the Chief Ministership of the most populous state in the country, Uttar Pradesh—led to any radical transformation of Indian politics. As elsewhere, democratic politics in India is by its very nature a distributive zero-sum game (see Lal and Myint 1996). Given the politicized nature of the economy under the Nehruvian dispensation, political power also led to economic benefits for those successful in capturing the levers of the state. This inherent populism of democratic politics was enhanced by the Indian Constitution's stipulation that the backward castes and tribes should be given time-bound reservations for public posts and contracts. This provision has been used by populist politicians to create a vast extension of affirmative action for virtually the whole of the non–"twice born" caste population, while ignoring the time-bound injunction. It has also accentuated the need to assert one's caste identity to obtain these politicized benefits, and has made both caste identity and assertion a central part of political competition in India. The liberalization of the economy in the 1990s and the resulting reduction in the attractiveness of public sector jobs have meant that the fierce opposition to this casteist affirmative action by the upper castes has also become muted. But if the rising demands for reservations in the private sector build up and are met, there will be a serious threat to India's future economic growth prospects.

Two questions have puzzled many observers of the Indian polity. First, how has a country with such linguistic, ethnic, cultural, and economic diversity managed to maintain its unity? Second, how could a subcontinental democratic polity with its equilibrium of "rent seeking interests" deliver economic liberalization? On the first, it is important to remember that like medieval Europe after the fall of Rome, the subcontinent has for millennia had a cultural unity provided by its Hindu cosmological beliefs despite long periods of political disunity. Moreover, India has always been a potential imperial polity. Although the imperial unity of the whole subcontinent has been ephemeral in Indian history because of the centrifugal tendencies dictated by geography and cycles in fiscal predation, the imperial ideal has animated every ruler of India. The British were the last of its rulers to turn this ideal into reality, and modern India is in many ways a continuation of the Raj (not least, as discussed below, because it has found it expedient to maintain the old imperial language of English as its lingua franca). The country has disposed of various militant separatist movements with an iron fist, while the democratic polity and the absorptive power of its cosmological beliefs have provided a means to eventually coopt dissidents into the polity.

On the second, Rob Jenkins (1999) in an important book has shown how, despite the breakdown of the Congress Party's dominance in the 1980s, the political players in the succeeding shifting coalitions at the center have skillfully used both a rearrangement of the previous spoils system and the various conflicts of interests among the numerous rent seekers to institute and continue economic reform. In this they have been helped by the improved economic productivity following liberalization, leading to larger rents, so that the predators got an unchanged share of a larger pie. This economic success has changed the perceptions of Western political scientists: having written a book called *Democracy and Discontent: India's Growing Crisis of Governability* in 1990, Kohli later edited a book entitled *The Success of India's Democracy* (2001).

The English, caste mobility, modernization, and Westernization

Given the fluidity of caste, as Srinivas (1966) had hypothesized, the process of caste mobility and thence class mobility has been the outcome of Sanskritization and Westernization, with the lower castes trying to assert a superior status by imitating the social habits of the upper castes. One of the surprising features of modern India is that, despite the desire and attempts by nationalist leaders to replace English as the lingua franca of the subcontinent, its role has been strengthened since Independence. This is because, since being reconstructed by the British Raj, the Indian state is a multiethnic empire, much like the former Austro-Hungarian empire. Just as in the latter, an imperial lingua franca has been adopted in preference to any language of the ethnic groups comprising the empire. Doing otherwise would immediately put one ethnic group at an advantage and would be fiercely resisted by members of other ethnic groups (see Lal 2004).

It was Macaulay's famous minute of 1833 that created a new English-speaking caste. In it he summed up the aim of English education in India as being the training of an English-educated middle class "who may be interpreters between us and the millions whom we govern; a class of persons, Indian in blood and colour, but English in taste, in opinions, in morals, and in intellect" (Macaulay 1898, vol. xi: 385–386). In this, the Raj was successful.

Because it is the language group that determines people's cosmological beliefs (Hallpike 1986), the cosmological beliefs of the full-fledged members of the caste for whom English had become their first language were more likely to conform to the beliefs of their linguistic cousins in the West than those of their vernacular countrymen. They were Westernized in a way that those for whom English is a second or third language were not.

All the early leaders of the nationalist movement were thus Macaulay's children. Among them two branches can be distinguished: the Nehruvians and the Gandhians. Both believed that modernization and Westernization were linked. But whereas the Nehruvians, who, despite lip service to marrying Indian with Western culture, accepted the implication and sought to implement a particular secular set of Western cosmological beliefs, the Gandhians (whose cultural successors include the various Hindu nationalist groups) have sought to resist modernization for fear it would lead to Westernization.

But, as I argued in *Unintended Consequences*, this was a false choice. As Japan was the first to show, it is possible to modernize without Westernizing, a process in which the role of English would be instrumental. For the myriad district- and lower-level service functionaries whose first language remained their vernacular, the English they spoke as a second or third language already fulfilled this role. They were not infected by Western cosmologies like the English-speaking caste. Even though they were not Westernized, they could have been modernizers. It was fateful that during the nationalist struggle they were politically mobilized by Mahatma Gandhi, that other child of Macaulay. For unlike the modernizers, Gandhi was above all concerned with maintaining a refurbished Hindu equilibrium. But by equating modernization with Westernization he created a backlash not only against the cosmological views of the West, but also against its material beliefs. Many of the views of the Hindu nationalists and the various "poujadist" and "kulak" political parties reflected this confusion (Lal 1999)

The field was then left clear for the modernizers-cum-Westernizers, symbolized most powerfully by the iconic figure of Jawaharlal Nehru. The English-speaking caste was during this period at the apex of the social pyramid. But with the economic failure of the Nehruvian model, an unintended consequence was that its progeny could not find satisfying or remunerative employment at home, and large numbers of them emigrated to the West.

With the abandonment of the Nehruvian model, the "intermediate" castes for whom English was a second or third language came to the fore.

But to the surprise of many, they did not, as had been expected, eschew modernization like their Gandhian predecessors. This change was completed when the Hindu nationalist party, the Bharatiya Janata Party, once in power did not turn its back on the economic reforms and the globalization that are so essential for India's modernization. These intermediate castes have increasingly come to accept that it is possible to modernize without Westernizing, and that in this task English serves a useful instrumental purpose. This has meant that, as soon as any part of rural India becomes prosperous, one of the first investments made by its residents is in private English-language schools. Furthermore, many members of these intermediate castes have progeny who along with English as their second language have also acquired the new information technology skills, which besides bringing them prosperity at home also provide a ticket to employment abroad.

This has resulted in a strange paradox, namely that many of the children of politicians and the administrative elite of both branches of Macaulay's children are now in the West. The political consequence has been that one of the Bharatiya Janata Party's early election pledges, to allow dual citizenship to the by-now-substantial Indian diaspora, is about to be redeemed—but with an interesting twist. It is only to be granted to persons of Indian origin who live in countries that recognize dual citizenship, namely, Britain and United States. By imposing this restriction they prevent the entry to India of the large number of Bangladeshis and Pakistanis who could otherwise claim Indian citizenship, while allowing the children of the older and newer political and administrative elites to at least metaphorically return to India.

To provide some rough orders of magnitude, Tata Services' *Statistical Outline of India 1995–6* (Table 234) estimates that, in June 1987 about 12.7 million persons of Indian origin were residing abroad. Of these about 6 percent were in Canada and the United States, and another 6 percent in Britain.[12] They are mainly the children of the two wings of Macaulay's children (of either kind) who will be eligible for dual citizenship. What role they will play in future Indian politics, given their relative wealth, is an intriguing question. But the diaspora does suggest that the process of caste mobility through the acquisition of English as a first or second language is likely to cut through the familiar caste patterns, even though in the personal domain—as the advertisements for arranged marriages for non-resident Indians in Indian newspapers testify—the desire to maintain caste endogamy endures.

One final aspect of the role of caste and politics is worth mentioning. The process of modernization is by its very nature disenchanting as people have to move to unfamiliar locations and undertake new tasks. The resulting turmoil in many modernizing societies has provided fertile ground for radical movements, which feed on the ensuing anomie. Apart from a few outbreaks of radical violence in the rural countryside, this has not happened in India, much to the chagrin of those of a Marxist bent of mind. I would suggest that it is the continuing resonance of the caste system's cosmological beliefs which provides the answer. Louis Dumont (1970) maintained that the great divide in human societies was between those who believed in "Homo Hierarchicus" and those in "Homo Aequalis," which in turn was based on the division between polytheistic and monotheistic religions, with the latter being egalitarian. Indian caste society is a prime example of a society of "Homo Hierarchicus," and as such egalitarianism has not had much resonance—except in rhetorical political terms. Therefore the resentments that would have been bred in a country with more egalitarian cosmological beliefs have not materialized. Equally important is the role of caste affiliations in providing both a social safety net and a framework to overcome the anomie that modernization would otherwise breed.

The family, social security, health, and education

India has maintained its traditional extended family system. Despite the fears of cultural nationalists, the rising new middle classes still adhere to traditional family values (Lal 1998, 2006). These were common to all ancient agrarian civilizations. In *Unintended Consequences* I argued, following Goody (1983), that the Papal revolution of Gregory the Great in the sixth century overturned the traditional patterns of legal and customary practices in the domestic domain in the West. The traditional system, concerned with providing a male heir to inherit family property, allowed marriage to close kin, marriages to close affines or widows of close kin, the transfer of children by adoption, and concubinage. Gregory banned all these practices, even though there was no basis for his injunctions in Scripture, Roman law, or existing customs in the areas that were Christianized. The purpose of the ban was to prevent families from having male heirs so that they could instead leave their property to the Church.

As part of this family revolution, the Church also promoted individualism through proclaiming the independence of the young: in choosing marriage partners, in setting up their households, and in entering into contractual rather than affective relationships with the elderly. The Church promoted love marriages rather than the arranged marriages that had existed in all Eurasian civilizations. A major consequence of Gregory's family revolution was that the social safety nets provided by the family in most Eurasian societies had from an early date to be provided by the state in the West.

There has been a fear that modernization will also breed Westernization and erode these traditional family-based social safety nets in India. But this fear seems to be misplaced. Thus a recent survey of the attitudes of 18–35-year-old urban Indians in the vanguard of globalization found that 70 percent would rather live in a joint than a nuclear family; 71 percent would not consider an old-age home for an elderly person in their family; 75 percent would not want a live-in relationship with someone before marriage; and 88 percent find kissing in public unacceptable.[13] This implies that the problems of pensions and healthcare for the aged, which are increasingly facing the West and China, are unlikely to be a problem in India, given its shame-based culture and the continuing hold of its traditional cosmological beliefs, which require the care of the aged within the extended family.

Furthermore, with the dismal failure of the Indian state to provide the merit goods of education and health to its population, most are privately provided and financed by the extended family. The World Bank (2000) found "private delivery of health and education is expanding rapidly, to the public in general and even to the poor" (p. 21). The PROBE team (1999) found that one-fifth of the children enrolled in private schools came from casual labor and one-half from scheduled castes or backward caste groups. In Uttar Pradesh 36 percent of children attending school are enrolled in private schools. The best course for the public education system is for it to be privatized, with public expenditure being used to provide vouchers for the poor to send their children to school. Similarly for health, a National Sample Survey (GOI 1999) finds that the failings of the public health system are leading to rising demand for private health services. Of India's overall health expenditure, representing 6 percent of gross domestic product, nearly 80 percent is spent on private health care. As with education, current public health expenditure should be used to provide vouchers for the poor.

It seems, therefore, that India will be able to avoid many of the pitfalls of Western welfare states. It can continue to rely on traditional family-based social safety nets. And it may not have the need for the state welfare systems resulting from Gregory the Great's family revolution in the West, with all the social and economic dysfunction that it has entailed.

The future of international relations

We can conclude by speculating on the likely effects of India's burgeoning population on its role in the world order. Because the momentum of its population growth is greater than China's, India will likely be the most populous country in the world by the end of the twenty-first century. Economically, in a globalized world, size does not matter, as witness the notable examples of Hong Kong and Singapore. But in global politics, population size, if married to economic and technological might, can be decisive (see Lal 2004). Given the large disparities in per capita income between India and the West, even if India grew at 8 to 10 percent per annum it would take until the end of the century for India to catch up economically with the West. But, given the relative size of India's population, its total gross domestic product would surpass that of the United States by about 2050. Part of that increase in output will undoubtedly be put into military weapons and into attempts to close the technological gap, now so overwhelming, between India and the West. Also, there is the sheer number of warriors that India could put in the field. So what are likely to be the international aims of this economically growing large population?

In the eighteenth and nineteenth centuries India and China felt the brunt of European economic and military superiority through direct and indirect imperialism, which stood in sharp contrast to the economic and technological stagnation of what had hitherto been the leading and most prosperous imperial systems in the world. Their current conception of international relations is deeply influenced by the perceived humiliations of this European onslaught and marked by a fierce determination that history will not repeat itself.

With the reemergence of the Asian giants as growing economic powers, India and China are regaining their relative importance in the world. After their long relative economic decline (see Figure 1, in Lal 2004), they are now on the way to becoming, with the United States, the dominant economic powers in the world for the twenty-first century. Like the United States and Germany in the nineteenth century when the British provided a global Pax, India and China may at first be silent freeriders on the current US Pax, and then challenge it as their economic and military strength (given by both population and per capita income) matches that of the current global hegemon. Many in the United States (see Mearsheimer 2001) harbor such fears particularly about China, which is also a fear shared by India. I am more sanguine. For I note that in their long history both imperial states have largely been "status quo" powers whose expansion has been to defensible frontiers.

Historically, the main threat to Indian security has always been from the northwest, even though the Chinese incursions in the 1960s showed that the Himalayas were no longer an impregnable shield to the north. For the foreseeable future the twin threats posed on these frontiers are likely to determine India's policies in international relations, as they have for the last half century.

The threat from the northwest is more immediate and more insidious. A hostile nuclear state, Pakistan, within the Himalayan shield seeking to exploit the tensions within a multi-ethnic empire poses a difficult dilemma. Being a potentially failed state with a fragile economy, and with its only sense of national identity provided by being anti-Indian, it is a difficult neighbor to live with. But, if the recent attempt by General Musharaff to turn Pakistan into a more normal and economically viable state is successful, the vision which I heard Jawaharlal Nehru enunciate in one of his last speeches as foreign minister of the desirability of a subcontinental confederation of states might be the answer. This vision has surprisingly been reexpressed by the former hard-line Hindu nationalist BJP interior minister L. K. Advani. But one should not hold one's breath, expecting this outcome.

In the longer term, competition for Great Power influence in Asia with the other colossus, China, seems inevitable. This long-term economic and military competition between the world's most populous nations will no doubt be of great importance for international relations by the end of the century. But with both potential Great Powers increasingly integrated into the world economy and dependent for their growing economies on imported natural resources, they will have a clear incentive to cooperate in keeping the lanes of commerce open and free from predators. Because most natural resources are now internationally traded commodities on NYMEX, owning these resources is of little importance, as the opportunity cost of their use is given by their changing world prices. More important is to ensure the security of trading these resources from the depredations of the equivalent of pirates of yore. The three imperial powers—the United States, China, and India—are all actual or potential natural resource importers. They would have a common interest in maintaining open sea and air lanes. The current race for owning global natural resources by the Asian giants is questionable.

Finally, another prospect is reminiscent of the British Raj. One of the reasons India was the jewel in its crown was the large Indian army, paid for by Indian taxes and deployed by the Raj to maintain its Pax from Suez to the Far East. Today with the Islamist threat to the world's oil supplies and domestic order, and the perceived threat from China, US and Indian interests are converging. So it is not surprising that, since the United States launched its war on terrorism, the Indians are cooperating with the United States in guarding the sea lanes from the Arabian Sea to the straits of Malacca. The recent strategic partnership forged by President Bush and Prime Minister Manmohan Singh, which envisages technical cooperation in nuclear and missile technology, presages a growing partnership between these two democratic powers. In my view the aim of such a partnership should not be to contain China, whose rise is inevitable and, as it has embraced the liberal international economic order, likely to be peaceful, but to move toward an informal tripartite concert of imperial powers to maintain the global Pax. The United States seems to be using China in its prickly dealings with the North Koreans, which might presage such an alliance.

With its domestic and near-neighborly problem with Islamicists, it is easy to imagine a time when, as during the British Raj, India would join the United States in some form of indirect imperialism to maintain order in the Middle East. In the nineteenth century, during its rise to world economic superiority, the United States depended on the British Pax to protect it from the machinations of the European powers, while it took responsibility for maintaining order in its own hemisphere. Now it is possible to envisage a global concordat where, within an overall US Pax, the responsibility for maintaining a Pax in East Asia would be taken over by China, with Japan and the United States maintaining a shield to ensure China does not overreach itself; while India would assume the responsibility (possibly with Turkey, the older imperial power) for maintaining the Pax in West Asia. But this would have to await a rapprochement with Pakistan and possibly the burning out of the Islamicist fervor that has so destabilized the Middle East.

Like the previous imperial powers in the region, the Turks and the British, India has always been a multi-ethnic empire that has not sought to impose a universal ideology on its peoples. Both the United States and China are by contrast homogenizing empires seeking to impose a common set of values on their constituents (Lal 2004). This could backfire and lead to political miscalculations in the imperial task (as demonstrated by the aftermath of the Iraq war). A regional Pax maintained by a multi-ethnic India is likely to be more successful in dealing with the political fissures of West Asia. Even though with its current technological hubris the United States may not wish to forge an alliance, and given their prickly nationalism the Indians are unlikely to mobilize armed manpower to maintain the Pax of the current imperial power, future developments may lead to something short of a formal alliance between the current hegemon and a rising great power.

Reading the tea leaves for the rest of century is a near impossible task. Two things, however, are certain. India and China will be the most populous countries in the world. If their current economic progress continues (and there is little reason to doubt it will), they will also be the largest economies after the United States by mid-century. Despite fears expressed by many "declinists" (see Ferguson 2002), I do not expect the United States to lose its technological and economic superiority before the end of the century (see Lal 2004). But the United States will be under serious threat from the Asian giants. Given its dismal pre-university educational system, the United States has increasingly relied for its technological superiority on its open door policy of importing the best brains from around the world. In this new world economic order, human capital (including skills in governance) will be of prime importance in determining the relative wealth of nations. As the two Asian giants create the conditions for the efficient deployment of their human capital, they will eventually have an edge over other countries because of their large populations. Julian Simon had argued in *The Ultimate Resource* (1981) that, as natural intelligence can be expected to be normally distributed in a population, the number of geniuses in the upper tail would be higher, ceteris paribus, in a larger population. This might soon come to pass, with these Asian geniuses choosing to work in their own countries rather than as at present in the United States. Thus, if not the current, then the twenty-second century is likely to belong to the Asian giants, whose large populations instead of being their bane (as had long been feared) will be the source of their greatness.

Notes

1 A revised, updated, and abridged version of *The Hindu Equilibrium* was issued in 2005 (Lal 2005).

2 It might be worth noting that, at Nancy Birdsall's instigation, Martin Wolf and I were responsible for part I of the 1984 *World Development Report*, which is rightly seen as a marker of the shift in World Bank thinking on population issues. There we discussed, for the first time, the implications of the aging of the population in the West for its economies and those of developing countries in an interdependent global economy (see Lal and Wolf 1986).

3 Eberstadt (2005) has usefully distinguished between the neo-Malthusianism of the past, represented for instance by the famous study by Coale and Hoover (1958), which asserted that wealth and productivity would be sacrificed by countries that threw resources away on extra babies instead of husbanding resources for investment and growth, and the current "environmental Malthusianism," which asserts that "rising demands upon the planetary eco-system will result in catastrophic overshoot and collapse of the natural global systems that sustain us all" (p. 479). See Lal (2006) for a discussion of why I find this assertion unpersuasive.

4 Pecuniary externalities are indirect effects mediated through the price mechanism, when, say, the increase in the supply of a good leads to a fall in its price, which harms other producers of the good but benefits consumers. These externalities are Pareto-irrelevant in the language of welfare economics. By contrast, technological externalities like smoke from a factory are not mediated through the price mechanism and are Pareto-relevant, leading to "market failure," which could require corrective public action. See Buchanan and Stubbelbine (1962).

5 I eschew any discussion of the various statistical problems involved in Indian demographic data. Visaria (1987) provides a succinct discussion of the matter.

6 The slowing down of the population growth rate in the 1901–21 period was due to the frequent epidemics of plague and cholera and the influenza epidemic of 1918–19, which raised the death rate in the 1911–21 census period to nearly the level of the birth rate. The growth rate of population was also lowered in the 1941–51 period by the Bengal famine of 1943, which killed an estimated 1.5–3 million people (Sen 1982), and the slaughter associated with the 1947 partition of Imperial India and the dislocation associated with "the total postpartition migration of nearly 15 million persons to and from India" (Visaria (1987): 136). The decline in the mortality rate in the 1950s was due to the control of malaria through low-cost spraying with DDT and the control of infectious diseases, particularly tuberculosis, through the introduction of antibiotics. But the decline in the death rate has slowed since 1961–71.

7 The spike in the infant mortality rate in 1911–21 was due to the epidemics discussed above. Since then it has been steadily declining, with the birth rate—as theory predicts—following suit, except for the substantial fall and then rise in the latter during the 1940s–50s. Visaria (1987) confirms that this is not a statistical artifact. But subsequently the birth rate has followed the infant mortality rate downward, although with some sluggishness during the 1960s, an acceleration in the 1970s, and from the annual data for birth rates an apparent stability between 1979 and 1984, since when there has been a rapid decline.

8 The fall seen in 2001 is probably due to the improved coverage of females in the 2001 as compared with the 1991 census, and the same seems to be the case with the reported declines in 1951 and 1981 (see Dyson 2001).

9 There is also an implicit assumption in steady state growth theory that colors much thought on the population question. This was explicitly and succinctly outlined by Sir J. R. Hicks (1977). The assumption is that "a steady-state expansion, in which capital

per head was constant and there was no technical progress, would show no gain in productivity. The expanded population would be absorbed, but that would be all. In such a steady state there would be no rise in real incomes and no rise in real wages. But in this steady-state theory is there not an important element which is being neglected? Is it not the case that expansion as such, even population-based expansion, is favourable to productivity?" (p. 23). The Boserup model on the role of population growth in inducing technical change in agriculture, briefly discussed below, fits the Indian "facts" better than Malthusian explanations.

Moreover, even without any induced technical change, as the population expansion is absorbed in an open economy with constant terms of trade at an unchanged real wage, following the Rybczynski theorem, this does not imply a lower social welfare because many ethical systems (such as the Utilitarian and Catholic) would include the number of heads along with consumption per head as positive arguments in a society's social welfare function.

10 Pryor and Maurer (1982) formalize this model and also provide a more general model that includes both the Malthusian and Boserupian positions as special cases. Also see Lal (1998: Appendix) for a diagrammatic explication of the model.

11 Both China's and India's recent outward-looking policy stances risk the danger that rising protectionist pressures in the North might thwart their rapid expansion. Given the history of the inter-war years this possibility cannot be completely discounted; however, it is encouraging that the substantial changes in the international division of labor that have already taken place have been accommodated with little backlash. Perhaps the mutually beneficial gains from trade are at last being realized as such, except for the anti-globalization fringe. I argue in Lal (2006) that the fear of a breakdown of the current liberal international economic order cannot be altogether discounted. But that does not mean that India and China need to change their current course to forestall a small possible threat to openness in the global economy in the future.

12 One of the major differences between the period of globalization in the nineteenth century and the current one is that whereas there was completely free movement of labor in the earlier period, immigration controls have become ubiquitous since then. This is because of the rise of welfare states in Bismarck's Germany, Lloyd George's Britain, and Franklin Roosevelt's United States. A welfare state creates property rights in citizenship because it allows any citizen access to the purses of its fellows. This makes the granting of citizenship to new entrants with incipient claims on existing citizens a major political issue. This has meant that whereas in the nineteenth century there was large emigration of the burgeoning peasants from India and China to the West and its tropical colonies in the Caribbean, Africa, and Latin America, in the twentieth century the immigrants allowed into the West have been largely the skilled. The peasantry from the subcontinent who settled in Britain entered just after World War II and before immigration controls were imposed in the 1960s. Most of the first-generation Indian diaspora today in the West thus consists of its relatively highly skilled rather than its peasantry. The latter have, however, found lucrative temporary jobs in the oil-rich countries of the Middle East. Today, with the aging of the population in Europe and the United States, immigration is being encouraged in part to deal with the problem of future pensions, but it is highly selective, being biased toward the skilled. This has meant that, whereas in the nineteenth-century period of globalization, migration of the unskilled was as important for the international convergence of factor prices as foreign trade (see O' Rourke and Williamson 1999), today trade is the major though less potent force leading to factor price convergence.

13 "Sex, society and the family," *India Today International*, 31 January 2005, pp. 34–37. These results are based on a poll conducted by AC Nielsen-Org-Marg of a cross-section of the population aged 18–35 years across ten major representative urban centers.

References

Ahluwalia, I. J. and I. M. D. Little (eds.). 1998. *India's Economic Reforms and Development.* Delhi: Oxford University Press.

Ahluwalia, M. S. 1998, "Infrastructure development in India's reforms," in I. J. Ahluwalia and I. M. D.Little (eds.), pp. 87–121.

Akerlof, G. 1976. "The economics of caste and of the rat race and other woeful tales," *Quarterly Journal of Economics* 90(4): 599–617.

Bardhan, P. K. 1979. "Labour supply functions in a poor agrarian economy," *American Economic Review* 69(1): 73–83.

———. 1984. " Determinants of supply and demand for labour in a poor agrarian economy," in Binswanger and Rosenzweig (eds.).

Barro, R. 2005. "The case of Asia's 'missing women,'" *Business Week*, 28 February.

Bayly, S. 1999. *Caste, Society and Politics in India.* Cambridge: Cambridge University Press.

Becker, G. 1981, 1991. *A Treatise on the Family.* Cambridge, MA: Harvard University Press.

Bhalla, S. 1979. " Measurement errors and the permanent income hypothesis: evidence from rural India," *American Economic Review* 69: 295–307

———. 1980. "The measurement of permanent income and its application to savings behavior," *Journal of Political Economy* 88: 722–743.

Bhat, P. N. Mari. 1998. "Contours of fertility decline in India: An analysis of district-level trends from two recent censuses," in Martine et al. (eds.), pp. 97–168.

Binswanger, H. and M. R. Rosenzweig (eds.) 1984. *Contractual Arrangements, Employment and Wages in Rural Labour Markets in Asia.* New Haven: Yale University Press.

Birdsall, N., A. C. Kelley, and S. W. Sinding (eds.) 2001. *Population Matters.* Oxford: Oxford University Press.

Blaug, M., P. R. G. Layard, and M. Woodhall 1969. *The Causes of Graduate Unemployment in India.* London: Allen Lane.

Boserup, E. 1965. *The Conditions of Agricultural Growth.* London: Allen and Unwin.

Buchanan, J. M. and C. Stubbelbine. 1962. "Externality," *Economica* 29: 371–384

Cassen, R. M. 1978. *India: Population, Economy, Society.* London: Macmillan.

Chaturvedi, V. (ed.) 2000. *Mapping Subaltern Studies and the Post Colonial.* London: Verso.

Coale, A. J. and E. M. Hoover. 1958. *Population Growth and Economic Development in Low Income Countries: A Case Study of India's Prospects.* Princeton: Princeton University Press.

Dandekar, V. M. 1988. "Indian economy since independence," *Economic and Political Weekly* 23(1–2):

Das Gupta, M. 1998. "Fertility decline in Punjab, India: Parallels with historical Europe," in Martine et al. (eds.), pp. 65–96.

———. 2005. "Explaining Asia's 'missing women': A new look at the data," *Population and Development Review* 31(3): 529–535.

Das Gupta, M. and M. Bhat. 1999. "Intensified gender bias in India: A consequence of fertility decline," in M. Krishnaraj, R. M. Sudarshan and A. Shariff (eds.), *Gender, Population and Development.* Delhi: Oxford University Press, pp. 73–93.

Deaton, A. 1990. "Savings in developing countries: Theory and review," *World Bank Annual Conference on Development Economics*, pp. 61–96.

Domar, E. 1970. " The causes of slavery or serfdom: A hypothesis," *Journal of Economic History* 30(March): 18–32.

Dumont, L. 1970. *Homo Hierarchicus.* London: Weidenfeld and Nicholson.

Dyson, T. 2001. "The preliminary demography of the 2001 census of India," *Population and Development Review* 27(2): 341-356.

Eberstadt, N. 2005. "P. T. Bauer on the population question," *Cato Journal* 25(3): 471–481.

Ehrlich, P. 1968. *The Population Bomb.* Baltimore: Ballantine.

Evenson, R. and H. Binswanger. 1984. "Estimating labour demand functions for Indian agriculture," in Binswanger and Rosenzweig (eds.).

Fei, J. C. and G. Ranis. 1964. *The Development of a Labour Surplus Economy*. Homewood, IL: R.D. Irwin.

Ferguson, N. 2002. *Colossus*. London: Allen Lane.

Goody, J. 1983. *The Development of the Family and Marriage in Europe*. Cambridge: Cambridge University Press.

———. 1990. *The Oriental, the Ancient and the Primitive*. Cambridge: Cambridge University Press.

———. 1996. "Comparing family systems in Europe and Asia," *Population and Development Review* 22(1): 1–20.

Government of India (GOI). 1999. "Survey on Health Care," 52nd Round (July 1995– June 1996) Schedule 25, NSS Organization, Department of Statistics.

Gulati, A. 1998. " Indian agriculture in an open economy: Will it prosper?," in I. J. Ahluwalia and I. M. D.Little (eds.), pp. 122–146.

Hallpike, C. R. 1986. *The Principles of Social Evolution*. Oxford: Clarendon Press.

Harrod, R. F. 1948. *Towards a Dynamic Economics*. London: Macmillan.

Hicks, J. R. 1977. *Economic Perspectives*. Oxford: Oxford University Press.

Inden, R. B. 1990. *Imagining India*. Bloomington: Indiana University Press.

Ishikawa, S. 1967. *Economic Development in Asian Perspective*. Tokyo: Kinokuniya.

Jeffery, R. and P. Jeffery. 1997. *Population, Gender and Politics*. Cambridge: Cambridge University Press,.

Jenkins, R. 1999. *Democratic Politics and Economic Reform in India*. Cambridge: Cambridge University Press.

Kaldor, N. 1955–56. "Alternative theories of distribution," *Review of Economic Studies* 23: 83–100.

Kelley, A. C. 2001. "The population debate in historical perspective: Revisionism revised," in Birdsall et al. (eds.), pp. 24–54.

Kohli, A. 1990. *Democracy and Discontent; India's Growing Crisis of Governability*. Cambridge: Cambridge University Press.

——— (ed.). 2001. *The Success of India's Democracy*. Cambridge: Cambridge University Press.

Kumar, B. Gopalakrishna. 1993. "Quality of life and nutritional status: A reconsideration of some puzzles from Kerala," in P. Bardhan, M. Datta-Chaudhuri, and T. N. Krishnan (eds.), *Development and Change*. Oxford: Oxford University Press.

Kuper, A. 1994. *The Chosen Primate*. Cambridge, MA: Harvard University Press.

Kuran, T. 1995. *Private Truths, Public Lies*. Cambridge, MA: Harvard University Press.

Lal, D. 1983/2000. *The Poverty of "Development Economics."* London: Institute of Economic Affairs; Cambridge, MA: MIT Press, 2nd US edition.

———. 1988/1989. *The Hindu Equilibrium*, 2 vols. Oxford: Clarendon Press.

———. 1988a. "The determinants of urban unemployment in India," *Indian Economic Review* XXIII(1): 61–81.

———. 1995. "Ecofundamentalism," *International Affairs* 71(July): 22–49.

———. 1997. "Ecological imperialism: The prospective costs of Kyoto for the Third World," in J. H. Adler (ed.), *The Costs of Kyoto*. Washington, DC: Competitive Enterprise Institute, pp. 83–90.

———. 1998. *Unintended Consequences*. Cambridge, MA: MIT Press.

———. 1999. *Culture, Democracy and Development*, Golden Jubilee Seminar Series. New Delhi: NCAER.

———. 2000. "The new cultural imperialism: The greens and economic development," inaugural Julian Simon memorial lecture, Occasional Paper 5, Liberty Institute, New Delhi.

———. 2004. *In Praise of Empires*. New York: Palgrave-Macmillan.

———. 2005. *The Hindu Equilibrium: India c.1500 BC–2000 AD*, revised and abridged. Oxford: Oxford University Press.

———. 2006. *Reviving the Invisible Hand: The Case for Classical Liberalism in the Twenty-First Century*. Princeton: Princeton University Press.

Lal, D., R. Mohan, and I. Natarajan. 2001. "Economic reforms and poverty alleviation: A tale of two surveys," *Economic and Political Weekly* XXXVI(12): 1017–1028.

Lal, D. and H. Myint. 1996. *The Political Economy of Poverty, Equity and Growth*. Oxford: Clarendon Press.

Lal, D. and I. Natarajan. 2001. "The virtuous circle: Savings, Distribution and growth interactions in India," in D. Lal and R. H. Snape (eds.), *Trade, Development and Political Economy*. Basingstoke, Hampshire: Palgrave, pp. 213–228.

Lal, D. and M. Wolf (eds.). 1986. *Stagflation, Savings and the State*. New York: Oxford University Press.

Lee, R. D. and T. Miller. 1990. "Population growth, externalities to childbearing, and fertility policy in developing countries," *Proceedings of the World Bank Annual Conference on Development Economics 1990*, pp. 275–304.

Lewis, W. A. 1954. "Economic development with unlimited supplies of labour," *Manchester School*, vol. 22, pp. 139–191.

Lipson, C. 1985. *Standing Guard*. Berkeley: University of California Press.

Macaulay, T. B. 1898. *The Complete Works of Lord Macaulay*, 12 vols. London.

Mamdani, M. 1972. *The Myth of Population Control*. New York: Monthly Review Press.

Martine, G., M. Das Gupta, L. C.Chen (eds.). 1998. *Reproductive Change in India and Brazil*. Delhi: Oxford University Press.

Mayer, P. 1999. "India's falling sex ratios," *Population and Development Review* 25(2): 323–343.

McNeill, W. H. 1979. *A History of the World*, 3rd edition. New York: Oxford University Press.

Mearsheimer, J. J. 2001. *The Tragedy of the Great Powers*. New York: W. W. Norton.

Mehra, S. 1966. "Surplus labour in Indian Agriculture," *Indian Economic Review* 1.

Modigliani, F. 1970. "The life cycle hypothesis of savings and inter-country differences in the saving ratio," in W. A. Eltis, M. Scott and J. N. Wolfe (eds.), *Induction, Trade and Growth*. Oxford: Oxford University Press, pp. 197–225.

O'Rourke, K. H. and J. G. Williamson. 1999. *Globalization and History*. Cambridge, MA: MIT Press.

Oster, E. 2005. "Hepatitis B and the case of the 'missing women,'" Harvard University Center for International Development, Working Paper 7, Cambridge, MA.

Panayotou, T. 1994. "Population, environment and development nexus," in R. Cassen (ed.), *Population and Development: Old Debates, New Conclusions*. New Brunswick: Transaction Publishers, pp. 149–180.

PROBE Team. 1999. *Public Report on Basic Education in India*. New Delhi: Oxford University Press.

Pryor, F. L. and S. B. Maurer 1982. " On induced economic change in pre-capitalist societies," *Journal of Development Economics* 10(3): 325–353.

Rosenzweig, M. 1978. "Rural wages, labor supply, and land reform: A theoretical and empirical analysis," *American Economic Review* 68(5): 847–861.

———. 1980. "Determinants of wage rates and labor supply behavior in the rural sector of a developing country," in H. Binswanger and M. R. Rosenzweig (eds.).

———. 1988. "Risk, implicit contracts and the family in rural areas of low income countries," *Economic Journal* 98(Dec.): 1148–1170.

Sen, A. K. 1966. "Peasants and dualism with and without surplus labour," *Journal of Political Economy* 74: 425–450.

———. 1982. *Poverty and Famines*. Oxford: Clarendon Press.

———. 1990. "More than 100 million women are missing," *New York Review of Books*, 20 December: 61–66.

Simon, J. 1981. *The Ultimate Resource*. Princeton: Princeton University Press.

Sivasubramonian, S. 2000. The *National Income of India in the Twentieth Century*. Delhi: Oxford University Press.

Srinivas, M. N. 1966. *Social Change in Modern India*. Berkeley: University of California Press.

———. 1996. *Village, Caste, Gender and Method*. New Delhi: Oxford University Press.

Summers, L. H. and C. Carroll. 1989. "The growth-savings nexus," paper presented at the NBER Conference on Savings, Maui, Hawaii, January.

Tendulkar, S. D. 1998. "Indian economic policy reforms and poverty: An assessment," in I. J. Ahluwalia and I. M. D. Little (eds.), *India's Economic Reforms and Development: Essays for Manmohan Singh.* New Delhi: Oxford University Press, pp. 280–309.

United Nations. 2002. *World Population Prospects: The 2002 Revision.* New York: United Nations Population Division.

Visaria, P. 1987. "The demographic dimensions of Indian economic development since 1947," in P. R. Brahmananda and V. R. Panchmukhi (eds.), *The Development Process of the Indian Economy.* Bombay: Himalaya Publishing House.

Visaria, P. and B. S. Minhas. 1991. "Evolving an employment policy for the 1990's: What do the data tell us?," *Economic and Political Weekly* XXVI(15). Reprinted in U. Kapila (ed.), 1993, *Indian Economy since Independence*, Vol. 4. Delhi: Academic Foundation, pp. 136–174.

Williamson, J. G. 2001. "Demographic change, economic growth and inequality," in Birdsall et al. (eds.), pp. 106–136.

World Bank. 2000. *India: Reducing Poverty, Accelerating Development.* New Delhi: Oxford University Press.

Wrigley, E. A. 1988. *Continuity, Chance and Change, Cambridge.* Cambridge: Cambridge University Press,.

Wyon, J. B. and J. E. Gordon. 1971. *The Khanna Study.* Cambridge, MA: Harvard University Press.

Population and the Natural Environment: Trends and Challenges

J. R. McNeill

The relationship between population and environment is simple at first glance and distressingly complex if one takes the trouble to look more closely. It is simple because, as a first approximation, more people means more environmental change. But getting beyond this generic, and sometimes inaccurate, proposition has defeated many fine minds. Taking all the variables and contingencies into account leads to a hopeless muddle. Even the general proposition that everything is connected to everything else, offered in many a "wiring diagram" in the field of global environmental change, underestimates the complexities involved. The earth's biological and physical systems are full of surprises that are difficult to depict and quantify. In particular, there are nonlinear effects. Soil erosion can proceed for decades with no discernible effects on yields, but when the process approaches bedrock, yields suddenly plummet. Fishermen might pursue the North Atlantic cod fruitfully for 500 years, but when their efficiency (perhaps combined with other cod-related factors) reaches a threshold, cod populations can collapse, and undersea food webs reorganize with new predators so that cod fingerlings have only remote chances of reaching breeding age. Furthermore, societies can exert their own unpredictable and nonlinear influences that affect the global environment. For example, industrial societies might release chlorofluorocarbons into the atmosphere for decades on end, with deleterious consequences for the planet's stratospheric ozone shield. But then, suddenly, as a result of new scientific findings, widespread alarm, and concerted political action, they might (as indeed they have) agree to stop.

Beyond the nonlinear effects, one must bear in mind that the relationship is mutual: environmental considerations affect population levels, and in changeable ways. Not only does a habitat's "carrying capacity" change with alteration to the environment, but, much more dramatically, disease environments help govern population levels. These environments are anything but stable, and in the modern world are precariously maintained by ongoing interventions by public health services.

All this is to say that generalizations on the relationships between environment and population must be treated with extreme caution: to paraphrase Marshall Sahlins, interdisciplinary generalizations take the uncertainties of one discipline and multiply them by the uncertainties of a second discipline. To this one must add—or perhaps multiply—the inherent uncertainties of the future, of which more later. With these opening remarks, I now plunge into the realm of uncertainty, taking up the relationship in terms of population growth, urbanization, and migration, then concluding with comments on how population and environment interact with yet other sorts of variables, notably technology and politics.

Population growth and its impacts

The secular rise of human population over the last 250 years is one of the most curious and consequential elements of modern history, far more important than most historians choose to recognize. It has certainly been of major importance to modern environmental history, although probably not as central as environmentalists choose to see it. Here I consider its environmental impacts in terms of three categories: land use, water use, and pollution. The basic population data are presented in Table 1, drawn from UN sources. Note that the projection to the year 2050 is one that has been declining with each iteration and on the global level carries a margin of error of a billion or two, depending on assumptions, mainly about fertility (Cohen 2005).

Land use

Rising global population required more food and fiber. Through the 1920s this generally meant converting more land to agricultural purposes, because raising yields was beyond the capacity of most farmers. From the 1930s,

TABLE 1   World and regional population trends, 1850–2000 and projection for 2050 (millions)

Region	1850	1900	1950	2000	2005	2050
Africa	95	120	224	812	906	1,937
Asia	749	937	1,396	3,676	3,905	5,217
Europe	266	401	547	728	728	653
Latin American and Caribbean	33	63	167	523	561	783
North America	26	81	172	315	331	438
Oceania, Australia	2	6	13	31	33	48
World	1,200	1,600	2,519	6,086	6,465	9,076

NOTE: Figures for 2050 are medium projections.
SOURCES: For 1850 and 1900: Reinhard, Armengaud, and Dupâquier 1968: 680–681. For 1950–2050: «http://esa.un. org/unpp».

however, the relationship between land and food production became more
elastic, thanks to chemical fertilizers, pesticides, scientific crop breeding, and
a vast expansion of irrigation. Globally, these effects became statistically visible in the 1950s. Without these developments, the twentieth century's great
spike of population growth would have been much muted. While it would
have been possible to clear more land for farming, it would not have been
possible to clear much good land. The earth has about 133 million square
kilometers of land not covered by rock, sand, or ice. The long-term trajectories of land use appear in Table 2, which shows the decoupling of agricultural area and population. From 1950 to 1990, for example, population more
than doubled but cropland grew by less than one-third, and pasture land
by less than one-half. Without the spectacular rise in yields, we would today need another North America to feed the globe.

Whether these remarkable improvements in yield will continue is an
open question with large and direct implications for both land use and population levels. The Dutch National Institute for Public Health and Environment and the UN's Environment Programme (RIVM/UNEP 1997: 57–60)
suggest that a 42 percent increase in world croplands (1990–2050) will be
achieved, together with grain yield improvements ranging from 60 percent
in Europe and North America, to 150 percent in the Middle East, and 130
percent in Africa over the same interval. In this scenario, farmers will need

**TABLE 2 Approximate evolution of global vegetation cover to 1990
(million km²)**

Date	Forest and woodland	Grassland	Pasture	Cropland	World population
8,000BC	65	63	0	0	5–20 million
AD1700	62	63	5	2.7	680 million
1850	60	60	8	5.4	1.2 billion
1890	58	55	13	7.5	1.5 billion
1900	58	54	14	8.0	1.6 billion
1910	57	52	15	8.6	1.8 billion
1920	57	51	16	9.1	1.9 billion
1930	56	49	19	10.0	2.0 billion
1940	55	47	21	10.8	2.3 billion
1950	54	45	23	11.7	2.5 billion
1960	53	41	27	12.8	3.0 billion
1970	51	38	30	13.9	3.7 billion
1980	51	35	33	15.0	4.5 billion
1990	48	36	34	15.2	5.3 billion

NOTE: This table vastly simplifies land cover categories and ignores distinctions within them and the (controversial) process of desertification.
SOURCE: McNeill 2000; Klein Goldewijk 2001; RIVM 2002; Klein Goldewijk and Ramankutty 2004.

to find 6 million square kilometers of new cropland. In reality they would need rather more, as some of today's farmland will be retired because of erosion or salinization in the meantime. Kazakhstan's Institute of Soil Management, for example, predicts that half that country's cropland will be so degraded as to be abandoned by 2025 (UNFPA 2001). Thus an area roughly equivalent to the continent of Australia will need to be converted to crops if these projections about yield are right. Of course, it is conceivable these estimates for improvements in yield are too conservative, in which case correspondingly less new cropland will be required. Moreover, should world population stabilize (or decline) after 2050, and improvements in yield continue, then some cropland will likely revert to spontaneous vegetation. Indeed, Ausubel (2002) anticipates that the world's farmers might raise yields by 2 percent per annum for the next 60–70 years, allowing half of today's cropland to return to nature. I expect, however, that the world's poorest farmers will continue to clear forest land.

Whereas in the nineteenth century most of the world's new cropland was converted from grasslands, after 1950 most of it came at the expense of tropical forests. The frontier epic of the North American prairies, South American pampas, and Australian bushlands ended in the early twentieth century. The last great plowup of steppe grassland took place in Russia and Kazakhstan in the 1950s, although a slower one is still unfolding in China (see below). Since then all the great expansions of cropland have come from forests, mainly in West Africa and Southeast Asia, but also in Central and South America. This will likely be where the new cropland is found between now and 2050, because that is where many of the additional people will be found, and it is the only place where land is nearly free for the taking. There are better soils now returning to forest in Europe and North America, but they are not cheaply acquired. Of course by 2050 climate change may shift the geography and quantity of suitable cropland somewhat in ways that are difficult to forecast (Rosenzweig and Hillel 1998).

One of the implications of extension of arable land, and particularly the reduction in tropical forests, is loss of biodiversity. The last century witnessed a modest reduction in species diversity, although just how much is impossible to say. (Estimates of the number of extant species range from 3 million to 80 million.) Since 1900, about 1 percent of bird and mammal species, a bit easier to count than beetles, have gone extinct. Many more became endangered. On present trends, the next 50 years will see a far sharper reduction in biodiversity, mainly because of the conversion of many remaining patches of rain forest to arable or pasture land. The expansion of agriculture before 1950 took place mainly in lands with low levels of species diversity, but that situation has changed since the rain forests became the most active frontier zones, for rain forests are by far the most biologically diverse provinces on earth. Most rain forest conversion is driven by population growth, so in this case the reduction in species diversity is fairly clearly a result of mounting human numbers in the American, African, and (less clearly) Asian tropics.

Of course, rain forest environments may fight back, curbing population growth. The AIDS epidemic is an example of what can happen when humanity inserts itself into unfamiliar environments. It has emerged as demographically significant in Southern and East Africa. It is entirely plausible that other potential human pathogens exist or are currently evolving in the world's rain forests, waiting, as it were, for the opportunity to find a human host (or for a sufficient density of human hosts to allow them to stay in circulation and break out of their original locales). If such pathogens moved from host to host more efficiently than does the AIDS virus—much as smallpox did or as tuberculosis and influenza do—the implications for 2050 population projections could be large and grim.

Water use

The earth has plenty of fresh water. The world's annual streamflow, not counting flood runoff, is about 2,000 cubic meters per person. With the floods, it is about 7,000. But that streamflow is inconveniently distributed in space and time. So arranging a sufficient supply of fresh water has occupied many societies in the past and will continue to do so in the future (Hunt 2004).

Historically, world water demand was driven chiefly by population growth. That is because most water use went for irrigation for food production, and some of the rest went for domestic use in cooking and cleaning. In the twentieth century that link weakened because industry took a growing share of the world's fresh water, and industrial production levels did not vary tightly with population. Table 3 shows the historical trajectory of world water use.

Table 3 suggests that over the long haul, the growth of population had much to do with total levels of freshwater use. In the 250 years before 1950, per capita use increased 3-fold but total use rose 12-fold. Since 1950, per capita use is up by half and total use by nearly 4-fold. In the period 1850–1970 industrialization disproportionally drove the rapid growth in water use, but after 1970 industry's share stabilized as water efficiency in industry improved, partly as a result of water pollution regulations. The fastest growth lately has come in municipal demand, connected to the hectic pace of urbanization. Today water use increases at about the same rate as global population, which means a new Rhine-equivalent must be found each year (UNFPA 2001).

These global figures will probably continue on much the same trajectories for a few decades. Total withdrawals can easily grow at the same pace for some time to come, and cities can take a larger share and irrigation a smaller one. If per capita use stays constant, by 2025 we would use water equivalent

TABLE 3 Estimated global freshwater use, 1700–2000, and projected use in 2025

Year	Withdrawals (km³)	Withdrawals per capita (m³)	Uses (percent of total)		
			Irrigation	Industry	Municipal
1700	110	170	90	2	8
1800	243	270	90	3	7
1900	580	360	90	6	3
1950	1,382	550	83	13	4
1970	2,526	680	72	22	5
1990	3,633	690	66	24	8
2000	3,973	662	64	25	9
2025	5,235	662	61	22	12

SOURCE: McNeill 2000: 121, elaborated from Shiklomanov 1993 and L'vovich and White 1990; Shiklomanov 1999.

to 70 percent of the global annual streamflow—a feasible level of use, especially if we become more adept at storing flood runoff, which is far greater than streamflow. But it should also be easy to improve efficiency, especially in agriculture, which on a global basis wastes about half of the water withdrawn for irrigation. Pricing water use normally raises efficiency sharply.

But acute difficulties arise on the local and regional levels. China has plenty of water, but north China does not: the Yellow River now runs dry some 600 kilometers inland in most years. Several northern Chinese cities pump out groundwater far faster than underlying aquifers can recharge. Some 20 or 30 countries in Africa and Southwestern Asia are, by the conventional measures of hydrologists, short of water. They are, for the most part, societies with high population growth rates. As their populations and their cities expand, water shortage will surely become more burdensome. The United Nations estimates that 1.7 billion people live in river basins where water is scarce (defined as less than 1,000 cubic meters per person per year), and that in 2025 some 2.4 billion people will. This stands to have repercussions for health, as people of necessity turn to unclean water, and for politics, as struggles to procure larger supplies will preoccupy states and, equally, rival claimants to water within states. These worries are justifiably emphasized in analyses of public health and environmental security. Fresh water is the only natural resource for which shortage is an imminent and significant concern. Of course, unforeseeable technological changes, cheap desalinization of seawater for example, could revolutionize this disconcerting prospect.

Air pollution

The links between population levels and air pollution have always been weaker than those between population and water. Energy regimes and technology exerted stronger influences than did population in contributing to air pollution. This will likely prove even more the case in the future.

Air pollution levels climbed quickly in the twentieth century. Lead emissions to the atmosphere increased about 8-fold, sulfur dioxide about 13-fold, nitrogen oxides 14-fold, and carbon dioxide perhaps 17-fold (McNeill 2000: 360). Much of this pollution increase took place early in the century, and in North America and Europe most of it was over by 1985, since which time lead and sulfur emissions have declined sharply and nitrogen and carbon emissions have stabilized. The concentrations in the atmosphere of these latter two, however, continue to climb. And in East Asia emissions of all of them are rising very quickly.

In the twentieth century population growth, mainly in industrial countries, raised pollution levels through demand for manufactures and especially through demand for automobiles. As long as smokestack, chimney, and tailpipe emissions went unregulated, or ineffectively regulated (which was the case until the 1940s), and as long as technological change did not fundamentally affect pollution levels, population remained a crucial variable. However, even in the first half of the twentieth century most industrial economies reduced the energy-intensiveness of production, so that pollution levels did not rise as fast as levels of industrial production. And then, from the 1940s and especially from the 1960s, regulation of pollution became standard, thus altering technologies considerably. Meanwhile, energy-intensiveness continued to fall, especially after the 1970s because of the 10–12-year era of high fossil fuel prices. All these developments weakened the link between population and air pollution. It will grow weaker still in the decades to come, presuming that states do not roll back regulation of pollution significantly.

The dominant concern related to air pollution at present is greenhouse gas emissions, owing to their role in contemporary global climate change. The major greenhouse gas is carbon dioxide, released to the atmosphere mainly by fossil fuel burning (c. 80 percent), but also by burning of forests (c. 20 percent). A rough calculation (McNeill 2000: 272) suggests that in the twentieth century, population growth accounted for a bit more than a fifth of the growth in CO_2 emissions. Other studies, focusing on the late twentieth century when population growth was highest and emissions rates slowed slightly, offer figures of 32–45 percent (McNeill 2000: 273 for a review). These global aggregates conceal a lot. Greenhouse gas emissions derive mainly from combustion. The enormous increase in sub-Saharan African population since 1950 did not raise the global total of combustion by much; the modest increase in, say, the number of Germans probably had a greater effect, because Germans drove cars, heated their homes, and in general used far more energy per capita than Africans. The implication of population growth for CO_2 emissions depends entirely on how the additional people live, which in turn depends mainly on where they live.

Since 1970 the CO_2 emissions of rich countries have stayed fairly stable at about 3.5 billion metric tons per year. The key variable has been technological change and "decarbonization" of the rich economies: they cleaned up or shut down many of their polluting industries. The fastest growth in CO_2 emissions since 1970 has taken place in poor countries (rising from about half a billion to about 2.7 billion mt per year).

In the near future the poor countries will outstrip the rich ones in CO_2 emissions, and China will overtake the United States, which now contributes one quarter of the total, as the single largest CO_2 polluter. Population growth will matter mainly in three ways: 1) when it occurs in countries where industrialization (and therefore energy use and combustion) depends on the size of the internal market, 2) when it occurs in countries that are taking up the automobile as the general means of transport (e.g., South Korea, Mexico, and Brazil at present; China and India soon), and 3) when it drives further deforestation (e.g., Central America, Peru, Cameroon, Central African Republic). If this analysis is correct, population growth will continue to matter importantly in climate change, although the processes of industrialization, motorization, and technical change will in every case govern how critical population growth will be.

The significance of population growth for environmental concerns will remain even as population growth rates decline. The modern rise of population dates from the eighteenth century. Since that time, it has probably been second-most in importance as a driving force of environmental change, behind only the energy regime. In the future, even though population growth rates will presumably continue to slow, annual increments will remain large for decades and growth will be more likely to prove environmentally destabilizing. This is because population growth will take place in poor countries and often in weak states, where environmental management carries a low priority, where feeding additional mouths requires clearing further land, and where fresh water is already scarce. The nineteenth and twentieth centuries reduced the ecological buffers—partly through rapid population growth—so that further population growth will probably prove more difficult to accommodate, even if it occurs more slowly. Technological changes, especially in the energy system (see below), could alter this unsettling picture.

Urbanization

The extraordinary growth of cities, together with the general crowding of the earth, is the greatest social transformation of modern times. For most of the past 10,000 years, fewer than 2 percent of people lived in cities. Leaving aside small city-states, the first societies to surpass the 10 percent mark were probably seventeenth-century Holland and Japan. The first to reach the 50 percent mark was Great Britain, in about 1850. By that time the historic constraints on city life were breaking down, as agriculture slowly grew more productive, transport systems reached out into the countryside, cities came to dominate their hinterlands more commonly, and public health systems began to check the ravages of infectious disease that had formerly made cities into black holes for humanity: London in 1750, for example, was lethal enough to cancel out half the natural increase of all England (MacFarlane 1997: 22).

The world in 1800 had only six cities with half a million population. By 1900 it had 43, mostly in Western Europe, eastern North America, and on seacoasts of export-oriented Asian regions, and some 225 million people lived in the world's cities. By 2000 about 3 billion lived in cities the world over. There also were cities of a size never seen before: by 2005, some 25 cities topped 10 million people (Brinkhoff 2005). Half the world's people lived in cities, 13 times the number of 1900 and perhaps 100 times that of 1800.[1]

This remarkable transformation resulted from accelerated migration from rural areas and, what was new, the improved health of city life. In the 1880s city dwellers in Austria and Bavaria had longer life expectancies than their country cousins, the first time in the world (as far as I am aware) that this had ever happened. By the 1920s this situation obtained in China. Cities were no longer black holes, and were free to grow as fast and as large as their food, water, and energy supplies would permit. These proved very elastic constraints in most cases, hence the spectacular urban growth of the twentieth century.

But this growth spurt appears to be a passing phase. City life has proven inimical to childrearing. In what is probably an extreme case, Vienna around 1930, the net reproduction rate dipped to 0.25, meaning that, absent in-migration, the next generation would be only one-quarter as large (Kirk 1946: 55). Sub-replacement fertility became characteristic of cities and, as citified ambitions and morals spread to the countryside, of entire societies. London today, as in 1750, would eventually vanish without in-migrants, and now they must come from the Caribbean and South Asia, because rural and small-town England does not generate enough. It remains to be seen whether city life will discourage childbearing in Lagos and Lima as much as in London.[2] But if it comes anywhere close, then cities around the world will return to their historic role as demographic black holes: this time not because they kill people so quickly but because they cause them to reproduce so slowly.

The ecological effects of urbanization were, and are, vast. Locally, it amounted to a total transformation: Chicago arising out of lakeside swamps or Canberra blooming on the Australian grasslands. But the ecological implications of city growth always extended much farther than their city limits. Cities draw food, water, energy, and other materials from afar, and they export goods and wastes. On the analogy of organisms, they have metabolisms. They have ecological footprints too, the area affected by their metabolic activity, both their intakes and their outputs.[3]

Their actual spatial footprint grew 10- or 20-fold between 1900 and 1990, to 1–2 percent of the earth's surface (McNeill 2000: 289–291). New Delhi increased its area 13-fold in these years, while Beijing doubled in the 1990s alone. Simultaneously, cities sprouted to the sky and burrowed underground. Cities were home to a greatly reduced variety of plant and animal life, especially where motorized transport replaced horses, camels, and donkeys. These were utter transformations—but they only affected the space of the cities themselves, which in 2000 was roughly equivalent to the area of Costa Rica.

The ecological footprint extended much further. Cities imported energy from hundreds of miles away in the nineteenth century, and from oilfields several thousand miles distant after 1950. Food imports, at least to seaport cities, came from thousands of miles away as early as the 1850s. Water was transported less easily, although lengthy aqueducts date from ancient times and Libya is building even longer ones today. Taking food, water, and carbon emissions into account, recent calculations suggest that rich-country cities now have an ecological footprint 100–200 times the size of their actual areas (Rees 1996). Highly urbanized countries, such as the Netherlands, require a space about 15 times the national area to keep their appetites supplied.[4] Most of the area affected is timberland, pasture land, or farmland. But the impacts of what is done there—logging, ranching, farming—would be only a little smaller if the people in question were country folk rather than urbanites. Cities have big ecological footprints because they have big populations: dispersing that same population would have modest effect. In some respects a dispersed population implies greater environmental impacts than does a concentrated one, because there are economies of scale in cities, especially in transport and heating, and therefore in energy use, but also in sewage treatment.

Cities' impact on ecological sinks is much more intense. The production of solid wastes by 20 million people in Mexico City (about 10,000 tons a year) is much more problematic than the wastes generated by 20 million villagers, because it is much more concentrated. In the last 50 years the pace of urban growth often outstripped the capacity of governments to provide sanitary services, so that morains of garbage arose around Manila, Maputo, and Medellin. New York City, which 100 years ago dumped garbage barges in Long Island Sound and in the 1940s built the world's largest landfill on Staten Island, now exports garbage to Virginia, where landfill space is cheap (and some communities are eager for the cash that comes with the trash). In Surat, a port north of Mumbai, accumulated garbage helped sustain a rat population that spread a brief epidemic of bubonic plague in 1994. Quick response by public health authorities limited the death toll to 57. So far, perhaps improbably, the sanitation and health risks posed by giant cities have remained risks and not become catastrophes.

Urban air pollution, discussed above, was much more deadly than urban garbage. The noxious emissions from a million cars or chimneys when concentrated in an urban space are quite a different matter from the same emissions dispersed over a broad territory. Urban air pollution killed perhaps 25–40 million people in the twentieth century, roughly 1 percent of the total deaths and roughly equal to the loss of life in the 1918–19 influenza pandemic (McNeill 2000: 103). In the 1990s its annual toll reached about half a million, a bit less than the global annual toll in car crashes (McNeill 2000: 103, citing Hall 1995: 77 and Murray and Lopez 1996: 28). By 2002, according to a World Health Organization estimate, air pollution killed 3 million people worldwide, which is a little more than the annual toll from malaria (Earth Policy Institute website: www.earth-policy.org/Updates/update17.htm [accessed 2 October 2005]). The discrepant figures testify to the methodological difficulties inherent in making such estimates. But in any case, urban air was, is, and for years to come will remain lethal to hundreds of thousands, if not millions, of city folk. Thus cities had ecological effects that were locally intense and, at lower intensities, rippled out across the world. In the half century to come, the urban proportion will surely rise, perhaps to 75 percent—the current level in both North and South America. If this population attained the consumption standards of Vancouverites today, we would need (all other things held equal) about three or four extra earths to accommodate their appetites. This assures that all other things will not remain equal, or else that consumption standards will remain unequal. Both outcomes are likely. The efficiency with which food and water are produced and used will rise, because there is so much slack in both systems. And the poor people of Veracruz and Vladivostok probably will not attain Vancouver's consumption levels. While the total impact of cities will continue to grow, the pace at which they bring about environmental changes should slacken, for the rate at which cities grow will decline as saturation approaches.

International migration

The pace of migration to the cities must inevitably slow, but international and interregional migration need not. Migration has been of great historical significance for land and water use and for deforestation and soil erosion. Its future social and political importance will probably mount, while its ecological significance dwindles.

The period 1830–1914 was the first great era of world migration, far outpacing earlier flows such as the African slave trade to the Americas (Klein 1999: 209–211; Cohen 1995). Indeed it was the winding down of the slave trade that helped set people moving. Millions of villagers from India and

China left home for the plantations and mines of the Caribbean, South Africa, the Indian Ocean islands, and elsewhere. Some 60 million Europeans departed for the Americas, Australia, New Zealand, or Siberia. Some of these migrants contributed to urbanization, but many of them went from one rural landscape to another.

Between 1865 and 1930 the prairies of North America received a few million settlers, mostly from humid environments in eastern North America or northern Europe. These migrants brought with them ideas and practices about farming, which they proceeded to follow in the semi-arid steppe from west Texas to Alberta. In wet periods the results were bumper crops and prosperity, but the outcome turned disastrous when the rains failed for years on end, as they did in the late 1920s and 1930s. The dust bowl was a matter both of drought and of in-migration by people ignorant of the requirements of agricultural life on the prairies. Analogous episodes of quick environmental change—usually soil erosion—took place with the Anglo-Irish settlement of Australia, the Soviet Virgin Lands scheme in Kazakhstan in the 1950s, and the Indonesian program of "transmigration," that is, the settlement of Javanese on the outer, nonvolcanic islands of Indonesia. Indeed, every instance of frontier agriculture, whether on the world's grasslands or its tropical forests, involved the migration of people who inevitably practiced farming as they knew it in new places where doing so proved wasteful and disruptive. It seems to take a generation or more to learn (or to be obliged by nature to adopt) new ways. Today the North American prairie soils are still eroding, but at much slower rates than in the 1930s.

The great flows of international migration slowed sharply with World War I and the turn to more autarkic government policies in the interwar period. Only in the 1960s did international migration bounce back, when fast-growing economies with slow-growing populations opened their doors somewhat. By the end of that decade, perhaps 75 million people lived outside their country of birth. Today some 2 million legal migrants move across international borders annually, and nearly 200 million people live outside their country of birth, about 3 percent of the world's population. But this great resurgence has different environmental effects from those of earlier periods.

The great majority of international migrants today (as they will continue to do in the future) head for cities, not for wide-open prairies. And they head for cities in rich countries. Their migration has environmental implications, in both their homeland and their adopted city. Consider the Salvadoran peasants who leave home to work in construction in Washington, DC. Their departure reduces the pressure on Salvadoran soils and forest. Their arrival in Washington eventually results in additional vehicles (pickup trucks are the most popular), more heated and air-conditioned housing, and thus a net increase in CO_2 emissions. The main purpose of contemporary migration is to get richer and change one's lifestyle. Insofar as it is successful, each act of international migration transforms a person who used little energy into one who uses a lot, and one who caused little pollution into one who causes a lot. The average American is responsible for perhaps six to eight times more CO_2 emissions than the average Salvadoran (and 16,000 times more than the average Somali). At the same time, however, each migration, in this example, transfers someone from a place where making a living involves soil erosion, and possibly deforestation and biodiversity loss, to somewhere else where the migrant has almost no such effects. That is to say, the environmental effects of such migrations are considerable, although they are of different sorts in the sending and receiving countries.

Two significant exceptions to this general picture exist, cases of rural-to-rural migration in which ignorant agricultural practices continue to have notable effects. The first is the ongoing settlement of the world's tropical forests. The settlers mostly come from other kinds of environments. They typically lack the detailed knowledge necessary to raise food (or other crops) in rainforest environments without accelerating erosion, nutrient depletion, and in some cases laterization of the soil. They probably also lack the incentive to husband soils, because they have insecure tenure on the lands they clear. And many such migrants will in future hope, as their counterparts often do now, that their sojourns as pioneer farmers will be temporary: their long-term stake in the lands they farm will be nil.

The second case involves the grasslands of Inner Asia (see Reardon-Anderson 2000). Over the centuries Chinese farmers repeatedly tried to settle the semi-arid grasslands of the eastern Eurasian steppe (today's Inner Mongolia and Mongolia, as well as western Manchuria). Until 1760 they were usually repulsed, sooner or later, by the military power of nomadic herders. Since 1760 the farmers have, through the military efforts of the Chinese state, had the upper hand. A gradual settlement of favored regions took place under the last dynasty (i.e., to 1911), and in Manchuria a faster one during the era of Japanese control (1931–45). With encouragement from the People's Republic since 1949, millions of Chinese peasants moved north, testing the ability of the grasslands to support farming. This proved a success in that it provided a place for the millions of hungry people to go, and in that the epic of frontier settlement fitted nicely into the image of a vigorous new China propagated by the state. But it was, and is, extremely costly in ecological terms, as the steppe soils easily blow away into the Sea of Japan and the Pacific Ocean. This is not a great plowup on the scale of the North American prairie or of the speed of the Soviet Virgin Lands, but rather a long-term, gradual encroachment upon the grasslands, a last echo of earlier pulses of grassland settlement around the world.

In sum, migration continues to have significant environmental effects. The nature of those effects will continue to change. There will be less rural-to-rural migration, although I do not expect it to vanish altogether by 2050. Instead, there will be more urbanization, and in particular migration from rural areas in poor societies to cities in rich ones, a process that thoroughly changes the environmental implications of human settlement. But frontier transformation of ecosystems, a frequent feature of past millennia and a major feature of the twentieth century, is winding down fast.

Much will depend on the future scale of migration. Since the 1960s, the global proportion living as immigrants has remained in the range of 2–3 percent. That is likely to climb, at least until receiving countries choose to close their doors effectively (and that would prove difficult in practice). One reason, among many, that willing emigrants will be plentiful is the environmental degradation of places such as Central America and North Africa. "Environmental refugees" eagerly become immigrants if they can. The nineteenth and twentieth centuries witnessed several examples of this phenomenon (e.g., McNeill 1992), and the twenty-first will see more. But, as always, the volume of migration will be determined by many factors, most of which have little directly to do with environment.

Volatile uncertainties

Over the course of 50 years, it becomes probable that something improbable will happen. Indeed, in the field of environment this seems particularly likely, because the contemporary world has pared away many of its ecological buffers and has harnessed the earth much more tightly than ever before. The high degree of global interaction now means that perturbations can easily spread worldwide, whether a nasty microbe or a loss of confidence in the dollar (the US current account deficit is a house of cards). With reduced buffers, the chances increase for the unexpected, the nonlinear effect. Beyond that, the current emphasis on scientific and technological research, also unprecedented, is sure to yield path-changing results. So the future is less accessible, less predictable now than at almost any other time in history.

Technological trajectories are particularly unpredictable in their timing and effects. One plausible development that would radically alter the environmental future is a basic change in the energy system (see Committee on Alternatives and Strategies for Future Hydrogen Production and Use 2004). Although the United States has lately deepened its commitment to a fossil fuel energy regime, market forces and international politics seem to favor the development of alternative energies. Most analysts foresee no durable oil supply shortages before 2020 (but see Deffeyes 2001), and some see none until after 2050. But in the transport sector especially, the relevant technological advances seem to be occurring anyway. A breakthrough in storage technology could make renewable energy—geothermal and solar mainly—easily able to meet global demand at competitive cost. Brilliant and well-funded people are working on nuclear fusion. Energy efficiency (mainly a matter of technology) will be crucial: Shell's projections for world energy demand in 2050 vary from 50 to 200 gigajoules per capita depending on efficiency (Shell 2001). Sooner or later, it is certain, fossil fuels will fade out as the heart of the energy system, and when that happens, the pollution and climate change equations will be changed fundamentally. The future of urban air pollution and climate change depends on how soon it happens: the difference between, say, 2020 and 2070 would (ceteris paribus) be of major import for CO_2 concentrations in the atmosphere.

As a further example, genetic engineering of crops, animals, and perhaps humans will quite likely make a big difference, although not necessarily in the ways the biotechnologists imagine. Recent centuries are replete with examples of biological invasions, cases in which a species when introduced to new environments without predators or pathogens underwent a population explosion, sometimes causing expensive havoc. Australia's rabbit plague is the classic example; North America's zebra mussels a recent one. Newly created species, surely, will occasionally behave like newly introduced ones, escaping constraints and disrupting ecosystems exuberantly. And in the unlikely event that the fruits of biotechnology always obediently follow the careers planned for them, they will still have significant ecological effects. New pollution-eating bacteria, for example, are on the drawing boards.

Politics will help select the future. It, too, is volatile. Energy and environmental policies will shift frequently in the next 50 years. They will be embedded in larger political and ideological programs. I hazard the prediction that the current trend toward weaker regulation and greater reliance on the market, in general and in environmental policy, will last for another decade or two, but not much beyond (see Portney 2000 for an opposing view). The past, on my reading at least, shows pendular swings between states and markets as the dominant institutions shaping economy and society (see Schwartz 1994). In the era 1850–1914 markets achieved great freedom from state regulation in the Western world and, to a lesser degree, in much of the rest of the world too, thanks to imperialism on the part of liberal states. But the social changes generated by that era of liberal trade, investment, and migration policy led to resentments that fed nationalism. That sentiment turned a local dispute into a World War in 1914, during which state regulation of economic and social life became a refined art. For the next 30 years of depression and war, states exercised much stronger control. They began to relinquish it slowly after 1945, acquiescing to an American-led system of regulated sovereignty, and then relinquished it rapidly, if involuntarily, after the world economic turbulence of the 1970s. Since then markets once again have been in the ascendant.

But to assume that the current arrangement is natural or indefinitely preferable is naive. As in the period 1850–1914, a liberal order today is reshuffling fortunes in ways that create deep resentments, which will be harnessed to political programs that threaten the current order. The liberal order will lose its moral and intellectual legitimacy, and eventually crumble politically. If I am right about this, then at the very least the regulatory regime for environmental issues will tend toward the "legislate, regulate, and litigate" end of the spectrum and away from market-based incentives, which have achieved intellectual and political supremacy, especially in the United States since 1980 (Kosobud and Zimmerman 1997). Such an outcome would also spell greater difficulty for international environmental regulation, which has met with modest success to date (for example, accords on international trade in toxic wastes and CFC emissions). And, unthinkably perhaps, it could lead to far worse things, analogous to the events of 1914–45. Whatever it will lead to, I expect we will have a good idea well before 2050.

The future locus of sovereignty is also in doubt, and trends there will shape environmental policy. The conventional wisdom foresees a weakening of national sovereignty by a devolution of power to local, state, or provincial authorities, and a simultaneous transfer of some powers to supranational bodies. This has been the recent pattern, notably in Europe, and it has begun to change the face of environmental policy. The European Union sets identical standards for beach cleanliness in Greece and Germany. But the validity of this conventional wisdom is not certain, contingent as it is upon a failure of nationalism to rear its venerable head.

Politics will affect the relationship between population and environment not merely in the realm of policy. Indeed, in the past the greatest importance of politics to the environment lay not in environmental policies and politics, but rather in the unintentional side effects of conventional politics, the quotidian quests for wealth, power, security. Nationalism, for example, led to state and societal behavior with myriad environmental and demographic consequences: Brazil's effort to develop Amazonia after 1960 so as to deny it to neighboring countries and, later, to more distant countries; Ceaucescu's attempt to maximize the number of Romanians after 1966, one of the more effective if short-lived pronatalist policies; Mao's effort to surpass British steel production levels in the demographically and environmentally disastrous Great Leap Forward, 1958–61 (Kligman 1998; Shapiro 2001).

Among the ways in which political changes could have large impacts is through public health regimes. In the twentieth century humankind stole a march on the microbes that previously did so much to keep us in check. From the 1880s we built sanitation infrastructure that curbed waterborne diseases in particular. From the 1910s we instituted vaccination regimes that checked several contagious diseases; and from the 1940s we used antibiotics against bacterial infections. These measures of course applied, and still apply, quite unevenly around the world. But their cumulative influence on health and population was widespread. By far their greatest impact came after 1950, in comparatively favorable political circumstances. But such regimes can decay, as has happened in Russia in recent decades, and they can collapse, as they have in Congo in the last eight to ten years, during which disease and violence claimed between 2 and 4 million lives.

The success of antibiotics, vaccination regimes, and sanitation infrastructure all depends on propitious political circumstances. Antibiotic resistance is on the rise, and reversing it would require great civic-mindedness on the part of physicians, patients, and farmers (most antibiotics are fed to livestock) around the world. Devising new drugs could blunt the impact of rising resistance, but new drugs are likely to be more expensive than old ones. Vaccination regimes have eroded widely, mainly because of their very success, but in chaotic societies for simple practical reasons. Further decay is likely in cases where markets acquire full ascendancy and health care is rationed by price, and collapse is certain in cases of state breakdown. All this is to say that since 1950 world politics has been unusually stable, and effective public health regimes unusually easy to install and maintain. We should not assume this set of circumstances will last.

Conclusion

The general practice in the twentieth century was to harness nature as tightly as possible to make it perform in the ordinary interests of individuals, organizations, and governments. These entities pursued traditional agendas of self-aggrandizement and security. Such agendas are likely to dominate the next 50 years too, because they are deeply rooted within our institutions and probably within us—the default settings of our brains as they developed over the long haul of hominid (and presumably pre-hominid) evolution. Cultural practices can blunt the thrust of these agendas for some people some of the time, but, on the evidence of history, not for all people.

Further population growth will tighten nature's harness considerably, but by just how much will be decided largely by new technologies. In recent decades a "green bias" has developed in technology: it is harder than before to promote a new technology that is manifestly bad for the environment. New ones are selected, partly, for their minimal or benign environmental impacts. This is likely to remain the case, because environmental anxiety is unlikely to fade, notwithstanding the hostility of some governments to environmental regulation. So new technologies will be, on balance, more resource-efficient and less polluting than older ones. How much so, and how fast they come, will be matters of politics as well as science and engineering. Perhaps the key question for global environmental issues will be how quickly new technology diffuses to the fast-growing populations and the newly industrializing regions. It is theoretically possible that these regions might "leapfrog" into a greener future, bypassing the dirtier stages of industrialization. But to do this they will need the cooperation of firms and governments in the countries that produce new technologies, which is and will likely remain a small club composed of Japan, South Korea, Western Europe, and North America, although others, such as China and India, may yet gain admittance. That cooperation is by no means assured; indeed on present trends I would guess it is unlikely. To transfer the latest technologies, the firms in question will want fuller ownership of enterprises in India and China than populations and governments in those countries will sanction. But China has formally committed itself to technological "leapfrogging" and may have the capital and expertise with which to do it (Lovins 2005: 82). If it is true that world population will begin to decline before 2100, and that technologies will carry a green bias, then the long-run prognosis for environmental health and stability is good. The difficulty will come in trying to get there from here, trying to squeeze 9 billion people, as it were, through the eye of the needle.

Notes

1 These data come from McNeill 2000: 281–287 and Brinkhoff 2005. Drawing on UN estimates, Cohen (2005: 48) says the global population will be half urban in 2007 or so.

2 Family structures, which exist in exuberant variety, may offer differing incentives to parenthood, so that higher fertility might survive in cities with a family structure conducive to childrearing.

3 Considerable methodological difficulties surround the procedures of calculating ecological footprints. Criticism has been particularly directed at inclusion of a notional forested area needed to offset a city's greenhouse gas emissions.

4 See Netherlands Committee for the World Conservation Union [n.d.] for a nuanced assessment.

References

Ausubel, Jesse. 2002. "Maglevs and the Vision of St. Hubert," in W. Steffen, J. Jaeger and D. Carson (eds.), *Challenges of a Changing Earth*. Heidelberg: Springer Verlag. See «http://phe.rockefeller.edu.sthubert».

Brinkhoff, Thomas. 2005. "The principal agglomerations of the world," «www.citypopulation.de» (accessed 1 October 2005).

Cohen, Joel. 2005. "The human population grows up," *Scientific American* 293(3): 48–55.

Cohen, Robin (ed.). 1995. *The Cambridge Survey of World Migration*. New York: Cambridge University Press.

Committee on Alternatives and Strategies for Future Hydrogen Production and Use, Board on Energy and Environmental Systems, Division on Engineering and Physical Sciences, National Research Council and National Academy of Engineering of the National Academies. 2004. *The Hydrogen Economy: Opportunities, Costs, Barriers, and R&D Needs*. Washington, DC: The National Academies Press.

Deffeyes, Kenneth. 2001. *Hubbert's Peak: The Impending World Oil Challenge.* Princeton: Princeton University Press.

Hall, Jane V. 1995. "Air quality policy in developing countries," *Contemporary Economic Policy* 13: 77–85.

Hunt, Constance E. 2004. *Thirsty Planet.* London: Zed Books.

Kirk, Dudley. 1946. *Europe's Population in the Interwar Years.* Geneva: League of Nations.

Klein, Herbert. 1999. *The Atlantic Slave Trade.* New York: Cambridge University Press.

Klein Goldewijk, Kees. 2001. "Estimating global land use change over the past 300 years: The HYDE database," *Global Biogeochemical Cycles* 15: 417–433.

Klein Goldewijk, Kees and N. Ramankutty. 2004. "Land cover change over the last three centuries due to human activities: The availability of new global data sets," *GeoJournal* 61(4): 335–344.

Kligman, Gail. 1998. *The Politics of Duplicity: Controlling Fertility in Ceausescu's Romania.* Berkeley: University of California Press.

Kosobud, Richard F. and Jennifer M. Zimmerman. 1997. *Market-based Approaches to Environmental Policy: Regulatory Innovations to the Fore.* New York: Van Nostrand Reinhold.

Lovins, Amory. 2005. "More profit with less carbon," *Scientific American* 293(3): 74–82.

L'vovich, Mark I. and Gilbert F. White. 1990. "Use and transformation of terrestrial water systems," in B. L. Turner et al. (eds.), *The Earth As Transformed by Human Action.* New York: Cambridge University Press, pp. 235–252.

MacFarlane, Alan. 1997. *Savage Wars of Peace: England, Japan and the Malthusian Trap.* Oxford: Blackwell.

McNeill, J. R. 1992. *The Mountains of the Mediterranean World: An Environmental History.* New York: Cambridge University Press.

———. 2000. *Something New Under the Sun: An Environmental History of the 20th-Century World.* New York: Norton.

Murray, Christopher J. L. and Alan D. Lopez (eds.). 1996. *The Global Burden of Disease.* Cambridge, MA: Harvard School of Public Health.

Netherlands Committee for IUCN. [n.d.]. "The Netherlands and the world ecology," «http://www.nciucn.nl/english/projects/econ_ecol/nwe/fsecology+.htm».

Portney, Paul R. 2000. "Environmental problems and policy: 2000–2050," *Journal of Economic Perspectives* 14: 199–206.

Reardon-Anderson, James. 2000. "Land and society in Manchuria and Inner Mongolia during the Qing Dynasty," *Environmental History* 5: 503–530.

Rees, William E. 1996. "Revisiting carrying capacity: Area-based indicators of sustainability," *Population and Environment* 17(3): 195–217.

Reinhard, Marcel, André Armengaud, and Jacques Dupâquier. 1968. *Histoire générale de la population mondiale.* Paris: Editions Montchrestien.

RIVM. 2002. «http://www.rivm.nl/env/int/hyde/index.html» [= Rijksinstituut voor Volksgezonheid en Milieu]

RIVM/UNEP. 1997. Bakkes, Jan and Jaap van Woerden (eds.), *The Future of the Global Environment.* Bilthoven: RIVM.

Rosenzweig, Cynthia and Daniel Hillel. 1998. *Climate Change and the Global Harvest: Potential Impacts of the Greenhouse Effect on Agriculture.* New York: Oxford University Press.

Schwartz, Herman. 1994. *States versus Markets: History, Geography, and the Development of the International Political Economy.* New York: St. Martin's Press.

Shapiro, Judith. 2001. *Mao's War Against Nature.* New York: Cambridge University Press.

Shell. 2001. *Exploring the Future: Energy Needs, Choices and Possibilities.* London: Shell International Global Business Environment.

Shiklomanov, Igor. 1993. "World fresh water resources," in Peter Gleick (ed.), *Water in Crisis.* New York and Oxford: Oxford University Press, pp. 12–24.

———. 1999. "Information about world water use and water availability," «http://webworld.unesco.org/water/ihp/db/shiklomanov/index.shtml».

UNFPA. 2001. *The State of World Population 2001.* «http://www.unfpa.org/swp/2001».

Seeking Sustainability: Cities, Countryside, Wilderness

DAVID G. VICTOR

In this chapter I explore the implications of past and future changes in popu-lation for cities, countryside, and wilderness. The motivation for this inves-tigation is the growing interest in promoting "sustainable development," by which most people envision some orderly improvement in the human con-dition (cities and countryside) as well as some protection of environments where humans rarely or never trod (wilderness).

My plan is to examine the human sphere and the natural sphere sepa-rately and to explore, in the course of the analysis, the dividing lines between the two. Throughout, I emphasize three themes. First is the importance of institutions—that is, norms that govern the ways humans interact. The in-creasingly urgent attention to sustainability reflects a concern that trajectories, left to their own momentum, are diverging from goals. Changes in behavior are needed to bring the two into line, and that leads to institutions. The big news in development studies is that institutions, primarily those that operate within countries, are the key to development. Outsiders can play a role, such as with development assistance, but their ability to exert leverage is limited.

Second, I examine the problem of values. Assessing the sustainability of trajectories and estimating the ways that human institutions may respond requires a theory of values that is useful over the 50-year time horizon of this study—a tall order within a given society and more so when prognosti-cating at the global level.

Third, I explore how trends in the human occupation of nature are affecting the dividing line between mankind and nature. In the past, indus-trialized societies have defined that line by expanding the geographical area of the human sphere and fashioning nature into an aesthetically pleasing countryside. Through the garden movement of the nineteenth century, na-ture and countryside were made synonymous; nature's protectors defined their mission as ordering and managing the greenery. The frontier—beyond the space occupied by humans—attracted explorers and adventurers but was seen neither as threatened nor as needing protection for its own unmanaged sake. With the rise of a view that values nature for its own unmanaged sake—wilderness as wilderness—lines are being drawn around man's garden. According to this new view, the goal is not to keep wilderness out but gardens in.

My argument is that the human sphere increasingly operates as a single organism because the institutions in cities and countryside are becoming integrated as information, equipment, and ideology spread worldwide. In large measure those institutions operate on principles of markets. The connections as well as the efficiency of markets are speeding the diffusion of technology; in this chapter I use examples of technologies of electrification, but similar technological diffusions are taking place in essentially every field of economic activity, including telecommunications, transportation, and agriculture. I also argue that this change in technology can be good news for wilderness, or it could spell disaster. The problem for wilderness is that only a tiny fraction of the world population seems to value wilderness for its own sake. Wilderness has not been protected in response to a groundswell of public pressure. Rather, to date, the best protector of the wilderness has been its sheer remoteness. However, the same technological changes that are integrating city and countryside also make it possible for humans to put footprints anywhere on Earth. Jet aircraft have reduced travel times; technological and managerial improvements in tourism have lowered the real cost of travel; for much of the world, incomes have swelled—a trend that seems likely to continue in the future. For the same fraction of time and income available every year, most households can travel further. Will they fly between New York and Chicago more often, or will they spend time and money commuting to ranchettes in the Amazon? Over the time horizon of 50 years, the fraction of the world population that could have access to and interest in the distant wilderness will probably grow dramatically. Will they tread lightly?

Sustainability

Before exploring the implications of the sustainable development movement for cities, countryside, and wilderness, it is essential to understand the concept of "sustainability" itself. As a political agenda, "sustainable development" is arguably one of the most successful examples of the last three decades. Even as scholars have become more skeptical of sustainable development as a wooly notion that is unable to focus serious research programs, politically its appeal has grown for the same reason: it is sufficiently elastic that it can include a wide array of views, while not so amorphous that it lacks all meaning.

The concept has persisted for two reasons. First, it is the only concept that provided a durable bridge between the conflicting aims of industrialized and developing countries. In international politics, the power of devel-

oping countries has risen steadily since the 1950s when many of these countries did not even exist as independent entities. The rising power of the
South was widely discovered only in the aftermath of the first oil shock in
1973. The New International Economic Order symbolized that power, even
if the NIEO itself was the engine of almost no tangible achievements. The
endless negotiations over the Law of the Sea, in particular on the provisions for sharing revenue from hypothetical deep sea mining, underscored
the lesson that future diplomacy would be required to contend with problems of underdevelopment, the core of the developing-country agenda.

In that environment, the Brundtland Commission received its charter
in 1982 to explore the long-term prospects for protecting the environment.
Their report in 1987 crafted the definition of sustainable development that
has become the most often cited ever since:

> Humanity has the ability to make development sustainable—to ensure that it
> meets the needs of the present without compromising the ability of future
> generations to meet their own needs.

> Yet in the end, sustainable development is not a fixed state of harmony, but
> rather a process of change in which the exploitation of resources, the direc-
> tion of investments, the orientation of technological development, and insti-
> tutional change are made consistent with future as well as present needs.
> (WCED 1987: 8, 9)

The Brundtland definition has become widely cited not only because it was
first (see Clark and Munn 1986) but also because it did not run afoul of the
main North–South political currents. It embraced protection of natural resources, an agenda in the North, while also embracing the South's agenda for
fair economic development. It was largely silent on whether Nature should
be protected for its own sake—a growing agenda in parts of the industrialized
world. It avoided fixing specific obligations toward present and future, noting
only that exploitation of resources should be "consistent" with future needs.

The key intellectual contribution of the Brundtland definition—what
kept it from being dismissed by analysts—was its prominent embrace of
technological change. The concept of sustainable development, along with
Brundtland's entire report, underscored that sustainable development was
not a static state of affairs. The hypothesis that there were rapidly advancing
"limits to growth," posited vigorously in the early 1970s and attacked with
equal fervor at the same time, had run aground on exactly that point.

The problem of values

The real problem for sustainability is valuation. What are the priorities of
Western societies? What are the priorities of other societies? How do we
order choices when priorities conflict? How do we take account of future

generations? Some of these questions can be answered; for others, it is possible to provide outlines of answers. But when making hard choices about the allocation of investment and the protection of natural resources, it is hard to provide precise answers to all these questions simultaneously. The problem of valuation across societies is difficult to solve because there is no universally accepted mechanism for resolving differences in valuations. The problem of valuation over time is especially difficult to solve not only because values change but also because decisions to protect a resource for the future often entail tradeoffs that have other intergenerational consequences. In particular, knowledge is an intergenerational public good: decisions to protect a resource and possibly slow economic growth in one period can slow the accumulation of knowledge and degrade the many benefits that multiply from knowledge accumulation. Essentially the same issues have arisen in other theories of justice. Rawls (1972) explicitly rejects the notion of a single application of his theory of justice that pertains across nations (but see Beitz 1985), and the weakest aspect of attempts to put Rawls's theory into operation concerns his imaginary dialogue between generations behind the veil of ignorance.

These problems of sustainability and priorities, so far, are unsolved. The only answers rely on informed political dialogue as a process through which priorities are shaped and agreed upon. Thus, one way to assess the priorities for sustainable development is to examine the priorities that have emerged from focused dialogues. Table 1 shows the priorities from two recent global dialogues about sustainable development issues: the Millennium Summit of 2000 and the 2002 Monterrey Summit on Financing for Sustainable Development. The listed goals are drawn from the final communiqués. Having cut through the boilerplate and diffuse aspirations that suffuse these documents, the items listed in Table 1 emerge as concrete statements derived from intense political bargaining focused on the objective of sustainable development and the areas where current trajectories are inadequate. The goals of Table 1, known as the Millennium Development Goals (MDGs), have been parsed by the UN Secretariat into specific targets and indicators. These goals suffer because they were invented by conference elites and do not reflect much depth of agreement among the participating states. I remain skeptical about the value of global goals because the tradeoffs that comprise sustainable development ultimately arise at the local level (Victor 2006); nonetheless, the MDGs are a start.

Before turning to particulars, it is worth noting that all the goals listed in Table 1 focus on the human sphere. Not one concerns wilderness, which should make one suspicious of whether wilderness plays any role in a globally confirmed concept of sustainable development. Certainly the need to protect wilderness is a central part of the concept of sustainable development advanced by many stakeholders, especially in the advanced industrialized countries, but the depth of that concern in the nations that represent

TABLE 1   Goals from the Millennium and Monterrey Summits

1. Between 1990 and 2015, to halve the proportion of people whose income is less than $1 a day and the proportion of people suffering from hunger.

2. To ensure that by 2015 all children will be able to complete a full course of primary schooling.

3. Eliminate gender disparity in primary and secondary education, preferably by 2005, and at all levels of education no later than 2015.

4. Reduce by two-thirds, between 1990 and 2015, the under-five mortality rate.

5. Reduce by three-quarters, between 1990 and 2015, the maternal mortality ratio.

6. To have halted by 2015 and begun to reverse the spread of HIV/AIDS and begun to reverse the incidence of malaria and other major diseases.

7. To integrate the principles of sustainable development into country policies; to halve by 2015 the proportion of people without sustainable access to safe drinking water and basic sanitation; and to have achieved a significant improvement by 2020 in the lives of at least 100 million slum dwellers.

8. To develop a global partnership for development.

SOURCE: From UN Millennium Declaration (8 September 2000) and Monterrey Consensus (22 March 2002), adjusted through UN diplomatic processes and summarized compactly in World Bank/IMF (2005).

most of the world's 6.5 billion inhabitants is not great. The problem of valuation rears its head.

Cities

The long-term trend in human movement and habitation is to large cities, and essentially every projection envisions that this pattern will continue for the next half century and beyond. Table 2, for example, shows projections to 2030 reported by the United Nations Centre for Human Settlements (UNCHS 2001). The causes of urbanization are complex, but it is not too simplistic to claim that urbanization and economic development go hand in hand. The most highly developed regions of the world have the highest levels of urbanization; areas of widespread poverty—Africa and South Asia, in particular— have the lowest. Average incomes in cities typically exceed those of rural areas by a large margin. Active policies that are needed to prevent people from moving to urban areas, such as the apartheid-era system of requiring low-income workers (i.e., nonwhites) to prove employment to earn urban residence, reveal the draw of large cities; when such programs falter, rural dwellers rush in. So far, when people are allowed to vote with their feet they head to cities; no matter how terrible the failings of urban life, it usually surpasses the boredom, squalor, and lack of opportunity in the countryside.

To a first approximation, then, the current and future challenge of sustainability is a challenge of urban development. Greater numbers will accu-

TABLE 2   UNCHS projections for levels of urbanization and numbers of rural dwellers in 2015 and 2030

Region	2000	2015	2030
Urbanization (% urban)			
Africa	37.9	46.5	54.5
Asia	36.7	44.7	53.4
Europe	74.8	78.6	82.6
Latin America	75.3	79.9	83.2
Northern America	77.2	80.9	84.4
Oceania	70.2	71.2	74.4
World	47.0	53.4	60.3
Total number of rural dwellers (billions)			
Africa	0.49	0.58	0.64
Asia	2.33	2.40	2.27
Europe	0.18	0.15	0.12
Latin America	0.13	0.13	0.12
Northern America	0.071	0.066	0.058
Oceania	0.009	0.010	0.011
World	3.21	3.34	3.22

SOURCE: UNCHS (2001).

mulate in urban areas, and the more successful we are in meeting the challenge of urban sustainability the more rapidly people will accumulate further in urban areas—further concentrating (and probably easing) the task of sustainable development. That conclusion seems to sit uneasily with romantic notions of pastoral, rural life; it also sits uneasily beside fears that urban concentrations will become hotbeds of activism and discontent. Pastoral ideal is no match for urban opportunity; discontent is a symptom of other failings in government.

Inadequate water supply and poor sanitation are chief among the causes of human illness and feature prominently in the goals listed in Table 1. Table 3 gives a snapshot for selected countries in Africa, Asia, and Latin America of how rural and urban dwellers fare in their connections to water and sewerage infrastructures, measured here as in-house piped water and in-house toilets. The data are far from perfect. Urban areas are probably more likely to attract unregistered (and thus uncounted) households that go without piped water or sewerage connections, which may account for some of the difference between urban and rural areas. Moreover, some of the difference between urban and rural performance is due to differences in income. Urbanites usually enjoy political advantages that allow them to channel public resources for their infrastructures. But the central point remains: without exception, urban dwellers fare better. The cause of this difference appears to stem from the density of urban life. The cost of infrastructures is

TABLE 3   Water and sanitation services in urban and rural areas of selected countries in Africa, Asia, and Latin America

Country and year	Piped water inside (% of housing units)	Inside toilet (flush and non-flush, % of housing units)
Africa		
Botswana 1996		
Urban	100.0	23.6
Rural	53.1	3.3
Kenya 1989		
Urban	84.8	28.7
Rural	16.6	0.4
Senegal 1994		
Urban	80.0	77.4
Rural	23.2	16.4
South Africa 1996		
Urban	66.0	78.1
Rural	10.9	8.6
Asia		
Iran 1996		
Urban	96.3	99.6
Rural	70.8	96.2
Malaysia 1991		
Urban	90.3	94.1
Rural	51.4	79.5
Pakistan 1998		
Urban	58.3	35.7
Rural	12.7	26.3
Latin America		
Argentina 1991		
Urban	82.4	99.0
Rural	39.9	97.8
Brazil 1998		
Urban	92.8	96.9
Rural	49.7	65.5
Mexico 1996		
Urban	69.9	84.5
Rural	17.6	29.2

SOURCE: UNCHS (2001), Table A.6.

lower when households are packed tightly. Costly spurs that serve few households are avoided; network effects from linked infrastructures multiply; fixed assets, such as sewage treatment plants and water purification facilities, can be amortized over many customers. Similar arguments explain why telecommunications, postal service, and other networked services are more abundant in urban areas than in rural zones.

The task of urban development is not fundamentally different from the task of development itself, about which much has been written. The current consensus seems to focus on four elements:

—participation of (and accountability to) civil society, lest the actions of those who govern become disconnected from the interests of the people (WCED 1987; UNDP 2005; Sen 1999);

—balanced budgets, lest the burden of servicing debt overshadow other functions of government (Easterly 2003; World Bank 1998);

—"rule of law," lest individuals (including investors) find themselves unable to predict and contain the behavior of government and other individuals (UNDP 2005; World Bank/IMF 2005);

—reliance upon markets to allocate resources, including market competition with foreign suppliers, lest governments and firms squander resources and fail to find innovative ways to supply services (World Bank 1998; World Bank/IMF 2005).

The full list is much longer, and no two experts can agree on the priorities, which vary by context. All of these conditions for development have posed difficulties at different times and in different places. Participation and accountability have caused democratic congestion—as in India today, where major elements of environmental policy are now being decided by courts because democratic institutions have proved unable to deliver decisions. In many other settings, including throughout much of Africa, public participation is merely a front for unaccountable cronyism, made worse by the absence of independent media (Zakaria 2003). Subsidies, such as those supplied for electric power by Indian states, have caused severe misallocation of scarce capital resources and have also made it hard for governments to supply other basic services, such as health (Tongia 2006). In countries, including Russia, without a strong tradition of legal independence, efforts to empower legal institutions have caused further entrenchment of interests rather than the rule of law.

But the real battleground is on the role of the market. Left to themselves, market forces do not necessarily deliver the priorities of sustainable development. Markets do offer the promise of efficient delivery, provided that market structures are conducive to private investment and competition. Additional regulation and planning are needed. The experience with privately owned water and transport infrastructures has been spotty, though promising where consumers have been able and willing to pay, where populations are not so transient that they have no interest in long-term investment in collective goods, and where rule of law exists to safeguard property rights (Kessides 2004; see also Harris 2003; Ros 1999). This last point seems particularly important because key resource infrastructures—energy, water, sanitation—are potentially attractive to outside investors only if they believe they can recover their investment. The last decade has shown those investments to be extremely risky. In electric power production, notably, the fashion in the 1990s was to entice foreign investors to build plants that would sell electricity on conditions set by long-term power purchase agreements (PPAs). As long as economies grew and demand for electricity rose, PPAs were honored; in the downswing, such as after the Asian financial crisis, PPAs unravel. Provisions for sovereign guarantees and binding international arbitration are ignored. Having sunk the capital into assets bolted to the ground, investors are forced to supply power at lower yet unpredictable costs (Woodhouse 2005).

Even if governors of particular cities, acting alone or with national authorities, were able to create the conditions for market supply of basic city services, it is unclear whether markets would be trusted or effective. In transportation, for example, the two most often cited examples of effective city services—Curitiba, Brazil and Portland, Oregon—owe their success to long-term urban planning, not to market forces. In its most fundamental sense, city planning is just that—planning, not markets.

Countryside

According to the projections of the United Nations Centre for Human Settlements, some time around 2015 the absolute number of rural dwellers will peak—at about 3.3 billion, or somewhat less than half the world's total population that year—and then decline steadily. What might be the causes and implications of this great rural emptying out?

It is quite possible, perhaps likely, that the decline in rural population will be rapid, rather than gradual. This could be a surprise for demographers, much as the crash in birth rates came as a surprise. The cause of this exodus is, in part, innovation in rural activities, mainly agriculture, which tends to spare employment and release people in search of other opportunities. They will leave the countryside for cities, where innovation and economic growth tend to generate jobs with higher average wage levels than farming. (Poor skills, however, may shut many out of skilled job markets.) Indeed, the success of rural development programs—advanced, often, with the aim of keeping rural populations in place—may actually speed the pace of rural-to-urban migration. Successful development brings electricity and telecommunications, and with it regular news by telephone, radio, and television of urban opportunity. Success in rural education provides skills that increase the chance that urban opportunity offers higher wages. Of the major elements of rural development strategies, only housing, water, and health programs seem unambiguously to make rural areas less likely to empty. Yet governments rarely invest only in rural development strategies focused on those needs; they make similar investments in housing, water, and health for urban zones—increasing their magnetic power.

The great exodus, by itself, will not solve the problems of rural life, if only because billions will still live in rural areas and the predicaments of rural life are many. I have already noted the lower penetration of piped water and sewerage connections in rural areas, so here I focus on energy. By far, the world's number-one air pollution problem is indoor air pollution—mainly in rural areas and caused mainly by burning wood, crop residues, and waste (WEC/FAO 1999). Table 4 shows results from a typical survey that compares measured concentrations of indoor air pollutants with WHO standards for safe levels and makes the point, now well known, that breathing indoors in a poor rural household is a hazardous business (Smith and Mehta 2003; Kammen 1995). These hazards are not exclusively rural—extremely poor households in urban areas also burn wood, dirty coal, and even some crop residues—but the vast majority of the estimated 2 billion people who do not have access to modern energy services live in rural areas. The consequences of how they use energy are felt not only in the lungs but also in time budgets; rural dwellers, especially women, spend inordinate amounts of time collecting wood and wastes for burning (Levine et al. 2001). They also devote significant fractions of time to collecting water, a task that would be greatly reduced by electric pumps and often extremely modest investments in infrastructure.

By conventional economic analysis, a wide range of energy choices is available to serve rural areas. Connections to the electricity grid, it seems, are just about as costly as installing small hydroelectric plants for local minigrids or installing various wind or solar technologies. In practice, though, in most areas of the world the choice is connection to the grid. This occurs not only because grid-connected electricity is familiar and often the least costly option in areas that are not too distant from main grid lines but also because alternative options are perceived as second-class. People want to connect to the grid not only to enable them to use one or two light bulbs for a few hours every night, or a radio. The first connection is a stepping stone for

TABLE 4   Typical indoor air pollution measurements due to cooking with traditional fuels compared with WHO safe levels

	Indoor concentration of pollutants from a typical cook stove (mg/m^3)	Safe levels (mg/m^3)
Carbon monoxide	150	10
Particles	3.3	0.1
Benzene	0.8	0.002
1,3-Butadiene	0.15	0.0003
Formaldehyde	0.7	0.1

SOURCE: WHO (2004).

further consumption of electricity—an iron, television, or refrigerator. All these "new" uses for electricity take precedence over finding alternatives to the dirty coal, wood, and dung that are burned for heat and cooking.

Over the past century, the advanced industrialized countries underwent a similar process of rural electrification, and their experience helps to elucidate what may happen over the next 50 years in the developing world. Essentially all of the industrialized countries adopted policies to connect rural areas to the grid, with the result that the cost per mile of new wires dropped sharply—a classic "learning by doing" phenomenon, along with economies of scale—and the economics and culture of rural life became integrated more tightly with the rest of the country. Rural electricity spread the benefits of clean and safe lighting, radio, and eventually television to rural areas; it was critical to the spread of refrigeration, which in turn sharply reduced the cost (and improved the safety) of food, even for people who lived right at the farm gate. Almost simultaneously rural and urban dwellers had access to similar information, bought similar products, and started having similar lives.

A similar integration of rural and urban life will probably accompany the spread of electricity in the developing world. I focus on the economic dimension to make the point. Electrification is only part of a broad trend away from traditional fuels and toward fuels traded in commercial markets. Figure 1 shows the steady decline in noncommercial fuels as a fraction of total energy supply; although the exact path of this "commercial energy transition" varies, the basic shape of the trajectory does not.

What drives down the share of noncommercial fuels is, first and foremost, the much greater quantity of energy consumed when people rely on commercial fuels. The density of energy in a bottle of liquefied petroleum gas or a liter of gasoline far exceeds what a villager could collect in crop residue or waste in a whole week, and the commercial fuels burn hotter, with greater precision, and more efficiently: their relative advantage in terms of useful energy is even greater than with respect to their total energy content. The key economic consequence of this transition is that fuel costs become a budgeted expense; along with crop prices they are one of the first connections between rural household economics and the rest of the economy. Although some of these rural energy forms are often subsidized, governments are under strong pressure to reduce subsidies to tame their budgets. One hypothesis, to my knowledge not yet investigated, is that a tighter connection between rural and urban households will favor rural-to-urban migration because the opportunities to earn cash—the stuff of normal market transactions, rather than the barter and sweat that are the mainstays of noncommercial energy systems—are much greater in urban economies. Indeed, much of the rural economy is already urban, inasmuch as the main source of cash is often remittances from relatives who live and work in urban areas.

**FIGURE 1   Percent of crop and residue waste (CRW) in total
primary energy consumption as a function of income, 1961–2000**

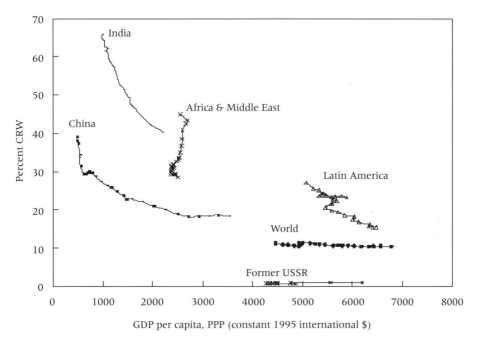

SOURCE: FAO (2002): World Bank (2002): BP (2002).

The economics of rural electrification are particularly interesting because electricity is costly to store, and thus investments in the electric power
system must be planned according to peak load. Figure 2 shows recent data
for peak loads during a typical winter week. (In very hot climates where
incomes are high, maximum annual peak load typically occurs during summer afternoons when air conditioners operate at full blast.) The South African market is typical of less wealthy countries, where air conditioning is
unaffordable to most; moreover, the country's cooler climate means that
demand for air conditioning is less than in tropical climes. The spread between the daily peaks—one in the morning and one in the afternoon, associated with diurnal heating and cooking as well as evening lighting and television—and the baseload is expected to increase over the next decade by 15
percent to 20 percent. This is a direct reflection of the success of electrification programs, especially in rural areas, already evident in the top segments
of the figure. By contrast, baseload demand for electricity, mainly from mining and smelting operations that drone on day and night, barely changes
during the day. Fluctuations in the demand for electric power in the mining industry depend mainly on world metal prices, not the diurnal cycle.

    The net effect of this shift to higher spikes in peak loads is the need
either to increase peak generation capacity or to find ways to level the load.

FIGURE 2 Typical weekly peak electricity winter loads in South Africa, 2002

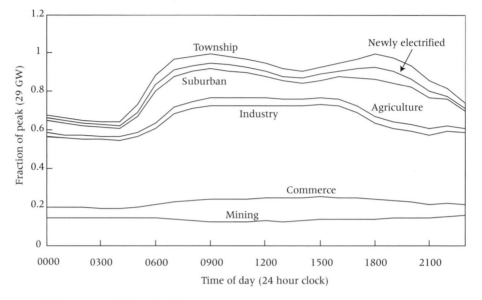

SOURCE: Data courtesy of Eskom, South Africa, and plotted by author.

Both solutions are costly and both have implications for rural life. Investing in new electric generating capacity requires either getting government to supply the capital or creating a financially self-sustaining power system that can attract private investment. In much of the world, governments are either unwilling or unable to supply capital for infrastructure. In most countries, creating a financially self-sustaining system will require a large rise in tariffs. South Africa, for example, currently enjoys some of the cheapest electricity in the world—a product of cheap coal, few environmental controls, and pressure from the government to keep costs low. Attracting investment in new capacity will require higher tariffs or substantial government subsidies.

When the capacity of government to subsidize rural life wanes, the basic structure of the electric power market seems destined to raise the price of electricity. Compared with a rural economy powered by dung, firewood, and soft coal sold by street hawkers, the impact on the rural household budget will be dramatic. Energy services will consume a large share of the budget. Rural life will look even less attractive when compared with urban alternatives. Few countries have allowed the market to put proper prices on rural power, but the trend is in that direction because pressure to control budget deficits seems destined to compel governments to shift the cost of power to households.

A similar story of costly rural service could be told for other infrastructures. These factors help to explain the emptying out of rural areas and suggest that the great rural-to-urban migration could proceed much more rapidly than now projected.

What will happen to the land left behind? Part of the answer depends on whether abandoned rural areas are given back to wilderness, the subject of the next section. Part also depends on whether urban dwellers stay in the city. So far, we have treated rural-to-urban migration as a one-way event. At the same time, high incomes of city life have made it possible to afford parallel lives in the country—ranchettes, ski chalets, golf mansions, and the like that allow easy proximate assault on nature. Viewed globally, this phenomenon currently exerts little impact on the landscape because only a relatively small number of people have the incomes needed to sustain these dual lives and to travel between city and country on a regular basis. Perhaps no more than 10 million households worldwide have the income of approximately $100,000 per year that is needed to sustain two or more homes, but by 2050 that number could rise substantially. Indeed, perhaps the greatest deficiency in long-term prognosticating is the nearly complete failure of analysts to explore the numbers and behavior of the super-rich who will have the capacity to exert a large and lasting influence on Earth.

It is possible to make some predictions about the contours of double and triple lives—for sake of a term, call it the "Hamptonization" of the countryside. Travel time budgets will probably chiefly determine which parts of the countryside become occupied. As shown in Figure 3, average time devoted to travel is an anthropological quasi-constant of approximately 1.1 hours per day that does not vary with income. Thus homes that are destined for regular use must be close (in travel times) to the cities that are their real lifeline to money and culture. Yet these homes must also be in "the country." The result is likely to be a donut of rural affluence that grows up around cities—outside the urban boundary line, within semi-commuting distance, and managed for its rural attributes. These rich greenbelts will be regulated tightly to keep them green—a modern version of the nineteenth-century garden. Barring new forms of high-speed transportation and more efficient "modal splits" (the transfer time between modes of transportation), these green donuts are unlikely to have a radius of more than 30 to 45 miles around cities. Bigger donuts require longer transportation times, which violates the 1.1-hours-per-day average, or faster transport systems.

Air travel, because it is fast, allows escape from the hometown donut for the semi-commuter. The commuter who has a pied-à-terre five minutes from his office accumulates nearly ten hours of "unused" commuting time every two weeks, allowing him to travel great distances (by jet) to airports that define the center of other living networks and then shorter distances (by car or helicopter) to the green donuts.[1] Direct commercial flights from New York to Vail, Colorado allow this kind of network Hamptonization already, although the true potential of commercial transport is severely hampered by

FIGURE 3   Average hours per day devoted to travel as a function of income per head

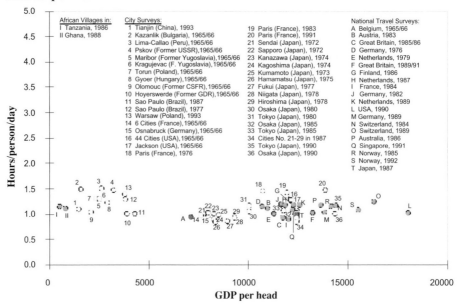

SOURCE: Schafer and Victor (2000).

the modal split inside airports. On that particular route, for example, the rig-marole of navigation within the airport roughly doubles one's travel time.

It is worth considering the effects of travel times on the behaviors of the societies of the super-rich and the very poor. The super-rich, because they most easily afford the fastest transport, will be the first to escape the estab-lished networks for donuts. Purely private subsonic jets already allow the semi-commuter to fly between Bozeman, Montana or Santa Fe, New Mexico and the urban epicenters of New York or Los Angeles. The advantages of private aircraft are not pure speed, since commercial jets move at the same pace once they are airborne; rather, they allow flexibility in route and much shorter modal splits. Private aircraft traveled the New York–Vail route long before direct commercial flights could attract a sufficient and regular number of paying customers to be financially viable. Several innovations will extend the effects of private travel—or, in other words, extend the travel behaviors of the super-rich to more ordinary income ranks. Smaller and cheaper very light jets (VLJs) will cut the cost of private jet travel. Fractional jet ownership allows many users to pool their demand for travel since very few flyers can take advantage of the approximately 500 revenue hours per year that repre-sents the optimal use of private aircraft. Fractional ownership, already widely available in the United States and Europe, allows strangers to pool their capi-tal along with other services, such as aircraft maintenance, pilot training, and logistics. On the horizon are innovations in supersonic private aircraft that will quadruple the time range for the semi-commuter: parts of the Amazon or Nepal might become the new Aspen or Telluride.

For societies that are considered very poor, these basic patterns of settlement also hold. The anthropological constant of 1.1 hours per day is evident in the poorest villages as well as the richest societies. Hamptonization patterns of settlement probably also prevail. In Bangkok, Lagos, Nairobi, and Rio de Janeiro urban cores are increasingly surrounded by pockets of green that are settled by the richer members of their societies. Presumably, with development more people will move to such areas (thus filling in the green donut) because they can afford more flexible and faster forms of transport. The bigger challenge for our predictions is the problem of underinvestment in public goods, such as infrastructure, that tends to arise in poor societies—indeed, it is one cause of underdevelopment. Poor transport infrastructures will impede Hamptonization because only short distances can be covered. Such a phenomenon may tend to produce "pocket cities"— those with no single core (e.g., São Paulo or, increasingly, Beijing). They may inspire the traveler to innovate as a way of finding faster modes of transportation. Examples are the helicopters that clog São Paulo's skies and the relatively inexpensive chauffeuring that allows the wealthier commuter to accomplish other tasks while on the move.

So, the great exodus from the countryside may not literally empty the farmlands and forests of people. Older generations left behind as the young leave the country for better city lives will be replaced, in time, with older generations of super-rich who leave their children (if they have any) and retire simultaneously in the city and country. The size of the green sphere that rings the cities will depend on travel times. Near transport infrastructures the human footprint will remain and even intensify; away from easy mobility the countryside will be in limbo.

Wilderness

Literally, "wilderness," in the sense of untouched areas, probably no longer exists on Earth. The impact of humans from pollution—heavy metals that accumulate in ecosystems and atmospheric pollution such as increased levels of CO_2 that spread over long distances (even globally)—makes it possible to measure the consequences of human influence everywhere near Earth's surface, including in shallow sediments (McKibben 1989). In the deepest sections of the ocean, away from downwelling zones, there are still environments that bear no sign of human influence. Slowly, though, the human presence is extending even there—evident, for example, in the radioactive isotopes from atmospheric testing of nuclear weapons. Aside from such semantics, I focus on wilderness as the terrestrial zone where humans have no regular presence.

Essentially all wilderness on land is in mountains, deserts, tundra, and forests. Mountains, deserts, and tundra are inhospitable places and their sheer physical attributes will probably protect them, at least from residents if not from drillers, miners, and other commercial prospectors. Forests are under greater threat, and I focus on them here.

The vast uninterrupted tracts of forests that existed 10,000 years ago at the end of the last glacial period have since been cut to about four-fifths of their original size. Most of the remaining areas of "frontier forest" are in Russia (Siberia), Brazil (Amazon), northern Canada, and Congo, and they remain protected by their remoteness. Let me suggest two ways to approach the question whether humans will occupy these spaces.

First, we can look at the potential for reducing pressure on forests. Jesse Ausubel and I have calculated the potential impact of improving productivity on agricultural lands and timberlands (Victor and Ausubel 2000). We examined those two activities because, worldwide, farmers and foresters are the two largest threats to forests. Improved productivity would allow them to deliver more product from smaller areas of worked land, thus leaving the rest of forests for nature, watershed protection, and other nonindustrial purposes. We called that projection the "Great Restoration," as shown in Figure 4, and contrasted it with a business-as-usual projection in which humans continued to cut and shave further areas of the world's forests because farming and agriculture did not become more productive at achievable rates. The Great Restoration would liberate large areas of land—about one billion hectares—that over 50 years could lead to a much larger global forest estate. We mapped out a policy program for achieving the restoration, and we outlined some clear milestones for measuring progress. The political, technical, and economic potential is great.

Second, we can examine strategies for protecting wilderness areas. While the potential for liberating land (and for reducing pressure on existing wilderness areas) is great, what will ensure that free land is not subsequently occupied? The traditional answer is regulation. I am not sure that approach will be effective, however. Today, only about 8 percent of the world's forests is formally designated as protected area. While accumulation of protected areas varies considerably across countries, there is also a common pattern: the process of delineating protected areas is running out of steam. Huge areas have been set aside in the early years of protection efforts, but over time the process follows an s-shaped logistic curve and saturates. Today, many efforts at protection focus not on setting aside land but on public–private arrangements—as in Brazil, where rules require that a fraction of privately owned forests be set aside and protected for the public benefit. The result is a fragmentation of forest lands organized around human occupation—the antithesis of wilderness. Outside those areas, protection occurs because it is not cost-effective to occupy the land, but technological change will make it easier to exert a presence in the wilderness, from

FIGURE 4   The potential for restoring the world's forests

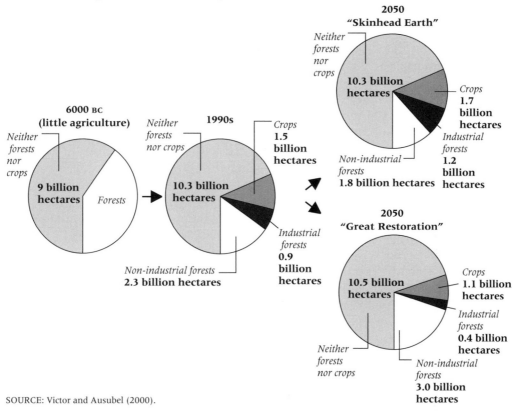

SOURCE: Victor and Ausubel (2000).

jet trips to remote ranches to logging of exotic species facilitated by helicopter transport. In much of the world this pattern of "protection" does not trouble decisionmakers because wilderness for its own sake is not valued.

I do not know which of these forces—the potential for protection versus the ever-expanding capacity to occupy the land—will win out. The predictions I have presented about settlement patterns and travel times suggest that networks and donuts will define the human settlement of all land areas, including areas that today we call "wilderness." Remoteness will be defined by distance from transport networks, notably airports. Areas proximate to transport networks are ripe for settlement, although outside urban areas the frontier of such settlement is likely to be occupied by the itinerant user of the land rather than the permanent inhabitant. The ecological footprints of casual settlement are not preordained. They could be disastrous if they fragment ecosystems, or they could be relatively benign if ranchette settlements are built with a light footprint. I do not have a theory to predict which way we will settle, but I suspect that the latter may win because it is nature and remoteness that, after all, draw the itinerant settler from the city. The biggest dangers may arise, however, with settlements that look natural (and thus meet the itinerant user's image of the garden) but are ecologically disastrous. Such dangers include fragmentation by roads and building lots, invasive species from gardens, and disturbances to energy and water flows.

Conclusion

I have argued that the problem of human sustainability is increasingly one that is focused on urban areas. Populations are concentrating into urban areas, and the human sphere is likely to concentrate even further as market institutions give favor to more efficient dense packing. At the moment the world's population is approximately evenly split between urban and rural inhabitants; the transition from rural to urban could occur very rapidly in the coming decades, with a great emptying out of rural areas.

For ecological sustainability the questions will increasingly center on what happens to the land left behind and to areas of wilderness. If we protect the areas that are liberated from human occupation or were never trodden, the result could be an even larger wilderness in the future. However, in most countries there seems to be little incentive to protect wild areas. Economic considerations have protected wilderness in the past, but technological change is eroding the advantage that wilderness has conferred on humans.

Notes

I thank many colleagues I met originally through the International Institute for Applied Systems Analysis—Jesse Ausubel, Arnulf Grübler, Nebojša Nakicenovic, and Andreas Schafer—for many discussions since I first visited the Institute in 1989. I am grateful, too, for editorial help from Becca Elias and for assistance on the figures from Nadejda Victor.

1 I will not deal here with what "counts" as green. Aspen, though semi-urban, may count as green because of its physical and ideological proximity to "greenness." The nodes in the network that exist solely for the purpose of escape may not demonstrate donut-like settlement behavior.

References

Beitz, Charles R. 1985. *International Ethics*. Princeton: Princeton University Press.
BP (British Petroleum). 2002. *Statistical Review of World Energy 2002* and supporting data tables, posted on «http://www.bp.com/centres/energy».
Clark, W. C. and R. E. Munn (eds.). 1986. *Sustainable Development of the Biosphere*. New York: Cambridge University Press.
Easterly, William. 2003. "Can foreign aid buy growth?," *Journal of Economic Perspectives* 17(3): 23–48.
FAO. 2002. FAOSTAT and supporting data tables, posted on «http://www.fao.org/forestry».

Harris, Clive. 2003. "Private participation in infrastructure in developing countries: Trends, impacts and policy lessons," World Bank Working Paper No. 5. Washington, DC: The World Bank.

Kammen, Daniel. 1995. "Cookstoves for the developing world," *Scientific American* 273(1): 72–75.

Kessides, Ioannis N. 2004. *Reforming Infrastructure: Privatization, Regulation, and Competition.* Washington, DC: The World Bank.

Levine, James, Robert Weisell, Simon Chevassus, Claudio D. Martinez, Barbara Burlingame, and W. Andrew Cowar. 2001. "The work burden of women," *Science* 294(5543): 812.

McKibben, Bill. 1989. *The End of Nature.* New York: Random House.

Rawls, John. 1972. *Political Liberalism.* New York: Columbia University Press.

Ros, Agustin J. 1999. "Does ownership of competition matter? The effects of telecommunications reform on network expansion and efficiency," *Journal of Regulatory Economics* 15: 65–92.

Schafer, Andreas and David G. Victor, 2000. "The future mobility of the world population: Results from a new model designed for aggregated long-term projections," *Transportation Research A* 34: 171–205.

Sen, Amartya. 1999. *Development as Freedom.* New York: Random House.

Smith, Kirk R. and Sumi Mehta. 2003. "The burden of disease from indoor air pollution in developing countries: Comparison of estimates," *International Journal of Hygiene and Environmental Health* 206: 279–289.

Tongia, Rahul. 2006. "The political economy of Indian power sector reforms," in David G. Victor and Thomas C. Heller (eds.), *The Political Economy of Power Sector Reform: The Experiences of Five Major Developing Countries.* New York: Cambridge University Press.

United Nations Centre for Human Settlements (UNCHS). 2001. *The State of the World's Cities.* Nairobi: UNCHS.

United Nations Development Programme (UNDP). 2005. *Human Development Report 2005: International Cooperation at a Crossroads: Aid, Trade and Security in an Unequal World.* New York: UNDP.

Victor, David G. 2000. "What roles can international law and institutions play in restoring world forests?" presented at The Great Restoration: A Vision for the World's Forests in 2050, Washington, DC, 20–21 January. «http://greatrestoration.rockefeller.edu».

———. 2006. "Recovering sustainable development," *Foreign Affairs* 85(1): 91–103.

Victor, David G. and Jesse H. Ausubel. 2000. "Restoring the forests," *Foreign Affairs* 79(6): 127–144.

WEC (World Energy Council)/FAO (Food and Agriculture Organization). 1999. *The Challenge of Rural Energy Poverty in Developing Countries.* London: World Energy Council; New York: United Nations.

Woodhouse, Erik J. 2005. "A political economy of international infrastructure contracting: Lessons from the IPP experience," Working Paper. Program on Energy and Sustainable Development. Stanford University.

World Bank. 1998. *Assessing Aid: What Works, What Doesn't, and Why.* Washington, DC: The World Bank.

———. 2002. *World Development Indicators,* CD-ROM.

World Bank/IMF. 2005. *Global Monitoring Report 2005.* Washington, DC: The World Bank.

World Commission on Environment and Development (WCED). 1987. *Our Common Future.* Oxford: Oxford University Press.

World Health Organization. 2004. "Indoor air pollution: The killer in the kitchen," «http://www.who.int/mediacentre/news/statements/2004/statement5/en/», based on the UNDP/DESA/WEC World Energy Assessment.

Zakaria, Fareed. 2003. *The Future of Freedom: Illiberal Democracy at Home and Abroad.* New York: W.W. Norton.

Managing a World
on the Move

Aristide R. Zolberg

Quite remarkably, despite epochal changes in social and material conditions since nation-states emerged from Europe's tumultuous history, contemporary states continue to adhere to the normative assumption that they consist of self-reproducing populations, and to assess their situation from this antiquated perspective, in relation to which emigration and immigration are constructed as disturbances. As a consequence, state actions have always played a major role in shaping international population movements. Hence in this sphere, today and in the foreseeable future, demography is inseparable from politics.

In the era of demographic scarcity, concern focused mainly on emigration (Zolberg 1978). In keeping with Jean Bodin's aphorism, "*Il n'ya de richesse ni force que d'hommes,*" emigration to another realm was prohibited; however, this did not apply to outward movement to populate the sovereign's newly acquired lands, even overseas. Occasionally, a ruler might expel or drive into flight valuable subjects, usually because they resisted pressures to adopt or maintain the approved faith (Jews in Iberia; Huguenots in France). But such acts were widely understood as heroic sacrifices meant to demonstrate the ruler's selfless piety; and when they occurred, members of the target group were usually eagerly welcomed by his competitors. Concomitantly, the prevailing stance regarding immigration was acquisitiveness; this also motivated the slave trade and prompted the elaborate rationalizations that rendered it legitimate.

Acquisitiveness did not imply "open borders," however. As Emerich de Vattel reasoned in his foundational mid-eighteenth-century treatise of international law, control over the entry of foreigners into the realm is a sine qua non of sovereignty, since in its absence hostile armies could just march in. Hence, while immigration tended to be welcome, the expansion of mobility in the early modern era gave rise to a proliferation of physical barriers with designated administrative checkpoints, coupled with standardized official documents identifying the "nationality"—a concept more precisely expressed by the German version of the term, "state belongingness"—of the border-crossers (Torpey 1999).

In relation to the prevailing system, the United States emerged at the end of the nineteenth century as an aggressive norm-violating intruder, which actively encouraged Europeans to break the emigration rules and ignore the obligations of their allegiance by permanently altering their nationality (Zolberg 2006). Initially the Europeans responded by tightening controls on exit. However, the moment coincided with a radical change in Europe's socio-demographic configuration: the onset of a rapid decline in the death rate, coupled with the "industrial revolution," one of whose offshoots was a revolution in transportation. The attendant dislocations also fostered the beginnings of the welfare state. Under these new conditions, within a few decades emigration from northwestern Europe to the United States was transformed from a "problem" into a "solution," even in the case of the United Kingdom, which was also seeking to establish white colonists in some of its overseas possessions. Similar developments occurred somewhat later with regard to emigration from southern Europe to South America.

Concurrently, development differentials between regions fostered large-scale internal migrations, often driving populations from culturally distinct peripheries toward the industrial centers (e.g., Irish to Manchester, Birmingham, and Glasgow; Auvergnats and Bretons to Paris; Flemings to coal mines in Walloon Belgium). In the final decades of the nineteenth century, development differentials within Europe itself turned its advanced industrial countries into alternatives to overseas emigration (Zolberg 1997). France, which, for reasons historical demographers are still debating, achieved "zero population growth" in the middle decades of the nineteenth century, emerged as a distinctively "immigration country," with most of the newcomers originating in adjoining Flemish Belgium, northern Italy, and Spain; around the turn of the twentieth century Poles began arriving as well. Despite its still growing population, the newly unified German industrial giant also experienced substantial immigration, largely from Poland.

The international migration regime as we know it came into being around the beginning of the twentieth century. As markets expanded in a surge of economic globalization, further developments in transportation radically lowered the cost of long-distance travel and expanded its domain to encompass a much larger segment of world population, while the rise of international political tensions and their eruption into more frequent and bloodier conflicts fought by mass armies rendered concern with control over outward and inward movement more urgent than ever. With refoulement (forced return) at the border increasingly inconvenient and risky, states resorted to "remote control"—that is, the requirement of obtaining permission to enter before embarking on the journey, by way of a visa entered in the passport by an official of the state of destination (Zolberg 2000). Remote control amounted to a projection of the country of destination's borders into the world at large. Elaborated in relation to the technology of railroad travel, it was most effective when border-crossing took place at sea, since ships constitute containers whose loading and unloading can be supervised, with transportation companies made to function as ancillary border police. In the twentieth century, the advent of air travel vastly facilitated further elaboration of the system; but it was simultaneously severely undermined by the spread of automotive vehicles and the proliferation of roads.

On the eve of World War I, even as economic and demographic differentials between the more and less advanced economies generated ever-growing international movements, Germany, Britain and its overseas dominions, and the United States had all adopted or actively considered measures to restrict the rapidly growing flows. The outbreak of World War I not only interrupted ongoing movements, but generated a hyper-nationalist reaction that subsequently fostered the adoption of more severe restrictions on entry, such as the literacy test and national origin quotas adopted by the United States. Although the war and its aftermath also produced large-scale forced movements, notably an "unmixing of peoples" in the Balkans—similar to today's "ethnic cleansing," but carried out by states with the approval of the international community—and flight from the Bolshevik Revolution, by the mid-1920s ordinary migrations were much reduced. Temporary labor migrations resumed, however, and in many cases expanded well beyond prewar levels. Restrictions at the point of entry were further reinforced at the outbreak of the depression, when many temporary migrants were brutally expelled, while totalitarianism and the subsequent resumption of international armed conflict once again produced a combination of draconian immobilization and forced migrations, with lethal consequences of unprecedented scope.

The fact that modern economic migrations usually involve movement between regions (within or between countries) that are culturally distinct, and hence result in the intrusion of "others" on the social scene of the receiving region, is not incidental but a constitutive feature of the phenomenon. Not only does the spatial unevenness of economic development often coincide with preexisting zones of cultural differentiation, but differential development itself exacerbates established differences. Consequently, the source region is usually beyond what the host society perceives as the boundaries defining its identity (Barth 1969). From the perspective of employers in the more advanced region, the less developed region constitutes a pool where workers can be obtained at bargain rates; concomitantly, for the workers in question the more developed region provides an opportunity to secure higher income. Within the receiving country or region, the menial functions immigrants are generally made to serve and the living conditions to which they are subjected reinforce their construction as "ethnic others."

The process generates a syndrome I have termed "Wanted but not Welcome," which arises from the tension between two sets of concerns, represented as orthogonally related axes—the one expressing economic interests, the other cultural or social interests, with a focus on "identity" (Zolberg 1987, 2000). However highly prized on economic grounds, the massive internal migration or outright immigration of culturally distinct labor-market competitors triggers considerable uneasiness among the receivers on "identitarian" grounds. Although this is especially marked among the general populace, who perceive the newcomers as labor-market competitors, it also prevails among higher social strata, who are not economically threatened by the newcomers, but see them as a threat to the established social and cultural order. The presence of such "others" nearby contributes to the crystallization of the dominant group's distinctive identity and also, by way of the material advantages it affords, reinforces its hegemony; but given the vagaries of human behavior, especially in the sexual sphere, the presence of others is also constructed as a standing threat to the dominant group's purity.[1] Because indigenous workers seldom have the power to prevent the immigration, it does take place; but the foreign workers are usually maintained in a state of segregation by way of an internal boundary. This facilitates their economic exploitation while minimizing their cultural impact.

The classic and most extreme case is that of racially distinct slaves. Where the newcomers could be constructed as racially distinct, as in the case of Asians in the United States and the British overseas dominions, the situation might be managed by instituting formal social differentiation that denied them the possibility of acquiring citizenship and integration into the host society; they remained "workers" without ever turning into "immigrants." Although the Chinese were eventually excluded altogether from the United States, other "different" workers were substituted for them—in California, Mexicans; in Australia, southern Italians—which again led to friction. To varying extents, these tensions were channeled into social movements arrayed in defense of traditional "national identity," which themselves often were mobilized by political entrepreneurs seeking to challenge the status quo. Notorious examples included the precocious "Know Nothing" movement in the United States in the 1840s and 1850s, the Dreyfus Affair in France, German anti-Polish agitation of the 1880s and 1890s (in which Max Weber was involved), and Karl Luger's anti-Semitic municipal party in turn-of-the-century Vienna, which inspired a young painter named Adolf Hitler.

Whereas the downside of these configurations is manageable in traditional and colonial societies, it becomes steadily more problematic in democratic societies, and even more so in democratic welfare states. The governing insight here is Weber's distinction between stratification on the basis of "status" and of "class." As status distinctions become unacceptable, the "others" in question acquire a latent claim to membership in the host society, a claim that comes to be recognized by some within the majority. Over time, these claims become stronger, and under conditions prevailing in contemporary liberal democracies, they are irresistible. Hence immigration moves to the fore as a challenge to the host society's internal boundaries—those of identity, broadly speaking, and those of of political citizenship, more specifically (Zolberg and Long 1999).

An additional problem arises when the host societies are constituted as welfare states. The issue concerns the boundaries of "social citizenship" (Marshall 1950). In its most elaborate form, the welfare state provides for its members "from the cradle to the grave," and even beyond, since in effect it provides for the transmission of social benefits to successive generations, notably in the sphere of education. As the share of income drawn from the welfare state's services expands, labor importation is profitable to the extent that workers can be denied some of these services. This is generally the case with temporary workers, with the most notorious instances involving those employed in the "informal" sector, or altogether illegally. Access to social citizenship by way of a transition from temporary worker to permanent immigrant status is therefore very costly from the host's perspective. While explicitly demanding that immigrants accept the established identity and assimilate into it so as to disappear, the receiving society also has an interest in reinforcing existing barriers to integration, such as citizenship laws, but then often blames the immigrants for failures to which its own actions have contributed.

In the light of recent developments, it should be noted that from the late eighteenth century onward, immigration also came to be viewed as a source of politically dangerous subversion. For example, the American founders responded to the European upheavals of the late 1780s and early 1790s by adopting a spate of "Alien and Sedition Acts," as well as prolonging the waiting period for naturalization; and a century later, the use of terrorist tactics by various social movements loosely grouped under the label "anarchist" again triggered the enactment of a spate of measures designed to screen and deter dangerous individuals. In the same vein, in most European countries foreign residents were subjected to special police surveillance. This was the case in the United States as well in response to the social upheavals of the post–World War I period, and in the wake of the Cold War.

Migration patterns and policies, 1945–2000

The postwar world was inaugurated by widespread international migrations. They again included vast "unmixings of peoples" in Central and Eastern Europe, as national borders were moved about and bearers of the wrong ethnicity—now mostly the descendants of ancient German eastward migrants—were deliberately expelled or driven into flight. "Unmixing" now spread beyond Europe, to South Asia following the partition and independence of India and Pakistan in 1947, and to the Middle East and North Africa following the partition of Palestine and the independence of Israel a year later. However, most of the forced migrants were quickly absorbed by receivers of the appropriate nationality, except for the Palestinian Arabs, who, as the result of the lasting international political tensions in the Middle East, remained permanent refugees, uniquely reproducing as a refugee population over several generations to date. Concurrently, a large part of world population was immobilized within totalitarian states: the Soviet Union and the East and Central European countries under its influence, as well as mainland China after 1949. In addition, the movements of much of the population of Asia, Africa, and the Caribbean remained governed by colonial regulations, which by and large immobilized them within the respective colonies, unless labor policies dictated relocation to another colony or to the metropole; and with very limited exceptions, such regulations offered little opportunity for youth in the respective metropoles to receive training to become modern colonial elites.

Labor migrations

From the perspective of international human mobility, the deliberately reconstructed international political economy was founded on a profound contradiction: although the "Bretton Woods" commitment to greater international movement of finance and expansion of international trade also entailed facilitation of the international movement of labor and of travel, there was little or no interest in international migration, which by consensual silence remained entirely within the purview of national policy. Shaped as before by concerns of national identity, and enhanced by security concerns arising from the conflictual nature of international politics, as well as by the protectionist concerns of indigenous workers, which moved to the fore with social democracy, these policies tended to be highly restrictive. Far from envisioning the launching of an unprecedented "age of migration," the OECD countries operated on the informal understanding that, within the framework of Keynesian-type economies, temporary labor migrations were especially advisable (Zolberg 1991). Concomitantly, faced with the perennial difficulty of absorbing rapidly growing working-age populations, governments of the independent "South" looked upon emigration as a partial solution; decisionmakers in the still dependent countries often did so as well, and in any case were driven primarily by the interests of their metropolitan center. Concurrently, in a totally unrelated development, the rapidly rising standard of living in the OECD countries, reflected in the wide availability of the automobile and the application of war-time technological developments to civil aviation, fostered the spectacular development of tourism, initially mostly domestic but quickly spilling over to the international level.[2]

"Guestworker" programs rapidly proliferated on both sides of the Atlantic, even as the receivers maintained highly restrictive immigration policies. Conceived of as "temporary" by the receivers, the migrants, and the sending countries, many of these programs sought to deter settlement by recruiting males only, prohibiting the entry of family members, and providing low-standard, dormitory-style housing. Nevertheless, these movements generated longer-term settlement and, even more importantly, contributed to the formation of vast transnational networks that facilitated subsequent migrations.[3] Moreover, the proliferating comings and goings of workers—as well as of tourists—contributed to the decisive transformation of international borders, from forbidding barriers into permeable gates.

After providing for the exceptional admission of a few hundred thousand European refugees, in 1952 the United States reaffirmed the restrictive national origins quota system adopted in the 1920s, as well as the even more draconian barriers against Asian immigration, and responded to the forthcoming decolonization of European dependencies by erecting unprecedented barriers against immigration from those countries. At the same time, however, it expanded its war-time guestworker program, involving largely Mexicans; US employers also expanded their use of illegal border-crossers, who constituted a more profitable labor force. Recruitment extended also to the Caribbean, including not only English-speaking West Indians, but also US-ruled Puerto Ricans. Because nationals of independent countries in the Western Hemisphere were not subject to US quota limitations, Mexico rapidly rose to the first rank of source countries for legal immigration, while also moving to the fore as the principal source of informal settlement. Concurrently, the nationalization of the labor market induced huge internal migrations, including a resumption of the great northward movement of blacks from the South, which within a short time fostered a radical alteration of the country's racially ordered social relations, as well as migration of both blacks and whites from the Midwest and South to California.

As they gained political power in the United States, the southern and eastern Europeans targeted for exclusion under the established immigration system sought its reform, finally succeeding in 1965. The conservatives, who were by then more concerned over "brown" immigration from Latin America and black immigration from the Caribbean, obtained as a counterpart the imposition of unprecedented limits on immigration from the Western Hemisphere. Thanks to more generous provisions for family reunion, however, the new system allowed for the rapid expansion of "chain migration," reflected in escalating totals. At the same time, despite the formal termination of the postwar *bracero* program in 1964, Mexican workers continued to gain access to the informal American labor market in ever-larger numbers.

In postwar Britain, which maintained the restrictive immigration regulations adopted in the early decades of the twentieth century, guestworkers continued to be mainly Irish. It is noteworthy that even after Ireland gained its formal independence, its nationals retained the right of free movement to the United Kingdom. Initially Britain also turned to Poles but, in the face of hostile labor union responses, instead recruited West Indian colonials—a move designed also to dampen radical agitation in the source region by relieving unemployment. Concurrently, by virtue of the political bargaining that occurred in the process of creating the "Commonwealth of Nations," nationals of India and Pakistan gained the right of free entry into Britain. Although movement was initially limited to elites, these pioneers provided the makings of networks that fostered an expansion of entry, to which Britain responded beginning in the late 1960s by progressively closing its gates—except, as always, to the Irish. Nevertheless, the flows of the early postwar decades gave rise to substantial Asian and Caribbean minority communities in most British cities.

During this period, France resumed recruitment of its less developed neighbors: Italians and Spaniards, and later Portuguese, to whom were now added Arabs and Berbers from still-colonial Algeria. Belgium also sought out Italians, Spaniards, and Portuguese, and later Moroccans. Engaged in massive reconstruction, West Germany benefited from a huge influx of Germans displaced or fleeing from Central Europe (Poland, Czechoslovakia, the Soviet Union), as well as from the Soviet occupation zone. These flows contributed as much as wise financial and fiscal policies to the "German economic miracle" of the 1950s. After the supply of workers was cut off by the Berlin Wall in 1960, Germany turned to the less developed southern European countries (Italy, Greece, and Spain) and, once that supply proved insufficient, pioneered an opening to the southeast, notably Yugoslavia and Turkey. Over time some workers were rewarded by being allowed to bring in wives and children. However, Germany continued to deter settlement by maintaining its highly restrictive nationality legislation (Brubaker 1992).

Except in Britain and to some extent the United States, foreign workers remained so marginalized in the receiving countries that their presence evoked little or no political concern until the late 1960s. The situation changed abruptly in the early 1970s, when the "oil shock" and the accompanying inflation appeared to signal the "end of growth." Although the receivers shut their gates and sought to return surplus workers to the source countries, they largely failed to do so in the face of workers' passive resistance to repatriation. Although this resistance might have been overcome by determined action, the ultimate resort to forcible expulsion was in effect ruled out by the constraints under which postwar liberal democracies operated. Willy-nilly, decisionmakers concluded that the best way of overcoming the objections and anxieties triggered by the presence of clusters of young males from minority groups was to transform them into families. The oil crisis had an even more severe impact on the non-oil-producing countries of the developing world, while the loosening of controls on exit in the ex-colonial countries and the greater accessibility of long-distance transportation rendered the international labor market more accessible to their nationals. Hence rather than diminish, the foreign-born continued to slowly increase in the liberal democracies, and the process of settlement in turn gave rise to ever larger permanent communities of foreign origin, which came to be perceived as highly problematic.

Forced international movements

The international community established the beginnings of a refugee regime in the 1950s and expanded it in the 1960s. However, this was designed to deal with what were still considered "exceptional" situations, initially sequelae of World War II and of decolonization, as well as of the incipient Cold War, and it was imagined that the regime ultimately would be self-liquidating (Zolberg, Suhrke, and Aguayo 1989). As of the early 1960s, only a few hundred thousand refugees had been assisted by the United Nations High Commissioner for Refugees (UNHCR). Many were Europeans, remnants of World War II and even the 1917 Bolshevik revolution; apart from the Palestinians, who were cared for separately by United Nations Relief and Works Agency (UNRWA), the only significant non-European refugee populations were Algerians displaced by the war of independence against France, and Chinese who had fled to Hong Kong after the revolution on the mainland.

Numbering around 6 million in the mid-1960s, refugees rose to about 10 million by the end of the decade, but then fell to a postwar low of about 2.5 million in the mid-1970s, when it looked as if the phenomenon were a thing of the past. Then, in the mid-1970s the refugee population in the developing world began to climb steeply, doubling twice to reach nearly 18 million in 1989 (of whom 14.9 million were "persons of concern to UNHCR") (Schmeidl 2001: 66; US Committee for Refugees 2001; United Nations High Commissioner for Refugees 2001). As of 1992, the refugee population in the developing world, excluding the 2.5 million Palestinians registered with UNRWA, exceeded 14 million: 5.4 million in Africa, 7.2 in Asia, 0.9 in Latin America, and 0.6 in Oceania. North America and Europe together hosted 5.4 million refugees, most of whom were in Europe.[4]

Refugee movements reflected the unfolding pattern of social conflict and international relations in the second half of the twentieth century. The process of decolonization was in some places violent, while elsewhere it set in motion new social conflicts. As the victims turned up in neighboring states, the hitherto European-oriented international refugee regime started to assist and recognize beneficiaries in the developing world. Many of the newly independent states adopted authoritarian regimes with little or no respect for human rights, determined to use brutal means to gain or maintain power. In addition, two structural conditions accounted for the dramatic increase of refugees in the developing world.[5] One was the underlying demographic growth, which, like the expansion of the formal international system, enlarged the universe of potential refugees. From 1950 to 1990 the world's population increased from 2.5 billion to 5.2 billion, most of it in the developing countries. The equivalent inflation of refugee numbers is strikingly illustrated by the small African state of Burundi: in 1972, widespread ethnic pogroms generated some 150,000 refugees; but when the events were repeated two decades later, they resulted in an outflow of at least 700,000.

The other structural factor pertained to the international political arena. For more than 40 years, the Cold War constituted an overarching, determining principle of international relations. Generally, the more fluid conditions in the developing world enabled the two bloc leaders to intervene directly or indirectly to gain incremental power advantages (Art and Waltz 1993). For a time, even the People's Republic of China entered into the fray. These probings and confrontations were usually accompanied by vast flows of weapons. In its most extreme form, the logic of competitive intervention led to warfare by proxy, as happened in southern Africa, the Horn of Africa, Central America, Afghanistan, and Southeast Asia.

In the predominantly multiethnic states of sub-Saharan Africa and South Asia, conflicts were generally waged over state formation. These essentially involved the definition of membership in the "nation," with boundaries drawn along ethnic lines. When ethnic groups were interspersed, conflict typically took the form of pogroms or spontaneous inter-ethnic violence; when ethnic groups had a distinct territorial base, conflict in its extreme form meant a reorganization of political communities along ethnic lines as existing states were partitioned, or—short of that—experienced inconclusive secessionist warfare. In some parts of Africa, social revolutionary struggles defined in the prevailing Marxist terms of that period merged with regional or ethnic divisions to create multidimensional conflicts that readily became linked to the Cold War.

Conflicts of a revolutionary kind were the other main cause of large-scale refugee movements. These occurred in East and Southeast Asia and Central America. In Asia east of Burma, Confucian-influenced, peasant-based agrarian states experienced a different trajectory of change. Class rather than ethnicity defined the lines of conflict, which came to focus on issues of social order and social justice rather than group membership. Revolutionary struggles also developed in Central America's oligarchic agrarian states, where social conditions generally fit the structural prerequisites for peasant revolutions. Further south, in Chile, Argentina, Uruguay, and Brazil, widespread conflict over the social order gave rise to systematic repression. Because the main protagonists were the military and the forces on the left—trade unions, professionals, and intellectuals—the struggle tended to be formulated ideologically in terms of Communism versus anti-Communism. The Cold War orientation was accentuated by the hegemonic role of the United States in the Western Hemisphere. US policy significantly shaped the evolution of conflicts in Latin America as well as the refugee flows they generated.

Both types of conflict could produce large outflows of people seeking to escape the fighting and its eventual outcome. But ethnic minorities or refugees from secessionist struggles often had a "homeland" where they could seek safety, either in a "liberated" separatist region or in an ethnically related state that offered some form of right to return. Successful revolutions, on the other hand, typically created one-way, irreversible, and often massive outflows of people with no alternative "homeland." The adverse external economic conditions that faced most developing states during the 1970s and the 1980s also shaped the pattern of conflict and associated refugee flows.

The age of migration?

The number of foreign-born persons enumerated worldwide grew substantially from about 75 million in 1965 to about 120 million in 1990 and 150 million in 2000 (Zlotnik 1998; International Organization for Migration 2000). Of the migrant population at the dawn of the twenty-first century, about 120 million were "voluntary," propelled by economic necessity and opportunity; the remaining 30 million were "forced" migrants, of whom about 20 million were formally recognized as "refugees."

The popular notion that the late twentieth century was "the age of migration" (Castles and Miller 1993) has to be qualified in light of the fact that the proportion foreign-born remained at the same level between 1965 and 2000, approximately 2.3 percent, indicating that international migration grew at about the same rate as world population. Although in the 1990s migrants grew slightly faster than world population, in 2000 the foreign-born still constituted only about 2.5 percent of the total population.

Within the developed world, however, immigration did become a more salient phenomenon, as the proportion of foreign-born grew from 3.1 to 4.5 percent—an increment of nearly half—while among developing countries it decreased from 1.9 to 1.6 percent.[6] The prominence of immigration as a feature of affluent societies was further accentuated by the fact that the receiving countries constituted a declining share of world population: whereas in 1965 the West (not including Israel) accounted for 16.5 percent of world population and hosted 35.7 percent of the migrant stock, in 1990 the proportions were respectively 12.8 and 42.7. The major growth poles for immigration were the "oil kingdoms" of Western Asia (from 7.4 percent in 1965 to 10 percent in 1990), Northern America (from 6.0 percent to 8.6 in 1990, and an estimated 11 percent in 2000), and especially Western Europe, from 3.6 to 6.1 percent (with a record rate of increase in the decade following 1965). As of 1990, 20 percent of the world's immigrants were located in Northern America (United States and Canada), and another 19.1 percent in Western Europe. It is therefore appropriate to speak of a "revival" of immigration in North America after a generation's hiatus (from 1930 to 1965), and an even more dramatic surge in Western Europe. However, it should be noted that the developed parts of East Asia (i.e., mainly Japan and Taiwan) had less than 1 percent foreign-born in 1990. If nothing else, this indicates very clearly that immigration is neither a necessary condition for economic development, nor its necessary consequence.

The character and direction of migrant flows changed significantly as well. Although migration between developed countries increased somewhat, the more noteworthy development was a vast expansion of flows from the developing "South" to the developed "North." In the United States, for example, the percentage of migrants from developing countries grew from 41.9 in 1960–64 to 80.3 in 1995–96; but the shift was even more marked in Canada (from 12.3 in 1960–64 to 78.4 in 1990–94), and especially in Australia (from 7.1 to 72.7). There was also a marked diversification. For example, in Sweden, the number of source countries accounting for 75 percent of migrants grew from four in 1965–69 to 12 in 1995; in Germany from 5 to 19; and in the United States from 18 to 26. Overall, the top senders were in South Asia (Bangladesh, Sri Lanka, Pakistan, India), with numbers rising from an annual outflow of about 250,000 in 1987 to nearly four times higher a decade later.

The end of the Cold War brought about an abrupt liberalization of exit, immediately translated into outward movement in search of economic opportunities, as well as an outburst of ethno-national conflicts, rooted in local history, that had been successfully averted by the authoritarian Communist regimes throughout their rule. The impact of these developments fell mostly on Central and Western Europe. Despite this diversification, however, the number of countries that are major sources of emigrants to the West is still quite low. Nevertheless, there was every reason to believe that the source pool would continue to expand, hence that the total size of the pool of potential movement would expand further as well.

In the United States, for example, immigration climbed to an average intake of 1.3 million persons a year in the 1990s, a historical record with regard to both numbers and diversity (US Census Bureau 2002). About two-thirds of the newcomers were legally admitted, mostly as ordinary immigrants; the remaining one-third were illegal border-crossers and visa overstayers. Because they are in effect a tolerated segment of the population, increasingly male and Mexican, which supplies low-skilled, inexpensive labor to a variety of sectors from agriculture to retail, border-crossers and overstayers should be viewed as an essential part of the American immigration system, which doubled its size in the 1990s to reach 8.7 million in 2000—amounting to about 2.5 percent of the total population. As a result, the United States is once again a "nation of immigrants," with an estimated 31.1 million foreign residents as of March 2000, constituting about 11 percent of the population—an approximate doubling since 1960, when the proportion reached its lowest level since Tocqueville visited a country he characterized as "Anglo-American."

Migration as a security threat?

In the final decade of the twentieth century, the massive movement of human beings across international borders came to be regarded as one of the most intractable problems the affluent democracies faced in the new post-Communist world. Long a marginal subject even for demographers and social scientists, in the 1990s international migration ascended to the status of a security "crisis," imperatively requiring attention in the highest places.[7]

The change was abrupt. As late as 1991, a review of global population issues from a security perspective, originally presented a few years earlier to a US Army Conference on Long Range Planning, attributed a limited role to migration and suggested that, overall, "the demographic significance of international migration has decidedly diminished" because "the territories of the globe are now divided among standing governments, virtually all of which limit the absorption of new citizens from abroad in some fashion." Consequently, "opportunities for voluntary migration for most inhabitants of the Third World remain very limited" (Eberstadt 1991: 125). The following year, however, the late MIT political scientist Myron Weiner proclaimed that international migration had become "high international politics" and cited in support of this assertion numerous instances in which it created conflicts within and between states (Weiner 1992/1993, 1995).[8] He suggested that it is therefore necessary to supplement the international economy approach with a "security/stability framework for the study of international migration that focuses on state policies toward emigration and immigration as shaped by concerns over internal stability and international security."

International migration's rise on the security agenda was further boosted by the influential pronouncements of the historian Paul Kennedy. Singling out the "global population explosion" as one of the most challenging issues of the twenty-first century, Kennedy suggested in 1993 that in view of the imbalances in demographic trends between "have" and "have-not" societies, one should expect "great waves of migration in the twenty-first century" because "desperate migrants are unlikely to be deterred" by immigration policies (Kennedy 1993: 44). Citing the difficulties France encountered in ridding itself of unauthorized immigrants and the United States encountered in keeping them out, he further pointed to the 15 million persons living in refugee camps, "hoping for somewhere to go.... While they, and those already on the move via Mexico and Turkey, may encounter obstacles, many of them are getting through." A year later, in a flamboyant *Atlantic Monthly* article titled "Must it be the rest against the West?," Kennedy and his coauthor evoked an impending apocalypse: "Many members of the more prosperous economies are beginning to agree with Raspail's vision: a world of two 'camps,' North and South, separate and unequal, in which the rich will have to fight and the poor will have to die if mass migration is not to overwhelm us all" (Connelly and Kennedy 1994).

The reference is to a dystopic novel published two decades earlier by the conservative French essayist, Jean Raspail, in which a horde of third world paupers from the shores of the Ganges manages to commandeer a huge flotilla of derelict ships and sets sail for the promised land of affluent Europe. As the blood-thirsty invaders prepare to land on the French Riviera, the white world falls prey to a collective paralysis induced by political correctness, reflecting the loss of its "racial will" to fight for survival. The French army abandons the south, leaving the local population to scramble for refuge. The scene is reenacted elsewhere as the successful invaders inspire imitators in other parts of the third world. The only successful holdouts are the Afrikaners and the Australians, still in possession of their "racial will." Alas, as we know in retrospect, not for long. When published in the United States by Scribner's as *The Camp of the Saints* in 1975, Raspail's novel evoked dismissive outrage from mainstream reviewers in *The New York Times* (13 August 1975: 32) and *Time* (4 August 1975: 63–64). However, the ascending neoconservatives were quick to identify a soulmate, and *The National Review* launched a campaign on the novel's behalf. Evoking the scandals triggered by avant-garde works earlier in the century, its Senior Editor reported that "In freer and more intelligent circles in Europe... the book is a sensation and Raspail a prize-winner.... Raspail is to genocide what [D.H.] Lawrence was to sex" (Hart 1975). A few months later (5 December 1975: 1412), Hart anointed the novel as "the most powerful political fable of our time" and included it in an intellectual "survival kit" for conservatives, along with George Orwell's *1984* and James Burnham's *Suicide of the West*. Although the novel quickly faded from the mainstream publishing scene, it was repeatedly reprinted by anti-immigration organizations and, after Connelly and Kennedy endowed it with unprecedented respectability, was reissued once more by the Social Contract Press of Petoskey, Michigan, which proudly

excerpted the *Atlantic Monthly* article on the novel's cover.[9] The cover illustration depicts a formidable group of blanket-clad Asians huddled on a beach,
with a tiny cargo ship in the distant background, immediately recognizable
as a scene from the widely reported incident involving the *Golden Venture*, a
rusty tramp steamer transporting nearly 300 Chinese seeking to enter the
United States surreptitiously, which ran aground off the borough of Queens
in New York City in the early hours of 6 June 1993. The implications were
clear: Raspail's doomsday prophecy has come to pass, the dreaded invasion
has begun, whites must get their guns and prepare to defend their race.

Restating in more sensationalist form some of the arguments previously set forth in *Preparing for the Twenty-First Century*, in their 1994 article
Connelly and Kennedy accepted Raspail's premise "that a combination of
push and pull factors will entice desperate, ambitious Third World peasants
to approach the portals of the First World in ever-increasing numbers." Indeed, they argued that "the pressures are now much greater than they were
when Raspail wrote," not only because of the additional people on the planet,
but because of the communication revolution as well as the prospect of widespread chaos in the developing world, as depicted by Robert Kaplan in the
same magazine earlier in the year (Kaplan 1994). Around the same time,
another writer suggested that the international migration crisis was exacerbated by the onset of environmental degradation and scarcities, either indirectly, by way of the contribution of such conditions to violent conflict or
simply by forcing people to move abroad in order to survive (Homer-Dixon
1994); and the Sierra Club in effect joined the anti-immigration camp, a
move that subsequently led to internal turmoil (Bouvier and Grant 1994).
Having participated in numerous Washington seminars and workshops in
the early- to mid-1990s, I can testify that these shrill warnings had an elec-
trifying impact on foreign affairs and defense officials saddled with the task
of thinking about the "new" international and security issues and formulating appropriate policy.

Bringing the apocalypse yet closer to home for Americans, in 1995
Random House published the decade's anti-immigration blockbuster, *Alien
Nation: Common Sense About America's Immigration Disaster* (Brimelow 1995).
Characterizing the 1965 reform of American immigration policy as a misguided effort, Peter Brimelow warned that, unless drastic counter-measures
are adopted, the "colored" groups will achieve a numerical majority by the
middle of the twenty-first century. Presenting himself as a sort of refugee
who came to America with his twin brother in 1967 "when for various reasons we decided all was lost in England" (p. 221), Brimelow views the United
States as a fragile lifeboat "that is towing the economy of the entire world"
but whose scuttles were opened to let in a multitude of colored aliens, and
as a result "is now developing an ethnic list, and may eventually capsize"
(pp. 18, 249).

At the beginning of the new millennium Patrick J. Buchanan issued his own jeremiad, *The Death of the West*, whose terminal illness is made explicit in the subtitle: "How dying populations and immigrant invasions imperil our country and civilization." Buchanan's book climbed onto *The New York Times* best-seller list in early 2002, undoubtedly helped by the 9/11 tragedy, which anti-immigrant advocates quickly turned into a demonstration of the soundness of their cause. For example, the spokesman for an anti-immigrant organization told the US Senate, "While it is absolutely essential that we not scapegoat immigrants,…we also must not overlook the most obvious fact: the current terrorist threat to the United States comes almost exclusively from individuals who arrive from abroad," and concluded by arguing: "Thus, our immigration policy, including temporary and permanent visas issuance, border control, and efforts to deal with illegal immigration, are all critical to reducing the chance of an attack in the future" (Caramota 2001). In a more extreme vein, Buchanan urged an immediate moratorium on all immigration, an expansion of the Border Patrol to 20,000 officers, a radical reduction of visas issued to nationals of states that harbor terrorists, and the expedited deportation of "the eight-to-11 million illegal aliens, beginning with those from rogue nations" (Buchanan 2001).

The affluent democracies' incapacity to control undesired immigration is supported by academic authorities. For example, Douglas Massey, a leading specialist on US immigration and an international migration theorist, has expressed considerable skepticism regarding the effectiveness of US regulations in determining the level and composition of US immigration in the twentieth century, both legal and unauthorized (Donato, Durand, and Massey 1992; Massey and Singer 1995; Massey 1995). In the same vein, the editors of a comparative study of immigration policy and policy outcomes in nine industrialized democracies concluded that "the gap between the goals of national immigration policy…and the actual results of policies in this area…is wide and growing wider in all major industrialized democracies. . ." (Cornelius, Martin, and Hollifield 1994: 3). Their book's perspective is well illustrated by a cover photo entitled "Too hungry to knock," depicting a group of young men jumping down on the northern side from the border fence separating the United States and Mexico.

My own assessment of the situation echoes Amartya Sen's warning regarding the "population bomb," namely that "the emergency mentality based on false beliefs in imminent cataclysms leads to breathless responses that are deeply counterproductive." He suggests further that Western anxiety over population growth in the developing world arises from "the psychologically tense issue of racial balance" at the global level (Sen 1994). Viewed in this light, the works just cited can be seen as the most recent expressions of the "fear of population decline," which has gripped the West intermittently since the beginning of the twentieth century and was voiced at that time by the German Emperor as "the yellow peril" (Barraclough 1967: 65; Teitelbaum and Winter 1985). There is no gainsaying that if world population is grouped into conventional "racial" categories—the common practice in public discourse among Europeans and their overseas offshoots—"white decline" is a genuine historical trend; however, from a less parochial perspective, the Asian and African shares of world population are presently still below their 1650 or 1750 level.

Overall, the crisis-mongers surmise more or less explicitly the operation of a causal chain: population growth in poor countries induces a massive disposition to emigrate; most of those who aspire to leave have the wherewithal to do so; hence this massive disposition is translated into a massive capacity to go, while potential receivers lack the capacity to restrict their entry. However, Sen questions the solidity of the third link in the chain, contending that vast uncontrolled flows are unlikely to occur because immigration is in fact strictly controlled by the countries to which people might want to go. He contends further that the second link in the causal chain is quite weak as well: the large movements from South to North that have taken place in recent decades "owe more to the dynamism of international capitalism than to just the growing size of the population of the third world countries. The immigrants have allies in potential employers." But these employers tend to be quite selective in their sources, usually drawing their workers from a small number of countries selected on the basis of a variety of criteria, notably proximity—when there is a sharp economic differentiation between the receiver and the sender—or from other "traditional" sources such as former colonies. Approaching the subject as an economist, Sen neglects the additional movements that have been generated by the dynamics of the international politico-strategic system; however, today as before, these movements also tend to be patterned by established international linkages.

In a similar vein, an examination of "ecomigration" concludes that environmental degradation exacerbates conflicts in the arid regions of the developing world, thereby contributing to massive uprooting and refugee flows. However, this has little or no impact on the North, and therefore "The use of environmental concerns to justify immigration restrictions plays more on perceptions than realities, especially in North America" (Wood 2001).

The sense of "crisis" is undoubtedly attributable largely to the fact that the liberalization of exit worldwide has shifted the burden of control to potential receivers. But although this abrupt turn of events caught many of them by surprise, developed states certainly do not lack the resources to deal with this matter. Indeed, one of the most striking developments of the last several years is the generalization of "remote control" by way of visa requirements and the like prior to embarking from South to North. But these regulations coexist with steadily more accessible transportation, providing greater opportunities for surreptitious entry. As with other illegal activities, the availability of a larger market also leads to better organization of the activity in question. In short, illegal border-crossing has become a big business, comparable in every respect to the international traffic in prohibited drugs. While the "crisis" label does not survive serious scrutiny, there is no denying that international migration is a source of genuine problems.

Forthcoming challenges

A recent US National Intelligence Estimate sought to assess the weightiness of these problems in the light of likely developments over the next 15 years (National Foreign Intelligence Board 2001). Prepared on the basis of contributions by leading nongovernment experts, the report confirms the "crisis" literature's key assertion that "Globalization, population growth, and demographic imbalances between OECD and developing countries, and interstate and civil conflicts are fueling increasing international migration, much of it illegal. During the next 15 years, migrants will seek to move to a growing number of countries in both the industrialized and the developing world" (p. 11). However, the report concludes with a more balanced assessment of the implications of this development than the crisis literature provides: "This large-scale movement of people in search of a better life will benefit most sending countries and those receiving countries that manage it effectively." Nevertheless, it also suggests that "migration flows will exacerbate social and political fissures in many countries."

The National Intelligence Estimate is founded on a restatement of the classic "push and pull" dynamics, taking into consideration the changing configuration of structural factors. It is predicated on the realistic assumption that global economic inequality will largely persist, albeit with some local changes resulting from both successes and failures. Even rising wages in developing countries experiencing economic growth will leave a considerable gap between them and the more industrialized countries. Moreover, the further spread of information through technology and education will enhance worldwide perceptions of opportunities available in the more fortunate countries. Transportation facilities will continue to develop as well, notably the penetration of vehicular roads into hitherto isolated locations. Given established demographic dynamics, some 45 million people in developing countries will enter the job market each year; out of the many who will fail to find work, some will emigrate, legally or illegally. In addition, developing countries are especially vulnerable to harsh fluctuations in economic circumstances.

Because the worldwide gap in economic conditions is unlikely to be narrowed in the foreseeable future, rational human beings will continue to seek to improve their condition by moving, even at a high cost. While the policy with the best track record for accelerating stay-at-home growth is free trade, helpful trade and investment policies may have counter-productive effects in the short term, especially if the wage gap between sending and receiving countries is large and well-established migratory networks flourish. Under such conditions, relatively successful development is likely to produce a "migration hump" in the near future (Martin and Taylor 2001). Because successful growth is more likely to occur in developing countries located near industrialized neighbors with which they develop a special relationship (e.g., United States–Mexico; EU–North Africa–Turkey–Eastern Europe), we should anticipate the further development of "regional migration systems" combining legal and illegal or "informal" movement in various proportions.

Continuing illegal migration will be facilitated by the development of alien smuggling syndicates that constitute a veritable "growth industry," vying with drug traffic in its profitability. According to the International Labor Organization, alien smuggling is currently a $10–$12 billion-a-year industry that accounts for over half the transport of illegal immigrants globally; prices range from as little as US$500 for short trips across a single border such as between Morocco and Spain, or Mexico and the United States, to as much as $70,000 for circuitous journeys from Asia to Western Europe and North America. Trafficking in women and children for purposes of labor, including the sex industry, is also increasing dramatically, with some one million individuals believed to be trafficked globally as of the early 2000s.

A more measured view is appropriate with regard to refugees as well. Contrary to the widespread notion that the situation has steadily worsened, and in particular that the end of the Cold War has unleashed a myriad of new refugee-generating conflicts, in the 1990s the number of refugees declined, and beginning in the middle of the decade the number of refugee-sending countries declined as well. Concurrently, the number of internally displaced persons peaked at 27 million worldwide in 1994, but dropped by 6 million the following year (thanks largely to reduced numbers in Africa and Afghanistan). Moreover, contrary to Kennedy's analysis, population in itself plays a minimal role in generating refugee flows: in Schmeidl's (2001) study, none of the population variables could significantly predict refugee migration once political factors were controlled for.

Nevertheless, violent conflicts of the type that have given rise to refugee flows in recent decades are likely to recur, thereby triggering massive forced displacements, some of which will result in international movements. The scale of the violence is likely to continue being amplified by the parties' firepower, attributable to easy access to weapons by way of international traffic. To a lesser extent, some developing countries will experience severe deterioration of ecosystems and renewable resources, making for forced uprooting, some of which will spill over internationally; in the same vein, such countries are more likely to be affected by various forms of natural disasters. While affluent countries are likely to continue their attempts to tighten their asylum procedures, the reality of a "well-founded fear" of persecution—to use the US criterion—in a significant portion of the applications will act as a severe constraint against resorting to uncompromising measures to deter unjustified applications. Hence the asylum process will continue to function in part as a loophole.

With regard to the impact of sheer "population pressure," Mary Kritz has subjected the specific relationship between population growth and US immigration to statistical examination (Kritz 2001). One of her key findings is that countries with the highest population growth rates account for only 1 in 17 US immigrants; conversely, 2 out of 5 come from countries with lower growth rates. Similarly, most US immigrants do not come from the countries with the highest total fertility rates. However, population size is positively correlated with US immigration: nearly 3 out of 5 immigrants come from the 25 largest countries in the world. As one would anticipate on the basis of common sense, distance acts as a deterrent. In short, absent established network connections of the sort noted earlier, the dynamics of world population of themselves do not generate intense "immigration pressures" on the United States. As against global demographic dynamics, the strongest correlate of current US immigration is immigrant stock living in the United States, as measured by the distribution of foreign-born persons. Kritz's conclusions have been verified by Zlotnik for the world as a whole (Zlotnik 1997, 1998).

On the "pull" side, the major factors will be population aging and labor demand at both the upper and lower ranges of the market. Although all OECD countries will experience aging, this will be especially acute in the European Union and Japan, where fertility has already fallen below the replacement level. According to the United Nations Population Division's medium-variant projection of 1998 data with zero migration after 1995, the European Union's population would peak at 372.5 million in 2000 and then decline steadily, reaching 310.8 million in 2050 (Population Division 2001: 89–90). Concurrently, however, the population would experience accelerated aging, so that the working-age population would be reduced by 30 percent while the population aged 65 and older would steadily increase, resulting in a decline of the "support ratio" from 4.3 working-age persons per pensioner in 1995 to 1.9 in 2050—a situation in effect impossible to sustain. Alternatively, the medium variant with an average net immigrant intake at the current level (1995–2000) would still result in a support ratio of slightly under 2.0 in 2050. Moreover, the situation would in no way be remedied by the accession of East European countries to membership in the EU, since their demographic dynamics are, if anything, even less promising: extended to Europe as a whole (UN regional division), the same population projections suggest a decline from a peak of 727.9 million in 1995 to 600.5 million in 2050, with a concurrent decline of the support ratio from

4.8 to 2.0 (for the variant with immigration at the current level, the support ratio would fall to 2.1).

However constraining, these demographic realities are once again not necessarily determinative. Although aging populations require substantially more spending for pensions and health care, leading to growing public deficits and increased public borrowing—with attendant inflationary risks—the situation is likely to be mitigated by exploiting technologies for greater productivity, promoting the entry of more women into the labor market (especially in Germany and Japan), and extending the length of time spent in the labor force in keeping with the steadily expanding life span. Nevertheless, considerable gaps are likely to remain, for which immigration beckons as a solution.

Although there is considerable talk of "market shortfalls" in the developed world, the matter should be approached in a skeptical vein. Some of the literature on globalization suggests that postindustrial conditions render affluent countries ever-more dependent on imported low-wage labor to fill their expanding service sector (Sassen 1995). In reality, however, it is difficult to distinguish between "need" and "opportunity." For example, while the United States makes considerable use of illegal workers, especially from Mexico, in the construction, garment, and food industries and for personal services, it is impossible to suppose that these services would vanish in the absence of an assured supply of the workers in question. The same sort of question can be raised about the advanced technology sector: while Silicon Valley is indeed a heavy user of immigrant workers from Asia, setting a precedent that is being emulated by Germany and other European countries, to what extent is this attributable to the ease of supply? And to what extent does the ease of supply function as a disincentive for enhancing the American educational system's capacity to train workers with the appropriate skills? That being said, there is no doubt that under the circumstances that will prevail in the next couple of decades, such "demand" is likely to persist and even expand.

As many sociologists have pointed out, the tendency for immigration to generate further immigration is well accounted for by the formation of "networks," particularly those elaborated on the basis of kinship (Massey et al. 1993). Accordingly, the institutionalization and expansion of communities of immigrant origin within affluent societies provides a pole of attraction of unprecedented strength, except in the classic overseas immigration countries—and even there we have seen, in effect, a revival of a situation that had passed from the scene for the middle third of the twentieth century. Of course, the presence of networks alone does not automatically result in international migration: while networks foster a disposition to migrate and a lowering of the costs involved—by providing financial sponsorship, know-how, the assurance of hospitality, and the likelihood of psychological support—an additional necessary condition is the possibility of movement. Looking back on the twentieth century as a whole, it is evident that much of the world's population was immobilized for long periods of time by the country of origin's prohibitions against departure, usually founded on a combination of economic and political motives. At the same time, many of the potential immigration countries also adopted highly restrictive policies designed to prevent "networks" from resulting in immigration. In short, "immigration begets immigration" only if states do not seriously interfere with the process.

Within the receiving countries, as in the past, the "pull" founded on market considerations will coexist, and to a certain extent compete, with political considerations that are related to what is commonly termed "identity," and that echo the more traditional "nationalist" concerns. The dynamics involved here are not of an unchanging "us" versus "them," but rather a flexible shifting set of boundaries (Zolberg and Long 1999). In retrospect, it is evident that most of the affluent receiving countries, with the possible exception of Japan, have considerably changed in this respect since the end of World War II. For example, in the United States, southern and eastern Europeans, who were the main targets of the 1924–65 quota system, have now been incorporated into the "American nation." At one time Protestant, the United States became "Christian," then "Judeo-Christian," and, on the eve of 9/11, was well on its way toward becoming "Abrahamic"— that is, incorporating Islam and its followers. Similarly, persons of southern European origin (Italians, Spaniards, Portuguese), as well as Jews, have come to be fully accepted as "white" in the northern European countries.

These shifting boundaries are a product of the conjunction of several factors: interactions leading to the acquisition by the children of earlier immigrant groups of many of the cultural characteristics of the new homeland; the further expansion of human rights as part of the development of liberal democracies; cultural relativism, facilitating the acceptance of plurality and differences; guilt for past abuses; and last but not least, particularly in the United States, proactive exercise of political power by formerly excluded populations.

To what extent are these processes likely to operate in the future? Ironically, there is a conjunction of skepticism from the right and the left. Critics on the right charge that contemporary immigrants not only diverge more sharply from the receiving cultures, but are less willing to assimilate than their predecessors. Concurrently, some immigrant advocates suggest that insidious contemporary forms of exclusion prevent immigrants from integrating, while others insist on the desirability of certain forms of "multiculturalism" that, if fully carried out, would result in a sort of "separate and equal" society—or at least the sort of "pillarized" (*verzuild*) society that existed in the Netherlands until recently, reflecting the belated settlement of the Reformation's religious quarrels. It is also suggested that contemporary conditions foster "transnationalism," that is, the maintenance of a binational existence, making for split but necessarily segmented commitments to the two homelands.

On balance, however, the evidence suggests that wherever opportunities for integration are in fact provided, it is proceeding apace, albeit in a less "assimilatory" or "melting pot" form than in earlier waves. An important distinction is the modification of the concept of nationality, which is no longer regarded as involving exclusivity, and therefore is more accepting of binational or even multinational affiliations (Aleinikoff and Klusmayer 2001). It should also be noted that transnationalism facilitates the development and maintenance of networks that foster continuing migration.

Despite changing conditions, the presence of immigrants and the prospect of further immigration will continue to stimulate xenophobic or at least exclusionary sentiments, which will provide opportunities for exploitation by populist political leaders. In most cases, this will have the effect of reining in inclinations to "open immigration"—except between countries that have come to view each other as "similar," notably members of the European Union and between the United States, Europe, and Canada. Despite occasional agitation to that effect, however, it is unlikely that such pressures will lead to draconian immigration restrictions.

A major issue posed in many of the affluent countries is the "loss of control over the borders." For example, the aforementioned US National Intelligence Estimate suggests that "A wide range of political and legal constraints will limit the extent to which most OECD countries will be able or willing to adopt harsh measures against illegal or other would-be immigrants." These constraints include the steady reduction of controls over cross-border economic transactions; business interests in maintaining permissive conditions for labor flows; counter-pressures from human rights groups; and the risk of damaging relations with governments of the sending countries (National Foreign Intelligence Board 2001: 17). To this should be added the emergence of immigrants and their descendants as actors in the policymaking process of affluent democracies, with an interest in maintaining generous conditions for family reunion.

Among the constraints, a leading one arises from the growing importance of international travel, especially for tourism. International tourist arrivals grew at an average annual rate of 4.3 percent in the 1990s—including 3.8 percent in 1999 and 7.4 percent in 2000—reaching a total of 650 million per year at the end of the century (World Tourism Organization 2002a, 2002b). The leading destinations were Europe, where tourism grew at a rate of 3.6 percent for the decade, and the Americas, at 3.3 percent. Despite the weakness of major tourism-generating markets in 2001, arrivals worldwide grew by an estimated 3 percent in the first eight months of

2001; they then experienced a severe setback due to the terrorist attacks of September 11, making for a drop of 11 percent in the last four months, and a rate of –1.3 percent for the year as a whole. Nevertheless, the WTO expected—correctly, as it turned out—that the industry would pick up its habitual rhythm by the second half of 2002.

Despite the fact that tourist travel to the affluent countries tends to be restricted to the more well-off segments of the countries of emigration and the additional fact that the affluent countries generally require advance visas for their nationals, tourism nevertheless constitutes in effect a "side entrance" for would-be immigrants, who can thereby turn into unobtrusive overstayers or use the opportunity to file asylum claims. This is perhaps even truer of educational travel, which is a notorious source of eventual "brain drain."

Under contemporary conditions, border control is a staggering task. For example, France, the world's leading destination for international tourists, recorded 75.5 million arrivals in 2002—far more than its total resident population. In the United States in a given year, the Department of Homeland Security inspects some 450 million persons entering by land and another 100 million entering by air or sea, amounting altogether to approximately twice the entire population of the United States.[10] Leaving aside returning US citizens and foreign daily commuters with multi-entry passes, the number of foreign entrants is in the neighborhood of 60 million. In 2001, the United States issued 7 million new visas to foreign nationals, of which some 800,000 were awarded to immigrants proper, about 600,000 to students, and most of the remainder to tourists and business visitors. About half of all documented entries consist of visitors covered by the Visa Waiver Program, whose nationals are considered unlikely to overstay or to engage in criminal activity.

Conclusion

In recent decades, the "South"—which has now been joined by the "East"—has generated masses of persons who are driven by economic circumstances to migrate and who have the wherewithal to meet the costs of doing so. Concurrently, these regions have experienced conflicts that have generated a considerable number of refugees. These processes foster huge internal migrations as well as South-to-South movements; however, they eventuate in South-to-North migration only when certain facilitating conditions occur in the North. These include: (1) the presence of employers who have an interest in recruiting foreign labor from less developed countries, and the clout to persuade their governments to adopt policies to that effect, or at least not seriously interfere with the market forces that induce workers to relocate where jobs are to be found; (2) foreign policy considerations, or occasionally historic ties of obligation to particular groups, that dispose a given Northern country to exceed the limited obligations of asylum arising from adherence to the contemporary international refugee regime, and agree to admit a group of refugees for permanent resettlement; and (3) a positive stance by the receiving state toward family reunion initiatives generated by earlier immigrants, or at least relative permissiveness in relation to them.

Although significant, these facilitating conditions hardly amount to an "open sesame." Although this interpretation leaves out of account illegal immigration—much of which begins as legal entry, followed by overstaying—its importance has been vastly exaggerated. Considering that immigration control is undoubtedly more problematic in the United States than in most other affluent democracies, because of its long land border with a much poorer country and the long-established tradition of laissez-faire with regard to entry via that border, as well as widely publicized laxity in the enforcement of measures designed to deter access to the US labor market (employer sanctions), the United States is very far from the nightmare envisioned by Raspail. While the transformations that have taken place are irreversible, it is also evident that European states quickly took steps to narrowly limit future immigration, notably by tightening up procedures for family reunion and asylum. Although no country has achieved the tacit objective of "zero immigration," the tide has been effectively stemmed. While erasing internal borders, the expanding European Union has been elaborating its external boundaries, deliberately equipping outermost candidates for membership to function as external bulwarks. Although Europe is also vulnerable to penetration by enterprising risk-takers, the magnitude of unauthorized entry appears lower than in North America.

A more measured assessment of global migrants and global refugees provides the basis for a more effective and benevolent consideration of appropriate solutions. This entails two distinct approaches: one the one hand alleviating conditions that foster unwanted economically driven movement toward the affluent countries, and on the other alleviating or preventing refugee-generating conflicts in the developing world and in the ex-Communist world.

Although, as noted earlier, refugees do not "threaten" the affluent democracies because most refugees remain in their regions of origin, the fact that they are deprived of the protection and assistance that residents rightly expect from their states of origin creates irrefutable obligations for the international community as a whole. If the refugees are not provided opportunities for resettlement in the North, then the North must help them and their host countries in the South. But as with economic migrations, one should also consider solutions that attack the problem at its source.

Paralleling the notion that development will alleviate economically driven migrations, democratization is likely to reduce forced movements since most of the contemporary refugee-generating conflicts have been caused or exacerbated by authoritarian rule. In this light, independently of ethical reasons for supporting and fostering democratization worldwide, the affluent democracies should do so on "realistic" grounds. However, on the basis of Schmeidl's (2001) analysis of post–Cold War conflicts and other observations, it might be suggested that "democratization" produces a "refugee hump" that parallels the "migration hump" induced by free trade. There is growing evidence that management of ethnic and national differences from above, under Western colonial rule as well as under Communist rule, tended to exacerbate tensions between groups, in line with the old Roman principle of "divide in order to rule." Authoritarian rule acts in effect as a "lid" that maintains these tensions under control and thereby enhances the dependency of members of these groups, and especially threatened minorities, on the rulers' benevolence. When the lid is suddenly lifted, however, these tensions are given free play, with little or no opportunity for the groups involved to learn to manage conflict.

Most recent attempts to prevent conflicts by way of humanitarian intervention, and attempts to substitute humanitarian assistance for political and military intervention, have been ineffective. Hence there is a need to develop temporary protection arrangements for the kinds of large-scale refugee flows many regions of the world are now experiencing. Guidelines to this effect can be drawn in part from UNHCR practice in the developing world since the 1960s. Beyond this, however, the tendency for Western countries to focus exclusively on refugee situations that are thought to affect their security and to limit their assistance to countries that are perceived to be geo-politically important leads to neglect of other situations, sometimes more acutely threatening for the populations involved. Hence there is no choice but to revise and expand the protection side of the international refugee regime, and link it more effectively to institutions dealing with the assistance side. As this is done, one has to keep in mind that under contemporary conditions, asylum demands will unavoidably be inflated by the unavailability of other forms of legal entry.

With regard to the "welfare state," while immigrants and their progeny create a demand for additional social services, notably in the sphere of education, they also help bring about a more favorable ratio of economically active to retired population. The nature of the bottom line depends largely on the orientation of those drawing up the balance sheet. There is no gainsaying, however, that the presence of "others" challenges established boundaries of identity and is thereby a source of social and political tensions. These have been especially visible in Western Europe, where popular support for radical xenophobic parties has grown dramatically over the past two decades. Parties supporting ideologies that had been relegated to the lunatic fringe in the period after World War II have now established a significant and enduring presence in most western European states. Their electoral success has allowed them to expand their organizations, distribute racist literature, and more effectively propagate their extremist views, often at taxpayers' expense. Their success also legitimizes expressions of ethnic hatred and encourages intolerance and violence toward immigrants and those of immigrant descent. Most importantly, it affects policies—not only immigration policy proper, but also those relevant to the incorporation of the immigrants and their descendants (Schain, Zolberg, and Hossay 2002). Nevertheless, these parties do not pose a direct threat to democratic governance. The reasons have less to do with the attributes of the challengers than with the nature of the regimes within which they operate. In short, the extreme right-wing parties of the period between the two World Wars irrupted into a Europe that had been deeply traumatized by a bloody war and whose established political institutions had been severely tested or altogether destroyed. The losers were particularly vulnerable. By contrast, Europe's contemporary international environment definitely reinforces democratic institutions.

One of the major criticisms arising from right-wing quarters is the immigrants' resistance to integration. The material and administrative ease of travel, the proliferation of opportunities for temporary migration, the possibility of maintaining contacts with the country of origin, and a climate of juridical permissiveness fostering the rapid growth of multiple citizenship have led some observers to extrapolate "transnationalism" into a generalized state of affairs, and others to speak of the "denationalization of citizenship" (Glick Schiller, Basch, and Blanc-Szanton 1992; Soysal 1994; Bosniak 2000). However, things should be kept in proportion, and it is evident that, while transnationalism represents a significant and undoubtedly growing social process, it involves a small proportion of the world's population, and that, overall, citizenship remains bound to the nation and the sort of "supernational" citizenship that is emerging at the level of the European Union is contingent on national membership. The limited membership that is being generalized by way of the extension of rights to non-nationals in liberal democracies is more appropriately termed "cosmopolitan denizenship" (Zolberg 2000). In any case, it is difficult to establish to what extent transnationalism is likely to survive beyond the first generation of migrants.

While it lasts, transnationalism may be a source of problems. Immigrants or refugees may import conflicts from their country or region of origin: for example, Turks versus Kurds in Germany, pro-government versus anti-government Algerians in France; Indians versus Pakistanis in Britain. Immigrants or refugees may also generate or exacerbate international tensions between the sending and receiving country. UNHCR insists that the granting of refugee status does not necessarily imply criticism of the sending country; however, since the award is based on "well-founded fear" of persecution, in practice granting refugee status often creates an adversarial relationship with the source country. The extent to which it does so varies considerably, as a function of the extent to which the receivers use the refugees as a tool in interstate conflict. Under current world circumstances, this may involve terrorist activity.

The events of September 11, 2001 brought to the fore the danger arising from intrusion by foreign malefactors. But what lessons are to be drawn from the attack? To begin with, the events had nothing to do with immigration properly speaking. All of the known perpetrators entered the United States legally as tourists. Viewing the security challenge in perspective, approximately one of every 500,000 visas awarded in the two-year period preceding 9/11 went to a hijacker or one of his suspected associates. More precisely, some 120,000 visas were issued to Saudi nationals, of which approximately one per 8,000 went to future hijackers, or .01 percent. The one suspect convicted by the United States on charges related to the 9/11 attacks is a Morocco-born individual who had acquired French nationality and hence was admitted without a visa, making for an infinitesimal ratio of dangerous individuals among the millions of entrants from the 29 countries who are visa-exempt or students. The difficulty of designing border control to provide greater security is exacerbated by the division of the task between disparate bureaucracies inclined to protracted turf wars. Most notoriously, until the recent reorganization of the system, the junior State Department officials saddled with visa duty did not have access to the Immigration and Naturalization Service's database of individuals with past immigration problems, and the FBI refused to open its own database to either INS or the State Department; but even after the reorganization, FBI information is of little assistance in detecting foreign terrorists, because they are unlikely to have accumulated criminal records in the United States. Today still, the agencies that deal with border control and regulate admissions do not have access to data from the intelligence agencies that monitor threats emanating from the outside world.

Nevertheless, a murderous attack did take place, and it is hardly unique; nor is the United States the only target. Although over the long term, terrorism is subject to reduction by structural change, and containment of particular manifestations can be achieved by local intervention and diplomacy, overall the danger will persist for the indefinite future. Under the circumstances, the "Westphalian approach" founded on sovereignty still has much to recommend it. To be fully effective, however, security must not be focused on geographic borders or on the home territory, but projected outward. If there is to be a crash program, it should be directed at improving the capacity of the United States and others in its situation to identify dangerous operations in the making abroad. Such intelligence is in turn a prerequisite for the implementation of a more effective screening system for foreign visitors, which is fully possible under existing law. While vigilance is called for internally as well, nothing has emerged so far to suggest that extraordinary measures are required for this purpose. Hence, an equally urgent security task is to provide adequate protection to minorities victimized by the diffuse anger of the uninformed, and ensure that in their encounters with law enforcement they are accorded the full benefit of the procedural rights that constitute one of the major foundations of democracy. The contemporary world is a world ever more on the move. While it is possible to reduce the risk of criminal attacks in the air by inspecting baggage, carry-ons, and passengers more strictly, the struggle against organized terrorism necessarily depends on vast improvements in intelligence by infiltrating suspect organizations and international cooperation in sharing relevant information.

Notes

1 This analysis can be extended beyond "workers" in the ordinary sense of the term to distinctive groups imported (or allowed to immigrate) to perform instrumental functions such as money-lending and trade—notably Jews throughout medieval and early modern Europe, Chinese in Muslim Southeast Asia, and various other groups (Indians, Greeks, Lebanese) in different parts of colonial sub-Saharan Africa (Turner 1969; Curtin 1984).

2 The statistical series provided by the World Tourism Organization starts only in 1980; I have not been able to find estimates for the earlier postwar period.

3 In this section, I limit myself to the Atlantic world, with which I am more familiar; *mutatis mutandis*, much of this is applicable to the other OECD countries as well.

4 *The State of the World's Refugees*, Geneva: UNHCR, 1993. More extensive bibliographical references to particular cases can be found in the 1989 edition.

5 This section is drawn from an unpublished manuscript prepared by Astri Suhrke for a revised edition of *Escape from Violence* (Zolberg, Suhrke, and Aguayo 1989).

6 By a different reckoning, the foreign-born population of the OECD countries grew from 36 million in 1985–87 to 46 million in the late 1990s, an increase of about 28 percent.

7 Worldwide there was a vast increase in the capacity of the population of poor countries to emigrate, whereas the countries they sought to enter failed to achieve a commensurate increase in capacity to prevent their entry.

8 This seminal article was subsequently incorporated in *The Global Migration Crisis* (Weiner 1995), published in a popular college-level political science textbook series. Its cover sports a rusty ship filled with people. Since Weiner, who died in 1999, cannot respond to my somewhat critical comments, I take the opportunity to pay tribute to his distinguished scholarship in this and other fields. He was my graduate teacher and we remained collaborators and good friends.

9 The Social Contract Press operates under the umbrella of a foundation that called itself simply "U.S." and is itself supported by the Laurel Foundation, founded by Cordelia Scaife May of the Mellon family (Cockburn 1994: 225).

10 These figures are taken from Annual Reports of the Immigration and Naturalization Service; I am grateful to Fred Cocozelli for his assistance in gathering the appropriate data.

References

Aleinikoff, T. Alexander and Douglas Klusmayer. 2001. "Plural nationality: Facing the future in a migratory world," in T. A. Aleinikoff and D. Klusmeyer (eds.), *Citizenship Today: Global Perspectives*. Washington, DC: Carnegie Endowment for International Peace, pp. 63–88.

Art, Robert J. and Kenneth N. Waltz (eds.). 1993. *The Use of Force: Military Power and International Politics*. Lanham: University Press of America.

Barraclough, Geoffrey. 1967. *An Introduction to Contemporary History*. Baltimore: Penguin Books.

Barth, Fredrik (ed.). 1969. *Ethnic Groups and Boundaries*. Boston: Little, Brown.

Bosniak, Linda. 2000. "Citizenship denationalized," *Indiana Journal of Global Legal Studies* 7(2): 447–509.

Bouvier, Leon F. and Lindsey Grant. 1994. *How Many Americans? Population, Immigration and the Environment*. San Francisco: Sierra Club Books.

Brimelow, Peter. 1995. *Alien Nation: Common Sense About America's Immigration Disaster*. New York: Random House.

Brubaker, Rogers. 1992. *Citizenship and Nationhood in France and Germany*. Cambridge MA: Harvard University Press.

Buchanan, Patrick J. 2001. *The Death of the West: How Dying Populations and Immigrant Invasions Imperil Our Country and Civilization*. New York: St. Martin's Press.

Caramota, Steven A. 2001. "Immigration and terrorism: Testimony prepared for the Senate Judiciary Committee Subcommittee on Technology, Terrorism and Government Information" «http://judiciary.senate.gov/te10121 st-caramota.htm».

Castles, Stephen and Mark J. Miller. 1993. *The Age of Migration: International Population Movements in the Modern World*. New York: Guilford Press.

Cockburn, Alexander. 1994. "Follow the money," *The Nation*, 5/12 September: 225.

Connelly, Matthew and Paul Kennedy. 1994. "Must it be the rest against the West?," *Atlantic Monthly*, December: 61–91.

Cornelius, Wayne A., Philip L. Martin, and James F. Hollifield. 1994. *Controlling Immigration: A Global Perspective*. Stanford: Stanford University Press.

Curtin, Philip D. 1984. *Cross-Cultural Trade in World History*. Cambridge: Cambridge University Press.

Donato, Katharine M., Jorge Durand, and Douglas S. Massey. 1992. "Stemming the tide? Assessing the deterrent effects of the immigration reform and control act," *Demography* 29: 139–157.

Eberstadt, Nicholas. 1991. "Population change and national security," *Foreign Affairs*, Summer: 115–131.

Glick Schiller, Nina, Linda Basch, and Crysztyna Blanc-Szanton. 1992. *Towards a Transnational Perspective on Migration*. New York: New York Academy of Sciences.

Hart, Jeffrey. 1975. "Raspail's superb scandal," *The National Review*, 26 September: 1062–1063.

Homer-Dixon, Thomas. 1994. "Environmental scarcities and violent conflict: Evidence from cases," *International Security* 19(1): 5–40.

International Organization for Migration. 2000. *World Migration Report 2000*.: International Organization for Migration / United Nations.

Kaplan, Robert. 1994. "The coming anarchy," *The Atlantic Monthly*, February: 44–76.

Kennedy, Paul. 1993. *Preparing for the Twenty-First Century*. New York: Vintage.

Kritz, Mary M. 2001. "Population growth and international migration: Is there a link?," in A. R. Zolberg and P. M. Benda (eds.), *Global Migrants, Global Refugees: Problems and Solutions*. New York: Berghahn Books, pp. 19–41.

Marshall, T. H. 1950. *Citizenship and Social Class, and Other Essays*. Cambridge: Cambridge University Press.

Martin, Philip L. and J. Edward Taylor. 2001. "Managing migration: The role of economic policies," in A. R. Zolberg and P. M. Benda (eds.), *Global Migrants, Global Refugees: Problems and Solutions*. New York: Berghahn Books, pp. 95–120.

Massey, Douglas S. 1995. "The new immigration and ethnicity in the United States," *Population and Development Review* 21(3): 631–652.

Massey, Douglas S. et al. 1993. "Theories of international migration: A review and appraisal," *Population and Development Review* 19(3): 431–466.

Massey, Douglas S. and Audrey Singer. 1995. "New estimates of undocumented Mexican migration and the probability of apprehension," *Demography* 32: 203–313.

National Foreign Intelligence Board. 2001. *Growing Global Migration and Its Implications for the United States* (March).

Population Division. 2001. *Replacement Migration: Is It a Solution to Declining and Ageing Populations?* New York: Department of Economic and Social Affairs, United Nations.

Sassen, Saskia. 1995. "Immigration and local labor markets," in A. Portes (ed.), *Economic Sociology*. New York: Russell Sage Foundation.

Schain, Martin A., Aristide R. Zolberg, and Patrick Hossay. 2002. *Shadows Over Europe*. New York: Palgrave.

Schmeidl, Susanne. 2001. "Conflict and forced migration: A quantitative review, 1964–1995," in A. R. Zolberg and P. M. Benda (eds.), *Global Migrants, Global Refugees: Problems and Solutions*. New York: Berghahn Books, pp. 62–94.

Sen, Amartya. 1994. "Population: Delusion and reality," *New York Review of Books*, 22 September, pp. 62–71.

Soysal, Yasemin Nuhoglu. 1994. *Limits of Citizenship: Migrations and Postnational Membership in Europe*. Chicago: University of Chicago Press.

Teitelbaum, Michael S. and Jay M. Winter, eds. 1985. *Fear of Population Decline*. New York: Academic Press.

Torpey, John. 1999. *The Invention of the Passport: Surveillance, Citizenship, and the State*. Cambridge: Cambridge University Press.

Turner, Victor W. 1969. *The Ritual Process: Structure and Anti-Structure*. Chicago: Aldine Publishing Company.

United Nations High Commissioner for Refugees. 2001. Population Data Unit, Population and Geographical Data Section. *Global Refugee Trends: January–September 2001: A statistical overview of refugee populations, new arrivals, durable solutions and refugee status determination procedures in some 90 countries*.

US Census Bureau. 2001. Kevin E. Deardorff and Lisa M. Blumerman, "Evaluating components of international migration: Estimates of the foreign-born population by migrant status in 2000," Working Paper Series No. 58.

———. 2002. Joseph M. Costanzo et al. "Evaluating components of international migration: The residual foreign born," Working Paper Series No. 61.

US Committee for Refugees. 2001. *World Refugee Survey 2001*. New York: Immigration and Refugee Services of America.

Weiner, Myron. 1992/1993. "Security, stability, and international migration," *International Security* 17(3): 91–126.

———. 1995. *The Global Migration Crisis: Challenge to States and to Human Rights*. New York: HarperCollins.

Wood, William B. 2001. "Ecomigration: Linkages between environmental change and migration," in A. R. Zolberg and P. M. Benda (eds.), *Global Migrants, Global Refugees: Problems and Solutions*. New York: Berghahn Books, pp. 42–61.

World Tourism Organization. 2002a. "Tourism highlights 2001: Updated" www.world-tourism.org.

———. 2002b. "World tourism stalls in 2001" (News release) www.world-tourism.org/newsroom/Releases/more_releases'january2002/numbers_200.

Zlotnik, Hania. 1997. "Population growth and international migration," paper presented at the Conference on International Migration at Century's End: Trends and Issues, Barcelona, 7–10 May.

———. 1998. "International migration 1965–96: An overview," *Population and Development Review* 24(3): 429–468.

Zolberg, Aristide R. 1978. "The patterning of international migration policies in a changing world system," in W. H. McNeill and R. S. Adams (eds.), *Human Migration: Patterns and Policies*. Bloomington: Indiana University Press, pp. 241–86.

———. 1987. "Wanted but not welcome: Alien labor in Western development," in W. Alonso (ed.), *Population in an Interacting World*. Cambridge, MA: Harvard University Press, pp. 36–74.

———. 1991. "Bounded states in a global market: The uses of international labor migration," in P. Bourdieu and J. S. Coleman (eds.), *Social Theory for a Changing Society*. Boulder and New York: Westview Press and Russell Sage Foundation, pp. 301–335.

———. 1997. "Global movements, global walls: Responses to migration, 1885–1925," in Wang Gungwu (ed.), *Global History and Migrations*. Boulder: Westview, pp. 279–307.

———. 2000. "The dawn of cosmopolitan denizenship," *Indiana Journal of Global Legal Studies* 7(3): 511–518.

———. 2002a. "The archaeology of remote control," in A. Fahrmeir and P. Weil (eds.), *From Europe to North America*. New York: Berghahn Books.

———. 2002b. "Guarding the gates," in Craig Clhoun, Paul Price, and Ashley Timmer (eds.), *Understanding September 11*. New York: The New Press (on behalf of the Social Science Research Council).

———. 2006. *A Nation by Design: Immigration Policy in the Fashioning of America*. Cambridge, MA: Harvard University Press.

Zolberg, Aristide R. and Astri Suhrke. 1995. "Escape from violence: Conflict and the refugee crisis in the developing world," unpublished.

Zolberg, Aristide R. and Litt Woon Long. 1999. "Why Islam is like Spanish: Cultural incorporation in Europe and the United States," *Politics and Society* 27(1): 5–38.

Zolberg, Aristide R., Astri Suhrke, and Sergio Aguayo. 1989. *Escape from Violence: Conflict and the Refugee Crisis in the Developing World*. New York: Oxford University Press.

The Political Demography
of the World System,
2000–2050

Paul Demeny
Geoffrey McNicoll

By the end of the twentieth century the bipolar competition of the Cold War had ended and the market economy model was triumphant. Economic globalization—greatly expanded international trade and capital movements, and even, to a limited extent, cross-border mobility of labor—had spread beyond the developed countries and East Asia, although very unevenly. Thus the developing world, by then four-fifths of mankind, had become far less homogeneous in both its demographic dynamics and its income per capita than it had been at midcentury. It included many middle-income countries and several emergent economic giants, all of them intent on rapid economic growth and eventual emulation of the high-consumption economies of the West and Japan. The giants—China, India, and Brazil—additionally displayed nascent ambitions for regional and even global projection of influence in political, military, and cultural as well as economic domains. But the developing world also contained large regions of persistent economic backwardness and a few even of retrogression, conditions aggravated by still-rapid demographic growth. At the same time the forces of globalization had begun to create social and economic strains in the affluent countries that, in combination with aging populations, aging workforces, and incipient population decline, seemed to put in doubt the sustainability of their own gains in economic welfare and called into question the applicability of their economic success as a model for the rest of the world.

The social sciences offer no means of forecasting the evolution of this global economic and political system over the next half-century—not even of distinguishing, among the plausible drivers of change, those that will in retrospect be judged the most significant. Recall how little of the world of 2000 was foreseen in 1950. But while steering clear of prediction, we can at least lay out some of the trends that are underway and explore their implications. Moreover, in comparison to some other efforts at future-gazing, we can call on the relatively robust structural frame that demography supplies. Compared to the rate of turnover and obsolescence in physical capital and technology, people are long lived. Some 40 percent of the population of 2050 (and probably about the same proportion of the labor force) is already alive in 2005—whereas much of the technology and a large part of the capital stock of the economy in use in 2050 have yet to be created. Moreover, mortality and fertility also tend to change in fairly predictable ways with industrialization and urbanization, giving some assurance to population forecasts at least over the next several decades. (Based on past experience, uncertainties mount up rapidly thereafter.)

Population and economy: Forecasts to 2050

The near-worldwide decline of fertility over the second half of the twentieth century has taken the "population problem" off the agenda of international relations. That relegation is unfortunate. It misconstrues the likely role of the demographic factor in the world system during the coming decades.

The United Nations estimates for 2000–05 put the average total fertility rate (TFR) for the more developed countries at 1.6 children per woman, and for the less developed world at 2.9. There are large contrasts in age distributions between regions—still relatively youthful in the less developed regions, exhibiting advanced population aging in the developed world—reflecting the timing and pattern of past fertility and mortality declines. The medium UN projections envisage gradual convergence in demographic behavior and eventually also in age distributions. Over the coming decades, however, this convergence will not prevent continuing large shifts in relative population sizes between regions and among major countries.

The same UN projections foresee global population growth between 2005 and 2050 of 2.6 billion—a net increase larger than the total world population in 1950. That increase is distributed highly unevenly across world regions. Holding constant the categories of "more" and "less" developed (admittedly, labels that have become increasingly vacuous[1]), the population of the more developed regions is projected to grow by only 25 million. This is despite the assumption that net immigration into those regions will amount to 98 million during the 45-year period. Thus, 99 percent of the global growth is expected to occur in the less developed regions.

Among major regions, Europe (including Russia) shows the most pronounced loss in terms of relative size. Its population was 22 percent of the world's total in 1950. By 2005 that figure had fallen to 11 percent. In 2050 it is expected to be 7 percent. In absolute terms, Europe's population is estimated to be 728 million in 2005. Despite an assumed net immigration of 32 million persons during the next 45 years, a further improvement in its mortality, and a recovery of its fertility from the current TFR of 1.4 to 1.85 by midcentury, the continent's population would fall to 653 million in 2050—that is, 75 million below its present level.

At the other regional extreme, Africa's population is projected to continue its rapid growth. Africa's share of global population was 9 percent in 1950, increasing to 14 percent in 2005. It will be 21 percent in 2050. Its projected absolute population growth during the next 45 years is more than 1 billion.

Table 1 sets out the anticipated growth in the first half of the twenty-first century against the previous half-century for major countries and regions. The spacings in the table loosely delineate three North–South segments of the globe. Africa and Western Asia are reconfigured into sub-Saharan Africa (as the UN defines it) and a group of countries termed the "Muslim tier"—significant in this study especially as a major source of immigrants to Europe.[2]

This differentiated pattern of demographic expansion yields a new clutch of heavyweight countries in the world. Arbitrarily identifying these as countries with populations above 100 million, the picture given by the UN estimates for 2005 and medium-variant projections for 2050 is shown in Table 2. Some rearranging of the list takes place over this period, with India overtaking China, and Pakistan and Nigeria moving up in the size ranking. No country is forecast to drop out of the list in this period, but Japan and Russia are not far from doing so. Emerging demographic heavy-

TABLE 1   Population and population change by major country and region, estimates and projections, 1950–2050

Country/region	Population (millions)			Percent increase	
	1950	2000	2050	1950–2000	2000–2050
North America	172	315	438	83	39
Latin America and the Caribbean	167	523	783	213	50
Europe[a]	547	728	653	33	−10
(EU-25)	(350)	(450)	(450)	29	0
Muslim tier[b]	148	545	1,109	268	103
Sub-Saharan Africa	180	670	1,692	272	152
Japan	84	127	112	51	−12
China[c]	549	1,259	1,382	129	10
India	358	1,021	1,593	185	56
Southeast Asia	178	519	752	192	45
Other Asia[b] and Oceania	128	379	562	196	48
World	2,519	6,086	9,076	142	49

[a]Including Russia.
[b]Muslim tier taken as 20 West Asian and North African countries (see endnote 2).
[c]Including Hong Kong, excluding Taiwan.
SOURCE: United Nations 2005 (medium-variant projections); Taiwan *Statistical Yearbook*.

TABLE 2   Countries with populations above 100 million, 2005 and 2050 (estimates and projections)

2005		2050	
Country	Population	Country	Population
China	1,300	India	1,593
India	1,103	China	1,382
United States	298	United States	395
Indonesia	223	Pakistan	305
Brazil	186	Indonesia	285
Pakistan	158	Nigeria	258
Russia	143	Brazil	253
Bangladesh	142	Bangladesh	243
Nigeria	132	Congo DR	177
Japan	128	Ethiopia	170
Mexico	107	Mexico	139
		Philippines	127
		Uganda	127
		Egypt	126
		Viet Nam	117
		Japan	112
		Russia	112
		Iran	102
		Turkey	101

SOURCE: United Nations 2005 (medium-variant projections); China excluding Taiwan.

weights are Congo, Ethiopia, Philippines, Uganda, Egypt, Viet Nam, Iran, and Turkey. (Astonishingly—and implausibly—these projections place Afghanistan barely lower, reaching 97 million by 2050.)

No European Union member country appears in Table 2. However, if the EU with its current composition (EU-25) is taken as constituting a state-like entity, it would appear with a population of 460 million in 2005—third, after India and ahead of the US—and 450 million in 2050—still third, but by then some 20 million below its peak and within range of a still-growing United States. Of course, the EU may have expanded further by midcentury: accession of Turkey, should it occur, would alone raise its 2050 population by nearly one-quarter.

Such population figures take on a fuller meaning in combination with current economic conditions and their plausible future evolution. If so considered, they suggest a major gain in the coming decades in the economic weight and thence the geopolitical importance of the Asia-Pacific region and of South Asia, in comparison to the North Atlantic—the region which, at least for the last two centuries, has held a preeminent position in the global hierarchy of economic and military power, scientific and technological prowess, and cultural influence. China, and at a farther distance also India, may soon rival the United States in gross domestic product. For example, in recent forecasts by Goldman Sachs, China's GDP exceeds that of the United States around 2040, India's a few decades later. At purchasing power parity, by 2001 China's economy was already three-fifths the size of that of the United States, India's one-quarter. (In comparison, in that year by the same measure, Latin America's economy was 39 percent of that of the United States, Africa's 15 percent.)[3]

Major per capita income differentials between currently rich and poor countries will, however, persist. Continued faster economic growth in per capita terms in the less developed world in comparison to the rich countries—the broad experience of recent decades, though with important exceptions—must eventually close that income gap, but even under the most daring assumptions in most instances this process will be far from completed by midcentury. In the Goldman Sachs forecasts just cited, China in 2050 would have a per capita income roughly equal to the average of the developed world around the turn of the millennium. In the early phases of the catch-up process, of course, it is virtually an arithmetic certainty that absolute per capita income differentials between countries will further widen.

Finally, the staggered pacing of demographic transition among world regions is reflected in a remarkable variation in the forecast levels and rates of increase in the proportions of youth and the elderly (see Table 3). Provision of old-age support, private or public, has mainly entailed pay-as-you-go transfers from workers or taxpayers to retirees. The figures in Table 3 signal the increasing fragility of that mechanism as the proportions of the young and the old move in opposite directions. The order shown in the table corresponds to the comparative stage in the aging process: Japan and the EU in the vanguard, Africa bringing up the rear. China, with its precipitous fertility decline in the 1970s and 1980s, is two or three decades ahead of India.

TABLE 3   Projected proportions of population below age 15 and aged 65 and older, selected countries and regions, 2005, 2025, and 2050

Country/region	0–14			65 +		
	2005	2025	2050	2005	2025	2050
Japan	14.0	12.5	13.4	19.7	29.1	35.9
EU-25	16.4	14.4	13.4	16.4	22.6	29.9
United States	20.7	18.7	17.3	12.3	17.7	20.6
China	21.4	17.9	15.7	7.6	13.7	23.6
India	32.1	24.4	18.3	5.3	8.1	14.8
Africa	41.5	36.9	28.7	3.4	4.2	6.7

SOURCE: United Nations 2005 (medium-variant projections) and Eurostat.

Long-range forecasts of dependency ratios—as defined in demographic terms[4]—are sensitive to assumptions about fertility and longevity (especially life expectancy at older ages), both of which are straddled by substantial confidence intervals. (Levels of immigration also affect dependency, but, as noted below, not by much at the ranges that are likely to be politically acceptable to countries of immigration.) A fertility recovery that yielded family sizes nearer two than one is not impossible in Europe and Japan, albeit unlikely in the view of many observers. The course of mortality at older ages in the developed world is even more uncertain—a further consequential matter for the financial condition of pension funds. The nearing approach of high old-age dependency combined with these uncertainties pushes governments toward adoption of retirement schemes involving individual retirement accounts, in which savings and later dissavings take place over each person's life cycle.[5]

Migration and identity

Income differentials, in combination with relative population sizes and rates of increase, clearly point to the continuation and the likely intensification of migratory pressures, with the potential to generate massive population movements from poor to rich countries. To what extent such movements actually materialize is a different matter. Migrant-receiving countries seldom plan the number of migrants to be admitted beyond the next few years—and where plans do exist, they can be and are revised at will or altered by circumstance. The migration assumptions incorporated in the UN projections, such as those cited above, are arbitrary, hence purely illustrative. They typically assume, country-by-country, continuation of the volume of the migrant stream estimated for the most recent past, or at a somewhat reduced level. The actual number of migrants may turn out to be far greater than this. Mexican migration into the United States in the 1950s and 1960s, for example, poorly signaled the massive influx from Mexico in more recent decades.

Migration may also turn out to be smaller than simple extrapolations suggest. Public opinion in the main receiving countries, especially in Europe and more specifically in the European Union, has, on balance, increasingly favored less migration—a sentiment reinforced by recently heightened tensions surrounding Europe's Muslim minority and by the volume of unskilled migration into the United States. Strict enforcement of the rules adopted in this sphere could greatly restrict migration flows, both legal and clandestine. Yet enforcement is costly in economic terms and infringes on other values and preferences of the native population. Moreover, in every immigrant-receiving country there are numerous persons and interest groups strongly favoring relaxation of rules in particular cases or for particular types

of immigrants: their wishes often prevail over the weakly expressed preferences of the greater number of those favoring tighter restrictions.

Such differences in attitude are typically strongly correlated with position in the income or class hierarchy. Whether in their private capacity or as
entrepreneurs, more affluent segments of the population disproportionately
benefit from greater access to low-wage domestic service workers or to wage
laborers willing to work for wages below the rates that native workers would
demand. At the same time, wealthier persons are apt to have less exposure
to situations that may be seen by many as discomforting, such as the changing ethnic make-up in residential areas or in the schools their children at-
tend. Persons in lower income classes bear the brunt of such exposure.

An often-repeated argument favoring immigration invokes the economic and social problems associated with population aging and the "needs"
of the labor force. The influx of migrants, it is held, rejuvenates the age
structure and fills jobs that otherwise would go unfilled. Migrants, if employed, thus ease labor force adjustments and prop up the pension and health
care systems of the receiving country. But as demographers know, this, at
best, is a temporary remedy for population aging. Immigrants also age; they
eventually cease to be workers and taxpayers and become claimants on pensions and other entitlements. To maintain the rejuvenating effect would
require sustained immigration on a scale that over time would radically
change the numerical balance between natives and immigrants—a transformation unlikely to be welcomed by most persons in the receiving country. That transformation—David Coleman calls it the third demographic transition—is accentuated where native–immigrant cultural differences are large
and migrant acculturation to the mainstream is slow. Cases in point are
European cities like Rotterdam and Birmingham.

Within broad limits, modern industrial societies should be able to cope
with the economic and social problems caused by population aging without
recourse to immigration. The institutional changes required for that purpose are well known. The availability of an apparently "easier" solution for
those problems, through immigration, allows societies to avoid the needed
reforms—as well as to avoid thinking seriously about policies to encourage
higher birth rates.

In filling labor force needs, the advantages and disadvantages of immigration would have to be compared to alternative means of adjustment,
whether policy-induced or arising in response to market signals: mobilizing
labor reserves from the native population; developing and adopting technologies that substitute for labor; upgrading wage rates to elicit labor supply responses; and, not least, eliminating activities that could only be sustained with low-wage labor. Each of these adjustments, whether applied
separately or in combination, has its costs. Over time these costs may, however, prove to be lower than those entailed in the reflexive reliance on immigration.

The migration solution looks easy because of the magnitude of the supply pool of potential migrants—a function of income differentials and relative population sizes.[6] Although geographic proximity now has less influence on migration decisions than in the past, when transportation and communication costs were higher, the point may be illustrated by comparing migrant-receiving countries with potential sender countries in the same general geographic neighborhood.

The European Union provides the principal case in point. (The North American case is similar in many respects, apart from its higher native-born fertility levels and its more flexible labor market.) Consider the three EU countries with the largest net immigration—Germany, Britain, and Italy—and the three largest potential migrant suppliers in the EU's "southern neighborhood"—Egypt, Turkey, and Iran. In 2005, the comparative population sizes of each group are almost the same: 204 million in the three EU countries, 217 million in the three countries of the southern neighborhood. For the next 45 years, the UN assumes net immigration of 9 million into Germany, 6 million into Britain, and over 5 million into Italy and substantial, although less massive, emigration from Egypt, Turkey, and Iran. Nonetheless, the medium projections for 2050 show a major shift in comparative population size: a slight decline, to 197 million, in the three EU countries, but a 50 percent rise, to 329 million, in the southern three.[7] Per capita income (2002 estimates in purchasing power parity terms) was above US$25,000 in each of the three EU countries; it was about $6,000 in Turkey and Iran and less than $4,000 in Egypt.

Vastly greater pools of would-be EU migrants exist in other parts of Africa and West Asia. Indeed this whole region might, somewhat provocatively, be called Europe's "southern hinterland." Its relative size contrasted with the EU itself, past and projected, is shown in Figure 1. Clearly, there is the potential for immigration into the EU on a much larger scale than is assumed in the UN projections. The same is true for other high-income areas, not only the traditional immigration countries—United States, Canada, and Australia—but also Japan and other prosperous East Asian countries and perhaps some emerging Latin American countries such as Brazil. More to the point, the potential flows are larger too than envisaged by any of the migrant-receiving countries. Should such flows materialize, they would amount to only a modest downward correction to population growth trends in the sending countries but could radically change the demographic make-up of the receiving countries. Both historical experience and present-day indications suggest that such changes can have unwelcome consequences—cultural, economic, and political—whenever assimilation of migrants proves to be difficult, whether because of attitudes prevailing in the receiving society or attitudes of the migrants themselves.

The right to determine who is admitted as a migrant is fundamental to the modern state system. In practice, as suggested above, the complex mix-

FIGURE 1 Demographic background to European immigration: European Union (EU-25) compared to its "southern hinterland," 1950–2050

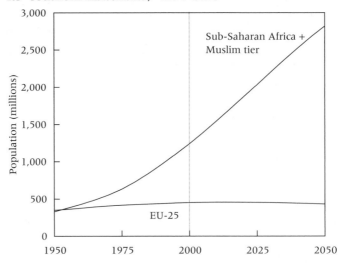

SOURCE: United Nations 2005 (estimates and medium-variant projections).

ture of gains and losses that are entailed and the interplay of interest groups with stakes in the outcome make the decisionmaking process inherently difficult. Moreover, sending countries may also claim a stake—through their concern for relieving domestic unemployment, for the well-being of their expatriate citizens, and, more tangibly, for the remittance flows that may be generated. This spread of claims has suggested to some a case for international regulation of migration. In the 1920s, Albert Thomas, then director of the International Labour Office, asked whether the time had come "for considering the possibility of establishing some sort of supreme supranational authority which would regulate the distribution of population on rational and impartial lines, by controlling and directing migration movements and deciding on the opening-up or closing of countries to particular streams of immigration" (Thomas 1927). Such ideas resurface in contemporary policy discussions in the international arena—for instance, Kofi Annan's remark in a 2004 speech that "migration is an issue that demands greater international cooperation—norms and policies to manage migration in the interest of all."[8] While any move toward sharing policymaking responsibility with sending states would no doubt be resisted by the receiving states, the issue introduces an additional level of uncertainty in forecasting the volume and direction of international migration in the coming decades.

For *temporary* labor migration, joint decisionmaking is certainly to be expected. Such schemes, bringing in migrants on work contracts for a fixed period, could be established to the mutual benefit of the receiving and the sending countries (justifying a quid-pro-quo in the form of material compensation for the sender), and, of course, of the migrants themselves. Although there are successful models for such guestworker arrangements, their potentials have not been much explored. An expansion of temporary migration, skilled and unskilled, has been under consideration in the United States in response to employer pressures and, in the unskilled case, as an offset to more stringent border controls. Such schemes should be of particular interest to countries in which popular sentiment is unequivocally against permanent immigration, such as Japan. Short of draconian administration, full enforcement of the return provision for guestworkers (presumably to be replaced by new recruits) is not to be expected, but that goal is not necessarily a condition for success provided return rates can be kept high. A side benefit of such a scheme could be its use in selecting participants to be offered permanent residence.

Migration within the countries of the European Union presents a special case of international migration. The label "international" is warranted, as EU countries retain major elements of national sovereignty. Treaties guarantee citizens of member countries the right to free movement, for whatever purpose, within the Union. (Labor migration from countries that joined most recently is subject to temporary restrictions by some members of the EU-15.) Through the Schengen agreement, involving a large subset of the continental EU countries, the right to free movement and settlement is also guaranteed to persons to whom any Schengen member country has granted permanent immigrant status. When differentials in income are minor, as in the case of the EU-15 countries, labor migration is likely to be small, an outcome reinforced by cultural and linguistic barriers. Few persons from Munich wish to take up work in Lyon, and vice versa. Labor migration from the rest of what is now the EU-25 has greater potential, evidenced by the labor inflow to Britain and Ireland (especially from Poland). But the most important migration type within the EU in the coming decades may turn out to be retirement migration—retirees attracted to parts of Spain, for example, in a pattern similar to that observed in Florida or Arizona in the United States.

Outside the EU, while free trade agreements have proliferated, the more radical integration involving common markets for labor has been rare. Australia and New Zealand have such an arrangement. Some regional groupings—notably ASEAN—have at times contemplated doing so.[9] The North American Free Trade Agreement, in contrast, has deliberately refrained from promotion of cross-border labor mobility—indeed NAFTA was originally seen by some as a kind of bulwark against unregulated inflows to the United States and Canada. A fortiori that would be true of any extension further southward, as in the Central American Free Trade Agreement or the bruited

Free Trade Agreement of the Americas (FTAA). In practice, as noted earlier, regulatory efforts to curtail migration reflect the diversity of economic and political interests in the matter, typically combining fairly strong if less than effective border controls with lax enforcement of employer sanctions.

This discussion is necessarily inconclusive, but it clearly suggests that migration flows from less developed countries to the rich countries during the next half-century—especially to North America and the European Union—will be at least as large as and possibly significantly larger than those observed in recent decades. At the same time, it seems probable that receiving countries will raise their expectations of migrant cultural assimilation and adopt more stringent control and surveillance measures (border security and registration or ID requirements), in part in response to xenophobic and nativist reactions by their citizenries. These measures notwithstanding, by midcentury both of these continent-size areas are likely to have populations far more varied by ethnic and cultural background and by geographic origin than they were at the turn of the millennium.

Fraying sovereignty: Fission and coalescence

Countries are creations of history: their continuity over time is not carved in stone. They can split into smaller units or merge to form larger entities. The post–World War II period brought a proliferation of national units. This was largely the result of the dismantling of the colonial empires, the last phase of which was completed with the gaining of independence by the 15 former republics of the Soviet Union. Disintegration of some artificial national constructs contributed to the process, such as the separation of Bangladesh from Pakistan, Singapore from the Malay Federation, Eritrea from Ethiopia, and the split of the former Czechoslovakia and Yugoslavia into their major constituent units. The division of Korea into two separate states solidified after the 1953 armistice. Southern Sudan is promised a future opportunity to break from the country's Arab north.

It is possible to see this pattern as the triumph of atavistic nationalist hatreds over the economic logic of market size, but closer examination tends to reveal the continued relevance of economic motives. Often the impulse to secede comes from an economically successful or fortuitously resource-rich subregion of a country, seeking to preserve or enhance its position by erecting barriers to entry.[10] The lessons of the economics of German reunification are read as proving the merits of disunity in rich South Korea; the economic success of Hong Kong holds a lesson for Shanghai as well as for China's several eastern provinces.

Subnational devolution of political power, short of national independence, is also in evidence, potentially offering the devolved entity greater economic returns (perhaps concealed in nationalistic rhetoric) while remaining under the security umbrella of the state. Quebec is an example, as are, in Europe, Scotland, Wales, Catalonia, Corsica, Wallonia, and Flanders. Far-reaching regional autonomy was built into the postwar reconstruction of Germany as a federal republic, and devolution by legislative reform gave greater powers to regions in France and Italy. Striving for movement in similar directions has been evident in many other countries as well, illustrated by the examples of Nigeria, Indonesia, Philippines, and Sri Lanka.

Is the present configuration of states approaching some near-permanent form or will the process of fission continue indefinitely? Working against further change is the entrenchment of the principle of national sovereignty in the United Nations Charter and in the everyday workings of international institutions. Efforts to override it by acknowledging a right to self-determination for some aspiring national entity (self-determination is also a UN principle)—or even to protect human rights in the face of egregious government violations—have been rare. A few states—perhaps Iraq included—may yet hive off separate nations; Russia could shed some troublesome Muslim territories along its southern borders. Ascendant powers, however, encounter few challenges in dealing as they please with minor would-be states on their fringes, such as Sikkim or Tibet.

The reverse phenomenon to fission—the consolidation of multiple political units into one—has seen few examples in the past 60 years. The most notable is the merger of the former East Germany into the Federal Republic. And of signal importance, although not classifiable under the traditional category of independent statehood, is the creation of the European Union. Starting with the six-country association under the 1957 Treaty of Rome, by 2004 the EU encompassed 25 states, with a population of 457 million, pledged to form "an ever closer union."[11] Member states preserve essential elements of sovereignty but cede by treaty many former state functions to a common, nonterritorial, political machinery headquartered in Brussels. Whether it should espouse more thoroughgoing federalist ambitions or settle for the less radical "Anglo-Saxon" confederate model remains a matter of disagreement among the member states, with far from predictable resolution.

East Asia has a number of efforts at regional integration. ASEAN, now including all Southeast Asian states except East Timor, is well established, seen by some as eventually growing into an EU-style entity. Institutional thickening can be measured in the continual invention of new ties among member governments, the progressive easing of bureaucratic barriers, and the profusion of meetings, dialogues, and working groups. There is no Brussels in view, however, let alone a regional parliament. It remains more an intergovernmental organization than a superstate manqué.

Integration across East Asia as a whole has not progressed as far but may have greater prospects. A Japan-centered East Asian economic system

seemed in the cards in the 1970s and 1980s, with massive Japanese investments in the region creating a set of burgeoning economies following in
Japan's train. (Lingering memories of Japan's colonial and wartime interventions precluded such relationships extending much beyond the economic.) But then came the dramatic slowing of Japan's economy in the
1990s, coinciding with China's economic take-off fueled by the rapid
strengthening of the investment and production networks of "greater China"
(China, Taiwan, and Hong Kong). By the end of the century it was apparent that any emerging East Asia–wide economic system would be centered
on China, not Japan.[12] A plausible institutional framework for an East Asian
community is the grouping known as ASEAN Plus Three (APT), adding
China, Japan, and South Korea to the ten ASEAN states.

Moves toward regional coalescence, at least in the economic sphere,
are also seen in the other major world regions. SAARC (South Asian Association for Regional Cooperation) formally brings together all South Asian
states, though it could also be seen as defining India's hegemonic reach—
aside from Pakistan's sometimes awkward inclusion and potential role as
spoiler. But India's rapidly increasing economic strength and place as an
emerging world power arguably gain little from that grouping.

Latin America south of Mexico, once to be accommodated by NAFTA's
transformation into the Americas-wide FTAA, is now more often seen as an
emerging region in itself, building on its two main existing trade pacts,
Mercosur and the Andean Community. An envisaged continent-wide South
American Community of Nations (CSN) would be explicitly modeled on the
EU—even to a common passport and currency. Brazil is set to remain the
region's heavyweight power: its GDP in 2004 was four times the size of
Argentina's, the next largest economy (though not yet surpassing Mexico's).
In the Goldman Sachs forecasts, it would be closing on Japan's GDP by 2050.[13]

The Middle East and North Africa, from the Maghreb to the Gulf, has
a loose political identity in the 22-country Arab League and has displayed
sporadic aspirations to unity. There is substantial labor migration within
this region but little basis for a strong regional economy. Finally, the African Union—successor to the Organization for African Unity—has a broad
integrative ambition, if as yet with scant accomplishment. In the words of
the African Union Commission (2004: 16), "Africa must form vast and viable internal markets to…pave the way for inter-African division of labour
according to relative domestic and external advantages, and confer on these
huge collective entities a genuine power of negotiation with the markets
already constituted on other continents."

The present and projected population sizes of the main regional groupings are shown in Table 4. Together these now make up 88 percent of the
world population, a proportion that would be maintained in 2050 under
the assumption of unchanged country composition. Market size, of course,

TABLE 4   Population sizes of major regional trade pacts or common markets (existing or in prospect), 2005 and as projected to 2050 (millions)

	2005	2050
European Union (EU-25)	460	450
NAFTA	438	577
CSN[a]	375	527
APT (ASEAN Plus Three)[b]	2,031	2,285
(ASEAN)	(555)	(749)
SAARC[c]	1,453	2,220
African Union	906	1,937

[a]Comunidad Sudamericana de Naciones (South American Community of Nations)
[b]Comprising the ten members of the Association of Southeast Asian Nations, China, Japan, and South Korea
[c]South Asian Association for Regional Cooperation
SOURCE: United Nations 2005 (medium-variant projections) and Eurostat.

would yield a different ranking, with the EU and NAFTA currently well ahead but ASEAN Plus Three rapidly catching up and SAARC also becoming a major market force.

The more general change that permits moves toward "ever closer union" in regional groupings, but that extends beyond regionalism, is a shift in the meaning of national sovereignty itself. Such a change is signaled by the popularity of adjectives like virtual or postmodern to describe certain countries. The "virtual state," analogous to the virtual corporation—a company "with a head but no body"—supplants the older trading state that was obsessed with territory and resources and worried about locating production within its borders (see Rosecrance 1996). Japan, Korea, and Singapore are in the vanguard of virtuality; China and Russia remain "territorial fetishists" (ibid.). Postmodernity as a political characterization appears in the work of international relations theorists like Buzan (1998) and Cooper (2003), who divide countries into premodern, modern, and postmodern. The modern group is made up of the conventionally-sovereign states that first emerged in seventeenth-century Europe and gradually became a universal model of statehood, spreading worldwide with the ending of the colonial empires. The premodern countries are the Somalias, Afghanistans, Sudans, and Liberias—characterized by "low levels of sociopolitical cohesion and poorly developed structures of government" (Buzan 1998: 223), whether not yet having reached modernity or having degenerated into political disorder and ungovernability. And the postmodern are those that have begun to relax their sovereignty. "Postmodern states have a much more open and tolerant attitude toward cultural, economic, and political interaction, and define a much narrower range of things as threats to national sovereignty" (ibid.: 221–222).

The postmodern world is the one taking shape in Europe, envisaged in the treaties underpinning the European Union ("a highly developed system for mutual interference in each other's domestic affairs, right down to beer and sausages"—Cooper 2003: 27), the Council of Europe, and the Organization for Security and Co-operation in Europe, with glimmers of a wider application indicated by a slew of international treaties on matters such as security, justice, and the environment. America, in this classification, is in many respects still a "modern" state, its concessions to internationalism (principally the WTO) often reluctant and subordinated, when deemed necessary, to national interests. In East Asia, China is modern, Japan postmodern.

Is postmodernity, in this political sense, the all-but-inevitable path for the world as a whole as globalization proceeds, or a fairly special outcome among a few groups of like-minded states? Consideration of demographic realities, undertaken below, would suggest the latter is the more likely.

Demography and globalization

The large income differences that drive contemporary international migration are the results of a long process of uneven development. In a stylized depiction of economic history, each country journeys from a position of poverty along a path toward greater material comfort. Some countries progress rapidly, others lag behind. The speed of advance is not uniform: overtaking and backsliding occur, gaps between countries narrow or widen. At least since the industrial revolution, however, Europe and its overseas offshoots, notably the United States, along with Japan, have led the pack. Their lead increased considerably over the last century.

The factors explaining the economic ranking at any moment are complex, intertwined, and often deeply rooted in the past. Among them are differences in acquisitiveness and in aptitude in seeking material advancement; ability to develop institutions conducive to thrift, trust, and cooperation beyond kin groups; interest in science and in its practical applications; favorable geographic location, climate, and access to natural resources; military prowess and skills in making and maintaining peace; and willingness to take risks and luck in having them pay off. A host of others could be added.

One of these factors, again in interaction with others, is demographic behavior. During their modern history, the presently rich countries benefited from the economic stimulus of spurts in population growth, yet they avoided the kind of expansion that, by natural increase alone, can multiply a population eightfold or more during a single century. Europe, in particular, could have built up a population that today would be a numerical match to China or India, or that could even have surpassed those countries in size. But, under the guidance of fortuitous institutional structures, Europe's aggregate population growth was kept in check during its modern history. By the late twentieth century, under circumstances of unparalleled prosperity, Europe was approaching zero population growth. Its countries developed elaborate welfare states, promising, and to a large extent providing, material comforts and security to every citizen. Europe seemed prepared to settle down to enjoy the pleasures of a stationary state.

Europe's offshoots in North America and Oceania retained much the same demographic pattern of moderate to low natural increase (births minus deaths). Their distinctiveness lay in tolerating and even promoting a large migrant influx, accommodated initially by an open land frontier and subsequently by similarly open labor markets—and, in the US case especially, more modest provision of an economic safety net.

Being born in one of these rich, stable societies in effect automatically imparts a gift—an unearned rent traceable to the wise demographic choices, individually or in their aggregate result, made by ancestors in a parade of generations reaching back into the deep past. Those seeking entry into these lucky countries by immigration can be thought of as trying to capture that same rent by the only other available route.

Threats to the European social model

Ironically, even before being fully able to realize its promises, this "European social model"—both in Europe and in its counterparts elsewhere—is now under threat. It is menaced from two developments, each of which has a key demographic component.

The first of these threats is overshoot in the reduction of fertility. Bringing fertility to a long-run replacement level is a historical imperative. Falling somewhat under replacement need not be differently characterized: fertility cannot be fine-tuned to 2.06 children per woman. For a long period, affluent industrial societies could certainly live with a slow decline in their populations and adjust to the economically less advantageous age structure associated with it, without suffering grim economic and social consequences. But should fertility settle at a level deeply below replacement, the rapid fall-off in population numbers together with the associated age structure— resembling, if plotted as an age pyramid, a pear stood on its stem—cannot be accommodated. Short of a policy-engineered revival of fertility, which, of course, has a long (20 years plus) lead time, mass immigration then becomes the only possible remedy. The scale of migration called for, however, elicits the kinds of responses discussed earlier in this chapter. Not least among them would be the erosion of political support for the redistributive measures of the welfare state.

The second population-linked threat is external: it arises from the processes of globalization, which draw mature postindustrial, post–demographic transition societies into economic interaction with materially much poorer societies—societies that have a different demographic past, different current demographic configurations, and different demographic prospects.

Economic theory supplies a convincing demonstration of the advantages of extending the scope of economic interactions from the narrowly local to the national and, beyond that, to the global level. Although the demonstration is studded with massive ceteris paribus assumptions that dictate caution, it is evident that larger markets permit greater division of labor, stimulate competition, specialization, innovation, and higher productivity, and provide their participants with access to a greater variety of goods. In so doing, the enlarged market delivers higher incomes and promotes economic growth: it makes individuals and countries richer.

Historical experience bears out the thesis. The first great epoch of globalization, the late nineteenth and early twentieth century, brought rapid economic growth in the leading industrial countries and sparked the beginning of industrialism throughout the rest of the world. The drastic curtailment of international trade by protectionist policies in the interwar years was associated with low growth and eventually with the misery of the Great Depression. After World War II, renewed efforts at international liberalization resulted in a vast expansion of international trade and unprecedented prosperity.

But that postwar success story was, in fact, geographically quite limited, and hence is a less than compelling argument for the merits of globalization. Much of the expansion of trade took place among the rich countries. These countries possessed similar or fast-converging levels of income, rendering them natural partners in trade. The second world—the Soviet Empire, with China nominally also included—was not part of the emerging free trade zone. Neither was India, an official admirer and would-be imitator of the Soviet prewar ambition of "socialism in one country." The countries of Africa mostly espoused and in part practiced "African socialism," and those of the Middle East similarly experimented with local varieties of the socialist model. Ideology also kept much of Latin America outside the revived world market: interaction with the "center" was seen as perpetuating peripheral status and solidifying economic dependency.

The conspicuous exceptions to these stand-apart regions were the market-oriented countries of East Asia. Guided by the visible but skillful hand of their governments, these "tiger economies" seized the opportunity for rapid industrialization offered by trade with, and unimpeded flow of capital investment from, the leading capitalist countries. Strategic considerations in the context of the Cold War helped to make the West a willing partner in these exchanges. But relative demographic size clearly facilitated that willingness. Even if Japan is included among the newly industrializing trading partners—and, of course, by the 1970s Japan was solidly positioned within the core of the capitalist world—their combined population, or, more relevantly, the combined size of their potential labor resources, represented a small fraction of the labor force of the leading capitalist countries. Any pain from losing industrial jobs to the East Asian tigers was clearly overshadowed by the economic gains generated by increased trade.

Not surprisingly, the lessons of success are eventually absorbed by others, and the recipes are adopted. The big turnaround came in China, marked by the Dengist reforms of the early 1980s that freed trade between China and the outside world and opened the Chinese market to foreign investment. The ranks of imitators thereafter grew rapidly. The latest major convert to the advantages of exploiting the global marketplace has been the formerly autarky-seeking, reform-socialist India. Today, despite the loud protests voiced at successive World Social Forums, ostensibly speaking on behalf of the world's poor, there are hardly any less developed countries that wish to shut themselves off from globalization.

For the industrialized countries, however, this new globalization of globalization presents an unprecedented challenge. It places them in competition with newly emerging industrial countries that possess labor forces, actual and potential, vastly greater in size than their own and does so under circumstances in which the former advantages that favored them in such competition are rapidly disappearing. The problem is highlighted in warnings insistently issued to the citizenry in the EU and, with less justification, in the United States: "You must work harder and longer than before; you must give up privileges to which you have grown accustomed; and even if you do so, your job may evaporate tomorrow." Why? "Because of globalization! You are in competition with countless millions of workers in faraway lands who are eager and able to do what you do and do it just as well, and are willing to do it for wages that are a fraction of yours."

Such rhetoric in part simply draws attention away from problems that have nothing to do with globalization but derive from features in the existing design of systems of social protection that are becoming unsustainable because of population aging. These problems require domestic reforms, regardless of the extent of exposure to foreign competition. But the element of truth the warnings contain, when considered alongside the demographic realities alluded to, warrants further examination. What is at issue is the viability of the WTO trade regime from the standpoint of the developed world over the lengthy period—perhaps decades—during which technological differences between the demographic giants largely vanish but substantial wage differentials persist.

Offshoring and the demographic overhang

In the past, the relatively high wages (and high non-wage costs) prevailing in the rich countries were routinely explained and justified by the higher productivity of their workers. That competitive edge derived from advantages that developing countries were once unable to replicate—a well-educated labor force that has privileged access to the best technology and to superior complementary factors of production such as management and marketing skills, organizational prowess, modern communication and transportation infrastructure, and a secure and healthy environment.

These advantages have fast been eroding as transnational corporations increasingly recreate them in locations where labor costs are much lower. Transferring industrial production to other countries then becomes an option favored by an elementary economic calculus. The wage differentials are initially seen in the "rubber shoes, bicycles, and umbrellas"–type manufactures. In the West, many one-time worriers about Japan's postwar economic predicament thought such products would be Japan's future way of earning a (modest) living through exports. Today no observer could miss the ability of China or India to produce a vast range of consumer and capital goods using the most advanced technologies, and their ability to sell such goods more cheaply than those manufactured in the high-wage industrial countries. China's Minister of Commerce, Bo Xilai, sought to defuse European objections to high levels of textile imports by remarking that China would need to sell 800 million shirts to afford one Airbus A380 (*China Daily*, 5 May 2005). A more significant calculation he did not essay was how long it would be before there was a Chinese-built A380.

Services are similarly prone to "offshoring" from high-income countries, and, as with manufacturing, skills in themselves offer no necessary protection. The criterion, as Blinder (2006) has noted, is whether the output of a job can be delivered electronically: "Janitors and crane operators are probably immune to foreign competition; accountants and computer programmers are not." Many jobs in the personal care industry—a growth sector in any country with an aging population—cannot be exported. And at least for a while, headquarters of transnational enterprises may remain in the centers from which much of the capital and most of the technology driving the new industrialization still originate. In this last case, however, even if such geographic specialization could be seen as permanent, favoring a well-compensated elite, not everybody in the former seats of manufacturing can be a banker, a lawyer, an advertising and public relations executive, marketing strategist, systems analyst, or management consultant. Moreover, research and development activities—the laboratories that power innovation and raise productivity—are among the strongest current candidates for outsourcing to China and India. The "symbolic analysts" who were to maintain the technical edge of the West's postindustrial economies are then as likely to be found in Shanghai and Bangalore as in Silicon Valley or the two Cambridges.

A more promising and steady jobs-assuring and export-earning large industry in the advanced stage of international specialization could be tourism—say, between the EU and the emerging modern Asia. In essence, Europe could be transformed into a huge theme park, geared for the entertainment of curious visitors, increasingly comprising the newly rich of Asia. In the ensuing equilibrium position, general material affluence might reign. But such a future, even on aesthetic grounds, would not appeal to countries with the memory of a quite different history.

Enthusiasts for globalization, whether seeing it as accelerating world development or as improving returns to capital, do of course recognize the major adjustment problems that offshoring imposes on developed-country workforces—even after taking account of the lower prices of the foreign-sourced goods and services and, partly in consequence, lower inflation. But they argue that any disadvantage is temporary: currencies will adjust to correct some of the trade imbalance, and industrial wages will quickly rise in the new locations. The problem with this expectation lies in the sheer demographic scale of the emerging economies. China and India, and many countries coming behind them, have large labor reserves in the traditional sectors of their economies that will not be exhausted for decades to come and will keep wages down. (That expectation is not belied by signs of upward pressure on wages, as observed recently in urban China. More probable explanations would point to temporary labor market frictions and educational bottlenecks.) For the West, moreover, a shift in manufacturing locations from China or India to Vietnam or Bangladesh would be no gain: the bottom line is the still-massive rural and fringe-urban populations in emerging manufacturing economies, providing several decades of something approaching an "unlimited" labor supply. As long as these populations exist and can be mobilized, permitting wage equalization upward would retard full modernization of the countries that possess them.

The absolute numbers of potential entrants to the modern economy are sobering. UN projections of urban growth extend only to the next 25 years, but they show proportions rural in 2030 still at 40 percent in China and nearly 60 percent in India (Table 5). In China, admittedly, that population will by then be aging rapidly; but elsewhere, notably in India, the cohort of entrants to the labor force shows only modest fall-off—even, as

TABLE 5   Rural population size and proportions rural in China and India, 2005 and 2030

	China		India	
	Rural population (millions)	Percent rural	Rural population (millions)	Percent rural
2005	784	59.6	786	71.3
2030	574	39.7	859	59.3

SOURCE: United Nations 2006.

TABLE 6   Youth cohort size, China and India: Age group 18–23 years, 2000–2050 (in millions, showing low- and high-variant projection range)

	2000	2010	2020	2030	2040	2050
China	116	137	108–110	85–121	74–131	61–119
India	111	134	139–140	124–157	104–165	86–160

SOURCE: United Nations 2005.

seen in Table 6, under the UN's most optimistic scenario of fertility decline. (Table 6 also indicates the mounting uncertainties in these forecasts beyond 20 to 30 years, reflecting different but still quite feasible assumptions about trends in fertility.) The overall demographic contrast over time with the United States and the European Union, the two main components of the West, is seen in Figure 2.

This line of argument is set out in only the sketchiest terms, and may seem overdrawn. But its consideration in the ongoing debate about the merits of globalization is likely to be unavoidable. The weight of academic opinion, especially among economists (for example, see Deepak Lal, in this volume), is on the side of pushing ahead along the track we are on. But popular opinion disagrees, and its potential for exploitation by populist demagogues is all too real.[14]

Are there alternative models for the organization of the international system over the next few decades that might lessen the opportunity for and

FIGURE 2   Demographic background to globalization: China and India compared to European Union (EU-25) and the United States, 1950–2050

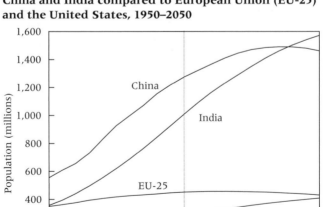

SOURCE: United Nations 2005 (estimates and medium-variant projections).

appeal of demagoguery? One that is worth fuller consideration (it is discounted by Lal) might be described as "regional quasi-autarky." What this entails is not a return to inward-looking protectionism at the country level: that has no attraction—if indeed it were even feasible. But a regional grouping of countries of comparable income levels, together offering a substantial productive base and internal market, could make good sense. A European Union is large enough, with nearly half a billion people, to exploit almost all conceivable economies of scale (perhaps only the Airbus actually requires a global market) and to provide a competitive environment assuring innovation and steadily improving product quality. Within its boundaries its rules already forbid protectionism. And it is large enough to provide balance—a diversity of industries and activities allowing for complementarities and unplanned synergies. How much more advantage can be squeezed out of extra diversity, in a region where Finns rub shoulders with Portuguese and Irish with Greeks? In short, as a region in itself the EU could flourish with a fair degree of autarky (energy excepted), working primarily to satisfy its internal market. The same recipe could fit North America or a larger Western Hemisphere grouping. And something similar could be fashioned from what some already call China's co-prosperity sphere, or an analogous region for India. These regions (say, those identified in Table 4) could live in peace with each other—a supposed attribute of democracies—and also trade. The EU needs some exotic spices; its citizens want to visit the Great Wall, the Grand Canyon, and the Taj Mahal. Mutatis mutandis, each of the other regions has comparable needs and desires. As with the EU and the United States today, there would be no objection to crafting special trade relationships in support of particularly backward economies.

In a more remote future, setting aside all that may go wrong, population pyramids around the world will even out—and, we can hope, will not have converged to the inverted pear-shaped structure. Worldwide economic prosperity of a sort will have been attained. In such a world, true globalization is likely to emerge as a real option. That future, however, not least for solid demographic reasons, is not within our grasp in the next 50 years.

An underclass of states?

The "global" in globalization and the global economy thus far and perhaps well into the future is less than all-encompassing. A significant number of countries have fairly negligible links with the major trading economies aside from the trickle of imports financed by foreign aid; others have substantial exports but deriving from extractive-industry enclaves with revenues diverted to a narrow elite in the society. For whatever reason—there are many candidates—these countries have not managed to find or hold to the development path taken by the successful emerging economies. Disproportionately they are located in sub-Saharan Africa.

Per capita GDP in sub-Saharan Africa, based on Maddison's (2003) calculations, has hardly moved since the 1970s. The two vaunted regional high-flyers, Botswana and Mauritius, are impressive exceptions but their combined populations amount to less than 0.5 percent of the regional total. The past ten years have seen an improvement in this dismal record, which some observers believe may presage a larger turnaround under which Africa would slowly regain the economic promise that it possessed in the immediate aftermath of decolonization in the 1960s. That, at least, is the vision promulgated by the Commission for Africa, whose 2005 report was endorsed by the G-8 and by major foreign-aid donor agencies. It is implicit in the rhetoric of the African Union and its NEPAD (New Partnership for Africa's Development) initiative. The factors militating against such a turnaround, though, are formidable.

The AIDS epidemic is one such factor. The bleak future for sub-Saharan Africa portrayed by Christopher Clapham (in this volume) has much to do with AIDS. The extraordinary fall in life expectancy at birth beginning in the 1990s in South Africa, Botswana, and Zimbabwe—by 20 years or more, to numbers not seen at a country level for many decades—presents huge development problems in addition to the tragedy it represents for individuals, families, and communities. Predictions of the future course of the AIDS epidemic vary widely—indeed, even estimates of current HIV prevalence rates are often questioned—but many analysts have retreated from earlier dire predictions of a continent-wide pandemic. Some countries that had experienced high rates of HIV prevalence and AIDS mortality in the early years of the epidemic have managed to reduce both; others, against expectations, seem to have largely avoided epidemic rates of infection. These outcomes apparently stem from some combination of health education, modifications in sexual behavior, interventions to prevent mother-to-child HIV transmission, and the fortuity of particular cultural practices (such as male circumcision, which apparently lowers infection risk). It is not wholly implausible that even without wide access to effective medical treatment—still a distant prospect for much of the region—the impact of the disease will gradually subside to a level that, while still serious, is more comparable to that of other health risks.

Heavy AIDS mortality over coming years but a less-than-dire scenario for the duration and spread of the epidemic are the assumptions made in the current UN population projections for Africa. As Table 2 showed, the medium projections for 2050 foresee a Uganda of 127 million, an Ethiopia of 170 million, a Congo of 177 million, and a Nigeria of 258 million. Overall, sub-Saharan Africa is expected to grow from 0.75 billion in 2005 to 1.69 billion in 2050; at midcentury, even though average fertility is assumed to have halved from its current level, the absolute annual increase in population would still be growing. This added weight of numbers will be a burden on development efforts and intensify already severe problems of governability. Glib assertions about economy-boosting demographic bonuses provided by favorable youth-dependency ratios—the potential reallocations from consumption and capital-widening expenditures to growth-enhancing investments—presuppose just those conditions of social order and administrative capacity that rapid population growth threatens.

A sanguine prognosis for the region would see some countries doing well (South Africa is the main hope among the larger economies) and many others, in one way or another, advancing at a pace sufficient to allow substantial improvement in social and economic conditions. Even under such a favorable outcome it is all but certain there will also be laggards and backsliders. States that combine poverty, economic retrogression, and pervasive domestic insecurity can be described as failing or, where these conditions have been longstanding, as "failed." African examples include Angola, Burundi, DR Congo, Guinea, Ivory Coast, Liberia, Sierra Leone, Sudan, and Zimbabwe. The category is far from clearcut and by no means precludes a state so described eventually regaining a foothold on the development path— though it may be starting from a much lower position.[15]

Failing or failed states are not found only in Africa. Afghanistan, East Timor, Haiti, Iraq, Nepal, North Korea, Papua New Guinea, and Yemen are among others that also fit the description. Few are populous: only in sub-Saharan Africa and perhaps the south-western Pacific do such states amount to a significant fraction of their respective regional populations. By some assessments, however, states "at risk" include Nigeria, Bangladesh, and Pakistan. That would lend the problem a truly ominous global dimension.[16]

But even a lack of significance in economic and demographic terms does not mean that failed states have no bearing on the evolution of the global economy and polity. The energy exporters among them obviously remain important in a tight suppliers' market for fossil fuels. Others figure disproportionately as sources of refugees and, through criminal and terrorist activity, as regional destabilizers or even threats to more distant states. And without functioning civil administrations, they are ill-equipped to combat infectious disease or environmental destruction, both with potential for damaging spillover effects beyond their borders.

Uncertainties and surprises

The varying assumptions underlying population forecasts like those of the United Nations concern the pace of fertility transition,[17] which in turn reflects the course of economic growth and cultural change. As was discussed above and in Chapter 1, such forecasts can go seriously awry over a span of half a century even without effects that would count as surprises. Interestingly, however, most of the dramatic events that are thereby ignored—wars, famines, floods, plagues—are barely visible at the broad regional scale and not at all at the global level. Thus the 1959–61 Great Leap Forward famine in China, perhaps the largest in history, killing some 30 million, can hardly be discerned in an East Asian population series. AIDS deaths in the tens of millions in sub-Saharan Africa go with a projected net addition of one billion persons in that region (150 percent) over the half-century to 2050.[18]

In his assessment of the risks of other such "fatal discontinuities" in this period, from asteroid collisions to microbes and nanobots, the geographer (and polymath) Vaclav Smil (2005a) finds most of the usual candidates for worldwide catastrophe comfortably distant or improbable.[19] Influenza and war are the main exceptions—with broadly similar risk-fatality profiles. A worldwide influenza epidemic is seen as unavoidable in the next few decades—the unknown being whether its fatalities can be kept down to a few tens of millions.[20] Precisely because its effects would be so widespread, however, a flu pandemic is not likely to be a destabilizing force in the global political economy. That is not true for war, which ample historical precedent shows can be genuinely transformational. While encouragement can be taken from the declining trend in major conflicts over the twentieth century,[21] what in the past have turned out to be transformational wars have sometimes been wholly unforeseen.

Discontinuities in the evolution of the global system can come about without mass fatalities. Environmental change offers several such scenarios, and doubtless many others that have not been imagined. The gradual atmospheric warming over the twenty-first century, predicted by general circulation models of the climate system, is the best known of these scenarios—its most severe effects coming later in the century but likely to be clearly visible well before. There are potentially large implications for the regional distribution of agricultural zones, for the prevalence ranges of particular infectious and parasitic diseases, and for coastal erosion and flooding from a rise in sea levels, in addition to drastic effects on the nonhuman biota. Rising fossil-fuel use and resultant greenhouse gas emissions, the main anthropogenic factor in global warming, owe more to economic than demographic expansion. But per capita emissions, bound to rise fast in China, India, and the other main emerging economies even under optimistic assumptions about abatement technologies, are multiplied by these countries' huge population numbers.

Wealth brings improved means to adapt to change, so global inequalities will be accentuated by these environmental effects. Many poor countries are particularly vulnerable. New food-deficit regions will probably emerge—and new areas of surplus—calling for major adjustments in the international trade in cereals. Coastal settlement will be affected: in more alarmist scenarios, "environmental refugees" would be created in great numbers.

Responsibility for damage, once assigned, elicits demand for compensation. In the international arena such claims are sometimes recognized—

for wartime occupation, for instance—typically through ad hoc bilateral negotiations. The possibilities of broad-scale damage to particular groups of countries through climate change may elicit claims of an altogether greater magnitude. The guilty parties—guilty of a kind of aggression, from one per-spective—would be the industrialized countries, many of them not only current large emitters but the main contributors to the build-up of green-house gases over decades past. Adjudication of such claims may well de-volve into more rounds of debate like those that have taken place in fol-low-up meetings on the 1992 Climate Convention (one of which produced the Kyoto Protocol), yielding treaties notably lacking in enforceable sanc-tions for nonperformance and with few repercussions on other spheres of international relations. Or, it may be that these distributional issues origi-nating in environmental change will become a dominant concern for the international system.

Climate modeling of the kind that underpins the projections of the Intergovernmental Panel on Climate Change yields smooth output trajec-tories—a warming, say, of a few degrees Centigrade by the end of this cen-tury. But sudden climatic shifts, beyond the predictive ability of current models, also seem possible. A widely publicized scenario of this sort is for ocean warming to disrupt heat circulation by ocean currents in the North Atlantic, and in particular to halt the moderating effect of the Gulf Stream on the climate of Western Europe. (Edinburgh and Copenhagen are on the same latitude as Moscow.) Research on the fine detail of climate history has uncovered many instances in the distant past of abrupt regime change—major (say, 10° C) rises or falls in mean temperatures in a region, some-times taking place in a period as short as a decade but lasting perhaps for centuries.[22] What can set off such events is unknown, but their existence adds to the range of uncertainty surrounding the effects of present trends in atmospheric composition.

Climate change aside, environmentalists also point to looming prob-lems of degradation of ecological services—the often unpriced benefits hu-mans receive from the various ecological systems they are part of. Examples of ecosystem services are crop pollination, fresh water supply from streams and aquifers, natural processes of soil formation and erosion control, nutri-ent cycling, and photosynthesis. Mounting evidence indicates that many such services are being degraded or drawn on at unsustainable rates, as a consequence of population growth, economic expansion, and poor man-agement practices.[23] Here too there are many possibilities for repercussions for human well-being and for economic and political systems beyond na-tional borders.

A particular class of ecosystem service has to do with the aesthetic val-ues humans derive from the natural environment. Those amenity values can in some measure be price-rationed like ordinary goods and services, thereby limiting adverse congestion effects for users. Population growth itself has been a factor in the enclosure or privatization of many common-access resources. But given the choice, most people would likely resist that privatization route beyond modest limits, preferring to retain open access. Unless other kinds of rationing can be devised, degradation through over-use becomes a serious risk. David Victor (in this volume) addresses these issues in relation to wilderness areas. The international spillovers implicated in wilderness preservation or wilderness destruction are mostly intangible—the satisfaction many people find in knowing of their existence, and the pain over their loss—but not a negligible element of welfare. Some conser-vation efforts attempt to translate those sentiments into monetary terms.

Futures for the demographic forerunners

In the very long term, beyond the time-horizon of this volume, full or near-full global convergence in demographic patterns might be achieved, along with—most would no doubt hope—a fairly stationary population or one trending slowly downward to a preferred global optimum. That is the fu-ture that the cosmologist Fred Hoyle (1963), in a brief foray into demogra-phy, called dull (his less-dull alternative was a time-series of population explosions and collapses), although a vision of human continuity is hard to reconcile with large departures from demographic stationarity. Dullness is not a risk over the next 50 years.[24]

The coming half-century is likely to see the ending of massive global population expansion—at least, if the UN medium-variant projections are borne out.[25] The demographic marginalization of the countries currently classified as "more developed" vis-à-vis those classified as "less developed" will proceed apace, with a ratio of 1:10 in births virtually unchanged over the period. The striking contrasts in age structures across countries and re-gions will also persist, although lessening by midcentury.[26] These differen-tials and trends have ramifying effects on the international political economy. For the more developed countries, they pose dilemmas for public policy, the chosen resolution of which will have profound implications for the so-cieties and cultures that emerge.

Low fertility was discussed above as one of the main threats to the European social model, as it is to Japan's also. Continuation of the ultra-low fertility now experienced in Japan, Russia, and parts of the EU leads to a rapid and hard-to-reverse downward trend in population. Under the UN low-variant assumptions, for instance, Japan's and Italy's populations would both diminish by nearly one-quarter by 2050, Russia's by more than one-third. Future levels of fertility stuck below 1.5 children per woman are quite plausible—even as a Europe-wide average—implying, if maintained, gen-erational population declines (aside from migration) of more than 25 per-cent. Accompanying those declines would be burgeoning proportions of the old and very old, requiring costly medical care (and invidious rationing).[27] As a long-run prognosis offered as an option in a policy debate, this demographic outlook might well be judged unacceptable. Its presence in the background sets the stage for consideration of expanded immigration on the one hand and pronatalist measures on the other.

Mere numbers, of course, are only the simplest of the issues that migration policy needs to be concerned with, but they are a convenient starting point. Low or moderate rates of immigration, combined with expectations of (and supporting measures for) integration, are unexceptionable responses to below-replacement fertility. Migration at rates that would be needed to significantly offset very low fertility, however, is a different matter. Integration then becomes far more problematic, and there is a likelihood of generating or further exacerbating serious cultural tensions. Even moderate inflows can yield high urban or fringe-urban concentrations of immigrants, impeding assimilation—and, in the subsequent generation, producing alienation and anomie among persons with cultural roots in neither their parents' society nor the one surrounding them.

Heavy reliance on migration, as earlier remarked, is in some sense an easy option for public policy, assuming that ethnic and cultural tensions can be kept in check. But in avoiding the institutional reforms that would be called for in adapting to a low-fertility, aging society, political leaders and their constituents are setting the stage for a deeper societal transformation. Historically, of course, that has happened often enough, but it entails a potentially huge loss of cultural patrimony. Such a calculation may no longer have much force in affluent, late-capitalist societies—with individualism triumphant and self-fulfillment acknowledged by many as a principal goal. But realization of impending transformation can also be a potent generator of populist reaction.

Maintaining fertility at a level that does not fall much below a two-child average—say, around 1.7–1.8—would largely avert this problem. Such levels (arguably creditable to some extent to supportive population policies) are found in some countries of Western and Northern Europe and in Australia and New Zealand; in the United States, fertility is even higher. But for those many countries in Europe—and for Japan—where levels are well below 1.5, that prospect is dim.[28] There are narrow limits to welfare-state generosity in bribing would-be parents, especially when the state is already overburdened with pension and health-care costs. There is a reluctance to make family allowances disproportionately high for third or later children—or for higher-income parents. There is lingering ideological resistance to the state trying to override personal preferences about childbearing. There is a strong economic interest in increasing female labor force participation, which, policy efforts notwithstanding, is a discouragement to childbearing.[29] And the state is powerless to counter cultural and value changes that favor low fertility or even childlessness. It is possible to imagine a spontaneous recovery in birth rates, like the prosperity-linked baby boom in the years after World War II or, more speculatively, through some radical cultural shift—a millenarian movement?—as yet unforeseen. The role for social policy in engineering an upturn, however, seems fairly marginal.[30] Even if an upturn were to happen, moreover, it would take a quarter-century before the new homegrown labor force began to be felt in the economy; the migration alternative is at hand and has no delay.

As this discussion makes clear, the post-transition demographic predicament of the low-fertility West—the European Union and Japan most notably—is both serious and intractable. That appreciation should argue for concentrated deliberation over what kinds of societies and economies these countries should be trying to construct for themselves and about how they might protect them through the remaining decades of the global demographic transition. Over most of that time they must expect to be continually challenged by low-wage but high-skilled competitors in the world's populous dynamic economies over the whole range of tradable goods and services; at the same time, they will face continued clamoring for entry to their societies by a stream of would-be economic migrants and refugees from fragile or failing economies. Against these formidable pressures they must seek to maintain the levels of social protection and leisure and the other components of the quality of life that affluence has won for them, in the face of further population aging and steadily diminishing numbers of native-born labor force entrants. If nothing more, the deliberation called for might begin a process of strategic thinking about these issues, helping to avert a day-by-day caving in of policy to narrowly based interests and recourse to least-effort political remedies. In the long run, if environmental and other dangers can be held in check, most human societies will have to find their way through the same demographic landscape, hence the experience of the forerunners should have much to teach.

In the United States, fertility has remained close to a two-child average, well above European and Japanese levels, and immigrants—even unskilled immigrants, provided they carry the requisite documents—are broadly welcomed. (The main caveat on migration applies to the large inflow from Mexico, seen by some as the making of a cultural—even political—*reconquista*.) Hence, there is no prospect of population growth ceasing in the foreseeable future. Medium Census Bureau projections show the 2050 US population at 420 million, almost 50 percent above the 2000 census count; decadal increases are undiminished, in the range of 25–30 million.[31] The words of the 1972 Commission on Population and the American Future, cited in Chapter 1 ("recognizing that our population cannot grow indefinitely," and recommending "that the nation welcome and plan for a stabilized population"—the population was then 210 million), have been decisively sidelined if not altogether rejected.

In its absence of a sense of national population *scale* or interest in stabilization, the United States is something of an oddity in the developed world.[32] What might eventually change that situation is unclear: localized congestion does not seem to. The contrast with other rich societies may extend to views of economic growth as well—albeit with elements of caricature on both sides. The vision Keynes spelled out in 1930, echoing John Stuart Mill a century earlier, plausibly resonates more in Europe and Japan than in the United States. The struggle for material goods, said Keynes (1963: 365–366), should not be "the permanent problem of the human race." He looked for a time when both material and demographic growth will have ceased, with attention turned to intellectual and aesthetic endeavors.

> [F]or the first time since his creation man will be faced with his real, his permanent problem—how to use his freedom from pressing economic cares, how to occupy the leisure, which science and compound interest will have won for him, to live wisely and agreeably and well.

A contrasting vision of the pursuit of happiness is that described by Richard Easterlin (1996: 153–154)—a perspective with a distinctly American flavor:

> The future, then, to which the epoch of modern economic growth is leading is one of never ending economic growth, a world in which ever growing abundance is matched by ever rising aspirations, a world in which cultural differences are leveled in the constant race to achieve the good life of material plenty.

The world in which either of these futures might be near to realization will also contain plenty of economic laggards. Some will be on an upward path—eased, no doubt, by flows of investment funds from the developed world, seeking economic returns wherever they can be found. But others might be more in the position of wards of the international community—though exposed to an ever-present risk of default on the part of that community and with their prospects worsened to the degree that any exceptional human talent they produce is siphoned off. Foreign assistance will still have a role, both in covering troughs in food production and in promoting development and demographic transition. Whether it can do so without repeating the many fruitless efforts of the past—by drawing on mature reflection on what should have been done in the last half-century—is far from certain.

Notes

1 As the earlier comments indicate, those labels are already highly tenuous. Convenience and convention are their only defense.

2 The term "Muslim tier" is used in Demeny (2003), where it refers to an arc of 25 predominantly Muslim countries from Pakistan to Mauritania (excluding former Soviet republics); here it is defined so as to exclude five of those 25 countries that the UN places in sub-Saharan Africa.

3 Goldman Sachs forecasts from Wilson and Purushothaman (2003); purchasing power parity estimates for 2001 from Maddison (2003).

4 Typically, the dependency ratio is defined as the population below age 15 and aged 65 and above divided by the population aged 15–64. This age range is of course arbitrary and, especially in advanced economies, at best a crude reflection of reality.

5 Individual accounts, however, offer no more protection than pay-as-you-go schemes against the risk of falling market value of accumulated capital caused by the shifting proportions of workers to retirees. On this "asset meltdown" prospect linked to population aging, see Poterba (2005).

6 Future latecomers to population aging, and economically disadvantaged countries in general, do not have recourse to such a solution. Its present-day use, therefore, has some characteristics of a Ponzi scheme.

7 The contrast is even sharper if the comparison looks only at workforce ages—say, the age group 20–59. In 2005 the 20–59 population in each of the two groups is about 110 million. Over 2005–2050, the EU group drops to 89 million, the southern neighbors increase to 172 million.

8 See Annan (2004). It is now often argued that the logic of globalization should lead not only to free movement of goods and capital but also to free movement of labor. For example, the report of the ILO-sponsored World Commission on the Social Dimension of Globalization (2004) called for "a multilateral framework for immigration laws and consular practices…that would govern cross-border movement of people," paralleling similar frameworks for "cross-border movement of goods, services, technology, investment and information."

9 At least for professionals. (Malaysia periodically expels undocumented Indonesian workers.)

10 Boniface (1998) argues on those lines, seeing the rush toward secessionism as driven by efforts of the territorially clustered rich to shed obligations toward the adjacent territorially clustered poor.

11 The impending entry of Bulgaria and Romania and, almost certainly, Croatia would add some 34 million to form an EU-28.

12 See MacIntyre and Naughton (2005). A recent conference report from the US National Intelligence Council (2004) foresees "China's benevolent dominance" of the region in economic and security affairs as likely to be in place by 2020.

13 World Bank (2005); Wilson and Purushothaman (2003: 9). Maddison's estimates for 2001 show Brazil's economy already one-third larger than Mexico's (Maddison 2003: 134).

14 A link between the demography of globalization and reactionary populism—but referring to immigrant European labor in the United States rather than to production outsourcing, and to the late nineteenth and early twentieth century rather than to the present era of globalization—is discussed by James (2001).

15 A summary of a recent conference of "top US experts on Sub-Saharan Africa" gives a more somber appraisal: "there is a class of African countries—which includes Burkina Faso, Central African Republic, Chad, Mali, Mauritania, and Niger—that are so burdened by their extreme climate, related problems of health and disease, and poor geographic position that it is not clear that any economic model offers them a path toward development" (US National Intelligence Council 2005).

16 A "failed state index" published annually by the magazine *Foreign Policy* lists no fewer than 60 countries "at risk," containing one-third of the world's population.

17 The assumptions concerning future trends in mortality and international migration are the same for each of the variants.

18 The low-variant projection shows a 118 percent increase over 2000–2050; the high variant, 189 percent.

19 Smil (2005a: 229) summarizes his findings and informed speculations on the risk and effect of "massively fatal discontinuities" in a simple graph plotting number of fatalities against probability of occurrence over the next 50 years on a double log scale. At 10 percent probability—a risk that many would regard as considerable reason for worry over that time interval—the three globally significant calamities are an influenza pandemic of a scale to cause around 50 million deaths, war (around 20 million deaths), and volcanic eruptions or tsunamis (1 million deaths). At 100 percent, the fatality expectations for the three events are about 25 million, 4 million, and 150,000 respectively. Asteroid collisions, the reader is pleased to discover, are not something to lose sleep over, with a 10 percent risk of about 50 fatalities. (An impact causing one million fatalities is put at .01 percent probability for the period.)

20 Other as yet unknown viruses with epidemic potential may well be in the wings, able in the right circumstances to cross to humans from animal hosts (see Lederberg 1988).

21 See the data and time-series compiled in Human Security Centre (2005).

22 See National Research Council (2002).

23 Bleak depictions are set out in great detail in the authoritative Millennium Ecosystem Assessment reports. See «www. millenniumassessment.org».

24 Smil (2005b: 636) concludes his two-part essay on the subject as follows: "[I]f you take a long look back and then try to discern what may come, if you ponder the reiteration of catastrophe throughout history and think about human irrationality, hatred, and drive for power and dominance, and about the fate of aerosols, bees, and bacteria, then you might conclude that, despite so many atrocities, failures, and fears, the past 50 years were an exceptionally stable and an unusually benign period in human history and that the probabilities of less benign events will greatly increase during the next 50 years."

25 The medium-variant of the UN long-range projections published in 2004 shows world population edging up from 8.9 billion to 9.1 billion in the half-century after 2050 and subsequently dropping back. (The low–high ranges, however, are large: 7.4–10.6 billion in 2050; 5.5–14.0 billion in 2100.) See United Nations (2004, 2005).

26 While in both regions the absolute number of the elderly will expand dramatically, the proportions will still be far greater in the more developed countries. The 80+ population in 2050 is projected to amount to 15 percent and 12 percent in Japan and Germany, 7 percent and 3 percent in China and India. The corresponding absolute numbers in this age group will be 17 and 10 million in Japan and Germany, 101 and 53 million in China and India. (United Nations 2005.)

27 Future technological breakthroughs, anticipated by some experts, may extend the human lifespan well beyond the business-as-usual extrapolations assumed by the United Nations. Within countries this could heighten the tensions inherent in allocative decisions on publicly financed health care (access could hardly be denied to those willing to pay). It also has the potential to generate analogous international dissatisfactions, or at least to amplify envy.

28 To an appreciable extent, very low levels of total fertility (TFR) defined at a given time are a consequence of women delaying their childbearing to later ages, rather than cutting back on their completed family size. That delay option has an evident biological upper limit which, as it is approached, may lead to some recovery in TFR. How significant such a recovery might be in practice is not known.

29 The main pronatalist policy mantra—make female labor force participation compatible with childbearing—has obvious limits: it virtually rules out families with three or more children, but not childlessness.

30 An avenue for social policy that for the most part has yet to be explored will be concerned with anticipated developments permitting genetic engineering in utero or in vitro. Parents would likely demand a major role in

what, in effect, would be grass-roots eugenics, but there is an equally evident public interest in the matter—albeit well short of *Brave New World* scenarios. International differences in the ethical premises and design of such social policy (the requisite know-how would rapidly spread among the technologically adept) may be substantial.

31 US Census Bureau (2005).

32 The reasons probably have to do with the concentration of immigrants in a few states and the design of congressional representation in the two houses. (Scale is also a matter to which economists pay little attention.)

References

African Union Commission. 2004. *Strategic Plan of the African Union Commission*. Addis Ababa.

Annan, Kofi A. 2004. "Why Europe needs an immigration strategy" «http://www.un.org/News/ossg/sg/stories/sg-29jan2004.htm».

Blinder, Alan S. 2006. "Offshoring: The next industrial revolution?" *Foreign Affairs* 85(2): 113–128.

Boniface, Pascal. 1998. "The proliferation of states," *The Washington Quarterly* 21(3): 111–127.

Buzan, Barry. 1998. "System versus units in theorizing about the Third World." In S. G. Neuman (ed.), *International Relations Theory and the Third World*. New York: St Martin's Press.

Commission for Africa. 2005. *Our Common Interest: Report for the Commission for Africa*. [London].

Cooper, Robert. 2003. *The Breaking of Nations: Order and Chaos in the Twenty-first Century*. New York: Atlantic Monthly Press.

Demeny, Paul. 2003. "Population policy dilemmas in Europe at the dawn of the twenty-first century," *Population and Development Review* 29: 1–28.

Easterlin, Richard A. 1996. *Growth Triumphant: The Twenty-first Century in Historical Perspective*. Ann Arbor: University of Michigan Press.

Hoyle, Fred. 1963. *A Contradiction in the Argument of Malthus*. Hull, UK: University of Hull Publications. (Reprinted in *Population and Development Review* 12 (3), 1986.)

Human Security Centre. 2005. *Human Security Report 2005: War and Peace in the 21st Century*. New York: Oxford University Press.

James, Harold. 2001. *The End of Globalization: Lessons from the Great Depression*. Cambridge, MA: Harvard University Press.

Keynes, J. M. 1963 [1930]. "Economic possibilities for our grandchildren," in his *Essays in Persuasion*. New York: W.W. Norton, pp. 358–373.

Lederberg, Joshua. 1988. "Medical science, infectious disease, and the unity of mankind," *Journal of the American Medical Association* 260 (5): 684–685.

MacIntyre, Andrew and Barry Naughton. 2005. "The decline of a Japan-led model of the East Asian economy." In T. J. Pempel (ed.), *Remapping East Asia: The Construction of a Region*. Ithaca: Cornell University Press.

Maddison, Angus. 2003. *The World Economy: Historical Statistics*. Paris: Organisation for Economic Co-operation and Development.

National Research Council. 2002. *Abrupt Climate Change: Inevitable Surprises*. Washington, DC: National Academy Press.

Poterba, James M. 2005. "The impact of population aging on financial markets." In Gordon H. Sellon (ed.), *Global Demographic Change: Economic Impacts and Policy Challenges*. Kansas City, MO: Federal Reserve Bank of Kansas City.

Rosecrance, Richard. 1996. "The rise of the virtual state," *Foreign Affairs* 75(4): 45–61.

Smil, Vaclav. 2005a. "The next 50 years: Fatal discontinuities," *Population and Development Review* 31: 201–236.

———. 2005b. "The next 50 years: Unfolding trends," *Population and Development Review* 31: 605–643.

Thomas, Albert. 1927. "International migration and its control," in *Proceedings of the World Population Conference, Geneva, 1927*. London: Edward Arnold.

United Nations. 2004. *World Population to 2300*. Department of Economic and Social Affairs. New York.

———. 2005. *World Population Prospects: The 2004 Revision. Volume I: Comprehensive Tables*. Department of Economic and Social Affairs. New York.

———. 2006. *World Urbanization Prospects: The 2005 Revision*—Population Database «http://esa.un.org/unup».

US Bureau of the Census. 2005. «http://www.census.gov/population/www/projections/popproj.html».

US National Intelligence Council. 2004. "Conference report on Northeast and Southeast Asia." (2020 Project Discussion Paper.)

———. 2005. "Mapping sub-Saharan Africa's future: Conference report" «http://www.dni.gov/nic/confreports_africa_future.html».

Wilson, Dominic and Roopa Purushothaman. 2003. "Dreaming with BRICs: The path to 2050," Goldman Sachs Global Economics Paper, No. 99.

World Bank. 2005. *World Development Indicators 2005*. Washington, DC.

World Commission on the Social Dimension of Globalization. 2004. *A Fair Globalization: Creating Opportunities for All*. Geneva: International Labour Organization.

AUTHORS

CHRISTOPHER CLAPHAM is a Research Associate, Centre of African Studies, Cambridge University.

DAVID COLEMAN is Professor of Demography in the University of Oxford.

PAUL DEMENY is Distinguished Scholar, Population Council, and Editor, *Population and Development Review*.

DEEPAK LAL is James S. Coleman Professor of International Development Studies, University of California, Los Angeles.

J. R. MCNEILL is Professor of History and holder of the Cinco Hermanos Chair in Environmental and International Affairs in the Walsh School of Foreign Service, Georgetown University.

GEOFFREY MCNICOLL is Senior Associate, Population Council.

EDUARD B. VERMEER taught at Leiden University and is an independent China consultant.

DAVID G. VICTOR is Director of the Program on Energy and Sustainable Development at Stanford University and an Adjunct Senior Fellow at the Council on Foreign Relations.

ARISTIDE R. ZOLBERG is Walter Eberstadt Professor of Political Science and Director of the International Center for Migration, Ethnicity, and Citizenship at the New School for Social Research.